Adult
Psychology

Adult
Psychology

LEDFORD J. BISCHOF
NORTHERN ILLINOIS UNIVERSITY

HARPER & ROW, PUBLISHERS
New York, Evanston, and London

ADULT PSYCHOLOGY

Copyright © 1969   by Ledford J. Bischof

LIBRARY OF CONGRESS CATALOG CARD NUMBER: 69–13744

*Dedicated to the brightest but lowest-paid form of
modern slave labor: The Psychology Graduate Assistant,
without whose efforts research would never get done.*

Contents

Preface

Excellent research and worthwhile concepts have come out of the efforts of child psychologists and adolescent psychologists. We have all learned much from their contributions. Now it is time for the adult psychologists (a new breed?) to speak out.

"We spend about one quarter of our lives growing up and three quarters growing old. It is strange, therefore, that psychologists and others have devoted most of their efforts to the study of childhood and adolescence." (Bromley, 1966) It is hoped that this book helps to complete the story of the aging process.

Most psychological literature on human growth and development starts with the ova and ends with the adolescent. This field of endeavor is usually called developmental psychology. The assumption appears to be that development completely stops with the end of adolescence. The next body of literature is devoted to geriatrics and gerontology: the medical problems of the aged and the science of studying the old. Aging has a strange connotation. It is as if aging is synonymous with being aged—*fait accompli*: To study aging is to study the aged. Yet others would maintain that the process of aging begins at the moment of birth and even in the embryonic state of existence.

Thus, between the infant and the infirm there is a hiatus. Most of us spend the greater part of our lives as adults: neither as infants, adolescents, or aged. The purpose of this book is to fill in this gap of knowledge.

The psychology of the adult, not too young and not too old, is more than a sad saga of proceeding from bifocals to trifocals and dentures to death. The middle-aged adult has as many problems to solve and pleasures to enjoy as any child or adolescent ever thought about. Since psychology broadly defined is the scientific study of behavior, the adult human animal is a worthy subject.

Browning's contribution that "The best is yet to be, the last of life, for which the first was made," may be poetical, but not pragmatic. Life continues to flow on from birth to burial, from cradle to casket, from womb to tomb. Somewhere in the middle there is a story to be told; that is what *Adult Psychology* is all about.

One final thought is necessary. Ten years from now an individual will not be able to write a book like this unaided. Having scoured the literature since 1964, one conclusion is inescapable: The "information explosion" is so vast and rapidly expanding that one person will be totally unable to assimilate or even collate but a portion of it. Even at this date fully one-third of the current research must be overly condensed, glossed over, or omitted in order to make this book commercially feasible. In the future it will take teams of scholars and writers to winnow down the vast mountains of information that will accrue. Two cases in point will illustrate amply. *Learning and Cognitive Performance in Adults* is solely a bibliography. It has 1,591 items. Ninety percent of the items date since World War II. The bibliography is a fitting posthumous tribute to the late Raymond Kuhlen, whose untimely death in July, 1967, saddened many psychologists.

Another bibliographical list only on gerontology and geriatrics contains 19,780 items as of April, 1968. (For further information, write to the Gerontology Research Center, Baltimore City Hospital, Baltimore, Maryland 21224.) The reader will soon note that gerontology occupies but one chapter in this book. Obviously more is left out than put in. Hurlock's 1968 edition of her monumental text, *Developmental Psychology* (too late to be treated in the body of the present book), is also an example of the problem of handling fantastic amounts of data.

How nice it feels for me to thank the good people who helped in preparing this book: To Linda Darner, Betty Richardson, and Jan Romanski, I am most grateful for typing skills. The dedication of this book is not in jest. Tim Marcy is a psychology graduate assistant, mine to be exact. I am proud and pleased to thank him in print for his underpaid, overworked, talented dedication in perfecting this book.

A final word of thanks goes to my wife Betty and teen-aged daughter Barbara for leaving father alone in his "writing shack" on the delightful scenic shores of Door County, Wisconsin.

L. J. B.

CHAPTER 1

Overview

WHY STUDY ADULTS?

Most people spend most of their lives as adults. The present book contends that not enough attention is being given to Mr. and Mrs. America, who happen to be between approximately 25 and 65 years of age. True, there are things being written and said concerning adults, but these are in some way deviant adults—mentally sick, in prisons, or physically incapacitated.

Perhaps what we may need in addition to "well-baby clinics" are also "well-adult clinics."

There appears to be a growing group of developmental psychologists who feel that the adult phase of life is the largest, the longest, and is even perhaps the goal of the growing child. It is just as interesting to discuss "what older people can do better as in finding what they usually do worse." Because aging begins at birth, the "implication is that development never stops" but continues in some ways until death concludes the life span. (Bromley, 1966)

Neugarten felt that "very little is yet known about adult personality." (Birren, 1964b)

Becoming an efficient adult is not an automatic process because the individual has lived a given number of years beyond adolescence. We may have to learn how to be middle-aged just as we had to learn to adjust to other periods in life. Some of the evidence indicates that becoming a grandparent for the first time, losing physical vigor, or being "locked in" an occupation requires adjustment and learning.

Birren states that "adult life, like that of a child, is always evolving." (Birren, 1964a)

A frustrating factor in studying child psychology is that we never know how the child turns out. What happens to the child when he eventually becomes an adult? Adults may be worth studying, from a psychological frame of reference at least, if for no other reason than to find out how the "story ends."

On a purely actuarial basis, one might make a case for studying adults simply because there are more of them. From the 1900 and the 1960 United States Census studies, we find that 4 percent of the population in 1900 was 65 years of age and older. In 1960, 8 percent of the population was 65 years of age and older. Approximately 3 million people in 1900 were 65 years of age and older, while 12 million in 1960 were 65 years of age and older. Looking at it another way, the median or middle age in 1900 was 16 years; in 1960, it was 31 years. The life expectancy tables indicate that for 40-year-old people in 1955, the prediction was for approximately 33 more years of life. (Vincent, 1961)

One of the conclusions from the above census data is that old age, or what was once considered old age, is now middle age. (Benaim, 1967)

Birren contends, "In a sense, the rewards of adulthood life take care of themselves; it is only the problems that demand attention." (Birren, 1964a) The study of adults may help us to delineate what these problems are. Who has them? How long do they last? Are they equally intense? Are they equally important? What happens *between* problems in adult life? "As yet we know little about the interactions between biological, psychological and social aging; but what we do know suggests their importance." (Birren, 1968a)

Hahn states, "Among our badly forgotten men and women are those who have completed their careers and who have successfully played career roles but are now caught in a professional trap." "Psychological practitioners can make a significant contribution to normal, mature, self-actualizing people between the ages of 30 and senescence." Hahn uses the term, "the forgotten people." (Hahn, 1967) (Hahn, 1962)

The adult years are indeed powerful. The peak earning capacity, according to the United States Department of Labor, lies somewhere between the ages of 45 and 65. (Vincent, 1961)

Ignoring the psychological study of adults may not be wise, because they possess economic power in our society. (*Time*, 1966b) (Desmond, 1956)

Despite some statements, parents are still the controllers of their children's environment. This is not a new idea. Carl Gustav Jung, for example, indicated that child psychology missed a major part of its efficiency when it studied the child only and in too many cases ignored the adults. To Jung, child psychology without 50 percent of its efforts directed toward parent psychology was "intellectual dishonesty." [1]

Some sources feel that middle-aged adults are "invisible indispensables." (*Time*, 1966b) (Vedder, 1965) Other sources call the middle years the "responsible years." (Benaim, 1967)

One possible reason for the neglect and misunderstanding of what happens to normal adults may be due to the current emphasis on our "youth-bound social science." (Birren, 1964a) It may be high time to tell the adult story. Surely there is more to human existence than childhood, adolescence, and old age.

If there is any value whatsoever to the idea of sequence in life (that is, that one is affected in his current period of life by what he did or what happened to him in a previous period of his life), then it follows that the field of gerontology suffers badly unless we study the previous age period. This sequence approach to life is particularly seen in the work of those psychologists who are promoting the idea that retirement does not begin at 65. Intelligent retirement begins somewhere in the middle years of life. These psychologists are saying that we do not suddenly retire. Adults should contemplate and plan for retirement 10 or even 20 years prior to the actual date of receiving a gold watch and attending the retirement banquet.

And, finally, an obvious response to the question of why one should study adults is the Socratic one: "The unexamined life is not worth living."

[1] Personal communication, April, 1960.

WHAT ARE THE ADULT YEARS:
OR WHO IS AN ADULT?

There are a number of opinions as to what constitutes the adult years of life, although none of them precisely agree. (Desmond, 1956) (*Time*, 1966b)

Abrahams says:

> The period of single "middle-age" is a matter of opinion, especially in regards to oneself! It is epigrammatically if imprecisely defined as the old age of youth or the youth of old age. The dictum of Cozalis (attributed to other more profound philosophers) that a man is as old as his arteries has been accepted as an attempt to establish some sort of standard or criterion. But nobody is capable of assessing the age of an artery, meaning thereby the measure of degree of deterioration or character of disease. [Ogilvie, 1962]

"Some say a man is as old as he is thought to be old by others— 'Abraham Lincoln was only 52 when he became president and 57 when he died'—yet we tend to think of him as an old, old man bearing the burden of his country during a civil war." (Havighurst, 1953b)

Some writers feel that adulthood is a horrendous stage of existence, more to be pitied and prayed about than to be lived through. Bergler in *The Revolt of the Middle-Aged Man* has some strong words to say in regard to the miserable condition of being middle-aged. "Man's Middle-age Revolt . . . is the sad story of an emotional second adolescence. . . ." "Middle-age without conflicts does not exist for man." In summary, Bergler maintains, "Adaptation to the reality of middle-age is as painful and as unavoidable as the infant's adaptation to the objective reality of his world. . . ." (Bergler, 1954)

British general medical practitioners have now instituted symposia on "The Hazards of Middle Age." (Benaim, 1967)

There are five possibilities of response to the question who is an adult or what is adulthood: historical considerations, biological and/or developmental aspects, psychological ramifications, statistical treatment, and miscellaneous categories.

Historical considerations

Table 1 illustrates the various events and influences on the lives of four men, whose ages in 1965 were 60, 50, 40, and 30. Though they are grouped together into one age level—the adult years—a short perusal of Table 1 indicates that their formative years were somewhat different.

THE 60-YEAR-OLD   The oldest of the four, now belonging to the "second half-century club," has come through ten Presidents of the

United States, two full-blown world wars, a Korean conflict, and is currently perturbed by the present Vietnamese situation, whatever its historical name may become.

TABLE 1. CHRONOLOGY OF FOUR ADULT MEN

YEAR	60	50	40	30	U.S. PRESIDENT	EDUCATION	CHARACTERISTIC EVENTS AND FEATURES
1905	1				T. Roosevelt		Heavy immigration
1910	5				Taft		Heavy immigration
1915	10	1			Wilson	60—1918—8th grade	World War I
1920	15	5			Harding	60—1922—High school	Roaring Twenties, Valentino
1925	20	10	1		Coolidge	50—1928—8th grade	Roaring Twenties
1930	25	15	5		Hoover	50—1932—High school	Depression
1935	30	20	10	1	F. Roosevelt	40—1938—8th grade	Depression, C. Gable
1940	35	25	15	5	F. Roosevelt	40—1942—High school	World War II
1945	40	30	20	10	Truman	30—1948—8th grade	
1950	45	35	25	15	Truman	30—1952—High school	Korea
1955	50	40	30	20	Eisenhower		The "Bomb"
1960	55	45	35	25	Eisenhower		Affluent society
1965	60	50	40	30	Johnson		Vietnam—Affluent society

He began life when the United States was in a heavy immigration period. He may even have been foreign-born and thus his early years may have been a bilingual struggle between the United States mores and the old stringent noncompromising attitude of his elders.

This 60-year-old person was 20 in the Roaring Twenties so ably chronicled by Hemingway, F. Scott Fitzgerald, and the Gertrude Stein coterie. Rudolph Valentino was the hero of the day, with slick hair and arched eyebrows.

He probably received a heavy indoctrination of chauvinism, with overtones of "down with the Kaiser," "let's get the boys out of the trenches," and all the nostalgic songs that Irving Berlin and others composed for World War I—"Over There," "Keep the Home Fires Burning," and so many, many other ditties, which the present ten-year-old is likely to think belonged to Moses or Lincoln or Washington or some ancient people. But this was his childhood, starting in 1905 and continuing to eighth-grade graduation on or around 1918 and, if he was one of the few, to a high school graduation in 1922. At high school, bloomers for the girls and Indian clubs for the boys constituted physical education: discipline the body for the boys and disguise the body for the girls.

The 60-year-old was about 25 years old, starting his family, when the great Depression of the thirties hit. Now he is likely not to forget a long depressing economic period or is he likely to let others forget what it was like when you sang, "Brother, can you spare a dime?" or "Happy Days are Here Again."

He was entertained by the first talkie movie, Al Jolson in the lachrymal *Sunny Boy,* the heterodyne radio, Sam and Henry. He noted with interest Ford Motor Company's switchover to a Model A from the reliable and bailing-wire-repairable Model T.

In 1932 Hoover was out and Roosevelt was in, and thus started a long line of federal governmental agencies rarely known by function but always known by alphabetical letters.

He went through a World War II experience either as a civilian with red stamps, rationing, spy scares, impounding Japanese in a concentration camp and all the panoply of another world war (What happened to the Kellogg-Briand Peace Pact? the League of Nations? Woodrow Wilson's 21 points?), or he learned the true import of being a "GI Joe" in the war turmoil of air, sea, and land. He was a hero in uniform despite the fact that no songs emerged such as he nostalgically remembered from his World War I experience as a youngster. If he did not have a uniform, he had a helmet issued by Civil Defense. Everyone pulled together and forgot former grievances except, of course, the ugly rumors of "hoarding" sugar, gas, tires, shoe coupons, or red meat stamps. This is what our 60-year-old remembers vividly about World War II.

Eventually Franklin Delano Roosevelt died and with him a long era of the "New Deal."

The Korean conflict came along at the age of 45, probably at the time he was involved in a second house, assuming a higher obligation with mortgages, and now with draft-eligible children of his own. The fifties may have slipped by quite rapidly, what with Eisenhower's Presidency, the ever impending bomb, and complete nuclear fission.

Now he is set and settled in his occupation, whether he likes it or not. He is about 60 years old. Lyndon Baines Johnson is President. The taxes are higher than ever. He makes more than he ever did or he is completely out of work and totally despondent, but the society is affluent.

What, then, is an adult? Perhaps it is a man or woman who has lived through all of these experiences and would like to share them with others but feels somewhat anachronistic to the current times and troubles. Draft evasion? "They called that being a 'slacker' back in my day."

In historical terms an adult is one who has lived through 60 years of history and has been touched by its events.

THE 50-YEAR-OLD   This individual started life 10 years later than the 60-year-old. The historical events that occurred in the lives of both the 60-year-old and the 50-year-old may have influenced them in different ways.

Two events may illustrate the above effects. When "Black Friday" of October, 1929, signaled the collapse of the stock market and subsequently the start of the Depression, the older man was threatened by the loss of his job and all income, but the younger man was still a sophomore in high school. Thus what may have been an ego-stripping period for the older man was perhaps an inconvenience for the younger man: he had to remain in high school longer.

Sunday, December 7, 1941, caught the 60-year-old male when he was 36 years of age. We can assume he was married, had children, was amortizing his mortgaged home, and his Selective Service Board would postpone action on him. The younger adult had no such option. Providing he was not 4F, he went into service through the avenue of enlistment or the draft. At the moment it mattered not whether he was married, a father, or had financial burdens; he became one of 13 million "GIs." He was 26 years old in 1941.

THE 40-YEAR-OLD   In 1965 the 40-year-old male has some memories of a war, too. His war was called the Korean conflict. At that time, he was 25 years old and very eligible for Selective Service. If he went into the Korean situation, the boundary lines of conflict were smudged. Victory was not as complete as in World Wars I and II. The war was more of an inconvenience than a total effect of a nation to protect itself. Thus we find that the same historical events have affected him differently than the other two adults described above.

THE 30-YEAR-OLD   For this individual much of what the other adults endured and experienced in a personal way was treated as current events for him in elementary school or high school. If he entered the service, it was for housekeeping primarily and not for conflict with an enemy. The two world wars, the Depression, are history to him and not personal experiences.

What is an adult? It is an individual who has lived for 30 or more years, but the events of history may have influenced each one differently, both personally and chronologically, depending upon his age at the time of the event.

Biological/developmental aspects

A second answer to the question of what an adult is may be provided by measuring the biological condition of the subject or the developmental phases of the physiological nature that the adult is now involved in. We shall only touch upon this particular aspect, leaving a much fuller treatment of what happens to the arteries, the heart, the whole physical system, to Chapter 8.

Despite the enormous amount of work done, there are no definitive guide lines at this point about the arteries or the cardiac system in the adult years. Can we call arteriosclerosis an older-adult index, or is there an incipient condition that would demark adults and their arteries? (Sobel, 1966)

Without a doubt the best measure of man's physiological rise and decline is the skeletal system, particularly the ossification of the wrist bones. This is probably the truest measure, though rarely used, and very little publicized, but more of that later in Chapter 8.

Selye's unique approach to biological aging may be pertinent at this point. Briefly presented, he advocates that all living tissue has a General Adaptation Syndrome, which means that tissue, when injured, goes through a triad of shock, followed by resistance, and then followed by exhaustion. The cycle is repeated at either short or long intervals, depending on the durability of the trauma and the success of the resistance. It is possible, of course, to resist and then collapse. Selye feels that all living tissue, specifically man, has just so much adaptation energy in its system from birth. This is the bank or battery from which reserves are withdrawn. Every withdrawal always depletes the reserve system. It is not possible, in the regular fiduciary way, to make withdrawals, deposits, or even collect interest. One is born with a storage battery full of so much adaptation energy. When it is used up, death results. A loss cannot be made up.

"One man may be much more senile in body and spirit and much closer to the grave at 40 than another person that's 60." (Selye, 1956)

"Development proceeds in stages which overlap. The transition from one stage to the next is more gradual than the events that signal this stage." Schneirla feels that adolescence is a stage triggered by menstruation, the event that signals it in the human female. In a different context, disengagement,[2] a concept about which we will have more to say later, can be thought of as a developmental stage, and retirement, the signaling event. The point of view is that if we knew and could measure and would agree on what disengagement is, we could then have a rather concise way of measuring the various points of adulthood.

Schneirla also states that beyond a certain point in time, it is not possible to reverse the process of maturation. (Birren, 1964b)

---

[2] Purposeful withdrawing from social obligations and contacts for one's own purposes and not because one does not have the vigor or is acceptable to the group.

Psychological ramifications

It may be possible that humans go from *goals* found in childhood and adolescence to being pushed, or adult *drives*. Is later adulthood that point in life when one is no longer goal- (future-) oriented but driven by the demands of everyday life? Once the middle years are met, are we concerned more, but certainly not exclusively, with solving our daily, weekly, monthly, problems, rather than with the "pie-in-the-sky" or "when-my-ship-comes-in" motivation?

The second psychological dimension to classifying aging may be that time of life when adults are more satisfied than less satisfied with themselves. If they have adequately handled their station in life and all that that means, they have passed successfully through infancy, childhood, adolescence, and much of the problems of being a young adult. Supposedly they are now on a happy plateau of having "arrived."

Charlotte Buhler wrote extensively on the changing needs in life, particularly on the variables in the life cycle. She suggested that life continues in a sense from premarriage to *expansion* and then in the 40s to *consolidation* of what one has gained. In the late 50s and 60s there is a period of *evaluation:* What do I have? Was it worth it? Is it better than the other fellow's? Do I want to keep it? Thus we have a system that would identify adulthood as consolidation and evaluation. (Birren, 1964b) (Buhler 1959)

A third attempt to answer the question revolves around the work of Carl Gustav Jung. Among the many things that Jung exposited, and not always in full clarity, was a concept that life consists of polarities: good and bad, right and wrong, male and female, god and devil. Human existence was composed of bringing together or balancing all of these polarities of life. This, to Jung, meant being a fully self-actualized human being. Jung felt that you did not have a true personality until you had reached middle age, because it was not until then that the human could balance organic needs versus cultural needs, physical energy versus psychic energy, the conscious versus the unconscious, progression versus regression, and extraversion versus introversion, and so on. (Bischof, 1964)

Birren discusses the term *disengagement,* or "load shedding," as a possible phenomenon of the adult years. He finds the research that he and others have done indicates disengagement to involve four things: less involvement with other people, a reduction in the variety of social roles played, greater use of mental ability rather than physical activity or social activity, and less physical strength to initiate and endure sustained activity. Possibly, if we could construct a scale or some quantitative device, we may have an instrument that tells us whether we are fully adult or not. (Birren, 1964a)

Within the rubric of disengagement, these may be six distinctive styles of success or failure in middle-aged or elderly adults: world of work, familism, living alone, couplehood, easing through life with small involvement, and living life fully. (Williams, 1965)

Peck categorically divides the last half of adulthood into two broad chronological periods—middle age (40s and 50s) and old age (from 60 on). (Birren, 1964b)

Kleemeier presents a classification system built somewhat around the family structure, "The distinction (is) between the family of late maturity—45 to 54 years—the family of preretirement—55 to 64 years —the family of early retirement—65 to 74 years—and the family of later retirement—75 years and on." (Kleemeier, 1961)

Neugarten states, "Clinical observations have been frequently made that aggressivity may be adaptive in youth but maladaptive in middle-age . . . just as rigidity may be maladaptive in young adulthood, but adaptive in older age." (Birren, 1964b) This suggests the possibility that nonaggression as compared to rigidity may be a rough but usable method for answering the question, what is adulthood, at least from a psychological point of view?

Statistical treatment

Approaching the problem from statistical considerations,

> There are probably certain broadly limitable periods, such as middle age and old age, but these are apt to be statistical artifacts describing the average person of 40 to 60 or some such span. There are bound to be some people of 65 who act, think, and feel like the middle-age group, while the other 65 year olds act, think, and feel very elderly. At least observations indicated that this is likely to be found. [Anderson, 1956]

Levine gives a second criticism to the statistical approach:

> The middle years as a span of life suffer from statistical vagueness. The person approaching middle age strives to delay its advent until the age of 40. The admittedly middle age persons insist on fixing its upper limit at 60. In an average life of 70 years this span from 36 to 55 would be nearer a middle allocation than 40 to 60. [Levine, 1957]

There is another way of treating adulthood in a statistical sense; however, the statistics possibly reach a ludicrous dimension.

For purposes of illustration, an individual who is now aged 50 (ignoring the leap years) has lived 365 days a year for 50 years or a total of 18,250 days. What has this person done during his 50 years of life?

He has slept, providing he sleeps every night, 18,250 times. Here, of course, being statistical, we are equating any human activity at the age of 2 as being comparable to any activity at the age of 22. In his 50 years of life, he has sat down and eaten approximately 54,750 meals. Assuming twice-daily trips to the bathroom, we find he has toileted himself 36,500 times. In addition to all of these figures in the number game, our 50-year-old human has breathed millions of times. Assume that he has laughed on the average of at least once a day—that comes to 18,250 laughs in his lifetime. Assume that he cries on the average, from his early childhood on through his fiftieth year, once a year. He has cried 50 times. Assume he has argued once a month. The result is 600 times. Our 50-year-old human has touched things, kissed and been kissed, walked, run, dressed, undressed, written words, read words, done literally hundreds and hundreds of activities through his 50 years.

Following this unusual treatment of a statistical approach for the very act of sexual intercourse, assuming a marriage at 25, and further assuming that the data of Kinsey, Pomeroy, and Martin have some validity, we find that our 50-year-old-male human in a normal course of love making has had approximately 2,600 orgasms in his 25-year-span of married life. (Kinsey, 1948)

Miscellaneous

Finally, in our pursuit of the answer to the question of what is an adult, we come to general, or miscellaneous, classificatory systems.

Vedder uses the ages of 45 to 65 to delineate the middle years of adult life. (Vedder, 1965) Disraeli is reputed to have said that "youth is a blunder, manhood a struggle, old age a regret." Gracian's maxim stated that "at 20 the will reigns, at 30 the intellect, and at 40 the judgment." And finally, a Greek proverb ruled that "childhood ends at 12, youth at 18, love at 20, faith at 30, hope at 40 and desire at 50." (Buhler, 1961)

Some developmental psychologists delineate life in decades:

0–10	Formative years
10–20	Frenetic-Flippant-Fluid-Future years
20–30	Foundation years
30–40	Family years
40–60	Middle years
60	Terminal

A middle-aged adult may be one who undergoes these four sources of stress: somatic, cultural, economic, and psychological. (Marmor, 1967) Other general classification systems usually follow approximately the order suggested below.

Infancy	2
Preschool	2–5
Childhood	5–12
Adolescence	12–17
Early maturity	17–25
Maturity	25–50
Late maturity	50–75
Old age	75

The most complete classification system divides the life cycle in 16 stages:

Period	Approximate Age
Zygote	conception
Embryo	up to 7 weeks
Foetus	after 7 weeks
Birth	38 weeks
Infancy	up to 18 months
Preschool	up to 5 years
Elementary	up to 11 to 13 years
Puberty and senior high school	11 to 16 years
Late adolescence	15 to 21 years
Early adulthood	21 to 25 years
Middle adulthood	25 to 40 years
Late adulthood	40 to 60 years
Preretirement	60 to 65 years
Retirement	65 years plus
Old age	70 years plus
Senescence	terminal illness and death

(Bromley, 1966)

Else Frenkel suggested roughly the ages of birth to age 40 as the *construction* period, the ages 40–50 as a *culmination,* and the ages of approximately 60 and over as a *reduction* period. (Frenkel, 1936)

Birren gives us as much help as anyone else in answering the question: What are the adult years? "Age is a useful and powerful index in classifying large amounts of information—knowing an individual's chronological age, one can make a number of predictions about his most likely anatomical, physiological and psychological and social characteristics." (Birren, 1964a)

ARE THERE THEORIES ABOUT ADULT DEVELOPMENT?

Investigators of human behavior operate under some theoretical basis when conducting research. Developmental psychologists labor under the difficulty of not following, or knowing exactly what is, their theoretical basis.

Neugarten feels the need for an adequate theory in regard to adult studies.

"Very little is yet known about adult personality, there are few theories that may be regarded as useful and few empirical studies are now available on which to build a developmental theory." "Over and above problems of method, the student of adult personality suffers from the lack of theory to guide him in conceptualizing personality change in making observations and determining the kinds of measures to devise." (Birren, 1964b)

Suggested here are at least twelve possibilities for theory formulation in studying the developmental aspects of adults. They are as follows: (1) stability, (2) life span, (3) reversal, (4) composite, (5) cultural, (6) critical periods, (7) resistance to change, (8) need hierarchy, (9) managerial, (10) masculine/feminine, (11) psychoanalytic theory, (12) *tabula rasa*. These twelve approaches to theory testing are unequal in value. Time and further research will indicate which rubrics are strong and which are weak. The order, or presentation, is no indication of their value. In most cases, the sources cited were not creating a theory. The present work interprets them widely for this purpose. Some of the so-called theories may be more appropriately called speculations or hypotheses.

Stability

(Theory) that aging produces stability. "Insufficient attention is paid in psychological research to the relatively stable years." (Bayley, 1963)

Life span

(Theory) that as the adult progresses through a life span, the individual's goals become easier to identify and define and may reduce in number. (Bischof, 1964, Adlerian concept)

Reversal

(Theory) that

A particularly attractive but erroneous theory regards the life cycle as reversing itself during the later years with adult personality regressing through an antique form of adolescence and falling into second childhood. This view had some support for a time from people who applied Freudian personality theory naively. Since the secretion of the sex hormones decreases after about the age of fifty, it was supposed that this decrease might lead to a kind of reversed puberty with concomitant personality changes. Such speculations have not proved valuable. [Birren, 1964][3]

Composite

"Genetic" (Theory) that barring accidents, an individual is born with a "built-in longevity table in his organic system."

"Counterpart" (Theory) that the investigator can relate or trace in later life the effects of early life origins.

"Wear and Tear" (Theory) that adulthood becomes somewhat "an accumulation of the effects of random events and accidents" so aging may be measured by the number of these occurrences that happen to an individual: the higher the number, the older the person. (Birren, 1964a) (Curtis, 1966)

Cultural

(Theory) that adults are more than products of environment but that with aging the adult finds it easier and easier to accept and adapt to the cultural milieu. (Slotkin, 1954)

Critical periods

(Theory) that as an individual progresses through life and achieves adulthood, he will have made more "choice points" at critical periods in his life. "If this hypothesis has merit, it may be expected that such events as marriage, becoming a parent or grandparent, or loss of spouse or job would influence in important ways the motivational pattern of an individual." (Birren, 1964b)

Resistance to change

(Theory) that the older an individual becomes, the more he will tend to resist personal and/or social change.

Need hierarchy

(Theory) that human aging will correlate positively to fulfilling the Hierarchy of Needs as expostulated by Maslow. (Bischof, 1964)

Managerial

(Theory) that a measure of adult status is the ability to manage the forces of society in a greater measure than other age groups. ". . . it is

[3] J. E. Birren (ed.). *Relations of Development and Aging,* 1964, Charles C Thomas, Publisher, Springfield, Ill.

those in the middle years who create and manage the society for both of the others." (Vedder, 1965)

Masculine/feminine

(Theory) that as individuals live through their life spans, males and females begin life uniquely homogeneous in behavior and manner. (Neugarten in Birren, 1964b) As individuals progress through life, the largest difference between maleness and femaleness may be found in the middle years of life. (Cameron, 1968) Then the gap closes, and in the very old we find uniquely homogeneous behavior quite parallel to early infancy. Aging may be measured on this scale. (Bromley, 1966) (See Chesterton's *What's Wrong With the World* and Jung's *Anima/Animus.*) (DeWit, 1963) (Bischof, 1964)

Psychoanalytic theory

(Theory) that at the middle years of aging, the adult is most efficient in utilizing the Freudian Defense Mechanisms to preserve and support his ego. Before and after middle age the individual is less adept at using the Ego Defense Mechanisms. (Kahn, 1965)

Tabula rasa

(Theory) that all human experiences, not just those of childhood, are written on one's "tablet of life," and once written are ineradicable.

> Personality theorists have not carried the same view of *Tabula Rasa* into adulthood. Psychoanalytic theory, tremendous as its influence has been, has given little attention to personality change after the crises of adolescence have been mastered. The personality is generally regarded as stabilized (if not fixed) by the time early adulthood is reached, and there are few developmental psychologists who have extended their theories upward in an attempt to look out for perceivable changes in adult behavior. [Birren, 1964b] [4]

DOES A SIMILAR PERSONALITY STRUCTURE CONTINUE FROM CHILDHOOD THROUGH ADULTHOOD?

Is adulthood nothing more than a continuation of the personality one structured during his formative years? If this be true, then there is little difference between child psychology and adult psychology. One is simply the equivalent of the other.

[4] J. E. Birren (ed.). *Relations of Development and Aging,* 1964, Charles C Thomas, Publisher, Springfield, Ill.

Oddly enough, the question has no easy answer. Most developmental research is of a cross-sectional nature. It compares adolescents with adults, infants with adolescents, infants with old people, and so on. The preponderence of cross-sectional research in developmental psychology is enormous and it usually shows that infants are different than adults and adults are different than infants. On the other hand, longitudinal studies concern themselves with following the events of a single human throughout the course of life. The problems involved here are enormous. There are few adults that psychologists have been able to follow for a life span, except after death in a biographical form. This, of course, permits them no manipulation of data or testing of hypotheses, but simply reportorial endeavors.

Using both approaches (cross-sectional and longitudinal), we shall try to answer the question: Does a similar personality structure continue from childhood through adulthood?

Birren feels, "Man is both the result and determiner of his environment." He states, "Rhythm of the life span is influenced by selective reinforcement of behavior." Man does have certain choices, but he cannot ignore his environment or change it completely to his own liking. (Birren, 1964a)

Neugarten feels rather strongly that not enough evidence has been accumulated to answer the question satisfactorily. In the Kansas City study and others, she feels they do find a continuity of personality over long periods of time and that there are certain definable differences in the personality changes in the adult years, which are not comparable to other life periods. (Birren, 1964b)

Jones in his work at the Institute of Development, University of California (1958), made some generalizations about physical, psychological, intellectual, and personality development. His point is well taken. "Conclusions were that the problem of age trend consistency is a more difficult one in the area of personality than in the other areas." "Among other reasons because the same research approaches can not be used with adults as with children and/or adolescents." (Birren, 1964b) (Jones, 1967)

In the next section we shall see how difficult it is to use the same instrument in measuring children, adolescents, and adults.

J. E. Anderson, long associated with the University of Minnesota, in a 1960 report gathered data on children from an entire Minnesota county. He began studying these children when they were in grades from the fourth to the twelfth. Some 5 to 7 years later he made a follow-up study of the subjects. From this enormous amount of data, Anderson came to the tentative conclusion that certain human characteristics did not change with age, while other characteristics did change with age. In what he called the cognitive measures—intelligence, skill, aptitudes, and particularly knowledge—there was definitely a change as the individual grew older. In most cases, the scores increased as the age increased. On the other hand, personality measures were what he called "age free." Some behavioral characteristics remain constant at a fairly predictable manner as age increased. On the other hand, measures of personality were apparently relatively unpredictable. (Birren, 1964b) (Anderson, 1959)

In *Relations of Development and Aging*, Kelly reports on a 1955 study made with 300 engaged couples. They were first studied in 1930 and then restudied in 1955, when they were about in their mid-40s. Kelly found that individual consistency was highest in the areas of values and vocational interest. He found very little consistency in these individuals 25 years later in regard to the ratings they made of themselves and other personality variables that he measured. His most outstanding finding was in individual variation, no matter what the area under consideration was. "Our findings indicate that significant changes in the human personality may continue to occur during the years of adulthood." (Birren, 1964b)

An interesting study done by Hans Thomae, reported in *Social and Psychological Aspects of Aging: Aging Around the World,* reports on a study he did with 150 male white-collar workers of approximately the ages 35–55. The subjects studied pictures and told stories about the pictures. The subjects also wrote autobiographical material, which was analyzed. Thomae strengthened the study by contacting, 3 years later, 70 percent of the original 150 subjects, and, 5 years later, 46 percent of the subjects. His conclusions are numerous and interesting. In regard to problems and adjustments for these 150 men, he found highly individualistic patterns very similar to the Adlerian life-style concept. There were general developmental laws or stages of development in the subjects he studied.

He further found, "Actually an intensive analysis of the autobiographies contained in our interviews, showed that major changes occur in the lives of older people almost to the same degree as in the lives of younger people."

Another condition, that at least Thomae found, was a period between the ages of 40 and 50, which he called a boredom period, in which the subjects began to have great ambivalence toward the future. The ambivalence, or indecision as to what to do, concerned itself with a longing for some kind of change, but the longing was hampered by a serious strain or fear of any changes, and especially of the consequences toward others that a change may make.

Another finding of Thomae's we find quite interesting. "The longitudinal analysis of our cases (following them for the eight year period) especially would show that the same person can work himself through the same theme again and again and again at different stages in life." This indicates support for the Adlerian life-style concept. One does not progress, one simply repeats the problems that one was unable to satisfactorily solve in previous periods of life.

Thomae concludes with, "Therefore, we might deduce from a thematic analysis of aging, the hypothesis that aging is a typical sequence of reactions toward certain typical social and environmental changes rather than a mental or motivational unity." (Tibbitts, 1962)

Apparently many developmental psychologists feel and would support the thesis of Sullivan that man must change or die. It is a question of, adjust to life from your babyhood ways, or abdicate from life. The current trend seems to be that the personality is not fixed in the strict psychoanalytic or Freudian sense. Some skills and intelligence may change very little. The question is, is intelligence or skill a part of one's personality or is personality a completely different facet of human behavior?

Still another study, by Symonds (1961), found a great deal of consistency in the behavior of his subjects. Using 28 subjects, which he first studied when they were from 12 to 18 years of age, he retested them at an interval of 13 years later, so the 12-year-olds were now 25 and the 18-year-olds were 31. Symonds found a high consistency in overt personality, by which he meant aggressiveness in response to both the interviews and the tests. Symonds felt that he had demonstrated "the remarkable persistence of personality over a 13 year interval and in particular, the fact that it is possible to estimate personality adjustment in later years from facts gathered about a person when he is an adolescent." (Birren, 1964b)

Two longitudinal studies are pertinent at this point. Rohrer traced a majority of the Negro adolescents who were first described by Davis and Dollard in their widely read book, *Children of Bondage* (1940). Rohrer reports in considerable detail on 20 of the Negroes who were interviewed 20 years after the original study. "Although the findings were not treated quantitatively, the net effect of these case materials is to highlight the great diversity of adult life patterns—not only partly predictable from observations made during adolescence." (Birren, 1964b)

A study by Meier, "Adults who were foster children," studied 66 men and women "between the ages of 28 and 32, who in their childhood had experienced 5 years of foster family care, and who had not returned to their own families while they were children." In part her finding concluded that there was an apparent

difference in impact upon boys as compared with girls. . . . we would start with the hunch that with girls the content of experiences which reflect upon *what* they are is of great importance, whereas with boys the kind of experiences which affect their sense of *who* they are, is of greater significance. [Meier, 1966]

One comparison found no difference between 47 British adults who as infants had spent an average of $2\frac{1}{2}$ years in foundling homes and 50 adults with no foundling-home experience. As adults, they were no different. Their abnormal behavior appeared to be related to "genetic factors." (Heston, 1966)

O'Neil, in his article "The stability of the main patterns of ability with changing age," which appeared in an Australian psychological journal, states, "The general conclusion to be drawn is that any age change in ability patterns which may occur seems to be minor, the predominant feature being one of stability." (O'Neil, 1962)

Two British pediatricians studied the childhood of 450 "unusual" men and women. Included were such widely known individuals as Nehru, Robespierre, Hitler, Brahms, Roosevelt, and Newton. The authors feel that there is "no single path to eminence, creativity, or evil" from childhood influences to adult behavior." (Illingworth, 1966)

Perversely we may find no better response to the question originally stated than, "The evidence indicates that the adult is a constantly adapting organism." (Birren, 1964a)

WHAT ARE THE PROBLEMS IN STUDYING AVERAGE ADULT POPULATIONS?

In this writer's experience, research with middle-aged people presents many unique problems: You cannot peek at them through one-way mirrors, they are most intelligent in ferreting out hidden meanings, and they demand explanations at times for problems and questions which the psychologists themselves are not quite sure about.

What are the problems in researching the dynamics of middle age? They are many and varied, and we should like to present twelve different ramifications.

Availability of subjects

Neugarten feels this acutely in her own work. Consider, for example, that there is no captive research group such as we have in elementary schools, high schools, and colleges. Adults are different: neither can they be forced into the research project, nor is their motivation the same. Mr. and Mrs. America have to be approached gingerly. Obviously this is not bad but at times becomes an insurmountable hurdle when one wants simply to study the people as they come in all walks of life and not just the deviants. The inability to find enough people to study has frequently stopped many a good research design or study problem when concerned with adults.

Willingness of subjects

One of the more productive research psychologists in this area, Botwinick, has realized this problem as much as anyone. (Botwinick, 1964) He has found middle-aged people to be frequently excessively cautious, quite rigid in behavior, and at times overly suspicious. One sometimes gets the feeling that some secret of theirs is to be found out and exposed to their peril. Again, obviously, this is the subject's privilege and no one in his right mind would have it differently. It does, however, curtail decent, well-thought-out research and investigative efforts. There is the hope, at least for the present writer, that some of this will be alleviated. If this book can do nothing else but to allay some of the reticence of adults to participate in psychological studies, the book will have earned its hard covers. (Preston, 1968)

British investigators have found that

> women are easier to recruit than men, but younger working-class men and women of average intelligence are difficult to secure. Older men of average ability are in relatively short supply, but there is an abundance of middle-aged men of high ability. Women schoolteachers are the easiest to recruit and the most reliable subjects. [Bromley, 1966]

Fact and/or fiction

Another author has concerned himself with the not unknown problem that what we think and what we know may be contradictory. (Kent, 1965b) This particular phenomenon has received, currently, at least, considerable effort under the rubric of "Cognitive Dissonance." Thus we have a gap between the general perception that each of us feels about the aging process and the actual facts as they emerge from good replicable research. As suggested, this is not a new problem; what we know to be true and what we want to have true may not jibe. In this particular case, the middle-aged subject is an intelligent, aware, conscious, thinking individual. He hears or reads about certain results of investigative efforts, and yet in his own personal experience he feels them to be totally false. His own self-perceptual system contradicts what he has been told by others. This phenomenon frequently has been a stumbling block to a further pursuit of whatever problem is being studied. This continues beyond the self-perceptual system to such general stereotypes as the cliché, "Fair, fat, and 40," or that all women suffer immeasurably through menopause, which we shall see in later chapters is not necessarily true. The person feels differently and thus refutes the data as they are known at that time. Such problems are not as universal when dealing with children. They do not read the results. They do not understand them; they couldn't care less. They simply go about their happy peregrinations on the playground. The adult research subject wants to argue about research results. That is his privilege. He should gain, however, as much data as possible and then exercise his democratic and God-given right to make up his own mind.

Age bias of experimenters

Dr. Wilma Donahue, long a worker in the field, made pertinent this statement at a 1955 American Psychological Association Conference:

> We should stop lumping all older people together. Perhaps the reason the older group (50 and above or 65 and over) is so frequently lumped together, is because it is the *young people who do the studies.* Their perception of the differences betwen 50 and 60 years of age isn't as clear to them as it will be when they are grown older too. [Anderson, 1956]

Again Donahue states in an article entitled "Relationship of age of perceivers to their social perceptions":

> After summarizing research studies which explore "Attitudes of Youth Toward Older People" and "Sources of Bias When Youth Are Interviewers of the Aged," attention is called to age-group membership as a circumstance "which conceivably may be affecting much of the data currently being collected from older people" and focuses on the urgent need for methodological studies in "examining and controlling the examiner effect." [Donahue, 1965]

This author heartily concurs with Donahue's statement and would extend it somewhat. It has been our experience to be somewhat irritated at times by the kind of research problems suggested and pursued by 25-year-old research psychologists and by 55-year-old research psychologists. Too frequently there seems to be a gap between the younger researcher, who wants to study the "old folks," and the older researcher, who would like to look around and find out what the others are like and possibly match his findings with his own experience. As we shall see later on, usually the research design or what is done is not affected by this age bias. However, the conclusions and summary too often receive negative overtones from the younger researcher and, as we might expect, are treated with much more sympathy by the older researcher, who is working on the adult subjects. This inconsistency is probably strongest in the area of rise, plateau, and decline of intellectual capacity. (Havighurst, 1966a)

White's revised book, *Lives in Progress,* focuses on normal individuals and avoids the "medical student's disease" of describing normal adults in medically abnormal terms. (White, 1966) Pressey asks that studies of the developmental problems of aged adults include "oldsters as co-investigators" beyond their involvement as experimental subjects. (Pressey, 1967) Posner felt that social caseworkers were not challenged by geriatric problems but preferred social work with children. (Posner, 1961)

One of the major difficulties in studying aging is that the research analyst is caught up in his own aging process. He has a sensitivity to the problem of aging, particularly when he is studying his own age level. (Bromley, 1966)

Difficulties of analyzing data

This is a very involved problem. The main portion could be divided roughly into two parts: What questions should we ask, and what do we do with the results?

There has long been a cliché in the research field that the good research scientist should, if he knows what he is doing, ask a $25 question of a $25 piece of equipment; however, as one might suppose, too frequently a 25¢ question is asked of a $10,000 piece of equipment. The lucky ones, of course, use 25¢ pieces of equipment to get the $10,000 answers.

It is quite possible and not unknown even in other areas of research. If you ask a foolish question, you get a foolish answer.

It must be understood by the researcher, although not always true, that if you ask a statistically oriented question, you will get a statistical answer. If you use a questionnaire or opinionnaire that has two answers (dichotomy)—yes or no—your results are going to come in a polar, or dichotomized, form. The distribution is either on one or the other, with a few undecideds in between, which you throw out because you don't know what to do with them. On the other hand, if you hope to have what is called scaling, in which the subject makes a choice on a point level between one through five, you discover most of your answers will average out to around a value of three. The question you ask mandates the kind of answer you are going to receive. This is a statistical trap not necessarily bad in itself, as long as one realizes what he is doing.

On the other hand, you can have as much difficulty in dealing with anecdotal kinds of responses. This is a situation in which you ask the subject to recount, or tell or tape-record, some personal experience. This avoids some of the statistical traps mentioned but gives you data that become enormously complicated, particularly when you try to measure any kind of differences. Length of statements, level of vocabulary, emotional tone, may fall apart in the actual analysis of data.

As suggested, this is such an enormously complicated methodological problem that all we can do at this point is recognize it and ask the reader to put up with it until something better comes along. (Maddox, 1965)

Measurement techniques

This could be, and certainly is for the present author, one of the most difficult problems to handle in doing research with middle-aged subjects. Most of the instruments we have were designed for either deviant populations or for children. Now to use these same tools and techniques with a good, average, *"gemütlich,"* middle-aged American adult is frequently ridiculous. What may measure children's behavior, and do so quite adequately, may seem absolutely childish and silly to an adult. For example, one of our tests in a popular individual intelligence test is to put together a cardboard mannequin. This is fine for children, but strikes the adult, as we might readily conceive, as a rather stupid thing to do for any grown-up. (Williams, 1963a)

The problem is frequently compounded in longitudinal studies. The instruments one has used with the subjects when they were children now become rather meaningless for them as adults. Yet, to make any decent comparison, one has to use the original instrument. One can't shift or change the measuring stick after the game is started.

One result of this technique difficulty is that children and adolescents frequently measure higher than adults simply because we are using a child or adolescent tool. This bemuses the current writer. Why not turn the tables? Use a good adult technique, such as driving an automobile, maintaining a home, giving a sophisticated party, filling out one's income tax, conducting a meeting of 200 people, to measure how well children can do? The answer is obvious. Adults are smarter, and will now measure better, than children because we will have now used an adult technique to measure children. (Bromley, 1966)

As ludicrous as this sounds, the writer must admit that too much research is frequently the victim of "technique traps."

Survival bias

Neugarten, as well as others, is extremely aware of the problem of "survival bias." (Bromley, 1966)

You cannot estimate the effects of survival bias. In other words, the weaker ones may die off and the stronger ones live, and this makes a difference in the data. Therefore, equating samples of young with old people is not necessarily possible. (Birren, 1964b) Thus we have some effect of the survival of the fittest. We may not be measuring the developmental changes in human lives. Not all of the original population is available to measure. Many of the characteristics of adults may be correlated with longevity rather than with what we think we are measuring. Though the good may or may not die young, if they do die young, they certainly die too soon to be subjects for adult studies. (Britton, 1966b) (Riegel, 1967b)

Developmental inconsistencies

This is a unique problem in the field of developmental psychology. There is a difference in what is called the "rhythm of change." What is meant here should seem obvious but is not always considered in developmental research data. One year in the life of a child is vastly different than one year in the life of an adult. Even more pronounced is the 12-month period of enormous development in the newly born up to its first birthday as compared to the imperceptible changes in the adult, say, from the thirty-sixth to the thirty-seventh birthday. Any cross-sectional study between children and adults is affected by this fact.

Historical influences

In a previous section, effort was made to indicate the effect of historical events on the lives of four males, aged 30, 40, 50, and 60. A world war is bound to have some effect on the personalities of both a human who lived through it and another human who did not. Even if this is not a crucial influence, as some would feel, it must be reckoned with as a problem in dealing with research questions for adult-aged subjects.

As Neugarten intelligently asks, "Do persons become more conservative with age? Or is it that older persons formed many of their social attitudes at a different time in history?" (Birren, 1964b)

Cross-sectional versus longitudinal

Again borrowing from Neugarten, "There are no longitudinal studies in personality yet available for individuals who have been studied in young adulthood or in middle adulthood and then again in old age."

There are some studies, such as Terman's studies of the gifted through a 40-year span. However, these are not average adult Americans.

The real issue in cross-sectional studies (comparing one age bracket with another) is that they may create more problems than they solve. (Bromley, 1966)

On the other hand, to find enough humans who will live long enough to be studied by the same methods is a goal not yet attained. The entire area of research in developmental psychology suffers from this problem. Contradictions in research findings are inevitable because of this problem.

Some investigators have advocated a "mixed method," combining the longitudinal and cross-sectional methods. In this case, "matched groups of 20-, 40-, and 60-year-old subjects are compared on some psychological dimension." Then, 5 and 10 years later, they might repeat their measurement, using the same or equivalent procedures. (Bromley, 1966)

Predictability

This is *the* problem in psychology as well as in almost all scientific pursuits.

Essentially what the psychologist is trying to do is to predict within given degrees of accuracy what to expect of any human. The problem of predictability, whether it be in the physical sciences or the behavioral sciences, is not unique. It is the most ubiquitous puzzle in all of scientific endeavor. Investigators find they are more accurate in predicting the behavior of a large group than in predicting the behavior of an individual. Although we may predict group behavior with a far greater degree of accuracy than individual behavior, most individuals do not care what the group is going to do. They care most about the behavior of the single individual, particularly themselves or members of their own family. Will my son or daughter finish college? Will my son and daughter make a compatible marriage? Will they succeed as a mother or father? Will they succeed in an occupation? To the lay person, this is the crucial issue in predictability. The psychologist frequently is efficient in describing human behavior and even explaining behavior. He is often as vulnerable as others in trying to predict human behavior.

Middle-class milieu

In the writer's own experience, and in that of Neugarten and others, a middle-class (most psychologists come from the middle class) researcher is frequently nonsympatico with a very low level economic group. His background is inadequate to understand their dynamics. He is highly suspect. He is likely to get responses that are stereotyped and "nice" or to receive total rejection. There is no one to blame. It's just the way the cards are played. We must recognize, however, that this is an over-riding problem in psychological research, particularly with adult-aged people. It is not so true when dealing with early-elementary-education students whose backgrounds are of a very low economic order. They are a captive audience.

Conversely, and in the writer's experience as well as in that of others, extremely wealthy people are practically inaccessible to any kind of penetrating research endeavors, especially for adult-aged groups. They look upon such psychologists' efforts as amusing, inter-fering, or threatening. This is the subject's privilege. It does not, how-ever, help in furthering our understanding of man's behavior, whether he is rich, average, or poor. The psychologists can only do as much as wealthy subjects will cooperate in.

The end result is that most studies have been conducted with middle-class people, who, for reasons we can only guess at (Are they perhaps pleased to be considered psychological subjects?), are more cooperative and less resentful than the wealthy or the poor. They seem, as a group, not as threatened in revealing information concerning their own lives.

Developmental psychological studies are primarily of a cross-sectional nature. They are unable to take into account differing edu-cational levels, cultural environments, and socioeconomic levels. Also, the very fact of being a male or female may cause a difference in the quality and quantity and significance of the subject's response.

Furthermore, there are few studies that compare Americans with Europeans or with Orientals. An enormous amount of cultural influ-ence is involved in trying to discuss what an adult human is like. It should come as no surprise that the middle-aged Oriental will operate under different sets of rules and dynamics than a middle-aged English-man or a middle-aged American. In many cases we have a sociological study, not a psychological one. This is healthy, but it must be acknowl-edged.

WHAT ARE THE METHODS MOST FREQUENTLY USED?

Most studies concerning the developmental aspects of adult-aged people are done, no matter what the technique, in two general ways: cross-sectional or longitudinal.

The actual methods of the developmental psychologist are as ingenious as the psychologist can devise. (Oberleder, 1967)

Probably one of the most widely used, because it is the easiest, threatens less, and gains the most data, is a survey technique. Usually the paper-and-pencil kind, such as a questionnaire or opinionnaire, gains as much material as any other technique. The researcher must decide how truthful the answers are.

A second method that is also frequently used, but much more expensive and time-consuming, is to interview adult subjects. Again, the sampling bias occurs, which we have discussed before (You may get different answers if a young callow-looking graduate student, aged 20, is asking the questions than if a 50-year-old man or woman is asking the questions of another 50-year-old man or woman). However, most psychologists do their utmost to eliminate the impurities of the interview technique as much as they possibly can. Usually the interviewers are very carefully selected. The length of the interview is considered. At times, totally unstructured, or free-response, questions are asked or are interspersed with highly structured questions that demand a definitive answer. The results of the interview are frequently taped and the depth or motivational analytical content is duly recognized. As one might suppose, the more practiced the interviewer, the better the data collected.

A third way the psychologist attempts to get his data is through biographical media. This uses diaries and any other writings, such as correspondence or reports from others, concerning the subject being studied.

A fourth method that may help to explain how the psychologist does research concerns itself with testing and measuring human behavior. Roughly speaking, there are two categories. The first are tests, such as intelligence tests, manual-dexterity tests, response measures to such phenomena as hand grip, pursuing a point on a rotor wheel, measuring the amount of eye-blink response, testing for comprehension in problem-solving or ability to memorize material, testing one's knowledge of a field. A second large area that testing concerns itself with is at times called expressive or projective measuring techniques. The intent here is to disguise somewhat the purpose of the research so that the respondent will not "rig," or make deliberate favorable or unfavorable responses, since he does not know what constitutes a passable or good answer. It is probably safe to say that the two largest of these are the Rorschach Ink Blot Test, a very widely used instrument especially for clinical psychologists, and a second equally important and widely used projective technique called the Thematic Apperception Test. These two instruments in themselves could well constitute one-quarter to one-third or even one-half of the research done with expressive or projective methods. Such other techniques as story telling, completing an incomplete sentence, drawing pictures, are also used. (Ames, 1966)

As we have stated previously, the ingenuity of the psychologist may be very important in eliciting a desired response from adult-aged individuals because most adult-aged people are perhaps cautious, suspicious, disinterested, and, contrary to children and other captive audiences, have freer choice as to participating in the research.

In reference to the cupidity that the researcher may employ, the present writer has found using humor is one of the most profitable and productive instruments with middle-aged subjects. Judging and responding to humor, it seems, is a nonthreatening task to perform and indeed seems to solicit excellent cooperation from this age-level group. Perhaps it is because our society considers having a "sense of humor" a good attribute. Obviously the intent is not on humor but on the differentiation of one's response to humor—verbal or cartoon—stimuli.

A fifth area of technique is the employment of physiological or organic measuring devices, such as the Electroencephalograph (which measures brain waves), the E.K.G. (electrocardiograph), and of course all the various devices and machines used by medical doctors in hospitals and clinics.

For some kinds of data, a pure census approach is used. These statistics usually come from the state or federal agencies or from the actuarial files of nation-wide insurance companies. In point of fact, the latter may be one of the most profitable data-producing sources. The subject's response is usually quite accurate because the insurance policy depends upon his accurate answers and in many cases it cuts across cultural and economic lines. However, insurance companies are not particularly prone to open their files to an interested developmental psychologist. This is, of course, their privilege.

The conclusions are that the psychologist uses every method he can possibly think of, whether it particularly fits his need or not.

Research
Suggestions

Knowledge concerning human behavior begs for replicable research evidence. In keeping with this quest, each chapter is concluded with suggestions for needed research in the field of adult development.

1. Can developmental theories that can be experimentally tested be formulated?
2. Is it possible to begin immediately to select populations most likely to be available for longitudinal studies?
3. Which areas remain the most constant over the years: cognitive, conative, or affective?
4. Will research discover a "boredom" period in middle-aged individuals?
5. Can more adult subjects be made available without "invasion of privacy" charges?
6. What is the effect of Cognitive Dissonance in adult research?
7. How can "age bias" in adult research be eliminated?

8. Can instruments be developed to specifically measure adult behavior?
9. What are the effects of historical influences on aging?
10. How can middle-class bias in developmental research be eliminated?
11. Can "adulthood" be determined by means of an instrument that measures disengagement?
12. What do most adults consider to be their greatest problems?
13. Can Selye's "General Adaptation Syndrome" be experimentally tested? In how many ways?
14. What are the changes in personality that occur in the adult years?

CHAPTER 2

Maturity

IS THERE AGREEMENT ON THE TERM *MATURITY?*

It is generally assumed that adults are mature. Assuming that adult-hood brings maturity, are adults inclined to remain mature, or is it possible to be a mature adult and then regress back to immaturity? Is maturity a process that one continually goes through; or is it a plateau; or is it a position; or is it a place; or is it a point in time? Chapter 1 considered the question of what are the adult years. This chapter attempts to clarify what a *mature* adult is. Adulthood and maturity may not be synonymous, but we may use some of the same approaches in considering possible answers.

Some writers regard maturity as more of an attitude rather than a collection of activities or worthwhile attributes. (Peck, 1959) (Clark, 1967)

Traditionally maturity is defined as

> the state or condition of complete or adult form, structure, and function of an organism, whether in respect to a single trait or, more often, all traits . . . maturity of behavior is nearly always given a commendatory connotation . . . a vaguely defined condition which may refer to (1) practical wisdom in contrast with intelligence; (2) steady and socially acceptable emotional behavior; or (3) mastery of effective social techniques. The term may be used relative to chronological age: a child is judged emotionally mature for his years . . . the arbitrarily set period between ages 21 and 65.[1]

The judgment of maturity may be highly subjective and in the eye of the beholder. When we contrast practical wisdom with intelligence and call it intellectual maturity, or witness behavior that we think is steady and socially acceptable and call it emotional behavior, or judge someone to have a mastery of effective social techniques and call it social maturity, we lack specific criteria and may be indulging in subjective wishful thinking. Are there any systems or ways of measuring maturity that call for a higher degree of objectivity? In the next section we shall examine this question and see what others have to say in regard to maturity and adulthood.

Some developmental psychologists consider maturity as being a process of "ripening," which subsumes a preparation for a future stage in life. (Wilson, 1967)

This concept is usually referred to as a "hypothetical construct." The psychologist refers to some kind of entity or process that is inferred as actually existing and also is amenable to being measured.

In theorizing about maturity in adults, we may also make reference to "operational definition." What are the operations or procedures that are employed in distinguishing maturity from other kinds of behavior? The meaning will ultimately rest upon facts of direct observation even though degrees of observational validity are obviously involved. (Wittenberg, 1967) (Steindl-Rast, 1967)

No matter whether the approach is to employ a hypothetical construct or an operational definition or subjective judgment, there appears to be little agreement on the term *maturity*, as we shall see in subsequent sections of this chapter.

[1] H. B. English and A. C. English, *A Comprehensive Dictionary of Psychological and Psychoanalytical Terms*, New York, McKay, 1958. Used by permission of David McKay Company, Inc.

HOW MAY WE MEASURE A MATURE ADULT?

What follows is an adaptation of the sources quoted, and it must be understood that the following authors are not necessarily discussing the concept of maturity.

One of Havighurst's many contributions to the field of psychology, and specifically of developmental psychology, is his concept of, "Developmental Tasks." Briefly stated, the idea of the developmental tasks is that there are certain skills or abilities or tasks that the human must master during a specific span of time in his life and that the mastery of these tasks is crucial to the individual's further development in the *next* stage or period of life. Havighurst's concept of developmental tasks is not universally accepted. It is without doubt, however, one of the most interesting contributions made in the field of developmental psychology to date (For a further elaboration of these developmental tasks, see Havighurst, 1953a.)

For the present, our interest is only in those developmental tasks that one should succeed in doing as he passes through the middle-adult span of life. Again, to succeed in these seven tasks is to make the next stage of life much easier, to fail in one or more of these tasks is to bring unhappiness and further failure in the next period of life following middle adulthood.

1. Achieving adult civic and social responsibility.
2. Establishing and maintaining an economic standard of living.
3. Assisting teen-age children to become responsible and happy adults.
4. Developing adult leisure-time activities.
5. Relating oneself to one's spouse as a person.
6. Accepting and adjusting to the physiological changes of middle age.
7. Adjusting to aging parents.

(Havighurst, 1953a)

Havighurst does not say that the successful mastering of these developmental tasks in middle age brings about a mature individual; it is the present writer who is making this suggestion and who feels it may be as defensible as any other concept of what maturity actually is.

Erikson is one of the few individuals who has been able to take Freud's psychoanalytic concepts and project them beyond the infant and child level of behavior. He has generated much reputable research and certainly wide interest in this field. (Neugarten, 1964a) (Erikson, 1959)

Perhaps we may define maturity as the successful resolution of the eight stages of ego development as they are postulated by Erikson. Each stage is expressed in polar extremes. The assumption is that physical maturity does not automatically resolve the tensions between the extremes and, further, that progress during life is seen as a continuum from one stage to the next.

The eight stages are as follows:

1. "Trust versus distrust" (early infancy).
2. "Autonomy versus doubt and shame" (later infancy).
3. "Initiative versus guilt" (early childhood).
4. "Industry versus inferiority" (middle childhood).
5. "Ego identity versus role diffusion" (adolescence).
6. "Intimacy versus isolation" (early adulthood).
7. "Generativity versus ego stagnation" (middle adulthood).
8. "Integrity versus despair" (late adulthood).

Thus one system of measuring maturity is to discern whether the individual has resolved the conflict of duality in each of the eight stages of ego development. It must be understood that each stage is not a stair step; once achieved, one does not retreat backward. Rather the preceding stages and the future stages at one given period of life are always in bipolar conflict. For example, at stage 4 (middle childhood), where there is conflict for the ego to be industrious and produce as against the feeling of being inferior and nonproductive, the individual may still not have totally resolved the conflicts of stages 1, 2, and 3 and at the same time be emerging into recognition and possible resolution of stages 5, 6, 7, and 8. At middle childhood, "industry versus inferiority" is nuclear. (Erikson, 1950) (Neugarten, 1964a) Whether this method proves to be a fruitful method of measuring maturity only time and research will tell.

Another attempt to solve the problem of what maturity actually is utilizes the work of Buhler. At her suggestion, it might be possible to consider maturity as the age of fulfillment. "Thus we arrive at the assumption of four basic tendencies of life. They are the tendencies (1) toward need satisfaction, (2) toward adaptive self-limitation, (3) toward creative expansion, and (4) toward the upholding of the internal order." (Buhler, 1961) (Buhler, 1959)

Havighurst feels:

Fulfillment is likely to come well before the end of life. In this case, how is a person to make a meaningful use of time in his later years? Most men and women in western cultures aim their life at a goal which is located in the middle years. Women feel fulfilled when their children are grown up and well started on their adult life. A working class man feels fulfilled when he has raised his family and paid for his house. A middle class man feels fulfilled when he has reached for the peak of his work career and has assumed a place of civic or professional leadership. [Kleemeier, 1961]

What is maturity? We have suggested, using the work of Buhler and Havighurst, that it is a period when we are fulfilled.

There is still another system that we may use in attempting to get a better picture of what is meant by maturity. Again, we do not distort the idea, but adapt the system to a degree probably never meant by its originator.

The General Adaptation Syndrome of Hans Selye has captured the interest of some psychologists. The essence of Selye's General Adaptation Syndrome is that man goes through, and all living organisms go through, cycles of shock-resistance-exhaustion. This pattern repeats itself throughout life either in short cycles or in very long cycles. Some of the cycles of the adaptation syndrome are parallel, some overlap, some are in sequence.

Selye is saying that life consists of a number of traumatic, or wound-producing, incidents. These may be biological or psychological but whatever their nature, they shock the system and may produce injury or harm. Once the animal or human system has received a shock, it then marshals all of its resources and resists the agency of shock. This resistance stage follows immediately upon the shock impetus. It is automatic. The length and severity of the shock, of course, control the amount and longevity of the resistance period. It is natural, then, that, in order to recover, the system will now go through an exhaustion stage. As we have stated, the whole triad of behavioral mechanisms repeats itself over and over again, depending upon whatever shock or injury the system is the victim of.

There is a possibility that we may measure maturity at that point in life when the General Adaptation Syndrome system is less efficient and begins to have used up its in-born battery of energy. (See also Chapter 1.) (Selye, 1956)

Once more we turn to the work of a noted psychologist for possible threads of evidence that may help us to better understand maturity.

The work of Carl Gustav Jung has been previously mentioned in response to the question of what middle age might be considered to be. However, at this point a fuller explanation is in order if we are to use the system for explanatory purposes.

The work of Jung is involved, complex, and we make no attempt whatsoever at this point to give the reader any more understanding than is necessary to handle the present question: How may we measure the maturity of an adult?

To Jung, all of life, all of living matter, all of the universe, exists on polarities. This rubric means that there are always two opposites to any and all things in life. As man is born and progresses through his infancy and childhood, he is faced with polarities that are inevitable. It is now his job, if he is to succeed in any degree, to balance or bring the opposing forces into equal positions so that he may have peace and productivity. The total process of achieving true polar equality is called self-actualization. Through a process of individuation, meaning that each of us has his own method and unique way of bringing a state of equilibrium between the polar factors of life, man first creates for himself a self system:

> The self, lying "midway between the conscious and the unconscious," is able to give equilibrium to the total personality: the psyche. It does more than balance the psyche; it also keeps the psyche in a relatively stable position. Man achieves this stability only, in most cases, in later life after he has emerged from the brashness of adolescence and the worldly orientation of the early adult. The attitudes of extraversion gradually are replaced by the attitudes of introversion as the individual lives through middle-age. During this period the middle-age person no longer needs the physical energy he once used to make a start in life, and thus, following the precepts of entropy and equivalency, he displaces physical energy with psychic energy to balance out the life picture. Likewise, the organic needs become less important, especially if he has managed to accrue some wealth and position, thus freeing more of his mental and physical energy.

> •   •   •

> It is very rare in Jungian theory for an adolescent or young adult to achieve full self-actualization. As the individual develops through his span of years, his primary energy source is organic and exists at the vulnerable, conscious level. It is only until he develops the counterpart of organic energy (psychic energy) that man can come near to a true self. The extraverted, impulsive behavior of children and youth must make room for the spiritual, or introverted behavior of adults, with their accumulated wisdom and value system based on deeper philosophical grounds. Actual chronological years are not the most important factor in this type of self-actualization through stages of development, but Jung considered most people in our civilization to reach this re-evaluation of values around the ages of 40 or 50. The age may vary through different cultures and civilizations. This aspect of Jung's personality theory can hardly be expected to appeal to younger people. [Bischof, 1964]

Jung goes on further to say that the process of self-actualization, which for most of us becomes a reality in our middle years of life, is greatly influenced by the number or amount of experiences that we have in order to gain full selfhood. In other words, the more variety we add to life, within reason, the greater number of things that we experience and profit from, the closer can we come to being self-actualized people.

It should be obvious at this point that the present writer is suggesting that self-actualization in the Jungian sense and maturity may have many common components. They may, perhaps, even be synonymous.

Using the very same word, "self-actualization," we explore the contribution of Abraham Maslow and its relationship to maturity. Like Jung, Maslow is not talking about maturity, but his hypothetical construct of self-actualization may well help us to answer our question of measuring maturity.

Maslow considers at least fifteen characteristics that are outstanding in truly self-actualized people. He even maintains that some people have come close to being self-actualized—Lincoln, Jefferson, Walt Whitman, Thoreau, Eleanor Roosevelt, Albert Schweitzer, as well as a number of less publicized and well known humans that Maslow has studied.

What is maturity? Perhaps it is akin to Maslow's concept of self-actualization and something that very few of us ever achieve.

The following fifteen items are the main characteristics of a fully self-actualized person:

1. Oriented realistically, efficient perception, good judge of others, quick to judge them.
2. Accepts self and others and the world for what they actually are, not for what he wishes they would be, not hypocritical.
3. High degree of spontaneity, unaffected in behavior, acts natural, may appear unconventional.
4. Problem-centered not self-centered, works on problem not self, not very introspective.
5. Inclined to be detached, great need for privacy at times, not entirely dependent on others, can amuse self, can detach self and concentrate alone, may appear aloof to others.
6. Autonomous within self and independent, dependent on self, serene.
7. Fresh appreciation of people and world, not dulled—not "I've been there before," but "every sunset is as beautiful as the first," "ten-thousandth baby as miraculous as the first."
8. Somewhat mystical or profound inner experiences, seems out of this world at times.
9. Identifies strongly with fellow man, but does not join in empathetic way, has older-brother personality, wants to help, truly interested in the welfare of man.
10. Deep and intimate relationship with only very few, has special friends or small circle of friends, highly selective in friends, gives absolutely to them, easily touched and moved by children.

11. Strong democratically oriented values, can relate and learn from rich or poor, acquaintance's class or race or position not important.

12. Understands difference between means to achieve a goal and the rightful ends to be achieved, strongly ethical and highly moral, though may differ with popular idea of right and wrong, focuses on ends and purposes.

13. Philosophical and whimsical inner-motivated sense of humor, does not laugh at cruelty, strong sense of incongruity, does not tell jokes as jokester but rather sees jokes in everyday things spontaneously.

14. Tremendous capacity to be creative, one of the *most* universal capacities in all self-actualized people, no special talent but new touches to life, creativeness of child, fresh way of doing things.

15. Swims against mainstream, very open to new experiences, resistant to conformity.

(Bischof, 1964)

Allport, who is much in the tradition of Maslow in that he actually cares about human behavior without being overly sentimental about it, has come to grips probably more realistically than other psychologists in delineating the aspects of maturity.

> Allport asks this provocative question and spends considerable time in discussing it: What is the fully developed self or what may we call a mature personality? He admits that neither he nor any other psychologist can tell us completely what normal, or healthy, or mature personalities are. However, there is a practical aspect which in our Western culture he feels does lead to considerable agreement as to what can be considered the mature personality or the fully developed self.
>
> Allport finds six criteria that all of us may agree upon. "The mature personality will 1. have a widely extended sense of self; 2. be able to relate himself warmly to others in both intimate and non-intimate contacts; 3. possess a fundamental emotional security and accept himself; 4. perceive, think, and act with zest in accordance with outer reality; 5. be capable of self-objectification, of insight in humor; 6. live in harmony with a unifying philosophy of life."
>
> Allport makes no claim to originality for the six criteria, but does feel that too often psychotherapy and counseling ignore these factors and overstress one or two. Also involved, and not too well handled, are our habits and developmental techniques in training children to become adults. It is the well-rounded individual who can meet the above six criteria. [Bischof, 1964]

Maturity may be defined as that point in adult life when the individual is capable of using the ego defense mechanisms in full support of his ego (Weinstock, 1967)

A daily syndicated newspaper columnist, Sidney J. Harris, adds still another worthwhile dimension in creating criteria for judging maturity.

The Conditions of Maturity

A college student in Kansas has written to ask me if I could define the word "maturity" for him. "The word is thrown around so loosely these days," he writes, "that it seems to mean everything to everybody."

I quite agree. In my time, when a girl threw a boy over, it was because he was a "jerk" or a "drip." Now she does it for the grand-sounding reason that he's "immature,"—when she may be just as immature herself.

It reminds me of the comedian I recently heard who explained he divorced his wife because she was "immature"—"She'd come into the bathroom while I was taking a bath, and sink all my boats!"

I wouldn't care to try a one-sentence definition of the word "maturity" because the idea covers too much ground. Besides, it's important to recognize that nobody is wholly mature in every direction, and that it is a goal we should keep aiming at, rather than a pinnacle we can ever attain.

But I do think it's possible to set down a list that will embrace the most important aspects of the word. And *the first condition of maturity is to use this list for judging ourselves,* rather than others.

If we can recognize, accept, and (most of the time) act upon the following nine maxims, I think we have a right to call ourselves grown-up:

1. Everything must be paid for, either in material or psychic coin.
2. The similarities between people are much greater than the differences; differences are accidental, similarities are essential.
3. The more we get to know someone, the harder it is to dislike him.
4. It is impossible to understand oneself without understanding others and impossible to understand others without understanding oneself.
5. Nobody can cheat us as we cheat ourselves; nobody can deceive us as we deceive ourselves; nobody can defeat us as we defeat ourselves.
6. Everybody is more or less irrational, more or less infantile, more or less tied to the past with invisible chains; therefore, we must not be quick to judge or quick to blame.
7. The sins of parents are handed down to the children; no law of heredity is more certain than this, or harder to accept.
8. What we call "intelligent self-interest" always fails in the end, for the more interest we show in the self, the less intelligent we become.
9. The means we use eventually change our ends; we become what we do.

[Harris, 1964]

"When—in the aging process, is physiological and psychological deterioration no longer compensated for by past experience?" Maybe this is what maturity is. "Generally, high social participation and being an active member of a matrix of personal interrelationships seems to be conducive to successful aging and may also have implications for physiological functioning." (Birren, 1964a)

Perhaps maturity is what Havighurst is talking about in the following selection:

> During and after middle-age there is an interaction of physical condition, social environment, and ego which produces the phenomenon of aging. The body loses energy and efficiency; the social environment changes its expectations and attitudes from those that apply to middle-aged persons; and the ego or the self relates to society in ways that are at least partly determined by the personality structure which is fairly continuous from middle-age to old age. [Havighurst, 1965b]

Thus, to this point we have a suggestion that maturity concerns itself with interrelationships or the possibility of interaction with one's physical, social, and psychological elements.

Some of the work of Cumming and Henry, as reported in their Kansas City studies, indicates (in a sampling of over 200 people aged 50 through 85, as reported in 1961) that the most marked changes appear around the age of 65. Following this lead, we may not know what maturity is, but this may be a thread of evidence showing when maturity ends. (Birren, 1964b)

From the same studies a theory may be formulated in regard to maturity as being a stable period or plateau. The suggestion is made that there may be but one major crisis in middle age; that is: being middle-aged. On the other hand, old age, like childhood and infancy, may have a number of stages in relatively quick succession. Are you mature when you have reached stability in life and must no longer face daily crises or very periodic crises? (Birren, 1964b)

It should be noted that there are at least two factors that tincture self-judgment in regard to how mature one is. Primarily growing out of the University of Chicago studies, the data are of interest, as social classes perceive maturity differently. Lower-class individuals gave 25 years of age as the prime of life or as marking a mature individual. As one goes up the social scale, the age of maturity rises, until those in the upper-middle class gave the mean age for maturity as 40. The data were for men. The upper-middle class felt that a woman was most good-looking or confident or mature or in her prime of life at a much higher age level than did the lower class. Whatever we think of maturity may depend upon how much money we have or what our class in life is. Equally involved could be the factor of being masculine or feminine. "Since women live longer than men and also mature about two years earlier, they are adults a somewhat greater proportion of their life span." The evidence seems to indicate girls mature earlier than boys. This may structure the entire consideration of maturity. (Birren, 1964b)

Not by way of summary or in conclusion, but because it is so neatly put, we end with the words of Sigmund Freud. In regard to maturity someone once asked Freud what he thought a normal person should be able to do; in other words, what is maturity? Freud's answer was very quick and concise: *"Lieben und Arbeiten"*—to love and to work.

Research Suggestions

1. Can a pragmatic objective scale that measures degrees or levels of maturity be constructed?

2. How can the utility and predictability of the Havighurstian Developmental Scales be tested?

3. Is there a way to test the conflict of duality in Erikson's Stages of Development? Are all conflicts dual in mature adults?

4. Is it possible to experimentally validate Buhler's "assumption of four basic tendencies of life?"

5. Can Selye's General Adaptation Syndrome be extended from biological to behavioral dimensions? For example, does the shock of the death of someone loved dearly go through the three stages that Selye expostulates?

6. Is there a way to experimentally test the hypothesis of Jungian psychology, which states that full self-actualization is not possible until middle adulthood or when the polarities of human existence are in balance?

7. Can Maslow's self-actualization rubric be validated? Is it possible to construct some objective quantitative device (a test) to measure the fifteen aspects of self-actualization?

8. Can Allport's six criteria for maturity be objectified?

9. Are there definite stages in middle adulthood, or is this age period a plateau?

10. How can the variance in masculinity and femininity with age be explored more deeply? Do men and women become more alike as they grow older?

11. Are there different kinds of maturity? What are they? How can they be measured? Can a man be mature in one area and immature in another?

12. How important are cultural influences in attaining maturity?

13. How do concepts of maturity differ in various countries?

14. How important is maturity to "successful" living?

CHAPTER 3

Self-image

WHAT IS SELF-IMAGE?

English and English indicate that self-image is "the self one thinks oneself to be. This is not a directly observed self-object but a complex concept: of one's personality, character, status, body and bodily appearance, etc. It may differ greatly from objective fact." [1]

To some developmental psychologists, the personality or self-image of the adult revolves around "self-concept," a feeling about the self

[1] H. B. English and A. C. English, *A Comprehensive Dictionary of Psychological and Psychoanalytical Terms*, New York, McKay, 1958, p. 487. Used by permission of David McKay Company, Inc.

that may be more physically oriented than intellectually oriented. (Brennan, 1967) Adults must think about the roles they play, which are bound to change in characteristics, such as parenthood, place in the world of work, relationship to a spouse either currently living or dead or divorced, memberships in clubs, and the entire panoply of the difficulty or inflexibility in wanting to change roles, which is never easy. There is evidence that the more successful adults are in single role playing, the more likely this may lead to rigidity or the inability to change role structure. (Rogers, 1967) (Tabachnick, 1967) The image the adult has about himself is that he is comfortably set in certain positions or roles in life, has discovered he plays them with more success than failure, and feels that it is not worth the time and trouble to, at least deliberately and with some expenditure of effort, change his role structure. It just does not seem to be worth the effort. (Hurlock, 1959)

Along the same line of thinking but using a different term, *ego energy,* the adult finds that his ego or feeling of importance about self not only has less energy as he perceives it but may become smaller and require less and less enhancement. (Birren, 1964a)

Donahue summarized five studies in this area. "According to the concepts of role theory, the well-adjusted older person is one who has learned a number of socially approved roles in earlier life and then continues to enact at least some of them during later maturity." (Williams, 1963)

Kuhlen, who reviewed a number of studies made in the middle 1950s, states: "Many people of quite advanced years often described themselves as middle-aged—half of over three hundred individuals whose ages were over seventy years of age in one of the studies and about thirty percent of those over seventy-five years of age in another study called themselves middle-aged." Kuhlen suggested the term *image maintenance* to describe this phenomenon. (Birren, 1964a)

"Sometime around the age of sixty in American society, a person is expected to begin to assume the roles appropriate to later maturity and old age. Ten years later by the age of seventy he is expected definitely to *live* the roles of the elder." (Birren, 1964b) [2]

Some adults hope to change their assigned role in life, and thus the image they have of themselves, by moving out of their previous environment. "For those who remain in the community of their adult life, the change of role tends to be less than for those who migrate in search of better climate or leave the metropolis to go back to the scenes of their youth." (Birren, 1964b) [3]

[2] J. E. Birren (ed.). *Relations of Development and Aging,* 1964, Charles C Thomas, Publisher, Springfield, Ill.
[3] *Op. cit.*

Neugarten and others consider the self-image of adults to consist of the biological functions, the cognitive functions, and the affect functions. It is possible that the self-image may be more related to health and disease than to increasing age, "the point is a reminder that chronological age has no meaning in and of itself, but is used only as a convenient index for representing the events that occur with the passage of time."

Neugarten proposes two terms that help to advance a deeper understanding of this phenomenon. "Analysis of individual cases leads to the conclusion . . . (there is) no sharp discontinuity with age . . . (and) coping becomes stable over time." Thus, as adults come to terms with their environments by coping, three behavioral components are suggested: to synthesize all of the impeding stimuli that surround the adult, to rationalize or make excuses for weaknesses, and to reorganize whatever events are occurring that do not seem to fit into a pattern that one wishes to recognize or can handle comfortably. The concept of coping is generally used in regard to children's and infant's behavior.

> The direction of the personality change, then, from middle to old age seems to be one of increased inner orientation; increased separation from the environment; a certain centripetal movement which leads to increased consistency and decreased complexity and in which the synthesizing and executive qualities, in maintaining their centrality, maintain also the continuity of the personality. [Neugarten, 1964a]

The same author finds that preoccupation with "inner life" increases as the adult ages. Forty-year-old adults see themselves as operating in a bolder manner where the rewards of taking risks are high. The adult at age 60 sees himself as more conforming and adjusting to outer-world demands. (Neugarten, 1964a)

Buhler, reporting on studies running from 1957 through 1962, finds that there may be three things that are emphasized in the adult years: meaningfulness of life, self-realization, and fulfillment. "For many people, life is a meaningful project involving self-determination toward goals with various episodes of self-assessment along the way and ending in fulfillment or failure." (Birren, 1964b)

CAN SELF-IMAGE BE MEASURED?

Psychologists, following Thorndike's early dictum that whatever exists, exists in some amount and is therefore amenable to measurement, have always spent great effort in measuring behavior. Self-image is no exception. Perhaps a more relevant question is the accuracy of measurement. The validity of a psychological test is always open to challenge. Instrumentation used to measure self-concept is no exception. Thus the question may be answered that self-image can be measured while the question of accuracy and validity is yet to be adequately answered. (Gergen, 1967)

The major types of measurement efforts are similar to those described previously in Chapter 1, "What are the methods most frequently used?" and in Chapter 2, "How may we measure maturity in adults?" Again, the primary emphasis appears to be in the projective-tests category.

One group, the Committee on Human Development (The University of Chicago), spent approximately 10 years, from 1952 to 1962, refining the techniques of measurement for their Kansas City studies on adults. After much experimentation they evolved a number of tests. One of them was a structured interview named the Life Satisfaction Scales, designed to measure successful aging in terms of the respondent's satisfaction with his present and past life. The scale measured five broad areas: zest versus apathy, resolution and fortitude, goodness of fit between desire and achieved goals, mood tone, and positive self-concept. Another test created by the Chicago group was a modified TAT technique primarily used in studying age-sex roles and personality for middle-aged subjects. Neugarten felt that some of the most efficient studies of adulthood might better follow inductive approaches coupled with "naturalistic observation rather than on the deductive and experimental." She concludes that the ". . . investigator of adult personality is likely to make faster progress in studying changes with age if he uses concepts and dimensions especially devised for his purposes rather than if he attempts to apply theoretical frameworks that have grown up in other areas of personality research." (Birren, 1964a) (Williams, 1963) (Neugarten, 1964a) (Rosen, 1960)

There is some evidence that other unique aspects of self-image may be measured. One's attitude toward death, especially as it involves the level of religious feeling, becomes an aspect of self-image. (Tibbitts, 1962)

Rotter's Level of Aspiration Test apparently was successful in measuring some, if not many, characteristics of self-image. The Rotter Test is an adaptation of a previous test by the same author. In this investigation, 39 white male institutionalized individuals, whose ages ranged from 70 to 86 years, were compared in the sentences they completed to 36 white male nursing assistants, whose ages ranged from 22 to 35 years. Briefly stated, the level of aspiration for both groups was quite low. However, in the older group there was less flexibility in adjusting to success or adjusting to failure. The older group also felt a greater need for self-protection and experienced a feeling of vulnerability. (Krugman, 1959)

One of the newest efforts to measure self-image is the result of the long-time efforts of Dr. Milton E. Hahn. Hahn is aware of the need for more research on middle-aged populations. As the result of his teaching, research, and private practice, he has created an instrument, "Self Study Projects," which is correlated with his book *Planning Ahead After Forty*.[4] (Hahn, 1967)

In summary, attempts to measure self-image are as variable and as useful as the psychologists can make them. Some preliminary success as reported by Neugarten is evident. However, psychologists are still looking for tools that are uniquely valid and useful for adult-aged subjects. (Hunt, 1967) (Denmark, 1967) (Osofsky, 1967)

DOES SELF-IMAGE CONTINUE TO CHANGE OR DEVELOP IN ADULTHOOD?

There appears to be some evidence that the individual's concept of himself does change through the adult years. (Meltzer, 1965a, b) (Shostrom, 1967)

The Kansas City studies on aging found a possible crisis occurring in the early 50s called the "middle-age depression." However, it appeared to be temporary, with a spontaneous recovery in the 60s. As usual, the findings emphasized unique social-class differences. Upper-middle-class subjects appeared to have better images of themselves than lower socioeconomic classes. (Neugarten, 1964a)

Contrary evidence from the same research sources indicates no difference between social classes and age groups on the basis of worries about being dependent upon others, losing one's health and vigor, and loss of income. The 40-year-old and the 60-year-old both were deeply concerned about these three factors in regard to themselves. Adults do not worry so much about "becoming" old as they do about "being" old, providing the above factors are present in old age. (Vedder, 1965)

Roughly speaking, the individual feels himself to be oriented outward toward the environment during the first two-thirds of the life span, but during the last third turns more inward toward the self. Sometime during middle age the ego restructures itself and becomes more concerned with mastering itself rather than the outside world. (Birren, 1964b)

Studies of young adults who tended to answer questions in terms of their social role compared to older individuals who tended to answer in terms of emotional tone or attitude toward their experience suggested a "progressive change in the self-image with age." (Anderson, 1956) (Preston, 1968) (Hickey, 1968)

A second study suggested that identifying with one's children and

---

[4] *Planning Ahead After Forty: The Process of Psycho-evaluation with Self-Study Projects*, 1967, Beverly Hills, Calif.: Western Psychological Services.

their successes provided a means of continued expansion when one's own life became stagnant. This is an interesting extension of one's self-image. It may be possible that when adult dreams are no longer being fulfilled, the self-image is fulfilled via the triumphs of one's offspring. (Anderson, 1956)

Utilizing a source published in 1962, *Aging and Personality,* further evidence seems to be present that personality and/or self-image changes for the adult years of life. This study was done with 87 aging men. "The real aging crisis for the men we studied occurred in late middle rather than in old age, particularly in critical transition in age status such as retirement. There was evidence that retirement was most stressful, especially in self-image, for our respondents just before it took place." The data suggested that older retired adults had greater ego strength (more realistic and responsible) than younger adults. Personal adjustment seemed to increase with old age. Hostility projection was greater for younger males who were not retired. Retired men were more "open and trusting in their attitudes towards others." (Reichard, 1962)

Buhler identified four groups who were concerned with their own self-assessment. We use her material now in supporting the case that middle-aged adults may have a different self-image than other ages.

1. Some felt that they had done their life's work and wanted to rest and relax.
2. Some felt that active life was never finished and thus continued striving to the end of life.
3. Some lacked strength or will power and thus found an unhappy sort of resignation.
4. The last group was frustrated because of meaningless lives, which eventuated in deep regret.

Buhler concluded that the critical thing in old-age adjustment is not functional decline and insecurity as much as it is the individual's feeling of self-assessment as to whether he did or did not reach fulfillment. (Buhler, 1961)

Other studies showed increased introversion in both the sexes in the late 40s and decreased extraversion through the middle adult years. (Birren, 1964b)

Kogan and Wallach reported that "older individuals are either more willing to admit unfavorable elements into their image of the ideal or that the very connotation of the concept evokes a more negative reaction in older persons whose age status renders unrealistic any aspirations toward an unrealized ideal self." (Kogan, 1961)

Havighurst reported that people who are accurate in calling themselves middle-aged, that is, actually were middle-aged, were better emotionally adjusted. A slightly amusing account reports that when older college professors took intelligence tests, they made 100 percent more self-belittling comments than did younger college professors. (From a study done by Sward in 1945) (Birren, 1964b)

Similar to Havighurst's report of 1953, Tuckman and Lorge in a 1954 study asked individuals to classify themselves as young, middle-aged, or old. From the conclusions of this study, we find that virtually every respondent below the age of 30 classified himself as young. The 60s and 70s classified themselves primarily as middle-aged and young rather than old. The authors felt that the respondent's self-classification as young, middle-aged, or old was definitely a function of self-concept. Changes in self-classification support the suggestion that self-concept is influenced by cultural attitudes toward aging and may have very little to do with actual chronological age. (Tuckman, 1954)

A large study conducted in England for a television series indicated that many respondents denied their age. "It seems that for some people, middle age is always twenty years older than they are themselves." Many middle-aged men and women felt they were not "living their life" but that their life was "living them" due to pressures and problems of current society. (Benaim, 1967)

Wertheimer found very similar results in a study reported in 1960. The findings lend "modest support" to the hypothesis that conceptions of one's chronological age appear to change in the life span. (Wertheimer, 1960)

Kuhlen and Johnson's study asked the question, "What would you like to be doing ten years from now?" The question was incorporated in a general survey of job satisfaction and adjustment for school teachers. This question was asked of 467 single women, 280 married women, and 218 married men, all of them teachers whose ages ranged from 20 to 65. In analyzing the replies by semi-decades, Kuhlen and Johnson felt there were marked changes in orientation with increasing age. After age 30 there was a shift from a marriage to a vocational orientation for the majority of the single women. For the married women schoolteachers, vocational goals were more secondary than they were for the single women and, as we may expect, married men were clearly vocationally oriented. However, for all groups, interest in retirement did not begin to occur until the 40s. This study, of course, concerns itself with the broader aspects of personality, but we are using this large concept in a narrower sense—as self-image. (Kuhlen, 1952)

Two additional studies used an interesting approach by having the subjects draw a human figure in whatever way they wished. The drawings give further evidence to the changeability of self-image, particularly in the middle years of life.

Lehner and Gunderson reported "that men tended to draw larger figures the older they got up to about the age of 30 and thereafter they drew smaller pictures. Whereas, women drew larger pictures up to the age 40 and then smaller pictures." It was assumed that in the drawing of a human figure the individual made projections of his own self-image. "It possibly may be inferred that these trends reflect trends in self-evaluation and that the picture is drawn larger until the individual senses that he has passed the prime of life." (Birren, 1964b)

In a very similar experiment done by Tuckman, Lorge, and Zeman, in which they were attempting to measure the self-image in aging, the hypothesis was that human-figure drawings show increasing inexactness with age. Their subjects were older adults: 104 men and women. The conclusions are tentative, although they did find sharp differences in detail between the drawings by younger subjects (children and adolescents) and those drawn by older adults. (Tuckman, 1961)

Rezler in a study of self-concepts of 546 women college graduates found differences in their feelings about themselves. Of particular interest were two groups: graduates after 5 years and graduates after 20 years in college. Unmarried women graduates felt themselves to be less ambitious, less easygoing, less idealistic, and less moody compared to those who had graduated 20 years ago. The older unmarried graduates felt they were more cultured. The age trends for the married graduates revealed somewhat the same self-concepts when compared to newly graduated students, with an additional factor: the older ones felt "less good looking"—not true for the older unmarried group.[5]

Summarizing the preceding material does indicate that the adult's self-image changes as the life span continues toward old age.

WHAT AFFECTS ADULT SELF-IMAGE?

Is it being wealthy or poor?

The evidence seems to be fairly clear that if you are a wealthy adult or if you are a very poor adult, your self-image is enormously affected by your socioeconomic status. (Chapman, 1966) (Kutner, 1956)

"Middle class individuals are prone to overidentify with, or be bound by, the aspirations of their parents, and their life pattern can be one of a continuing aspiration and striving for mobility." (Birren, 1964a) (Hollingshead, 1958)

Again, in confirmation of the New Haven Study, 1958, by Hollingshead and Redlich, we find Neugarten saying, "There is now

[5] Unpublished data supplied by Dr. Agnes Rezler, University of Illinois Medical College, 1966.

abundant evidence that emotional stability and social effectiveness tend to be positively related to social class." (Neugarten, 1964a)

Although we are not speaking directly of self-image, it is worth further exploration to study the effects of socioeconomic status on the dynamics of middle-aged people. For example, "Upper-middle class people have the best integrated, most adaptable personality systems." It was felt that the lower-middle class were the next best adjusted, while the very lowest class people, on the average, showed unintegrated, undifferentiated, and unresourceful personalities. So, "the social class differences in adaptability and adjustment, thus, are not only a matter of financial resources, but also of inner psychological resources." One gets the impression from this report that money may not be able to buy happiness but that it is likely to accompany talent in living and talent in adjusting and learning. In short, good things may go together. (Neugarten, 1964a)

As we stated in Chapter 1, however, the data are incomplete. It is very difficult to solicit wealthy adults as subjects in a psychological study. They are usually highly amused if they participate and are very quick to withdraw their support if they feel bored or threatened. Obviously, this is their privilege, although it does not help us understand the world any better. On the other hand, very poor adults living on a bare subsistence level also present some difficulties in conducting psychological research. In many cases, financially strapped adults will cooperate at times because they feel that not to do so will threaten or influence their ability to receive relief or welfare money. It should be stated that their negative responses may be quite blunt and, in a few isolated cases, vulgar. Again, this is their privilege. Fortunately, we have no laws that say you must participate in an experiment.

It is interesting to note that in Neugarten's reports, the 40s were reported as the "prime of life" by middle-class individuals, but not by lower-class or very wealthy individuals. She found that the middle-class individuals, somewhere in the 40s, seemed to display the first signs of major redirection of their egos from the outer world into the inner world or their own minds. (Birren, 1964b)

Kuhlen suggests that "among middle class Americans, for example, career drives are likely to take precedence over many other psychological needs and dominate the years of young adulthood, perhaps even to the point of resulting in minimal contact with family." Kuhlen states that if the middle-class individual does get ahead of his present station, he is quite likely to turn back to his family and community in later life as a source of gratification. (Birren, 1964b)

One study used two sociology classes at the University of Minnesota. Two hundred and eight students took questionnaires home for their parents to fill out. About 50 percent were returned. Because of the nature of the population, it was considered to be middle class. The general question asked was, "In general, how satisfied are you with your life?" There is some evidence that middle-class women who married at an age they consider as having been too young or too old are much more likely to be dissatisfied with their lives after their children have grown up than women who married approximately between the ages of 20 and 30. This was not true for men. The middle-class women who were dissatisfied felt that participating in social events was very important for life satisfaction. An inverse feeling regarding staying around the house was found for the men and women: Women wanted to spend less time around the home, and, even though the men were dissatisfied, the men wished to spend more time around the home. (Rose, 1955)

It seems evident from the previous research findings that the middle-aged person's self-image is strongly affected by how much money he has. Being wealthy, being average, or being poor does something to self-image. This does not seem to be a startling conclusion.

Is it being male or female?

What affects self-image in middle age may have a great bearing on whether one is a man or a woman.

Neugarten, for example, reports, ". . . sex differences have appeared in most studies." In summarizing the 1958 Kansas City studies, she finds that men, as they progress from the age of 40 through 70, shift from being active to being passive toward the outer world. Men in this study felt a lack of efficiency in coping with their own impulses. For the men in later life, there was a greater desire to conform to society and a much greater dependence on the superego, or the moral/conscience factors of life. Women also, from the ages 40 to 70, seem to have much stronger ego control over their impulses. There was some evidence that women had a better balance between maternal feelings and altruistic feelings in comparison to wanting to dominate either home or social situations. As the older subjects approached the age of 70, men and women role-reversed. Men and women approximately the ages of 40 to 54 saw man as a figure of authority. Men and women of ages 55 up through 70 reversed this and saw the older woman as a figure of authority and the older man as a submissive individual. ". . . women as they age, seem to become more tolerant of their own aggressive, egocentric impulses; whereas men, as they age, of their own nurturant affiliative impulses." Despite the fact that both men and women as they grow older have increased difficulty in managing their inner life, there were, "striking sex differences." Women, as they approach the age 70, were more willing to act out against their environment as they experienced it and not necessarily as the environment was. Men in the same age bracket were more inclined to act out against themselves and blame themselves. Older men felt that there was increasing stress on their own self-control. They felt they had lost some of their friendly adaptability as they aged. Women went through a period of altruistic, controlled, mother-type of behavior during their early years. As they got older and older they seemed to become more egocentric and impulsive. In some cases there was direct aggression against pressures they felt. Conversely, the older men had "passive mastery." They felt that even though they were failures, they were comfortable in their failure. There was much more rumination and more fantasy instead of action. The conclusions were, generally speaking, ". . . women do not confabulate an environment in which the goals of action are magically achieved; rather, they confabulate versions of reality which permit them to act in their accustomed and preferred way." (Neugarten, 1964a)

An additional factor is pertinent. Middle-aged women go through a menopausal stage. Men at that age go through a stage called climacteric. This factor in itself may cause differences in self-image. As we found in previous research, measuring the self-image of middle-aged women may be infinitely more difficult than measuring the same thing in men. (Gilbert, 1963)

Data from *Who's Who in America* indicate that older single women have a tendency to omit their ages from autobiographical sketches. This is not true for men. Perhaps this has something to do with self-image. (Birren, 1964b)

Morgan investigated the role perceptions of working college graduates versus nonworking college graduates. ". . . the results do not support the general hypothesis that career women deal with conflicting role expectations . . ." The women college graduates were remarkably similar in the perceptions of their own roles, despite the fact that one group worked and the other did not. There was a difference in how they felt about a career role for women in contrast to a career role for men. (Morgan, 1962)

A similar study found a difference in the changes in self-concept between mature women attending evening courses and a matched nonattending group of mature women. (Denmark, 1966)

Bieliauskas reviewed all the literature and research going back to 1955 that studied the differences between masculinity-femininity, particularly in regard to the development of the male and female self-concepts and with whom they identified. There seemed to be some evidence in the 10-year period (1955–1965) that there were outstanding differences between men and women in their interests, their feeling about occupations, and what they considered to be achievement.

Studies toward the later part of the decade indicated some cultural influence and change in the feeling of men and women. If further studies are to be done contrasting masculinity versus femininity, better operational definitions are going to have to be used. Just the fact that one is a male or a female is not enough differentiation. Factors such as one's working or nonworking, professional status, social class, health or nonhealthy, and others of this nature will have to be considered in future research efforts. (Bieliauskas, 1955)

Once again, it does seem to make some difference, even though the research results are not neat and irrefutable, whether one is a man or woman. We might add that it could make a difference whether the researcher was a man or a woman. We already know that it makes some difference in test performances for men whether they are being tested by another man or by a woman, and especially if she is a very pretty woman.

Is it being black or white?

This is an open question and is likely to remain so at least in the judgment of the present writer. After a rather exhausting search of the literature on developmental psychology, there are no research studies definable as such that draw differences in regard to the self-image of adult black humans and adult white humans. This lack of data may continue primarily because such differences may indicate a rather negative finding for black humans and thus offend the current emphasis on integration. Some writers even indicate it would not be fair or democratic to draw conclusions of black versus white, on the basis that the results would be discriminatory.

The reader is then left to his own devices, to make whatever hypothetical hunches he wishes to make. It is the rank assumption of the present writer that probably there are differences in the self-image of adult Caucasoids and adult Negroids. It must feel different to be a 50-year-old Negro man than it is to be a 50-year-old white man, just as much as the evidence seems to indicate that one feels different about one's self if one is 50 years old and very poor (black or white) or 50 years old and very wealthy (black or white). But for any real factual evidence to prove this assumption, we can only wait for the data to come in.

Is it being learned or a lip reader?

Although many studies of mentally retarded children have been undertaken, none of the studies particularly apply to self-image, nor does there seem to be any evidence whatsoever of studies done on self-image for adult mentally retarded humans. The reasons for this seem somewhat apparent. Many severely mentally retarded humans do not live to be adults. Their population is very small. Other difficulties involved in this kind of study would be the lack of ability of adult mental retardates to respond to any kind of sensitive measurement instrument that was trying to ferret out a self-image pattern.

However, there is and has been an outstanding research effort conducted for well over 3 decades by one of America's most renowned psychologists, the late Terman. For many years Terman and his followers studied a group of intellectually gifted men and women who are currently in their middle years. The literature on this group is rather voluminous, but we wish to point out only the factors in regard to self-image. What is sometimes called "Terman's Gifted Group" were asked how they felt about themselves now that they had achieved midlife. Their responses fall into five categories. They felt quite successful in each one of them. For example: (1) they felt they had realized their goals in life, had vocational satisfaction, and a strong sense of achievement; (2) they felt that they had happy marriages and home lives and felt more than moderately successful in bringing up their families; (3) they felt that they had an adequate income for very comfortable living; (4) they also felt that they were contributing somewhat to the welfare of mankind by helping others and possibly leaving the world a better place to live in; and (5) there was a general feeling of peace of mind and being able to adapt to stress or emotional control. The above findings, it should be emphasized, were not universally true of all the intellectually brilliant subjects in Terman's group, but well over 50 percent of them responded as above. It should also be noted that the above five categories are not listed in order of importance. (Terman, 1959)

From another source we find some indications that ". . . age is less important than intelligence in the personality adaptations over adult life." (Birren, 1964a)

We shall have more to say about the effect of intelligence on middle age in Chapter 8. At the moment we are only concerned with the effects of one's brain power on the capacity for creating self-image.

A major obstacle, it seems to us, in considering this question is to rule out the effects of previous training, individual differences, and the enormous difficulty of simply trying to measure basic intellectual capacity. To any well-trained psychologist who knows his Binet, this is not an easy task in itself, particularly in measuring adults.

Is it being healthy or handicapped?

Schwartz studied the effect of illness and the effects of age upon the aspects of personality. His study concerns only men. His approach was to use a sampling of 100 white male service veterans, of which 25 were young-sick (median age of 31) and 25 were old-sick (median age of 66). Both groups were patients in a Veterans' Administration Hospital. The researcher compared this group with two other groups somewhat comparable. The first of the groups compared consisted of 25 young-well men (median age of 32) and 25 old-well men (median age of 67). There was support for his hypothesis "of a disengaging effect upon self-concept as a function of the cumulative and interacting effects of illness and aging." (Schwartz, 1963)

In an entirely different vein and not concerned particularly with health or handicaps, a short report was made in regard to the over-estimation of one's height as compared to one's aspirations for power and feeling about male superiority. Although the evidence has not been fully accepted, there did seem to be a direct relationship between overestimating how tall the subjects were and having strong feelings of power as a superior male. (Shaffer, 1965)

We postpone further considerations of the state of health in adult-hood to Chapter 8, where the broader aspects of health are more fully considered.

We need not belabor the question. It is being healthy or handi-capped that affects self-image in middle age. Much of the data con-cerning state of health, no matter what the age level, seem to indicate an enormous effect upon the self-image, whether the individual is 6 years old or 60 years old. (Butler, 1967a and b)

CAN ADULT SELF-IMAGE BE IMPROVED?

The answer to this question has to be an unequivocal yes or we deny the entire value of all "helping professions" such as clinical and counseling psychologists, psychiatrists, family doctors, welfare workers, and all applied professions. (Frank, 1967) (Korman, 1967)

If the answer is yes, it now becomes a question of how much help, when is it needed, who should do it, how much will it cost, when should it start, and so on. Responding to this question in all its facets is not possible right now. To do so would mean writing another book at this point to defend and explain the value and efficiency of therapy. (Billig, 1957) (Dreikurs, 1967)

Thompson concludes that society in general fosters a rather dismal outlook for the middle-aged person and in so doing, increases the middle-aged person's stress. This may be due to an overpowering youth-oriented culture. (Thompson, 1955)

The most fundamental approach to the restructuring of any self-image, with or without a specialist's help, is for the self to recognize that its own self-image is cracked or tarnished. This is an unavoidable, undeniable, first step to benefiting from professional help. (Kutner, 1956) (Ziller, 1967)

IS DISENGAGEMENT A SPECIAL KIND OF SELF-IMAGE?

There has been a growing emphasis on the term *disengagement,* which came out of the work of Cumming and Henry. (Cumming, 1961)

In her work published in 1960, Cumming first began to discuss the aspects of the concept called disengagement. It was a suggestion then, but in further work with Henry in 1961, and in further modifications in 1963, the idea seems to have caught on, gaining support, and some criticism. (Havighurst, 1968)

Essentially, the idea of disengagement means a mutual withdrawal or disengagement between the self and others in any given social system. Although Havighurst prefers to deal with the idea primarily for individuals beyond 60, others have used it to describe behavior, and more specifically, how one feels about one's own behavior as beginning as early as the mid-40s. Thus, psychological disengagement would precede sociological disengagement. Disengagement is not considered to be eccentric or idiosyncratic. Probably a good synonym for "disengagement" would be "selective withdrawal." (Neugarten, 1964a)

Some investigators suggest that disengagement has three facets: physical, social, and emotional. (Williams, 1963a) (Brennan, 1967)

The suggestion is that people of, for, and by themselves become less concerned with the demands and expectations of the outer social and physical world. They reduce the amount of physical and mental energy *by their own volition* rather than because they are getting old and creaky. The individual becomes more frugal with time. He is likely to become happier with middle-age and old-age status. In a sense, the middle-aged and old-aged person is saying:

> *You* are not counting me out of the game. I do not *choose* to play. I will play only the kinds of games I enjoy and stop trying to compete with what I think society wants me to do. I no longer care always to do what society thinks I should do. I am now of an age when I think I want to do that which I enjoy, providing it harms no one else. [Benaim, 1967]

The disengaged adult withdraws emotional investment and energy from the environment. Having taken his involvement away from the demands of society, he becomes somewhat disengaged or transfers energy to his own life's satisfaction and to his own self-image satisfaction. Apparently this does *not* mean that the disengaged individual is passive and totally withdrawn, but that the bonds are weakened that tie the individual to his social environment. It may mean a good deal of rocking chair in action. It may mean, and be equally true, that one develops a carefree attitude combined with assertiveness: travelling where, when, and how, one would like to travel regardless of what some others may think.

In summary, disengagement means that somewhere in the later adult years the individual withdraws intense emotional attachments to people and objects. It means a lessened desire for approval. It means an increased freedom of choice. It means a much greater tendency to select activities that will give a shorter-run gratification. The individual does not do something because it will pay dividends 25 years from now. For example, when the individual is aged 50, he does something during the summer because he has always wanted to do it (the children are gone, his income is adequate, and so he takes a freighter trip to some remote island): an activity that may not have been at all suitable when he was a rising young executive and chose to spend his vacations at the most fashionable resorts so as to be seen and to see. (Birren, 1964b) (Buhler, 1961) (Williams, 1963a)

Support for the theory is not universally accepted. It certainly is an idea that may give us a much broader understanding of the mechanics of being middle-aged.

One interesting observation is made by Kuhlen in reporting on work by Filer and O'Connell to the effect that before disengagement can actually take place, one must have had to have been *engaged originally* in some kind of activity. Kuhlen further states, "The implication is that the disengaged state of affairs is something desired for its own sake and not a second-best role adopted as a means of avoiding the threat developing in more significant participation or as a result of societal rejection from more significant roles." Kuhlen feels that the concept or theory needs much more investigation. (Birren, 1964b)

From this viewpoint we may get the idea that disengagement is a term for rationalization for middle-aged people. People may disengage from activities not from choice but by force. They are simply not included, elected, or selected. This critique may be a moot point. (Birren, 1964b) (Maddox, 1964)

In the final analysis, the disengagement theory may be accepted or itself get disengaged, depending upon, not the investigator's efforts so much, as what middle-aged and old-aged people actually demonstrate to themselves in their own self-concept systems.

Research Suggestions

1. Does the ability to adjust and maintain roles for the adult indicate a better adaptation to stress and anxiety?
2. Is there an efficient and scientific way to measure "ego energy"?
3. How many role changes may the retired adult expect after retirement?
4. Is it possible to construct a table or measure of decreasing risk-taking as the aging process continues? Is risk-taking correlated with mental ability or with personality structure?

5. Does the measurement of self-image in adults require different techniques for the various socioeconomic levels?

6. Passing which age seems to have the most effect on self-image: 40 or 50? Is it more pronounced for men or for women?

7. Is it true that "sometime during middle age the ego restructures itself"?

8. Is the "progressive change in self-image with age" comparable for men and women, for black and white, for wealthy and destitute?

9. What socioeconomic group extends their self-image to their children the most? Do mothers or fathers do it the most?

10. Would the evidence indicate interethnic differences in drawing human figures? (Tuckman, *et al.,* 1961)

11. What methods would be most successful in measuring the self-images of mentally retarded adults?

12. Is there a measurable difference in the perception of disengagement between the researcher and the subject?

CHAPTER 4

Marital Status

WHAT IS MARRIAGE LIKE FOR ADULTS?

Marriage may be one of the biggest gambles that an individual will ever take in his life. There may be times when the true nature of the gamble is not discovered until later adulthood. It is at that time that the individual may discover whether the marriage was a good gamble or a poor gamble. (Kephart, 1967) (Parke, 1967)

As we shall see, it is not only the number of children that one has in the family, or one's economic level, that indicates a compatible marriage, but a number of diverse considerations. (Pickford, 1967) (Rabkin, 1967)

The home one lives in is actually a series of habits that have been formed since the day of birth. They consist of how to eat, how to dress, where to wash one's hands and face, and all of the thousands of little daily occurrences that comprise the course of life. If home is a series of habits, then it would also seem that marriage is a series of habits. The longer one is married, the greater is the web and complexity of the habit formations. This we shall discuss in responding to the question: What is marriage like for adults?

In 1890 the average expectation for married life was 31 years. During this time there were usually children in the home. Death terminated the marriage about 2 years prior to the marriage of the last child. In 1950 the average had risen to approximately 40 years and there were no children in the home for the last 14 years of the marriage. (Birren, 1959)

Using this time factor as a point of departure, Table 2 is an attempt to highlight some of the pertinent time factors that may be involved in the marriages of adult males. Beginning at the top of Table 2, we find that the 40-year-old man was born in 1926 and, assuming a marriage at age 23 in 1949, his oldest child would be around 17 years of age. He is not yet a grandfather. He may have memories of the earlier years of his married life, which began in the prosperity of post-World War II affluency. The factors affecting his current married life in 1966 may revolve around mortgage payments and upward occupational mobility patterns, and we might assume heavy involvement in PTA and all of the activities in which his elementary and high school-aged children are involved. Assuming his wife is younger than he is, he may feel that she still has a good figure but is possibly getting a little sloppy.

By way of contrast, we find that the 60-year-old individual, born in 1906 and married in 1929, might have a son or daughter as old as 37 years. It is possible our 60-year-old man, in the twilight of his middle years, is now a great-grandfather who is much more relaxed and tolerant of children than he was in the years past. The 60-year-old gentleman, when he was dating his current wife, lived through the Roaring Twenties, peace seemed assured, and the Japanese and the Germans were not threatening as yet. That picture would soon change, plunging him into a Depression almost immediately after his wedding and honeymoon. His current frame of mind probably concerns retirement. His attitude toward his wife we should like to explain more fully in a later section.

No theme is more recurrent in the field of psychological research than the problems of measurement. As we have seen before and must recognize now, the difficulty of measuring any facet of marriage is enormous. (Dean, 1966) The psychological literature attests to this difficulty: "Neither form discriminated significantly between groups of married differing in marital satisfaction." (Levinger, 1965) "The findings secured from a middle-class sample with these instruments indicated that there are no clear cut associations between the variables studied." (Hurvitz, 1965) "The sentence completion technique is explored for its potentialities for measuring marital satisfaction." (Inselberg, 1964)

All of the following psychological studies reported in this chapter must be interpreted with extreme caution.

At least one other cautionary statement should be accepted. Most of the studies reported appear to be done with middle-class subjects, probably because they are the most cooperative, whereas the very rich and the very poor may not be so.

One study found: "Men and women married to satisfy three basic needs—the need for love, sex, and parenthood." Other findings are what we might expect: social condition and patterns of life played an important role in the degree of adjustment to marriage. Pathology, either of a biological or psychological nature, would make any adjustment to marriage very difficult. (Stone, 1953)

A clue as to what constitutes the dynamics of a marriage may be found in a study done with 39 white couples, college trained, and for the most part residing in or around Lincoln, Nebraska. The subjects were between the ages of 20 and 40 years. The researchers paid particular attention to the relative influence of the husband and wife in forming and maintaining close friendships. The conclusions were that husbands have the greater influence in initiating friendship and also in determining who the best friends of the couple will be. All of the couples were of middle-class status. (Babchuk, 1963)

Another study attempted to find out if there were any differences in decision-making among Iowa farm and nonfarm families. The results seemed to indicate that there were no consistent or marked differences in the relative dominance of the husband or the wife in making decisions, whether they lived on a farm or did not live on a farm. (Burchinal, 1965)

Romantic marriage may be a twentieth-century illusion and it is a myth to expect marriage to continue as an endless romance. It is only in the fairy tales that they "lived happily ever after." A more realistic concept would be to consider a "workable marriage," in which "partners actively invest themselves to make the marriage work." (Steiner, 1963)

Marriage during the adult years of life may oversentimentalize family life in the past. What was really involved was a "struggle for survival." There was "little reason to believe individuals and families were physically, mentally, or emotionally stronger in the past." (Birren, 1964a)

One author feels that instead of mute and defeating silence in a

TABLE 2. THE TIME FACTOR IN MARRIAGES FOR MIDDLE-AGED MALES

AGE IN 1966	BORN IN	MARRIED AT AGE 23 IN	APPROXIMATE AGE OF OLDEST CHILD	GRANDFATHER ROLE	FACTORS OF EARLY MARRIED LIFE	FACTORS OF CURRENT MARRIED LIFE IN 1966	POSSIBLE ATTITUDE TOWARD WIFE
40	1926	1949	17	—	Prosperity begins and so does "Bomb" threat.	May still have heavy mortgage, occupational mobility upward.	Good "figure," maybe getting a little sloppy, still too easy on the kids.
45	1921	1944	22	Probably yes, and proud of it.	World War II, war marriage, war "hero," no new automobile, rent, food, and everything rationed.	Mortgage easing somewhat unless moved to new home, vertical occupational mobility easing up.	Not as pretty as some women he knows, flights into adulterous fantasy.
50	1916	1939	27	Grandfather more than once and has a favorite grandchild and in-laws able to help the "kids."	Hitler and Hirohito and Benito threaten world peace, "Let's get married, for tomorrow I may be drafted."	Still paying on house, may be locked in occupation, young people at work are pushing, "kids these days are either drinking, delinquent, or driving like maniacs."	She may not be beautiful but she is trustworthy, loyal, friendly, kind, faithful, and she's all I've got.

50	1916	27	1939	Grandfather more than once and has a favorite grandchild and in-laws able to help the "kids."	Hitler and Hirohito and Benito threaten world peace, "Let's get married, for tomorrow I may be drafted."	Still paying on house, may be locked in occupation, young people at work are pushing, "kids these days are either drinking, delinquent, or driving like maniacs."	She may not be beautiful but she is trustworthy, loyal, friendly, kind, faithful, and she's all I've got.
55	1911	32	1934	Grandchildren are too "wild" and need discipline.	No money, low paying job, but hope springs eternal, Depression, NRA, orange-crate furniture, short honeymoon if at all.	"How old can you get?" "World is going to Hell in a wheelbarrow," don't struggle at work, relax, protect your seniority.	Best wife a man could have had considering, of course, all things.
60	1906	37	1929	Might now be a great-grandfather, relaxed and more tolerant of kids, enjoys their occasional triumphs.	Dated in the Roaring Twenties, Stutz Bear-cat and raccoon coats, make it big in the stock market, peace forever.	"They should lower medicare age," displays watch for 40 years plus of service to employer, "Who's retiring where and how do others like it?"	Now we are free and the kids can do what they want.

marriage, a good marriage is based on "constructive quarrelling." (Ogilvie, 1962)

A British writer stated, "Marriage is the nearest adult equivalent to the original parent-child relationship. Thus, its success must revolve around the freedom to regress." If we follow this line of thinking, a successful marriage should have a mutual childlike dependence of the husband and wife on each other without censure or loss of dignity. This kind of marriage gives security knowing that the other partner accepts the occasional regression into childlike behavior. (Dicks, 1963)

Further studies advocate that a marriage, particularly in the early adulthood years, should be a parallel relationship rather than a converging one. The husband and the wife are each to play their own role rather than to assume the prerogatives and the behavior of the other partner. The husband is a man and he should act like it. The wife is a woman and she should not give up her womanly prerogatives. Only in the case of an extreme emergency is it possible to converge and adopt the role of the other. In regard to the middle years, "Marriage provides the most sensitive test of maturity." (Vincent, 1961)

An interesting case may be made for what constitutes a good marriage by extending the remarks of Birren. "The adaptive person continually modifies his behavior over time, thus aging 'successfully.'" Using this as a point of departure, it may mean that a novel and nonstereotyped way of behaving in a marriage would strengthen the marriage considerably. This would keep it from being dull and pedestrian. (Birren, 1964a)

Byrne conducted an interesting study using 36 married couples as subjects. Byrne measured the similarity in attitudes between husbands and wives. First he had the husband and wife respond to an opinion-naire as they themselves felt. Later on he had them guess how they thought their spouse would respond. There was a significant husband and wife correlation. They did have similar attitudes but felt they were more similar in attitudes than they actually were. This held true regardless of the length of marriage. (Byrne, 1963)

Socioeconomic differences in handling marital problems are indicated between middle- and lower-class women. The former were more open with friends and professionals but less with their relatives, while the latter confided almost exclusively with relatives. (Mayer, 1967a)

Perhaps we may find evidence that sex plays a decreasing role in the marriages of middle-aged people. Approximately 1000 men and 1000 women, primarily residents of New York City, were asked to respond to body-part preferences through the use of a questionnaire. "The age changes were most apparent in the devaluation of sex-specific parts [but] . . . of the parts common to both sexes, both males and females rated the tongue most highly." Could it be true that as men and women progress through marriage and grow into the middle years of their lives, they value sexual aspects less and communication more in their marriages? (Weinstein, 1964)

Hurlock suggests that there are at least six adjustment problems in the marriages of adults. These are: adjustment to changed roles, adjustment to one's spouse as the years go on, adjustment to change of sex relationships and sex behavior, adjustment to potential or actual marital instability, adjustment to changed family relationships as children and parents grow older, and adjustment to the possibility of divorce or death of the spouse. (Hurlock, 1959)

The effect of the length of marriage upon the marriage itself is a very complicated issue. This is true primarily because for most people children are involved and we find that ". . . parental roles took precedence over husband-wife roles." Some men and women have remained as husband and wife together only as long as the children were at home. The influence upon a marriage of not having children will be taken up in a further section. A number of studies indicate that as the marriage progresses, and particularly during the middle years of life, there is a tendency to change attitudes on authority in the family. Women tend to rise and men to decrease in authority, particularly in their late 50s and 60s, and especially is this true after retirement. (Birren, 1964a)

Some studies indicate there is a reversal in the image of the older person. Men become more nurturant and less dominant. Women become much more tolerant of their own aggressiveness and are inclined to excuse a display of their ego strength. (Neugarten, 1964a)

While the husband is at work, the wife must face different changes in her own life. Because she operates the home, her life may change drastically as the children grow older and leave, leaving her with less to do for them and more time for herself. The specter of death of a spouse is far more poignant for the wife than the husband. Assuming that physical appearance is somewhat less important for men than women, the wife in the family may feel more threatened. There is evidence also that menopause is more physically incapacitating for the wife than the climacteric is for the husband. The male has other pursuits and interests outside of the home and marriage relationship to keep him occupied. For women, especially in their 40s and early 50s, there is a "critical period" in the marriage. (Hurlock, 1959)

A 1955 study conducted with 300 engaged couples, of whom 278 were later married, has some interesting highlights. Sixteen to 18 years later a follow-up study was done. The most stable characteristics these married people possessed in common were their value systems and vocational interests. Couples who had very low positive relationships toward each other showed very little increase 18 years later. Apparently marriage did not bring them closer together. There appeared also to be considerable change for both the husbands and wives in their attitudes and in their ratings concerning themselves. The peak change occurred in their mid-20s and mid-40s. (Birren, 1964a)

Another study attempted to measure marital satisfaction over a 6-year-period. Two groups of 40 married couples identified in 1957 as satisfied or unsatisfied with their marriages were requestioned in 1963. The object was to discover any increase or decrease in the satisfaction they felt toward their marriages. Of particular interest is the fact that couples who were originally classified as satisfied with their marriages now scored lower on a test for marital adjustment, keeping in mind, of course, that tests of marital adjustment are at best not overly accurate. (Paris, 1966)

However, another study was made in regard to the "number of years married as related to personality perception and marital satisfaction." Using the same adjustment-measurement technique, 80 married couples were retested after approximately 8 years of marriage. The results indicate that the longer the couples were married, the more benevolent they felt toward their spouses. This was as true for couples who found their marriages satisfactory as well as for those who were dissatisfied with their marriages. Of particular interest is the fact that marital satisfaction had no relationship to the number of years a couple was married, but was very highly related to the number of years of schooling the couple had. It should be emphasized that staying longer in school does not cause one to be happier with one's marriage, but there was a relationship between length of education and satisfaction with one's marriage. (Luckey, 1966)

One of the most interesting sidelights in regard to length of marriage and its effect upon the marriage relationship comes from the Japanese culture.

> Within the all-important context of the family, the later years of an individual's life (in Japan anyway) are marked by a series of observances of the attainment of certain ages. Important among these are the dangerous years of life (Yakudoshi) regional variation aside. These are generally considered to be the 25th, 42nd, and 60th years of life for men; the 19th, 33rd, and 37th years of life for women. Of these the most dangerous for men is the 42nd, and the most dangerous for women is the 33rd. [Kleemeier, 1961]

Other intercultural studies indicate differences in the "marital power structure" for couples from the United States, France, Greece, and Yugoslavia. In the United States and France the husband's authority was related to educational level, occupational status, and income. The opposite was found to exist for Greece and Yugoslavia. (Rodman, 1967)

CAN THE SINGLE ADULT BE AS HAPPY
AS THE MARRIED ADULT?

Answers to this question have very little research evidence that applies to the middle years of life. The single middle-aged individual, whether man or woman, seems to fit a stereotype in our current culture. The considerations for being a bachelor man appear to be very different than for those concerning the bachelor woman. Being wealthy, middle class, or poor makes a difference in the lives of unmarried adults. There is little research data to substantiate this, but one gains the impression that being single and middle-aged is extremely rare for the lowest economic levels. Somehow or other these people manage to have been married at least once, providing, of course, they are not mentally or physically retarded. Single people of the middle-class status in life appear to be occupationally oriented. There is practically no data whatsoever on the characteristics of the bachelor man or woman at middle age who is extremely wealthy.

Keeping all of the above qualifications in mind, we may find the following considerations to apply to the bachelor man now somewhere between his fortieth and sixtieth year.

1. Single men are handy to have around to fill in on social engagements. They may be the matchmaker's target.
2. It is possible that the single male has remained so by preference, whereas this may not be so true of the single female.
3. Being single and middle-aged may create two kinds of feelings toward this individual by others who are now married: envy and/or suspect. The unhappily married middle-aged person may have a strong feeling of envy for the so-called freedom of the male bachelor. There may also be a feeling of deep but unstructured suspicion directed around the question that there must be something wrong with the person or he would have been married a long time ago, the way "regular" people are.
4. It is possible the middle-aged bachelor can afford to be very charming, dress quite well, and obviously travel about with a great deal of freedom. He does not have to sustain a relationship with another human or feel particularly responsible for a wife or children, provided, of course, that he does not reside with one or both of his parents.
5. Most evidence points to the fact that the middle-aged bachelor has a great deal more freedom in his sex life than does the bachelor woman. For her, an assignation may require considerable planning and have aspects of tawdriness. Prostitution and romantic interludes are much easier for the male bachelor to arrange.

On the other hand, a middle-aged woman not married or ever having been married seems not to cast the same kind of picture for most of society.

1. It is probably true that the bachelor woman is somewhat suspect as having failed in the primary mission of a woman in our society: married and with family. Society may feel that the man has managed cleverly to escape the entrapment of a woman. Society's feeling for a bachelor woman is that she has failed to "catch a man."

2. Whether it be compensation or not is beside the point, the bachelor woman is expected to be an occupational success in lieu of success in marriage. This may seem unfair to the single woman, but the mores of society are not structured along lines of fairness or unfairness. This is the way they are.

3. Continuing in the same vein, society is frequently not very understanding of the single woman. Again, it is assumed that she is not single by choice but by elimination.

4. The single middle-aged woman is, like the man, quite free to travel or at least indulge in romanticized ideas of travel.

5. Unlike the middle-aged bachelor, there appears to be an attraction among middle-aged single women toward each other so that they share living quarters, frequently dine together, travel together, and have a very compatible relationship.

6. Unlike men in similar positions, unmarried middle-aged women may turn to religious organizations in order to fulfill contact with others not possible in their solitary life.

7. Unlike her counterpart, the bachelor woman has very little outlet for sexual release. Other than the work of Kinsey and of Masters and Johnson, which we shall discuss later, practically nothing is known about the sexual life of the middle-aged bachelor woman. We may only surmise on flimsy evidence that her sexual life revolves around images, fantasies and, in short, is no different than that of other humans whose sexual contacts are limited.

It may make a vast difference whether the middle-aged single woman is very wealthy, of middle-class heritage, or extremely poor. There may be some truth, though it has never been proven, that society's concept of this person is highly influenced by the amount of money she has. The middle-class middle-aged single woman may have remained unmarried because of family responsibilities. These are usually centered around helping nieces and nephews or, in most cases, providing a home for an aged parent. Again society may feel about the extremely wealthy middle-aged but unmarried woman that she is either overwhelmingly clever and inclined to indulge her appetites or that she has been overprotected from overzealous suitors who were interested in only her money.

Again it must be emphasized strongly that the above lists have no basis in research. It must also be emphasized, certainly by this writer, that no censure whatsoever is intended.

From one source we find that approximately 8 percent of the adults have never been married and that there are more men than women in this classification. The statistic of 8 percent is actually very meaningless because it depends on whether we are speaking of rich, average, or poor and whether we are speaking of black or white adults. (Hurlock, 1959)

Landis in a 1950 study suggested that after age 45, the single woman's chances of being married are 9 out of 100. After age 45, the widowed woman's chances for being married again are 18 out of 100. After age 45, a divorced woman's chances for being remarried are 50 out of 100. Landis felt that the "desire to marry or remarry frequently is replaced by vocational goals." (Hurlock, 1959)

The same source also points out that the role of a single man in middle age is usually more favorable than that of the single woman in middle age. Reasons for this are that the single man usually does not have to take care of his parents in their old age, or if he does so, it is with financial aid. The single man in middle age appears to be much better rewarded by business in promotions, in earning more money, and in the way society views him. It is easier for the single man in middle age to marry if he feels lonely or now wants to change his way of life. He is much more warmly accepted by society and, as has been pointed out, possibly even envied. (Hurlock, 1959)

One author has attempted to handle the subject of longevity and the never-married. This author finds that there is an increased survival factor for the single individual, which has been found to be true both here and abroad, specifically in the United States and the Netherlands. This is felt to be a twentieth-century phenomenon. Two further findings were noted: If a single never-been-married individual lived to be beyond 70 years of age, his chances are extremely high of outliving another individual over age 70 but who has been or is now married. Once having achieved an age of at least 70, single unmarried women will probably live longer than men in the same classification. (Tibbitts, 1962)

Most studies of mental health indicate that the incidence of psychoses or neuroses is higher for unmarried than for married individuals. (Lowe, 1967) (Rallings, 1966) We shall spend considerable time in discussing this phenomenon in Chapter 8. For the moment we cite one study, which is indicative of many.

Data from the 785 interviews of married and never married respondents in a sample of the adult population of San Francisco are presented by marital status. It was found that more single men are maladjusted than single women or than married men, thus confirming and enlarging on the results of other studies. [Knupfer, 1966]

So what happens if you are middle-aged and have never been married? The vast evidence seems to be that society will be rather unkind and unfair, whether it is warranted or not.[1] But, you may live longer.

DIVORCE: DILEMMA OR DELIVERY FOR THE ADULT?

The potential for divorce is usually based on the infidelity of the husband or wife or both. The financial position of the individuals involved may have a large bearing on whether the divorce actually is gained or a "living arrangement" is tolerated while one or the other marriage partner participates in extramarital relations. At this stage in life, the cost in money, and particularly the cost in emotions, of breaking old ties and also explaining the desire for divorce to the children who are now young adults is not a minimal condition.

Actual divorce for men appears to be somewhat different than for women. Men appear to be more receptive to the idea of divorce than do women.

A husband's wanting to break the marriage contract is, according to one author, of a psychopathological nature. It involves "the act of searching out for a mother substitute." (Neugarten, 1964a)

There appears to be some evidence that the vulnerable years for divorce are in the first few years of marriage and in the early 40s (approximately 41 to 45). The latter is a time when there is more money (and divorces cost money) and the direct responsibility for rearing the children is lessening either because they are away from home or in the process of leaving it. The "other woman" syndrome is present. Some writers feel that the woman in marriage, now that her children are gone and no longer need her, tries to "raise" a husband in lieu of children. This results in a nagging wife. Also involved are sexual

[1]In the writer's counseling experience, it is sheer idiocy to assume that it is necessary to be married to be happy. The writer has dealt with too many married individuals in middle age who were quite miserable and now yearned for an unmarried status. Along the same line, unmarried men and women, and particularly women, become quite realistic as to their single status somewhere after the age of 40. This is not so true of widows and divorcees. The entire question must be answered with extreme caution because so much depends upon the individual case. To rule that being unmarried naturally begets unhappiness and misery is to place oneself in the ridiculous position of stating that nuns and priests, for example, know no happiness. This is patently not true.

incompatibility and the claimed irresponsibility of husbands. The evidence indicates that more often it is the husband who wants the divorce than the wife. (Hurlock, 1959) (Blumenthal, 1967) (Zybon, 1966)

A rather close and careful study done of 40 couples, through structured interviews and a measurement of need fulfillment and marital satisfaction, concluded: "Analyses indicate that marriage partners try to deal with their dissatisfactions by fantasy rather than real involvement, or by tending toward variety of a sexual nature rather than substituting fantasy or an emotional involvement." (Neubeck, 1962)

Many writers in this field are of the opinion that divorce rates are highly influenced by socioeconomic conditions. Divorce is more apt to occur during times of prosperity. Further involved is the high degree of urbanization and industrialization; the higher these two factors, the greater the incidence of divorce. These factors are independent of longevity of marriage or of the particular ages the marriage partners happen to be living in. (Pinard, 1966)

Evidence regarding the impact of divorce may be gained from a study published in 1956 that involved slightly over 2000 cases. Most of the divorces involved marriages that were against the wishes of the parents. Further data indicate the first marriage lasted slightly less than 6 years and the women remarried about $4\frac{1}{2}$ years after their divorce, when they were in their early 30s. As is the custom, the sole custody of the children was given to the woman. The evidence seems to indicate the children were pleased about the idea of the remarriage and liked the new father, who seemed to reciprocate in the affection. The woman had some affection toward the husband's children, if he had any, but not quite as much as for her own children. Evidence also indicated both the parents and the community approved of the second marriage.

In the same study involving over 2000 people, the divorced woman was approximately 34 years old, whereas the divorced man was 44 years old. Again, his first marriage was without the approval of his parents. It lasted about 7 years, not much longer than the 6 years for the woman. The children were in the custody of the first wife. In this case, the man remarried about $2\frac{1}{2}$ years after his first marriage. It will be remembered that the woman remarried $4\frac{1}{2}$ years after the first marriage ended in divorce. Because the man did not have custody of the children from the first marriage, they were totally indifferent toward his remarriage. He appeared to be quite fond of his second wife's children. In contrast with a divorced woman's remarriage, the community did not approve of the man's remarriage with the same degree of acceptance they had for the woman's remarriage, especially when children were involved. (Bernard, 1956)

"Divorce by no means invariably makes the participants emotionally free of each other. Especially if the reasons for the divorce were based on revenge or retaliation by a neurotic individual." (Good-enough, 1959)

There seems to be no definitive answer to the question of whether divorce is a dilemma or a delivery from problems during the years of adulthood. Once again, there are so many individual variations on the theme that the answer depends primarily upon the individual. We shall study the question of remarriage in greater detail later. One gains the impression from the research studies that it is a general tendency of middle-aged women to hold onto their spouse and their marital relationship. Men may be more inclined to overemphasize youth and start marriage with a newer, younger spouse.

IF DEATH INTERVENES, WHAT ARE THE PROBLEMS FOR ADULTS?

No author can answer the question as poignantly and accurately as a recently bereaved man or woman who has lost a marriage partner. The problems are overwhelming, until time and action resolve some of them. Time alone does not resolve problems. It may even deepen them as the habit of sadness persists. The best evidence indicates that the problems are never truly resolved, but more likely put away or mastered within oneself. Further evidence seems to indicate that the death of one's spouse may be less severe for men than it is for women. This is obviously not true when considering an individual case of bereavement. Some authors refer to the survivors as "incomplete families." (Benaim, 1967)

As we shall see, widowed men tend to remarry more frequently than widowed women. We can only guess as to the reasons for this. Possibly one reason may be because the man looks like a good marriage prospect to another single woman who may have been divorced or widowed. There may be the feeling that "he needs someone to look after him." In other cases, the widowed man may feel no urge or desire to remarry because he has an oldest daughter who can run the home in the tradition to which he is accustomed and be a substitute mother to the other children, thus relieving him of having to make drastic changes in his life pattern. Certainly it seems obvious, despite the fact that he has lost his wife through death, his job and his outside-of-the-home world continue very much as they did when his wife was living. It may also be true that society in general feels that the widowed man is unable to cope with his single-parent role and that society is more inclined to do something to help him by bringing meals, arranging for babysitters, and the like.

The widowed woman, on the other hand, certainly has a severe disruption in her income to run the home and raise the children if there are any. Even though insurance is involved, it can hardly be adequate to compensate for a lost income of from 5 to 10 years. This may lead to the necessary measures of gaining employment simply to meet the expenses of everyday living. In contrast to the widowed man, however, the widowed woman has been out of the job market probably for many, many years. She must now restructure her entire pattern of living and join the competitive world of work. It seems logical that the more children she has the less attractive she would be to another single male her age, who might be reluctant to take on the expenses and challenge of raising children who were sired by another man.

Whether the widowed man or woman remarries or not, the evidence seems to be quite clear that death idealizes the deceased.

One of the subjects discussed in the President's Council on Aging meeting in 1963, which considered, primarily, individuals over age 65, was that the average cost of hospitalization prior to the death of a spouse was $525, which did not include doctor bills. Thus the difficulty is compounded not only through lack of income, but the longer the term of illness, the greater the hardship and the more likely financial resources are to be wiped out. This would include, of course, the burial expenses. (Birren, 1964a)

Such authorities as Dr. Alvarez felt that with the length of life now increasing particularly more for women than for men, the number of widows is increasing much more rapidly than is the number of widowers. One suggestion he makes to this problem is that a "wise and kindly husband" should always carry adequate insurance. (Alvarez, 1955)

Despite the hard cold facts of economic necessity that are involved when one loses his or her spouse, the loss of marital status is an enormous disruption of highly personal habit patterns. There seems to be an overriding need for a partner who will continue to play the complementary role that one has become accustomed to while being married. The question becomes for the widowed an extremely complicated issue in which absolutely no one on earth can point to the right way to do things. Involved here are old vestiges and sentimental strings to the past, which, as we have pointed out, become overidealized, but also involved are the loneliness and the lack of direction for the future, whether children are involved or not. It seems obvious that a new life must be made, a new set of rules must be adopted, and all of this at a time in the middle years of life, when the individual is less flexible.

Aside from sheer companionship, other factors of daily living are important to a widow. "I miss terribly being taken out . . . to have someone buy a meal for *me* and pay the bill . . . instead of having to go out and always be self-sufficient all the time, I want to lean now and then." (Benaim, 1967)

Difficulties come about in the reaction of society to the bereaved. If the bereaved manage to control their emotions and pick up as best they can after the death of a spouse, some friends and acquaintances are all too inclined to think that the death could not have been much of a blow because the recovery was so quick and apt. This is of course not true; the sorrow and sadness that go on within the individual are simply not apparent to society. On the other hand, if the individual continues to be sad and weepy, never smiling, always crying or sighing on many occasions, society again makes it more difficult. This time the reaction is one of avoidance. Immediately after the funeral there is a great surge of help and understanding, which very quickly drops off if the bereaved continue to prolong their sadness.

The end result, all too often, appears to be a losing game. If you recover too quickly, there must not have been much love and the loss was not great; if you recover too slowly, you become a difficult person to be with and in short order you are avoided. It is not a question of being fair or unfair. It is simply the way the situation is structured by society that, for adults, is built on husbands and wives and children. If the individual does not fit into this pattern, society is somewhat at a loss to know what to do with such a widowed man or woman. (Benaim, 1967)

It seems even more unfair because more women are widowed than men and the disruption in the life of a woman is greater than it is for the man. However, there is little evidence to support the hypothesis that widowhood "triggers mental illness" particularly in retired people. (Simon, 1968a)

DIVORCED OR DEAD SPOUSE: SHOULD YOU REMARRY?

Probably the magnum opus concerning remarriage was written by Bernard, *Remarriage: A Study of Marriage*. (Bernard, 1956) Much of the following material comes from the above source. Of the 6 studies reported in the book, there was very little difference shown in the success of first marriages and the success of remarriages.

Divorce seems to serve a selective function. Divorce eliminates the divorce-prone from the remarried population more rapidly. It appears that after the first divorce, those individuals who are not good marriage prospects are inclined to be eliminated from another marriage. This should, of course, make the statistics for remarriage as good as, if not better than, those for first marriages.

Some studies suggest that the duration of remarriages is somewhat shorter than that of the first marriages.

Divorce works differently on different people. For some individuals, one divorce virtually leads to another divorce because it becomes actually a habit. For others, however, the first divorce serves as a stimulus to work much harder for success in the second marriage so as not to have to go through the trials and tribulations and emotional upsets of another divorce.

A number of factors may apply that would help us to understand why a remarriage may be successful, whether it be because of divorce or death of the spouse.

1. There is the experience gained from the first marriage as to how and what married life includes; this is not a factor in first marriages.
2. There is a deeper motivation in wanting success in a remarriage and probably less romantic ideas concerning what marriage actually is.
3. In a remarriage the two people are older, we may assume much wiser, probably can handle the vicissitudes of life much better, are now emancipated from their parents and from in-laws who may have interfered in a first marriage, and one cannot deny the factor of loneliness as a motivating force. Older people may also have much less exacting standards in regard to the person they marry, and accept the marriage on a far more practical basis, whereas first marriages are just the opposite.

"The second marriage . . . may be the major emotional enterprise of a lifetime, of great intensity or duration. When a remarriage is of long duration, stable, and in general similar to a first marriage, people tend to forget that it is in fact a remarriage." In many cases, those who remarry after a divorce have almost as high a percentage of success in their second marriages as the rest of the population has had in their first marriage.

One study based on personal interviews conducted all over the United States found that both bereaved and divorced persons are as well adjusted in their second marriage as those who have been married only once. In this study, divorced men showed a slightly less satisfactory adjustment than others.

Most of the studies in this field of remarriage indicate that courtship for the second marriage is far simpler and more direct than in the first marriage. The two people fool around less, seem to be more mature, know what they want and are doing, and act less adolescent with "stars in their eyes" than do the individuals approaching a first marriage.

Some studies indicate that remarriage has tended to be more common in the lower socioeconomic classes. Wealthier people take more time to remarry. They may have higher standards for a remarriage partner and, obviously, have more money to exist as single individuals. It is less a matter of economic necessity than one of choice for the wealthy.

Other studies indicate that a divorced person has a greater likelihood of marriage than others in his age and sex bracket who have never been married. Usually, remarriage after divorce takes place rather quickly. About 75 percent remarry within 5 years after the divorce. "The increase in the remarriage after death and after divorce is due in part to a shift in public attitudes."

In contradiction to Bernard's book on remarriage, we find one author, Landis, who feels: "Remarriages are less successful than first marriages and women seem to be a poorer risk in second and subsequent marriages than men." (Landis, 1950)

One statistic indicates that "about every 8th married person or about 12½ percent have been married more than once in the United States." (Bernard, 1956) Starting with the turn of the century, remarriage has been increasing and at a fairly rapid rate.

As we might assume, the younger the person at the time of divorce, the greater the likelihood of a remarriage.

> The remarrying population, therefore, is composed predominantly of men and women in their middle years. This fact seems to call for a re-evaluation of the nature of love and the relations between the sexes of the middle years. For the most part, students of human behavior have tended to limit their analyses of love primarily to the early years of adulthood. The growing incidence of remarriage calls for some considerations of love in middle and later maturity. [Bernard, 1956]

A study conducted in New York City between the years of 1945 and 1948, which surveyed 259,000 marriages, found that the median age for all remarried men in the population was 50. The same study seemed to indicate that a previous marriage seems to increase the probability of marriage for a woman as well as for a man at all age levels. The individual who has never been married and approaches middle age apparently has less of a chance for a marriage, when considering the group as a whole, than does the person who has gone through one marriage.

From England we find that in the age group of 40 to 60 "more than 20 percent of the people are living alone." (Benaim, 1967)

Reviewing all the studies on remarriage, there is definite evidence that a far more stringent and careful selective force operates in a remarriage than in a first marriage, especially if the first marriage terminated by divorce.

Courtship for middle-aged people who have never been married lasts almost twice as long as courtship where both the individuals had been married before. In the first case, the courtship lasts from about 20 to 24 months. In the second case, where marriage has occurred, the courtship lasts for approximately 12 months. Another interesting fact is the difference in two of the categories: where the woman has previously been married but the man has been single, the courtship is much shorter than where the woman has been single and the man has been previously married. One wonders if women previously married are more able to draw a single man into marriage than the man who has been previously married is able to talk the single woman into marriage. "In this culture the man pays court to the woman and bows to her wishes." (Bernard, 1956)

When a marriage occurs in middle age when neither individual has been married before, the form of the wedding, the size of the wedding, the cost and value of the gifts, all are much greater than in other types of marriage at middle age. The honeymoon is also a very expensive one. When a single woman marries a man who has been married before, she also has a long courtship and a good-sized wedding. Her honeymoon will be rather expensive, but according to one study she will receive only about half as many wedding gifts as the previously unmarried woman marrying the previously unmarried man.

Courtship and wedding patterns are extremely different when the woman has been married before. The wedding usually is small and inexpensive, the wedding trip is quite short, and the entire procedure has less elaborateness about it.

Two studies were conducted in Seattle, Washington. The first, in 1939, involved 1,947 people, and the second, in 1946, involved 13,000 people. These 2 studies concerned themselves with distribution of re-marriages and considered previous marital status.

1939 Study

	Percent
Single man—divorced woman	21
Divorced man—single woman	20
Divorced man—divorced woman	16
Widowed man—single woman	13
Widowed man—widowed woman	9
Single man—widowed woman	9
Widowed man—divorced woman	5
Divorced man—widowed woman	4

1946 Study

	Percent
Single man—divorced woman	29
Divorced man—divorced woman	23
Divorced man—single woman	18
Single man—widowed woman	8
Widowed man—widowed woman	6
Divorced man—widowed woman	5
Widowed man—divorced woman	5
Widowed man—single woman	3

About 25 percent of the men and women who remarry have children, approximately 75 percent of the women who remarry have custody of their own children, and about 33 percent of the men who remarry have custody of their children by a previous marriage.

Divorced women have an average interval between marriages of about 4 years. The average interval between marriages for men was 2 years and 3 years for divorced and widowed respectively.

A rather unique statistic was found: the remarriage of men with sons is more common than the remarriage of men with daughters. This was true for both divorced and widowed. The chances are that there are more father-and-son systems incorporating new mothers than there are father-and-daughter systems.

Some of the findings indicate that small children of widowed or divorced people, particularly sons, appear to welcome a second marriage for their parents; some little boys are almost eager to have a new mother.

On the other hand, older children, particularly daughters, may have strong antagonisms toward a new mother. Along the same line, adolescent boys resist considerably accepting a new father, whereas they would accept a new mother more readily.

One author suggests that there are at least five things that have to do with remarriage and the children's acceptance of this remarriage. (Bernard, 1956)

1. Some confusion may exist as to what you call your new mother or what you call your new father. This appears to be more difficult as the children grow older or are already older when the remarriage takes place.

2. A rather vexing problem is what to do with the mementos of the first marriage. How do you dispose of, or where do you put, such personal effects as pictures, scrapbooks, favorite chairs, favorite furniture?

3. Questions come up as to moving from the old home to a new neighborhood or the advisability of moving the children from their favorite environment to a brand-new environment with a brand-new mother or a brand-new father.

4. Another problem emerges in remarriages: what to do with the legality of the children? The adoption and legal rights of the children to their first father's or first mother's estate is involved. Some children bitterly resent the idea of adoption. Also involved is whether the child takes the name of the new father or retains, with some ensuing difficulty in explanations, the name of the previous father.

5. A final problem area to be considered in remarriages and the

children's acceptance of the remarriage has to do with myths. Many times the stepchild's stepmother myth acts as a stumbling block. The older child may gain erroneous ideas from a literary work such as Hamlet or the younger child from the story of Cinderella and assume a situation that does not exist in fact.

All things considered, a survey of 8 studies concerning the attitudes of men and women toward their children acquired through remarriage indicates that at the most about 5 percent of these adults actively rejected the children of the new marriage. However, the data do indicate it is harder for the mother to assimilate other children into the family structure than it is for the father. This seems natural, since it is up to the mother to enforce the rules around the home while the father is at work. Consequently there is an inclination to create an image of a cruel stepmother more than a cruel stepfather image.

One author suggests at least six situations in which competition occurs in the families of remarriage. This competition takes place with a child's affection.

1. Between the child's divorced and biological parents.
2. Between his new parent and his biological parent of the same sex.
3. Between the parents of the former spouse and the new spouse.
4. Between the new father and the children for the mother's affection.
5. Between the new mother and the children.
6. Among the children themselves.

Other considerations in regard to remarriage are as follows:

More men than women tend to remarry.

Single men were choosing previously married women for partners more often than they have in the past.

Negroes show a greater tendency to remarry than do whites.

The divorced tend to remarry more than do the widowed.

There is some evidence that divorce is, in effect, moving up the class ladder.

Previously married persons tend to choose spouses among those who have also been married before.

A large proportion, 75 percent of all divorced persons, remarry within five years. Of those widowed for five years, 50 percent of the men and 25 percent of the women have remarried. It appears thus that divorced persons tend to remarry sooner than the widowed persons.

There is some evidence to indicate the remarried woman is a 10 percent poorer risk than the remarried man.

There is some evidence to show that remarriage is becoming an increasing middle class phenomenon. [Bernard, 1956]

What happens when divorced partners marry each other? In a study of about 200 cases of divorced people who remarried, it was discovered that about 45 to 50 percent were quite happy. In other words, in the cases of people who were divorced and then remarried the first spouse, the chance of success is about 50–50.

One author suggested there were at least six reasons why a remarriage to your first spouse may be successful.

1. The partner is more mature the second time.
2. Although the wife may have longed for freedom, once it was attained she found she did not like what she thought was a free life.
3. The crisis that may have precipitated the divorce proved to be a mere infatuation rather than a real rival relationship.
4. Many of the outside pressures of one kind or another, which originally led to the divorce, have been removed by time passage or by death or by other causes.
5. Because the children had suffered in the broken home, the divorced partners decided to get back together again and, if for no other reason than to keep the children reasonably happy, are making additional efforts to make the marriage work.
6. The partners never really wanted the divorce in the first place; they may have been moved to it by causes outside of their own relationship.

There are some figures that indicate successful remarriage is a factor of socioenonomic class. In one study, professional people who had remarried each other after a divorce had about 30 percent successful remarriages; however, unskilled or semiskilled had only 12 percent of the cases successful.

There is very little data that show how remarriage, as distinguished from divorce itself, affects the children's chances of success in their own marriages. One source, in which 29 surveys dealt with delinquency involving 85,000 children, seemed to indicate that the children with stepparents contributed more than their proportional share to the delinquent population. However, the author wisely suggests there is a tremendous amount of evidence that the individual variations were enormous. The many variables involved in delinquency did not indicate that having stepparents was a primary cause of delinquency. (Smith, 1953).

To anyone trained and active in working at the professional level with human behavior, another factor is involved: the tremendous adaptability of children. This was particularly brought out in a study by Ann Roe concerning the children of alcoholic parents raised in foster homes. (Roe, 1945)

Like so many questions regarding human behavior, the answer as to whether one should remarry after divorce or the death of a spouse carries no conclusive answer. The best evidence seems to indicate that there is at least a 50–50 chance for success, begging the question of what is success in marriage.

The following considerations seem to apply in regard to widowed and divorced men and widowed and divorced women.

Divorced men

1. There seems to be evidence that the world soon forgets why and who in regard to divorce and just labels the individual as divorced. Divorce and remarriage for men may be awkward because of the children involved and particularly what one's business friends and associates may say.

2. Undoubtedly how much money one has influences divorce and remarriage. Divorce costs money. It is possible, although no one has adequately researched it, that poor people may separate and not go through divorce proceedings but still take up living with another individual.

3. The best evidence seems to indicate that men divorcing in middle age almost always do so to marry another individual and almost always a woman younger than they are.

4. Men who divorce and who remarry rather quickly after the divorce do not seem to be very adept at caring for themselves, that is, meals, laundry, and cleaning the house.

5. Almost all of the evidence seems to indicate that the divorced middle-aged man is groping for his youth, and desires to marry a younger person. Later studies in this chapter indicate he is all too frequently unable to have the vigor to be a young lover.

6. The remarriage of divorced men is obviously not a factor for Catholics.

Divorced women

1. It appears that it is much more awkward for a divorced woman to remarry than for a divorced man. In some sense she is a drug on the market, particularly if she has a large number of children and if any of them need special care.

2. Like the divorced man in remarriage, the divorced woman may wish to remarry a younger man and so regain her own visions of youth, but very little statistics that are meaningful apply to this phenomenon.

3. For some reason or other, society still continues to be less approving of the divorced woman remarrying than the divorced man,

although this attitude appears to be rapidly disappearing, with the old title of "grass widow" applying less and less.

4. Unlike the man, a divorced woman, especially in middle age, appears to be a threat to the friends whose husbands they think she may wish to marry.

5. Divorce and remarriage for women depends greatly upon the economic level of both individuals. There is indeed a trend for divorced people in remarriage to marry someone just a litle higher on the socioeconomic ladder than the previous spouse.

6. Remarriage for middle-aged divorced women may not be attempted if a large alimony is involved, which would be lost with the remarriage.

Widowed men

1. The remarriage of a widowed man frequently depends upon whether children are involved or not. A childless widowed man appears to be far more prone to remarry than a widowed man with many children. However, the statistics on this are inadequate.

2. Contrary to the widowed woman, the widowed man, especially if he is salaried, becomes an object of pity and he appears to be well "housebroken" and thus a good prospect for a second marriage.

3. Even though the widowed man may have children, the age of the children is a strong factor in remarriage. Adolescent children are inclined to idealize the image of the mother even though they did not get along with the mother during her life, whereas younger children, approximately age 6 and below, appear to accept the new mother with very little stress involved.

4. Some statistics indicate that in the 50s there are more remarriages than in the 40s, primarily we suppose because the children now have lives and plans of their own. Lonesomeness and approaching old age seem more threatening and the income level is higher for the widowed man, thus making him more attractive to other women.

5. Contrary to popular belief, there is some evidence that the bereaved man is not entirely heartbroken upon the death of his wife. The cliché is, of course, to the opposite. However, some men take the death of their wives as a sign of release and the opportunity to marry a younger woman, thus enhancing their own image. This may be particularly true when the husband has struggled through long years of complaining illness by his now departed wife.

Widowed women

1. The remarriage of a widowed woman also depends highly upon the age and number of children she has. The more emancipated the

children and the fewer their number, the greater are her chances of remarriage.

2. Though it is rarely reported in psychological literature, the amount of insurance or estate money left the widow has a great deal to do with her chances of remarriage. If she is extremely wealthy, there seems to be far less of a problem in finding a male interested in marrying her.

3. Like none of the other three groups, the widowed woman is a great recipient of all kinds of free advice from in-laws, other widows, and practically everyone she meets. This is not true for the widowed man. Whether the widowed woman wants it or not, she finds many people telling her what to do and how to do it, how to spend her money, what to do with the estate, whether to sell her home, and numerous kinds of unsolicited advice.

4. Most studies show that the widowed woman is more inclined to remarry a male widower than a single man or a divorced man.

5. Again, as in the case of the widowed man, widowed women may have greater chances for remarriage in the 50s than in the 40s, because of the involvement of children. In the 50s the widowed woman is more inclined to be free from mothering responsibilities and may have regained her composure because of the bereavement.

6. Unlike widowed men, widowed women appear to have a far greater tendency to band together with other widowed women rather than with divorced or single women. Frequently they will travel extensively with each other and more often than not share expenses in apartment living.

English studies show that the remarriage age for widowers has increased from an average of 50 years in 1931 to 58 years in 1961. The remarriage-age statistics for widows show an increase from 45 years in 1931 to 52 years in 1961. (Benaim, 1967)

Whether divorce or death separates the adult from his spouse, there is no answer as to whether remarriage is the thing to do.

A great deal depends upon whether children are involved, whether a large estate is involved, the condition of the first marriage—whether it was happy or not—and in the final consideration the individual alone can provide the best answer.

COMPATIBILITY IN MARRIAGES FOR MIDDLE-AGED ADULTS: FACT OR FICTION?

Most middle-aged couples married at least 20 to 25 years may have some difficulty in answering this question. They have been married for so long, they no longer think too much about being compatible or not; it's the thing they do, like wearing old and comfortable clothes. The question is not so much, "Do I like the clothes or not?" Rather it is a question of "this is what I wear. It is comfortable and I am used to it."

As we shall see later there may be a difference between what a young research psychologist age 25 considers to be a compatible middle-aged couple and what the middle-aged couple consider themselves to be in regards to compatibility.

One study of middle-class married couples found that their assumed agreement on issues far exceeded the actual agreement they had between themselves. Assumed agreement was positively correlated with marital satisfaction. (Levinger, 1966)

Other studies indicated that incompatibility for middle-class couples was based on psychological and emotional problems while lower-class couple's problems centered around physical harm and financial stress. (Levinger, 1966)

In a study of happiness-unhappiness in married couples, a rather unique approach was used. Four hundred and forty persons raised in large families were judged by their brothers and sisters according to whether they were happy or medium happy or unhappy. The results seem to reveal there was a considerable amount of marital unhappiness that had not reached the critical stage of separation, desertion, or divorce. A further finding in the study suggested that the crisis period for married women is in the late 40s and early 50s, and for men in the late 50s. (Bossard, 1955)

Fifty adjusted and 50 unadjusted middle-class couples were compared as to how they felt about themselves as husbands and as wives. There was a distinct difference between the adjusted and unadjusted couples. The greatest difference was in how they perceived themselves and their mates in regard to who was dominant and who was submissive. There seemed to be a stronger influence in the husband's ability to see himself and his wife in proper roles. The efficiency of the husband seemed to be more indicative of good marriage than the wife's. (Kotlar, 1965)

Most studies of the effect of similar religious backgrounds and compatibility agree: the more similar the background the better the marital relationships. (Stimson, 1966) (Christensen, 1967) There is some evidence that couples affiliate with the church beliefs of the spouse with the higher educational background when the marriage is an interfaith one. (Babchuck, 1967)

One investigation concerned 38 wives of men who at the time of the study were from ages 26 to 27. Approximately 12 years prior to the study the men had taken a personality test and on the basis of the test had what was called perfectly normal scores: no deviances or neurotic patterns. The follow-up 12 years later measured both the wives of the men and the men themselves, using the same test. They were also interviewed in their homes. The wives turned out to be at least as well adjusted as their husbands, if not more so. Also, the marriages were highly satisfactory to the partners. The marriages seemed "essentially mundane and dull" to the investigators! (Golden, 1963)

In conclusion we find that compatibility in marriage is practically impossible to measure. We have just seen that it depends upon whose viewpoint you are using. (Ryder, 1967) (Ladd, 1967)

Whatever compatibility means, it certainly involves one's spouse as a living partner in the daily affairs of life, as a sexual partner, as a parent of children, and the child of parents still alive, as an economic team working and paying for goods, and as a social team operating in a neighborhood and in a society. If all of these things involve compatibility in marriage, we may assume that marriage in the middle years of life may be no worse or better than marriage at any other period of life. (Udry, 1967) (Bernard, 1966)

IF ADULTS MARRY FOR THE FIRST TIME
LATE IN LIFE, WHAT CAN THEY EXPECT?

What can you expect if you marry late in life? One source states that "the older bride is less likely to try to remake the man she loves." This author finds that being in love and getting married in the later years of life as compared with love in youth is doubtless a subtle kind of relationship much colored by the pleasure of finding someone with whom one can share experiences. In addition to this, sex plays a rather unique role in older love when compared to younger love, partly because it is no longer associated with childbearing. Sex is no longer a great mystery, but it is still a major human experience. The author says, "it is more like a ballad than a tragic grandcomic opera. There is finally, more emphasis on friendship and companionableness than in 'sextasy.' " (Bernard, 1956)

First marriages late in life do not appear to have as wide an age discrepancy between the husband and wife as do remarriages. In the latter, the general trend was for both men and women to seek a younger mate. (Bossard, 1951) (Glick, 1950)

All studies indicate that unhappiness in marriage is much more common if marriage occurs prior to the age of 20. Conversely, there is very little dissatisfaction if the individual marries after the age of 30. Further data from the same source indicate that 40-year-old men are more inclined to marry within their own age group. This is not true of 50-year-old men (at least 75 percent in one study), who married women younger than they were by 5 to 10 years. The same facts seem to hold true for women at these age periods. (Hurlock, 1959)

So we return to the question, If individuals do marry late in life for the first time, what can they expect? The answer seems to be they can expect a lot of happiness. They can also expect to be marrying a person younger than they are. Those who marry late in life seem to appreciate more what they have, seem to do so with a clearer head, and their chances for success appear to be very great.

ARE THE HUSBANDS' AND WIVES' MARITAL ATTITUDES DIFFERENT IN MIDDLE AGE?

Most evidence indicates that men view marriage somewhat differently than women. However, there are contradictory reports. (McGinnis, 1967) (Inglis, 1967)

In one study we find, "less marked sex differences in interests in middle-age than during the earlier years of adulthood." This applies, of course, to more than just interests in marriage. Some authors feel that the increase in femininity by males increases with age, femininity meaning less active and less strenuous life and a greater interest in sedentary occupations. "After the mid-50's, there is little or no change in interests except a further narrowing down of interests already established."

Along the same line of interest, men appear to be inclined to be more clothes conscious in their middle age than when they were younger. However, there seems to be some evidence that women tend to be a little less clothes conscious in their middle years than they were in their earlier years.

Another contrast in the attitudes of men and women during the middle years finds that men are less worried about money if they are from the middle and upper classes, obviously, but the opposite is true if they are from the lower classes. On the other hand, women in the middle years and middle class tend to feel that money becomes more and more important, particularly to buy things for the home, educate the children, travel, and keep up with their friends. There is further evidence that as a woman grows older she becomes more security-minded for herself and her children, anticipating an earlier death for her husband than for herself. (Hurlock, 1959)

One of the most helpful studies in regard to answering the question of differences in marital attitudes for husbands and wives in middle age was done by Tharp. Tharp reviewed many studies in regard to both theory and research. He suggests that model marriage-role expectations do exist and are different for the sexes and that they have been established by parental identification. There seems to be other evidence that particularly during the middle years a husband is more inclined to imitate the behavior patterns of his father, while a wife is more inclined to imitate those of her mother. Regardless of husband/

father and wife/mother identifications in middle age, Tharp found that the husband's role was highly instrumental in the marriage relationship as far as promoting and moving the family toward different levels. The wife's role was more integrative. It appears that she plays the primary role in holding the family together. Marital happiness for both the husband and wife was more dependent upon the husband's role than the wife's role. If husbands were unhappy, it was more important to the marital happiness than if wives were unhappy. (Tharp, 1963)

Another writer, Levinger, is not so convinced that there is a difference between husbands' and wives' attitudes, particularly about marriage in the middle years. His feeling is that there are two needs in regard to this age level: complementary needs, which require both parties to fit their differences together in a compatible pattern, and similarity needs, in which the husband holds to his masculine role and the wife to her feminine role and they pursue life in a parallel form. (Levinger, 1964) (Tharp, 1964)

From the work of these two authors and many others it is obvious that marriage theory is lacking, whether it be for the middle-aged people or not.

One study concerned itself with the attitude of husbands who are approaching retirement. In this study there seemed to be an attempt by the preretirement husbands to make disparaging comments and be somewhat contemptuous of women as a whole. After retirement, the husbands changed their attitude and became more understanding and accepting. The author felt that "for some, retirement may be anticipated as threat to masculinity. Feeling no longer capable of doing a man's job, they may attempt to reaffirm their masculinity by disparaging women. In this way, they may disassociate themselves from a passive or feminine role." The data from this study suggested that anxiety about preserving masculinity, like many other kinds of anxiety, was greater in anticipation than in reality. (O'Neil, 1962)

Much has been written about the wife's search for identity and its effect on the marital relationship. There have been very few studies, however, created to examine this so-called dissatisfaction by middle-aged women. Most of the things written have been of the Sunday-supplement variety, with very little or no basis in researchable fact.

In a study of 37 cases referred to a clinic, the wife's search for identity truly affected the equilibrium of the marital relationship. This should come as no surprise. If either one of the marriage partners is unhappy about anything, we may fully expect that the equilibrium of the marriage relationship is going to be affected. (Dame, 1965)

Neugarten in her Kansas City studies of 1958 found an important difference between men and women as they age. Men seemed to be more receptive toward their own feelings for wanting to be loved, while women seemed to be more receptive and felt less guilty about their aggressive egocentric impulses. Although the above data do not apply directly to marital attitudes, they may be construed as affecting how one would feel toward his marriage partner in middle age. (Birren, 1964b)

From the writer's own experience with well over 100 husbands and wives in middle age in regard to their marital attitudes, the variety of responses was enormous. In a major number of cases, the attitude was less concerned with marriage per se than with their feeling about their particular mate. The question might better be put thus: Are husbands' and wives' marital attitudes different about each other when they are middle-aged than they were when they were first married? The answer seems obvious. Yes, they are different. Both husbands and wives, at least in this writer's experience, take a more benevolent attitude toward their spouse; they are less ambitious for themselves and much less ambitious for their spouse. The husband now admits his wife is a poor cook or not a very good mother or somewhat of a social recluse, but there isn't much he wants to do about it because he loves her for many other virtues. Wives, on the other hand, do not look on their husbands as strong, virile individuals anymore, as they did when they were first married. They consider their husbands more in light of the kind of money they can provide for the home and the children. They either become resigned to their husbands' weaknesses or somewhat defensive in discussing their husbands, wherein they will counterbalance each weakness named with a strength that they have come to enjoy and love. However, many thoughts of middle-aged husbands and wives do not apply to their own marriage but more specifically to their daughter's, as we shall see in the next chapter.

In general, however, and again, solely from the writer's experience with clinical cases, husbands appear to be more forgiving and less critical of the marriages of their contemporaries than do wives. It should be stressed that the above statements come from a very select population, all cases referred because of some problem area or another, and are not indicative of the population in general.

HOW IMPORTANT ARE SEXUAL RESPONSIVENESS AND SEXUAL RESPONSIBILITY IN MARRIED ADULTS?

There appears to be strong evidence that in the adult years of life there is a gradual decline in sexual behavior; but is it crucial?

Ilka Chase probably put sex in its proper perspective, at least for adults, when she described the difference between not being married to being married as going from the hurly-burly of the davenport to the deep sleep of the double bed.

Another source feels that, "many spouses indicate that when (sexual) harmony is achieved . . . no discussions about it need take place." (Ogilvie, 1962)

In other words, there is no need to have a long, drawn-out talk about success—you feel it.

There are few studies that concern themselves directly with the dynamics of sexual behavior for adults. Probably the two best sources of information are found in the work of Kinsey and his co-workers and the work of Masters and Johnson in their 1966 publication, *Human Sexual Response*. Both of these sources of information we shall discuss later, where appropriate.

A statistic never tells why. It can only tell how many. The intimacy of human sexual behavior is primarily a why question and not a census artifact. Marriage is an enormously complex, complicated ball of tangled memory threads. Sex is but one aspect of the organizational pattern of two people who chose to live together as man and wife.

Many writers feel as does Levine that ". . . sex role includes both a social and a physical set of expectations." (Levine, 1963)

There are probably more assumptions regarding human sexual behavior with little basis in fact than there are regarding any other aspect of human behavior, even though these assumptions and bits and pieces of folklore may have profound psychological significance. (Levine, 1963)

It should come as no surprise to any intelligent thinker about human behavior that sexual orgasms and sexual play diminish as the human gets older. So do most things. The overt form of sexual behavior may be considered to be supplanted by everyday intimacies. It is not a question of sublimation but of embellishment, diversifications, and greater subtlety.

As the adjusted adult husband and wife well know, marriage is not one long sexual orgy, but marriage is mortgages, PTA meetings, parental pressures, and the like.

Marriage in the adult years is a series of habits gained through the day-to-day contacts of two people living together. Sex is one of the habits.

The vast evidence indicates a different set of sexual behavior for men than for women.

Mode

Sexual excitation for men is gained through physical intimacy, rubbing, touching, which leads to the sexual climax, or orgasm. Man is the aggressor in the sexual act and needs an erect penis or no copulation takes place.

Conversely, women are the passive partners in the sexual act. They are the recipients. Most writers seem to agree that the sexual act is more psychical than physical for the woman. Hers is a greater demand for affectional intimacy.

Drive

The sexual appetite in males appears to be much stronger during adolescence than it is for women. Further evidence seems to indicate that the sexual drive reaches a peak earlier for men than for women.

In contrast to this, the sex drive for women is inclined to be fairly constant during the adult years, with some indication that it becomes stronger during the middle age.

Problems

Males appear to have greater genitourinary problems in middle age. The prostate and bladder systems do not function as effectively as in youth or early adolescence. Further, erection is not as spontaneous as previously. In order to reach full orgasm, therefore, the male may desire more deviant or quasi-perverted forms of sex play. Because of the greater difficulty in maintaining an erection and the taking longer to reach orgasm, the deviant forms of sexual behavior the middle-aged husband may require from his wife may disgust the wife and further alienate the male in the sex role. Unless the process is understood by both parties, this may threaten the male's masculinity, causing him to seek prostitution or a younger mate. Having created a deviant situation from past sexual patterns, the wife may want to be loved for herself alone as a reinforcement of her fading physical attractiveness and not be "all things" to her husband in his desperate attempts to achieve an orgasm.

One of the difficulties an older woman may have in sexual satisfaction in marriage is the strong sense of losing her Lorelei attractiveness in enticing her husband into a sexual relationship. There is some evidence that as the marriage progresses, and particularly in the middle years, the wife may lose some of her earlier inhibitions and develop stronger desire for sexual discharge than in earlier years of marriage. The situation then becomes one in which the men are declining in their sexual appetites while the women are not.

Dynamics

Much of sex is a mental factor utilizing imagery. It becomes more than a physical act, especially during stages of excitation.

Husbands and wives in their 50s have been having intercourse for a period of 30 years. It should come as no surprise that the novelty, the newness, the trying of new techniques, has long since been missing. Sex may become a habitual act rather than a romantic interlude. Such factors as these are involved:

1. Both the husband's and the wife's bodies are older, less attractive.
2. The physical appetite may be dissimilar, men decreasing, women comparatively on an increase.
3. Varieties of sex play have been exhausted.
4. Some embarrassment to indulge in initiating appetites with sex play (it is juvenile to kiss, fondle, and pet).

Within this set of circumstances we may then assume that sexual behavior between husband and wife in middle age may lead to immature attempts to adjust by fantasies, desertions, divorce, and remarriage to younger mates. This brings about adolescent behavior with young men or young women or depends upon commercial sources of sexual gratification, such as prostitution and symbolisms via pornographic literature. Bare-breasted waitresses may titillate the middle-aged male in an ineffectual attempt to recapture the naughtiness he once felt was a part of his youth.

MALE

The young groom loves his wife at least partly because she is a sexual object to him. The older man loves a woman who then becomes a sex partner to him. The active search for casual sexual relations without love is probably more common in the early than in the middle-years, in part because sex is more imperious in youth but in part also because *sex in the middle-years has become more commonly integrated into the total personality.* [Italics added] It does not so readily function separately and apart. To men in the middle-years and to middle-class men in particular, the partner is probably more important than sheer physiological drive so far as the meaning of sex is concerned. The subject of experience itself may vary in youth and middle-life. It is more localized, more genitalized in youth, more diffuse in middle-life. [Bernard, 1956]

No attempt is made herein to make an exhaustive report of the Kinsey studies (1948, male; 1953, female). For readers who are more interested in an exhaustive study of sexual behavior of adults, it is suggested that they read, in the original, the works of such writers as Kinsey, Deutsch, and Masters and Johnson.

The Kinsey studies have some value at this point in making generalized statements.

From the interviews Kinsey conducted, he came to the conclusion that "sexual activity in marriage is largely determined by the male." The results seem to indicate that men start higher in their sexual appetites and desires than women and then decline, whereas women appear to increase in their desire, at least through the age of 50. (Pressey, 1957)

Further findings from Kinsey note that desire for novelty in sexual partners for the male may have a temporary stimulating effect on the sex drive, but this does not alter the linear decrease over the adult life span. In short, the middle-aged man is kidding himself if he feels he has regained his youthful vigor in the bedroom.

From the Kinsey data we find that marital intercourse averages about 2½ times per week at approximately age 20, slightly less than 2 times a week at ages 36 through 40, and less than one active intercourse on the average per week at the age of 60. (Birren, 1964a)

Comparing the 1953 study of females, Kinsey found the rate of masturbation to be less in females than in males. However, the rate of masturbation declined much more rapidly in males than it did in females. The conclusion was tentatively presented that this may mean sexuality changes are less in the female than in the male. It must always be remembered that every bit of evidence and any kind of study made of sexual behavior in humans must of necessity grant that individual differences from the norm are enormous. Anyone who compares their personal sexual habits with an average is guilty of swimming in statistics.

Surveying the literature, we find that the climacteric for middle-aged men is a normal part of life's pattern that is different for men than for women. Such factors as these are involved:

1. Climacteric is a very slow rate of change.
2. Most studies indicate that climacteric is strung out at least through the 40s, 50s, 60s, and in some cases even in the 70s.
3. Males appear not to suffer the severe physical discomfort that is the pattern for some women. The endocrine imbalance of androgens and estrogens may produce a higher pitched voice and a decrease in the amount of hair.

When considering climacteric, therefore, the middle-aged neurosis about it is more psychological than physical. The entire issue seems to be wrapped up in the phrase, "anxiety about virility." (Hurlock, 1959)

FEMALE

For reasons not entirely clear to this writer, research data seem to be more abundant for the sexual aspects of the female than for the male.

Some of the following studies indicate this. (Chapman, 1967) (Fisher, 1967b) (Salzman, 1967)

In a study consisting of 417 women who had been married an average of from 17 to 19 years in which that data was gathered by questionnaire methods, one of the findings was that of "a marked positive correlation between frequency of orgasm and extent of enjoyment of coitus—orgasm is not necessary for the enjoyment of intercourse." (Wallin, 1963)

In another study, which concerned itself with menopausal symptoms in women, a checklist of menopausal symptoms was administered to 460 women whose ages ranged from 13 through 64. The study indicated that there were more symptoms common to women at menopause and at adolescence than at any other ages. (Neugarten, 1965c)

Contrary to popular belief and folklore, the University of Chicago studies done primarily in Kansas City indicated that most women adjusted quite well during the menopausic period. (Birren, 1964a)

Just as menses is a normal part of life's pattern, menopause is also a normal part of any female life pattern. One author suggests that admittedly with many variations, "early puberty usually means late menopause and vice versa." (Hurlock, 1959)

The androgen/estrogen imbalance of the endocrine system at middle age is likely to produce in the female more hair, a lower-pitched voice, larger pigmentation in the skin, flattened curves, and flabby breasts as milk glands atrophy. Contrary to the male, whose climacteric is long drawn out and has no strong physical reactions, generally three symptoms appear for the woman during menopause: flushes of the skin, primarily around the head and neck; profuse sweating, with feelings of differences in body odor; and hot flashes over the entire skin area.

Many writers feel that the psychological symptomology is more disturbing than the physiological. At this time come headaches, irritableness, insomnia, nervousness, vertigo, restlessness, and a concomitant feeling of frigidity. This may produce in the female at middle age a feeling of hostility, depression, and high criticalness of self followed by feelings of guilt. (Hurlock, 1959)

Most of the sexual activity for females takes place during menacme: "the period in a woman's life between puberty and menopause."

Still another research project attempted to study women's sexual responsiveness and the duration and quality of their marriages. By use of questionnaire data for women in their early and middle years of marriage, it was found that there tended to be an increase in wives' sexual responsiveness during approximately the first 5 years of marriage for those marriages characterized as positive. For marriages characterized as negative, there was a notable decrease in responsiveness as the marriage continued throughout the years. (Clark, 1965)

Many things have been written about infidelity in marriage, but very few of the studies have much meaning. Most of them are fictionalized and reported in a "Peyton Place"-like manner.

Indicative of one of the more valuable studies is the following one, done in Cleveland, Ohio, through the Family Service Agency, concerning 10 cases of female sexual infidelity. As we find in most of the other studies, there was "reflected character disorders which preceded marriage." Many of the cases in this study, as well as others comparable to this study, indicate a strong denial of their mother's love for them when they were children. The psychiatric explanation is that women in middle age are inclined to use the excitement of extramarital affairs to fill a void left by early lack of affection from the mother. (Garfield District Staff, 1962)

HIS AND HERS

When middle age comes for husbands and wives, the sexual appetites have decreased considerably. So have the appetites for many other things. Some authors are inclined to overemphasize the fact that because the husbands and wives spend less time in sexual activity, gross unhappiness will result. This strikes the present writer as illogical. It is just as sensible to say that the marriage is near divorce because the husband and wife spend less time playing tennis or going bowling or doing any of the infinite number of physical things they did when they had more energy in early adulthood.

The best evidence from all sides indicates that "sex differences in adjustment (at middle age) are specially marked." (Hurlock, 1959) This hardly seems a startling fact. The sexual equipment of males and females is different, their endocrine make-up is different, their jobs in life are different. Although "menopause may undermine a mother's confidence," she has a very narrow personality if sex is the only dimension in her character. Nevertheless, some studies, because of the nature of the questions they ask, may appear to overemphasize the sexual behavior of middle-aged men and women.

Turning once again to the Kinsey studies of males in 1948 and of females in 1953, sex may be called the "silent psychic factor." Again we find that studies such as the Kinsey report, which is a statistical treatment of data, may count what people do but never answer the question of why they do it.

Kinsey found that sexual behavior was affected by at least eleven variables—sex, race, age, age at onset of adolescence, marital status, educational level, occupational class, rural-urban background, religious affiliation, the extent of devotion to religious affairs, and parental occupational class.

Kinsey found that sexual behavior was not the same in a religious man as in a so-called nonreligious man, in an educated man as in an uneducated man, in a professional man as in a manual worker, and in an older man as in a younger man. The primary point was that the meaning of sex and the value placed upon it were psychological, socio-logical, and cultural rather than strictly organic. Further, Kinsey found that it should not be taken for granted that previous sexual experience is necessarily an advantage in forming a new sexual adjustment. "Kinsey's studies have shown that aging may also make the older woman a more attractive sexual partner, both psychologically because she has fewer anxieties about sex and sociologically because of her accumulated experience." It was further found by Kinsey that the decrease in sexual activity in the middle and later years (a decrease of one sexual act per week per decade) may not be wholly the result of organic change. He felt that it might be in part the result of psycho-social forces. Lastly, it is interesting to note that psychological fatigue also occurs in the sexual behavior of lower animals as they get older. (Kinsey, 1948) (Hurlock, 1959)

Clark comes to the conclusion that middle-aged men and women must make some emotional and physical adjustments in their sex life, and the success of these adjustments depends on the soundness and understanding of their marriage. This conclusion seems to be valid and, we might add, is also good advice in settling economic problems, parental problems, and problems concerned with where to spend a vacation. All adjustments apply to more than just the sex life of the middle-aged. (Clark, 1949)

Two final studies should be reported, both concerned with reli-gion and sexual gratification in the adult years of marriage. One study investigated the relationship between sexual enjoyment and marital satisfaction for those who score high on religiosity and those with low scores on religiosity. The major finding was that a deep feeling of religion or a high regard for religion reduced the effect of a woman's lack of sexual gratification. This did not occur for men. (Wallin, 1964)

A second study "Personality patterns among religious personnel" reported as follows:

Men and women college subjects were aggressively aroused by male examiner and then wrote TAT stories, two of which were elicted by cards with men dominant and two with women dominant. Both aggressive and sexual imagery were greater in this aroused group (64 cases) as compared to an unaroused controlled group (60 cases), thus suggesting that these motives are intimately related. However, men also increased in defensiveness while women did not. Almost all stories told

about the female-dominant cards had the dominance relationship reversed or changed, while this rarely occured for male-dominant cards.
Nearly all of the results suggested that men were more defensive about
the expression of these motives than women and further, that simple
extrapolation of American middle-class values regarding the expression
of the two motives will not predict these data on college students.
[Barclay, 1965]

It is necessary to emphasize one study of human sexual behavior
because of its unique nature and the to-be-expected impact on the
social scene (number 4 on the best-seller list, *Time*, July 29, 1966).
Published in 1966, *Human Sexual Response* is the work of William
Masters, an M.D., and Virginia Johnson, a research psychologist. The
book was written for a professional audience and not for the salacious
appetites of sensation seekers. To this type of reader the book will be
boring and dull. The research was conducted by two competent professionals who were well aware of their responsibilities in conducting
research in this highly sensitive area of human behavior. No intelligent
reader of their work can criticize the high level of skill and precautions
they utilized in conducting research concerning human sexual behavior. Whether they have achieved one of their goals of emancipating
man from his sniggering sexual attitudes is open to question. Not open
to question is the amount of data they have contributed toward knowing what actually happens biologically to humans during the course
of masturbation and copulation. Again, whether humanity profits
from this information is a moot issue. Masters and Johnson feel that it
is not moot but profitable to seek and disseminate openly such knowledge. They must believe in their research efforts. They spent 11 years
perfecting their investigation techniques and gathering data. They now
undergo the brutal scrutiny of writers and public, qualified or not,
asking: Why did they do it? Was it fun? What does it feel like to watch
people masturbating or copulating? The questions are not appropriate
or inappropriate. The questions do not apply. To any competent,
dedicated, research-oriented scientist, conducting an investigation is
a hard job. It requires intelligence, patience, long hours of study,
objectivity, and plenty of money among many things. Masters and
Johnson can hold their heads up and meet any challenge as to their
qualifications to do research as scientists.

Research procedures

Most of the data were gained by actual observation of the coital act.
Some data were obtained by interviews only. Both Masters and Johnson
were always present, whether the subjects were participating in actual
intercourse, automanipulation (masturbation), or being interviewed.
Without exception, all subjects in the study were volunteers. Some

received monetary rewards, some did not. All are completely anonymous.

The study began in 1954 to investigate the problems of human sexual inadequacy. It was conducted within the framework of the Department of Obstetrics and Gynecology of Washington University School of Medicine. Starting in January of 1964, the work has been done under the auspices of the Reproductive Biology Research Foundation. All research was conducted in the reproductive biology laboratory, where observations and anatomic and physiologic measurements were recorded.

Obviously, basic differences are in force in the sexual expressions and equipment of intrasexual and intersexual comparisons. However, the study emphasizes the parallels and similarities rather than the differences in human sexual behavior. (Masters, 1966)

Population

The original population studied consisted of 118 female and 27 male prostitutes. The prostitute population was not included in the final report: too migratory for extended study, and the varying degrees of pathology of the reproductive organs were considered to be too dissimilar to an average group.

The basic study continued for 7 years. The population statistics were as follows:

Males interviewed	654
Males selected as "active study subjects"	312
Males age range was 21 to 90	
Females interviewed	619
Females selected as "active study subjects"	382
Females age range was 18 to 80	

GENERAL FINDINGS (for all age groups in the study)

1. While there was great variation in the intensity of feeling and the length of female orgasmic experience, males had far less individual variation in ejaculatory reaction. Male patterns of climax are more standard than the female.

2. Females are more easily restimulated than males after orgasm.

3. For women there may be greater individual differences in the depth of emotional feeling and in the length of time orgasm takes place. The same variations in length and intensity may be expressed by an individual woman.

4. There are many "phallic fallacies," one of them being that the "larger the penis the more effective the male as a partner."

> . . . there certainly is no statistical support for the "phallic fallacy" that the larger penis increases in size with full erection to a significantly greater degree than does the smaller penis. The difference in average erective size increase between the smaller flaccid penis and the larger flaccid penis is not significant.

5. Still another "phallic fallacy" was studied and found to be nothing but a fallacy.

> . . . the size of the penis has less constant relation to general physical development than that of any other organ of the body. It has been presumed by many cultures that the bigger the man in skeletal and muscular development the bigger the penis, not only in flaccid but also in an erect state . . . there is no relation between man's skeletal framework and the size of his external genitalia.

The range in length of penis during the flaccid state for the subjects actively studied was from 14 cm in one male weighing 152 pounds and 5 feet 7 inches tall to 6 cm in another male weighing 178 pounds and 5 feet 11 inches tall.

6. There are also misconceptions concerning the female anatomy. "It becomes obvious that penile size usually is a minor factor in sexual stimulation of the female partner. The normal or large vagina accommodates a penis of any size without difficulty." If the vagina is exceptionally small, physical stress may be experienced by the female until "advanced stages of female sexual tension have been experienced."

7. Sexual continence during pregnancy is a highly individual matter. The customary medically advocated restricted periods of continence for 6 weeks prior and 6 weeks following delivery of the baby may do a disservice to the husband and wife. "Blanket medical interdiction of coital activity for arbitrarily established periods of time both before and after delivery has done far more harm than good."

8. Multiorgasmic experiences increase the sensual pleasure for women; the second and third episodes being more satisfying. Usually men reported the first ejaculatory experience as being the most pleasurable.

> Cultural demand has played a strange trick upon the two sexes. Fears of performance in the female have been directed toward orgasmic attainment, while in the male the fears of performance have related toward the attainment and maintenance of penile erection, and orgasmic facility always has been presumed.

About older women

1. Masters and Johnson wisely point out that having studied only 34 women 51 years and older in active laboratory situations, their

findings suggest clinical impressions rather than established biological fact. (One hundred fifty-two women gave sociosexual histories in an interview situation.)

2. "During coitus, nipple erection occurs in the aging female following exactly the patterns described for her younger counterpart. . . . However, the intensity of the reaction is usually diminished."

3. The development of the sex flush over the skin area of the entire body is limited in occurrence.

4. Postmenopausal women frequently complain of urgency to urinate immediately after coition. Many also complain of burning sensations of urination immediately after coition.

5. Although there is a wide variation at all ages in clitoral response, the postmenopausal women, in the study, "demonstrated the usual clitoral response patterns of younger women."

6. Childless women over age 40, in this study particularly, lose the heightened visceral responses of the sexual organs that once were present in earlier years.

7. During the orgasmic phase of coition, women over 40 develop contractions of the vagina exactly the same as younger women, except that the duration is shorter.

8. Sexual capacity and effectiveness are not confined to the premenopausal years. ". . . the aging human female is fully capable of sexual performance at orgasmic response levels, *particularly if she is exposed to regularity of effective sexual stimulation.*" (Italics added)

9. Endocrine imbalance may result in painful coition in the immediate postmenopausal years even though there has never been any discomfort prior to this.

10. The main contention of postmenopausal women is to adjust to a slower rate of sexual stimulation and gratification.

11. Women beyond 60 years of age, "suffering from all of the vaginal stigmas of sex-steroid starvation still will retain a far higher capacity for sexual performances . . ." providing that "opportunity for regularity of coital exposure is created and maintained."

12. Taking estrogen does not automatically increase the sex drive in postmenopausal women. The personality plays an equal, if not stronger, part in determining sex drive.

13. There is some evidence that inability to adjust and emotionally accept menstrual cycles prior to menopause may presage a difficult postmenopausal adjustment.

14. There is evidence also that increased levels of sexual desire and activity during the late 40s and 50s constitute a "second honeymoon" phase possibly far more satisfactory than the first honeymoon.

15. "The interview material (152 women beyond age 51 interviewed) suggests that a woman who has had a happy, well-adjusted, and

stimulatory marriage may progress through the menopausal and post-menopausal years with little or no interruption in the frequency of, or interest in, sexual activity."

16.

Masturbation presents no significant problem for the older age group women. The unmarried female who has employed this method for relief of sexual tensions during her twenties and thirties usually continues the same behavioral pattern during her forties and through her sixties. When heterosexual contacts are limited or unavailable the widowed or divorced woman also may revert to the masturbatory practices of her teens and twenties when sexual tensions become intolerable. As might be expected, there is reduction in the frequency with which manipulative relief is deemed necessary beyond 60 years of age.

17.

There is no reason why the milestone of the menopause should be expected to blunt the human female's sexual capacity, performance, or drive. The healthy aging woman normally has sex drives that demand resolution. The depths of her sexual capacity and the effectiveness of her sexual performance, as well as her personal eroticism, are influenced indirectly by all of the psycho- and sociophysiological problems of her aging process. In short, *there is no time limit drawn by the advancing years to female sexuality.* [Italics added]

About older men

1. As was true for the older women in the Masters and Johnson investigation of sexual behavior, ". . . the material . . . must be accepted in the light of an admittedly inadequate study-subject population." (39 men 51 years and older as active subjects, and 212 who gave sociosexual histories in an interview situation)

2. "As a rule, the urban male slows in tension (of the penis) increment before his rural counterpart."

3. "Many men in their middle or late fifties and in their sixties find that they cannot redevelop penile erection for a matter of 12 to 24 hours after ejaculation."

4. In young males, penile erection from an unstimulated flaccid state may take 3 to 5 seconds after the beginning of any kind of sexual stimulation. "This reaction time is at least doubled and frequently trebled as the individual male passes through his fifties and into the 60 and 70 year age status." Stimulative techniques do not seem to alter this.

5. "Full penile erection frequently is not attained by the aging male (particularly by those over 60) until just before the ejaculatory experience."

6.

The younger male can expel the seminal fluid the full length of the penile urethra under such pressure as to deposit initial portions of the seminal plasma 12 to 24 inches from the unencumbered urethral meatus. The man over 50 years of age exhibits markedly reduced ejaculatory prowess, 6 to 12 inches being the average distance that the seminal plasma can be expelled.

7. "Seconds after a 60-year old man ejaculates the penis may have returned to an unstimulated flaccid state."

8. Unlike younger males, the elderly male can "experience the seepage . . ." rather than ". . . feel the actual emission of seminal fluid . . ." Younger males go through a two-staged ejaculatory process while older males (over 60) may have only a single stage ejaculatory process.

9. Just as in the females, there is great variation in sexual capacity and performance between individual elderly males (60 years and over) and within the single individual from time to time. Furthermore, sexual dynamics comparing the sexual differences are quite parallel: the most important factor in the maintenance of effective sexuality for the aging male is *"consistency of active sexual expression"* and ". . . if elevated levels of sexual activity are maintained from earlier years and neither acute or chronic physical incapacity intervenes, aging males usually are able *to continue some form of active sexual expression into the 70- and 80-year age groups."* (Italics added)

10. However, possibly contrary to the female, "the incidence of sexual inadequacy in the human male takes a sharp upturn after 50 years of age."

11. "When the aging male is not stimulated over long periods of time, his responsiveness may be lost."

12. Probably of major interest to many middle-aged readers, both male and female, is the factor of "Monotony in Sexual Relationship," particularly in a marriage of long standing. Masters and Johnson feel that this is "probably the most constant factor in the loss of an aging male's interest in sexual performance with his partner." Oddly enough, no mention is made of this wanting variety in the aging female. Either we must assume sexual relationships with the same male do not become monotonous or, as is more likely, the Masters/Johnson study has not enough data to discuss women's feelings of monotony. As it stands, the aging males seem to feel that the sex act may become more monotonous, especially with the same partner, than do the aging females. The entire issue, it must be overemphasized, is totally unproved as far as the entire population is concerned. With this statement, Masters and Johnson would have no quarrel.

Apparently the ". . . ego of the aging male is especially vulnerable to rejection, either real or illusional." ". . . over-familiarity with the partner does influence sexual responsiveness (for the male)."

It should be emphasized that the boredom complaint is the male's, not the female's, according to Masters and Johnson. Thus it is the ego-oriented male who feels that ". . . the female partner has lost sight of the necessity for working at the marital relationship with the same interest in stimulating and satisfying her male partner that she originally may have demonstrated at the onset of the marriage." By their own admission, many of the women interviewed no longer showed either sexual interest in or sexual concern for their husbands.

Yet, one gets the impression from the above treatise that the male feels unobligated to promote the sexual act to the same obligatory degree he insists the woman have. It becomes sort of "I am available, but you must entice me as of old. My presence is prima facie evidence that I am a satisfactory sex partner. Do not ask me to stimulate the situation."

Admittedly the above interpretation is not found in the Masters/Johnson data. The extension is a device of the present author.

13. After depth interviews with the 212 male subjects aged 51 and over, five additional reasons were discovered that may help to explain the aging male's inability to promote and indulge in the sexual act.

    a. Overconcern by the male with desire for success in an occupation and accumulating wealth.

    b. Fatigue in which mental fatigue was considered to be a stronger factor in the involution of male sexuality.

    c. Excessive consumption of either food or alcohol or both is a contributory factor. This was felt to be particularly true of alcohol. "While under its influence, many a male of any age has failed for the first time to achieve or maintain an erection of the penis."

       Overconsumption of alcohol increases the problem beyond biologic factors: The male confuses cause and effect because of his inebriated state (it is not his prowess, but his organic system that has failed) and he attempts variety in sexual partners and/or practices to alleviate his involution. Alcohol compounds the problem even though it may delude the male into false feelings of love potency. "As this male (the true alcoholic) progressively deteriorates physically and mentally, his sexual tensions simply disappear."

    d. "In short, any acute or chronic illness, mental or physical in character, that reacts to impair the male's general physical condition or to reduce the efficiency of his body economy may be associated with lowered or absent sexual tensions."

Abetting this, particularly for the over-60 group, is the strong possibility of the female's physical infirmities.

e. Fear of failure appears to be a complex and growing complicated cause for involution in the sexual act. A single failure seems to have a disproportionate effect upon the male over 40 and his fear of ineffective sexual performance. It appears that the adult male may attach more importance to his ability to function as a sexual partner than does the female in the same age bracket.

Once impotent *under any circumstances,* many males withdraw voluntarily from any coital activity rather than face the ego-shattering experience of repeated episodes of sexual inadequacy. Not infrequently they vocalize, and eventually come to believe extraneous excuses for sexual withdrawal rather than accepting the clinical fact of a normal involutionary process. [Italics added]

14.

Sexuality is a dimension and an expression of personality. Culturally, sexual aggression has been accepted as a mode of expression for the human male, an integral part of the "plumage" of his dominant role. Currently, eroticism has become so synonymous with maleness that it has progressed beyond acceptability to desirability. It is presumed that only physical defect or the depletion of the aging process will interfere with the male's innate erotic interest and his ability to respond to sexual stimuli. Two conceptual errors defeat these basic presumptions: First, any fear of performance, displeasing sensation, or sense of rejection affects male eroticism as much as it does the physiologic effectiveness of his response; and second, age does not necessarily deplete the male's physiologic ability or (sic) psychologic interest in sexual performance.

Impressions of and comments on Masters and Johnson's study

1. One can only guess what an older adult reader thinks about this study on human sexual response. One type of response seems almost inevitable. Many adults may feel that the study concerns the obvious. They know all this. They have lived through and experienced in a unique individual manner the rise, plateau, and decline of their own sexual powers. They are their own experts. The study tells them nothing new. It may be news to the adolescent or the young adult. The aging adult has lived through sexual decline. True, the study may have added some comparisons he wondered about, but as for the major findings, he knew them all along from personal experience. He is, simply, not the man he once was.

2. A second type of unimpressed reaction by an older adult may be equally true. Again, this blasé response may be typified by "What's new?" This individual knows all of his processes have slowed down.

He wears bifocals. His hearing is less efficient. His breath is short. His reaction time has decreased. So why, then, should not his sexual prowess be affected by the same decrements. The study impresses him not. He feels animals, automobiles, appliances—everything—is less efficient as it grows older and older. Of course, the more you use it the better it works. The less you use it the rustier it gets. Thus, he feels, sexual behavior follows all the laws of decline just like everything else.

3. Still a third reaction is possible. It may be likened to the story of the little boy who was taken to the planetarium to watch the stars and the heavens unfold. After a thorough lecture of two hours he was asked how he liked it. "O.K., I guess," he said, "but it told me more than I wanted to know."

4. Finally, an anticipated response by older adults may be one of controlled shock, embarrassment, and annoyance at such a bold effort. A male and a female scientist actually witnessing couples during intercourse and measuring the physiologic responses seems too much.

Although Masters and Johnson may seem to have taken some of the romance out of sexual intercourse, they have also taken out some of the nonsense and folklore fantasies.

Through the conscientious efforts of two competent, qualified research scientists, knowledge about one of the fundamental behaviors of man now exists, where it did not exist before. The subjects volunteered for these studies. No unsuspected invasion of privacy was perpetrated. In some ways, this is more than we can say for the federal government's efforts to investigate income tax matters.

Masters and Johnson wisely state that their research is intended partially for the *armamentarium* of physicians and not intended for popularization.

Research
Suggestions

1. Of what does marital satisfaction consist? Is there a way to measure it objectively?
2. Is it the "novel and unstereotyped way of behaving" that makes a marriage successful (Birren, 1964a), or is it the "essentially mundane and dull" marriages which are most successful (Golden, 1963)?
3. What is the extent of the correlation between happiness in marriage and number of outside pursuits and interests? How do men and women differ in this respect?
4. Why do older, never-married individuals live longer than older married individuals?
5. How important is "freedom to regress" (Dicks, 1963) in maintaining a successful marriage?
6. Would research support the many beliefs about bachelor men and women?

7. Why do men with sons remarry more often than men with daughters?
8. Precisely what is the effect of the number of children on remarriage for men? for women?
9. What factors are responsible for the increase in marriage failure as age at marriage decreases?
10. What are the happiest years of marriage? Why?
11. How does the number of children affect marital happiness?
12. Can a study be designed to settle once and for all the controversy about the success of second marriages?
13. Do divorced people have personality characteristics that significantly differentiate them from those not divorced?
14. Why does "monotony in sexual relationships" affect males more than females?
15. Can more "old wives' tales" be discarded by means of a thorough study of the psychological aspects of sex in marriage?
16. Can ways be found to obtain marriage data on upper- and lower-class people?
17. What does the future hold for marriage? How will marriage change?

CHAPTER 5

Parents
and
Family

IS THERE ANYTHING SPECIAL IN
BEING MIDDLE-AGED PARENTS?

Prior to getting into the research data, there appear to be a few obvious factors about parenthood and middle age. During the middle years, the parents may have infant children of their own yet be grandparents of infant children of grown sons and daughters. Many of the studies to be cited are concerned with parenthood per se. The roles of parenthood may be more confusing than clarifying. Parenthood consists of four factors: being a mother or a father but also being a wife or a husband. In addition to this, one may have children of one's own and thus be a parent; but one may have one's own parents still living and thus be a child, at least in the eyes of his mother and/or father. In some ways, therefore, parenthood for middle-aged people may be more complex than at any other stage in life.

It has often intrigued this writer that the only commandment in the Ten Commandments that promises you anything if you fulfill that commandment is the fourth: "Honor thy father and thy mother that it may be well with thee and thou mayest live long on this earth." There is no intent herein to give a theological interpretation of this commandment. It is of interest, however, that one of the commandments gives a prize if it is obeyed. Long life is promised if the individual obeys his mother and father. May we presume that even as far back as Mosaic times obedience to one's parents could not be taken for granted. If this be true, the world has not changed much!

An interesting viewpoint of parenthood and its relation to maturity is proposed by another author. "We here operationally define the onset of middle-age not in terms of years, but in terms of their children's reaching the age of independence." (Vedder, 1965)

One special consideration of being parents during middle age may be found in the suggestion by Glick that married couples now have more years of togetherness after their children have married than did couples of earlier generations. Trends toward earlier marriage, smaller families, and individuals living longer have all produced the fact that ". . . couples now spend one-third of their married life with no unmarried children of their own in the home." (Glick, 1955)

Most of the research done in family relations has to do with marriage selection, the problems of early adulthood, and the influence of family life on children and infants. There is very little research on family relations for the middle-aged and old. We have few theories to account for the continuity in personality adjustments within the family. The demand for changes in behavioral patterns of parents to their children and vice versa has largely been unstudied. What may be fruitful are more longitudinal studies. (Gravatt, 1953) (Mercer, 1967) (Moore, 1965a)

Few studies concern themselves with the cycle of the family life from the viewpoint of middle-aged parents. It is these individuals who must make adjustments in playing the role of mother or father as their children progress from infancy to childhood to adolescence to being young married parents. At middle age the mother and father must learn new rules to play their roles of parents, because what worked for the first child does not seem to work for the second child, and so on. Even if there is only one child in the family, the adjustments for the parents may be difficult and disturbing. (Mitchell, 1967) They come to the realization that they must adjust as parents with each advancing year of their child. What worked with a lively, lonely 3-year-old does not apply in handling a 13-year-old child. The parents begin to feel that there is no plateau. Consistency as parents becomes very difficult to maintain. Parenthood of an only child becomes a continuous battle to keep up with the child's own development. What worked last year is not applicable to this year's problems. Further complicating the picture, of course, is whether the child is a son or daughter. One of the strong determinants of how one plays his or her parental role appears to be the social pressures and mores of the times: what are the other parents doing? (Hiltner, 1953)

Is there anything special in being middle-aged parents? Some writers feel that this may be the most difficult time in which to fulfill the parental role. Of primary importance is the parents' experiences with their own parents, "thus parent-child may well be a quality of parent-grandparent relationship." (Stringer, 1961)

One author studied the intergenerational family relationships and social role changes in middle age. One of the purposes of the study was to investigate the differences in social classes. Fifty-seven couples whose ages ranged from 45 to 60 years were interviewed approximately 8 months after their last child had married and left the home. Questions were asked to explore the extent to which family continuity was maintained, that is to say, were their children raising their grandchildren in somewhat the same manner as they had been raised? Family continuity was found to be inversely related to social class: the higher the class, the lower the continuity. "It appears that intergenerational family continuity is a more important factor than social class." (Sussman, 1960)

Another investigation, "Studies of three-generation households," gives some interesting data. A three-generation household was defined as a living arrangement in which the husband and wife were rearing a child or children under the age of 21, and in the same living arrangement one or both of their parents also lived. Three separate studies were conducted. The primary information came from the wife. Three-generation households were recognized as a very hazardous type of family living. The grandparents indicated a strong reluctance to relinquish any authority over their own children. Husbands and wives appeared to resent the threat upon their own independence and authority. Complications arose from the youngest generation's being baffled by the splitting of authority among their elders. Grandparents and parents would not agree, which created conflict with the child's own desires to be grown up and emancipated from any adult control. (Koller, 1954)

One study indicated that couples maintain closer relationships with the parents of the wives than with the parents of the husbands. (Droege, 1963)

One of the special characteristics in being middle-aged parents might depend upon what time in history you were living. Employing the census data, one author finds that in 1890 the birth of the last child would come on the average when the couple were in their early 30s. The same data indicated that in 1950 the birth of the last child would come on the average when the couple were in their late 20s. The last child would leave home on the average when the couple were in the mid-50s for the data in 1890. In 1950 the last child would leave the home on the average when the couple were in their late 40s. (Hurlock, 1959)

An interview in depth of approximately 100 middle-aged adults in England reveals some interesting facts of this age group in that country. Most of the findings were reported in a series of programs for British TV viewers. One of the greatest erroneous assumptions found was that mothers always enjoy their roles as mothers. They found many who did not. Contrary to the general belief that family life today is not as strong and good as "in the old days," the authors contend that today's families are far better in at least five ways: (1) status of the children in the family and society was much improved, (2) women in English families had far more privileges than in the past, (3) standard of living had made current family life far more tolerable, healthy, and safe, (4) medical and health standards had eliminated much suffering in inadequate home surroundings as well as reduced infant death, and (5) in their estimation, the moral tone of family life had improved. As a result, members of modern average English families were better able to become "total persons" and reach fuller personalities than in the nostalgic Victorian past. (Benaim, 1967)

WHAT DO CHILDREN THINK OF THEIR PARENTS?

Although there are no studies that can answer that question completely, a number of investigative efforts do give us some meaningful information. Underachieving boys perceived their mothers as exercising strong control. (Davids, 1967) The average mother or father probably makes an impression upon his or her child in direct proportion to the age of the child. (Kobashigawa, 1966) (Swift, 1966) Young children may idolize or eulogize parents. Teen-age children may despise or defy parents. Children who are recently married may look upon the folks at home as an ideal source of second-hand furniture. Children of middle-aged parents who themselves are now mothers and fathers may now look upon their middle-aged parents as wise and sagacious to a degree they never felt possible before. (Irving, 1966)

One research endeavor had 60 teen-age students (36 boys, 24 girls) rate the personalities of their fathers. The fathers' occupations broke down into two classifications: professional and nonprofessional. Although there were no differences in the ratings between the boys and girls toward their fathers' occupations, there was some evidence that the professional workers were rated higher on emotional stability and responsibility. The nonprofessionals' children rated their sires as being higher on sociability. (Smith, 1966)

What happens when you measure the recalled treatment by their parents of 83 university students, all male, and test the hypothesis that those students who remembered their parents as punitive, irritable, and unloving would have higher blood pressures than those male students who recalled their parents in a more favorable light? The results of the study indicate that at least for 83 university males there was absolutely no connection between their memories of their parents and the students' blood pressure. (Harburg, 1965)

Another study by Marzolf examined parental behavior as reported by college students. Marzolf took two samples of students, 300 in one group and 300 in another, and asked them to describe their parents' conduct. A few of the findings were as follows: desirable items describing their parents were most frequently reported, there was wide latitude in the items students chose as characteristic of their parents, and there was some evidence to indicate that students who were high in ego strength reported their parents as being quite self-assured. (Marzolf, 1965)

College girls who reported that their mothers had either ignored or rejected during their childhood appeared to have more insensitivity to social reinforcement. On the other hand, college girls who recalled their mothers as being rather low in control and "accepting" of their childhood behavior appeared to have personalities that functioned much more strongly. (Heilbrun, 1965c)

One study had a cross-cultural influence. In this study, reported in a British journal of psychology, two matched samples of 44 American and 44 German high school graduates participating in a foreign exchange program were questioned about the parent-child relationships in their own country. It may be of interest to note that the high school graduates of American parents reported them to be less strict and to have given them much more autonomy than the German parents. German high school graduates considered their parents to be much more punitive. However, for both American and German groups, the father was viewed as the main disciplinarian, and the mother was considered to be much more affectionate. There was some evidence that the German father appeared to be more strict. According to this one study, American mothers exerted much more achievement pressure than did German mothers. The total result of the study indicated that mothers and fathers are not the same in America as they are in Germany. (Rabbie, 1965)

A second study of cultural influence was reported in a Polish journal in 1965 in which three hundred essays written by girls and boys ages 12 through 18 indicated that approximately 75 percent of this group felt that the relationship with their parents was quite unsatisfactory. The main problem, particularly for the 15- and 16-year-olds, was the inability to get along with one of the parents. The greatest source of conflict for girls in the 13-to-18 age group concerned their strong desire for independence. This study may be of interest to befuddled American parents. It may give them some sense of satisfaction that things may be quite similar in Poland. (Sobanska, 1965)

When 245 adolescents were asked to indicate which parent punished more, was the boss in the family, they feared more, checked up on them the most, and gave them help with problems, there was a significant difference in the responses toward the mother's role and the father's role. Specific results indicated that boys stated affection and support was better from their mothers. However, half of the girls stated the above characteristics were gained from their fathers. Boys associated punishment with their fathers, girls with their mothers. Boys generally feared their fathers more than their mothers. On the other hand, half of the girls feared mother while half feared father. Both sexes expected help from the mother, but it was almost a unanimous feeling for the girls. There were pronounced differences in the response of these ninth-graders between the middle-class and working-class boys, especially in the area of punishment and fear. The lower-class boy felt the father's role was more potent. (Fitzgerald, 1966)

Tuckman asked college students to rank all the age periods in life's span in terms of in which periods they thought time would pass the quickest and in which periods the slowest. The results should not surprise anyone. The college students had a very strong negative attitude toward aging and felt that time would drag and drag as one got older and older. (Tuckman, 1965b)

Two psychologists wondered whether adolescent boys would identify more with their fathers and adolescent girls identify more with their mothers. The identification was relative to the source of control over their behavior. The results show that girls are likely to see their mothers as more powerful and boys to see their fathers as more powerful. (Grinder, 1965)

Other studies indicate that the older the subjects in the studies, the more benign a picture they recall of their early family life. Although distortion in memory was always present, the evidence seemed to be fairly clear. (O'Neil, 1962)

In one study, measures were obtained on about 350 male and 450 female college students to find out how college students perceived and accepted themselves, and this was then compared with the parents' perceptions and acceptance of the students. The study also attempted to measure the parents' attitudes toward the college students' academic pursuits. For the male college student, there was general agreement between how he accepted himself and how his parents accepted him in regard to academic effectiveness, but this did not hold true for the female college student. There appeared to be a wide discrepancy as to how females accepted themselves in general and how their parents accepted them. Male college students who had strong goal-seeking drives also had parents who agreed that a college education was primarily for intellectual broadening. (Wyer, 1965)

One approach to the question is in the technique used in guidance clinics particularly with teen-aged populations. In order to develop broader perceptions of each others' roles, adolescents and their parents are asked questions about each other that may indicate how much or how little they know about each other. Nothing magical results from this approach. There does seem to be evidence, at least in the experience of this psychologist, that more sensitive and deeper understanding may come about when one individual knows more about another individual. (Duvall, 1965)

The child answers questions about his parents

How Well Do You Know Your Folks?

1. How did your parents meet each other?
2. How long were your parents engaged?
3. Where did your parents get married, in a church, in a home; who married them?
4. When is the anniversary of your parents' marriage?
5. Who do you think is your father's best friend?
6. Who do you think is your mother's best friend?
7. In your opinion, how did (does) your father get along with his own mother and father?
8. In your opinion, how did (does) your mother get along with her own mother and father?
9. Approximately what is your father's present salary?
10. Can you describe what your father does for a living in his occupation?
11. Does your mother have a favorite hobby, pastime, or recreation? What is it? Why do you think she enjoys it?
12. Can you name or describe your mother's favorite club or organization or group with which she spends most of her time?
13. What do you think is your mother's greatest ambition for her own self-purposes?
14. In your opinion, how does your mother get along with her own brothers and sisters, if she has any?
15. What do you consider to be your mother's greatest strength?

16. What do you consider to be your mother's greatest weakness?
17. How far did your mother go in educating herself and what were her special interests or majors in education?
18. When your mother was in school, which subjects did she like the least and which subjects did she like the most?
19. How would you describe your mother's present state of health?
20. Does your father have a favorite hobby, pastime, or recreation? What is it? Why do you think he enjoys it?
21. Can you name or describe your father's favorite club or organization or group with which he spends most of his time?
22. What do you think is your father's greatest ambition for his own self-purposes?
23. In your opinion, how does your father get along with his own brothers and sisters, if he has any?
24. What do you consider to be your father's greatest strength?
25. What do you consider to be your father's greatest weakness?
26. How far did your father go in educating himself and what were his special interests or majors in education?
27. When your father was in school, which subjects did he like the least and which subjects did he like the most?
28. How would you describe your father's present state of health?
29. Keeping in mind that this is very confidential and will be treated as such, how would you describe how your mother and father get along with each other?
30. Is your mother or is your father more understanding of you? Why do you think so?
31. Considering absolutely everything about your mother and your father, is one of them more of a favorite of yours than the other?

The parent answers questions about his child

How Well Do You Know Your Child?
1. Name at least two friends of your child.
2. Which one would you consider to be a "best friend?" Why?
3. Which acquaintance does (he) (she) dislike the most? Why?
4. What school subject does your child like the most? Why?
5. Which one the least? And again, why?
6. What do you consider to be (his) (her) greatest fear? Why?
7. Worry? Why?
8. When left to (his) (her) own devices, what does (he) (she) enjoy doing the most? Why?
9. Who is your child's favorite teacher? Why?
10. What teacher does your child dislike the most? Why?

11. Do either of the above-named teachers resemble you in any way?
12. What does your (son) (daughter) dream about being when (he) (she) grows up?
13. When was the last time you had a strong argument or disagreement or fight between the two of you? What caused it? Who "won"?
14. What relative is (his) (her) favorite?
15. What relative does (he) (she) dislike the most?
16. If there are brothers or sisters, which one appears to be a favorite most of the time? Why?
17. If you were to die very soon, what kind of person do you think your child would prefer to have your spouse marry? How much does this resemble you?
18. If your child had 3 million dollars to give away, what three people do you think would get 1 million each?

The object of this guidance device is to compare the answers of the child with the answers of the parents. In reverse, the parents' answers are evaluated by the child.

In this writer's experience the confrontation of known to unknown frequently runs the gamut from hilarious to heartbreaking. Many parents do not know what their children think of them until they challenge it by trying to ascertain the facts rather than fictionalized and rationalized feelings. (Wakefield, 1966)

WHAT INFLUENCE DO CHILDREN HAVE ON THEIR PARENTS?

There can be no doubt that being a mother or a father has an enormous impact on the conduct of an individual's life. (Gilmore, 1967) The appropriate question might better be how much does it change one's life? It is possible that working and sacrificing for one's children may be the most powerful motivating force for adults in our society today. "Someday, son, this will all be yours," says the father who has worked hard all his life to create a business or a farm. "We do it for the children's sake," a cliché that could be attributed to any set of parents who have just installed an outdoor swimming pool, purchased a larger home with more bedrooms and more mortgages, borrowed money to purchase a summer home on the lake, or decided not to be divorced despite the fact that there was very little relationship left between the husband and wife.

A number of factors are involved in studying the effect that children have upon their parents. (Sprague, 1966) (Oakes, 1966)

Self-sacrifice

All the way from diapers to death, many mothers and fathers have
given unstintingly of themselves so that their children may have bette;
food, clothing, and an education. It is not uncommon for some parent
to consider their PTA membership as servitude on behalf of their
children. (Are there any adults who faithfully attend the PTA meeting
and serve on committees even though they do not have children cur
rently enrolled in the school and do this just for the benefit of al
children?) There are times in the private practice of this writer wher
he has been overwhelmed by the dedication and sacrifice of parents fo;
their children. Sometimes one gets the impression that mothers wil
work as menial slaves just to make certain that their children have
clothing, food, and educational opportunities at least as good as their
relatives and the neighbor's children have. Equally true is the patter;
of the father who will continue to work for years and years at a job h(
hates intensely.

Identification

Psychological literature includes many examples of parental identifica
tion with their children. Cartoons highlight this theme: The new fathe;
walks into the maternity ward laden with baseball gloves, bats, and
balls. He does more than identify. He *projects* all of his thwarted ambi
tions and desires upon his young son, not even 3 days old. Again we finc
that mothers in their mother/daughter matching dresses are equally
prone to identifying with their daughters and projecting their unful
filled ambitions upon the young child. The syndrome seems to be that
whatever the mother or father was unable to fulfill in his own life car
now be fulfilled through his children. This might be referred to a;
the "second-chance syndrome."

Substitute love object

The psychoanalytic concepts of Oedipal and Electra complexes are
pertinent here: mothers hold their sons as love objects and father
their daughters in the same manner. There is evidence that mother;
may transfer their love relationship from their unresponsive husband;
to their sons. This is especially true when the son is pliable and acutely
responsive to the protection and devotion of the mother. This may be
exemplified by the mother's remark, "Don't you think you are a little
too hard on him. After all, he's such a little boy." The father's use o;
the daughter as a love object may be found in the daughter's statement
"My mother will probably say no, but I can get almost anything ou;
of my dad."

Rivalry with spouse

Occasionally one finds a husband and wife in their roles as mother and father competing with each other. This may happen in a friendly or a nonfriendly manner. In such cases, both the mother and the father will strive to do their best in the appropriate roles, not wanting to be the lesser of the two parents.

One of the factors of parenthood in many societies is the desire for "upward mobility" for their children. Other than the fictional Fagin, it is as rare as the duck-billed platypus to find an adult who wants any children to go downward and be degraded. Obviously there exist mothers and fathers who demean their children, injure them, or totally ignore them. This behavior, however, is a pattern of the neurotic or psychotic and not of the average parent, and thus belongs in a special category.

For the middle-aged parents there is another effect on their lives. It is usually at this time that at least one or two of the children are married and are living away from home with families of their own. "One result of greater physical separation is an increase in what may perhaps be called 'routine visiting.' " We like the term of Nimkoff who considers parents whose married children are now living away as "modern circuit-riders." This is a twentieth-century phenomenon. Highways may be full of grandparents going back and forth across the nation en route to visiting their children and their children's children. Probably the peak of the modern circuit riders occurs during vacation time in summer and during the holiday season, particularly at Christmas time. (Friedman, 1963)

Murdock studied numerous cultures and suggests that there are at least four functions of the family and of parenthood that are basic to social life. These are (1) sexual functions, (2) economic necessity, (3) reproduction reasons for maintaining the race, and (4) educational functions necessary for passing down the knowledge of a civilization. Murdock feels that, particularly for the middle-agers, as the children mature, a good parent should have "twinges of loss" and "moments of nostalgia." Finally, Murdock gives some encouragement to parents by maintaining that the children's needs and the parent's needs must necessarily be in conflict many times. (Sutton-Smith, 1963)

One study indicates the effect children may have upon their parents' memory. The study was designed to measure the accuracy of parental recall for various aspects of their child's development. The subjects were well-educated members primarily from middle-class homes in New York City and suburbs. There were 39 couples studied, plus 5 mothers whose husbands were either lost, divorced, or otherwise not available to be interviewed. To test the memory of these parents, lengthy interviews were conducted. The results are quite interesting. The parents were grossly inaccurate in their memory of details about the child-rearing practices and early development progress of their children. Most of the inaccuracies in memory were toward recommendations the child guidance experts had made. This was more evident with mothers. Faulty parental memory is interesting, particularly because each set of parents had frequent rehearsal data in the 3-year study. The greatest inaccuracies were in regard to weaning, toilet training, thumb-sucking, and whether or not the child was on demand feeding. There was evidence that mothers recalled slightly more correctly than did the fathers as to when events occurred. Mothers who were working full time had far inferior memories for details than mothers who were staying at home or working part time. Oddly enough, mothers of boys tended to recall more accurately details of the boy's childhood than did the mothers of girls. On the same basis, fathers of boys also tended to recall more accurately items of the boy's childhood than did fathers of girls. As we might expect, mothers of single children tended to recall better than mothers of two or more children in the family. (Robbins, 1963) (Chess, 1966)

Another author felt that a 6-year-old child will produce greater alterations in maternal behavior than, for example, a 2-year-old child. The hypothesis was that a 6-year-old can manipulate the mother much better than a 2-year-old, at least in the mother's attitude and behavior toward the child. The "feedback system" is based on the difference in maternal behavior demands of the two age levels. Also, the mother perceives the child to have more of a personality as it grows older and consequently reacts more to the child. These processes of reaction to children may lie dormant for many years. The deeper parental feelings toward the children and the children's feelings toward their parents may not be displayed for as much as 10 to 20 years after a particular incident. Recollection of past incidents usually does not come until a crisis occurs. The author concludes that the understanding of the cause-effect relationships between parents and their children may be a very fruitful avenue for the study of longitudinal behavior. (Birren, 1964b)

Sussman came to the conclusion that the postparental period (that stage in middle life after the children have left) produces very little significant change in the satisfaction mothers felt toward their children in prior years. (Vedder, 1965)

Is it true that parents work harder because they have children and want their children to have "nice" things? The Kansas City studies reported in 1962 indicate, particularly for Middle West, middle-class people, that parents are normally in a higher social class at middle age than when first married. Some 37 percent of the subjects were highly upward mobiles, 13 percent were downward, and approximately 50 percent remained at the same socioeconomic status. One interpretation may be that having children does make parents work harder to raise their standard of living and to raise their social-class status. (Birren, 1964a)

Does it make a difference if children call their mothers Mom, Muzzie, Mumzie, if they call their fathers Pops, Pa, or Dad? No one knows the answer to this as yet, but a number of investigators are beginning to be interested in the nicknames children use for their parents. Some research psychologists feel such a study is a first step in the analysis of relationships within American families. Perhaps some psychologist will concoct a psychological test that measures the depth of family feelings by the nicknames children use for their parents. (Lewis, 1965)

Hurlock feels that "retirement from parenthood is as difficult for most adults as retirement from work." Parenthood in this sense means primary parenthood rather than secondary parenthood (being a grandmother or grandfather). It is difficult at this point to see how one ever retires entirely from parenthood (apropos of the modern circuit rider). The suggestion is made that retirement from primary parenthood and active involvement of children living in the home must depend on preparing for their leaving and that new interests must be developed. (Hurlock, 1959)

When children marry and leave home, parents do have greater freedom of movement and more money—providing that they have not undertaken much of the financial burden of the new couple. With more freedom and more money it is possible to take trips, design and build a new smaller home (or redecorate), and become more active in the community. Some writers feel that adult education is not totally possible until middle-aged people no longer are directly involved with having children in the home. Other writers feel that the level of parental adjustment is in direct relationship to propinquity: how far or how near the children live from the parental house. Psychologists and psychiatrists advocate that fighting the cutting of the parental psychic umbilical cord leads to gross unhappiness. Both the mother and the father should develop outside interests, begin to turn toward their own egos, and become somewhat "me" centered. The mother may feel the separation from her children more acutely than the father, who has his occupation to absorb his interest. After the children are married or in college, it is the mother who is being retired from her primary job, not the father. She may have greater adjustments in the mid-50s than the father and because of this earlier experience be better able to handle retirement at age 65 than her husband. (Hurlock, 1959)

Thompson and Streib discovered that the preretirement family (age 55 through 64) developed greater differences in family composition. There were four times as many widows as widowers. The children, with very few exceptions, had left the home because of marriage or for a career. (Vedder, 1965)

A study of 291 families showed an even flow back and forth between the assistance parents and adult children gave to each other. One exception was in financial aid, which went from the parent to the child. Parents place greater emphasis upon the ties they have toward their children than do the children toward their parents. Retirement of parents does not seem to have much effect on children's feelings toward their parents. (Streib, 1965)

One psychiatrist reported in 1966 that "psychopathological reactions to fatherhood probably occur with more frequency than is commonly recognized." After carefully studying 10 case histories and recognizing symptoms in other "new fathers," there was sufficient evidence to consider "Fatherhood as a precipitant to mental illness." (Wainwright, 1966)

Another 1966 study had a novel approach. An ambiguous child's voice was played over a tape recorder. One group of parents was told it was a girl's voice and the other group a boy's voice. "Results indicated fathers showed greater permissiveness toward girls than boys. Mothers showed greater permissiveness toward boys than girls." (Rothbart, 1966)

It would be ridiculous to maintain that children have no effect upon their parents. Certainly for those whose children are in infancy the effect may be quite pronounced. Much of the family life and much of the sleeping patterns of the parents are directly affected by an infant child. However, there may be evidence that as the mother and father progress through middle age, particularly in the late 50s, the children may have less and less effect upon the parents' behavior, feelings, and plans for the future.

WHAT INFLUENCE DO PARENTS HAVE ON THEIR CHILDREN?

More studies concern themselves with the effect parents have on their children than the effect children have on their parents. Many studies seem to indicate parents have a bad effect upon their children or are unable to guide and direct them in proper paths of human conduct. Certainly the most pronounced effect a parent has upon his child is having caused him or her to be born!

Research efforts run the gamut from accidents to homesickness. (Kurokawa, 1966) (Platt, 1967) Parents are blamed for making the transition from adolescence to adulthood difficult. (Conway, 1966) (Crawford, 1966)

Kagan uses the term *sleeper effect* to describe the time lag between the cause and effect of personality variables as they show up over long periods of time. For males who were inclined to be passive and had had a fear of bodily harm during their first 3 years of life, it was a better than average prediction that they would have love-object dependency as adults. Another sleeper effect had to do with girls and maternal practices. If a mother was very critical of her daughter up to the age of 3, the prediction was that the child as an adult would be a very high achiever. However, if a mother was very critical of her child past the age of 3 and up to the age of 10, there did not seem to be much relationship to the daughter's later achievement as an adult. If a mother was overly protective of her daughter during the daughter's first 3 years of life, the adult daughter would have withdrawal symptoms when stress was upon her. However, if she had large amounts of protection from the mother between the ages of 3 and 10, there seemed to be no consequent relationship in wanting to withdraw from stress as an adult. (Birren, 1964b)

One question that frequently occurs is how much effect the mother has and is it more than the effect the father has upon the children? Obviously families vary so widely that to give a definitive answer is to practice intellectual dishonesty. There are studies, however, drawn from representative populations, which consider the average effect of mothers and fathers upon children. (Heilbrun, 1966) One study of male and female high school students compared their scores on an anxiety test with their mothers' and fathers' scores. The data seemed to indicate that a boy's and girl's anxiety scores are much more related to the mother's than to the father's anxiety scores. (Adams, 1963) Again we find that mothers from low socioeconomic homes are blamed for strong authoritarian control and rigidity in handling their children. Mothers who have daughters and no sons appeared to be more democratic than those with only sons for children. (Edwards, 1966) Husbandless mothers are more concerned than married mothers in pushing their children toward high educational achievement. (Kriesberg, 1967) Children whose mothers were highly affectionate developed overly strong attachments to their mothers. (Livson, 1966) On the other hand, Peterson and many others conducted an in-depth study of parental attitudes. One of the primary conclusions was that fathers "were found to be at least" as important as mothers in creating maladaptive children. The implications are that fathers may be even more important in molding certain types of attitudes in children and that much more research should emphasize paternal behavior instead of only maternal behavior. (Peterson, 1968)

College students who had been extremely successful in high school but were failing in college were studied by Teahan. Mothers of low-achieving girls were dominant figures and had used strong disciplinary measures during the girl's childhood. Low male achievers had had possessive and dominating fathers. The feeling was that these students had been unable to develop sufficiently strong personalities to make it on their own. Conforming during high school produced high grades. High academic performance did not carry over into college when parents were not present. (Hamlin, 1966)

A team of psychologists studied one aspect of college dropouts and found a high positive correlation between parents who had dropped out when they were in college and their sons and daughters who did the same thing later on. College students whose parents had completed college were inclined to do the same thing. Dropouts beget dropouts and success begets success. (Warriner, 1966)

What affects family adjustment? If mother and father agree strongly on what the family should be, the evidence indicates the family will be well adjusted. If the parents' conception of an ideal family agrees with the actual family, there is also evidence of a well-adjusted family. The perception a person has of his family is an extremely important factor in the family's adjustment to each other and to outside pressures. (van der Veen, 1964)

Heilbrun asked the question: are daughters more similar to their mother than sons to their father? The answer, at least in this one study, is no. However, similarity to the same-sexed parent is positively related to personal adjustment for males and negatively related for females. The effect is greater in the case of son-father similarity than in the case of daughter-mother similarity. (Heilbrun, 1966)

How do college women perceive the dominance of one parent over the other and how is this reflected in their value orientations to college work? (1) Perceived parental influence is highly related to the socio-economic status of the father. (2) Fathers engaged in professional work and with a level of education and training higher than that of the mother exert a far greater influence on the female child. The father's idealized goals for the daughter were also internalized by the daughter. (3) The girl who identifies with her mother more often than with her father comes from a home where the father works at a skilled or semi-skilled level. (Kinnane, 1964)

Following the same line of thinking, Shaw and White studied students who were divided evenly into achiever and underachiever groups. There was strong agreement among the members of the achiever families. They thought the same and had the same value systems. This was found to be lacking in the underachiever group. In this study, achievers identified very much with the like-sexed parent. (Shaw, 1965)

Do parents influence children's political opinions? To find out, 440 students in sixteen American colleges responded to questionnaires in regard to their 1963 political opinions and beliefs. The study indicated that "almost as much deviation from, as conformance to, parental beliefs existed." Although rebellion to the right may be increasing, the strong prevailing direction is leftward from parental political beliefs. This may come as no surprise to a middle-aged parent who has a college student concerned with politics. (Middleton, 1963)

Another study found that the parents' role taking did not affect their children's political belief. This study was done with a random group of 17 emotionally disturbed children. (Copper, 1962)

On the basis of 2 studies, parents and children do not agree in their political beliefs.

A doctoral dissertation done by Kent using white Protestant middle-class mothers found no difference between authoritarian and equalitarian mothers in the psychological adjustment of their children. (Kent, 1965b)

A 1966 report on college students gave evidence that they were more anxious and maladjusted as adults if their parents had "remained angry at them for a long time and prolonged punishment when they had been children." College students whose parents had punished them quickly in childhood and did not prolong their anger were much better adjusted in college. (Perdue, 1966)

There appears to be evidence that the social class of parents does have a strong effect upon the children. (Edwards, 1967) (Hoffman, 1967) (Levine, 1967) A representative study indicated: (1) middle-class mothers tended to stress character development and morality more than other social-class levels; (2) higher-status-class mothers felt more effective in handling their children's social and emotional needs; (3) upper-middle-class children tended to accept maternal care less than lower-class children; (4) middle-class mothers, when interviewed but not when answering questionnaires, expressed great concern about their ability to perform their roles as a mother. Middle-class mothers are very ambivalent about their child-rearing role. This was not as apparent in the upper- and lower-class mothers, who felt more comfortable with their roles. (Swinehart, 1963)

Studying the intergenerational effect of 97 families whose 195 married children lived away from home suggests that despite the reduced emphasis on familism of the middle-class family, parents and their married children have a pattern of giving and receiving between them. All of these families were middle class, white, Protestant, and financially well-to-do, as well as highly educated. (Sussman, 1953)

What are the results when white and Negro women in middle and working classes are compared in attitudes toward child-rearing? Among whites, both in upward- and downward-mobility homes, there was a more favorable attitude toward change in child-rearing practices. Middle-class white women were more inclined to maintain the same child-rearing practices. Upward-mobile middle-class Negro women with working-class origins were less inclined to change their child-rearing practices. However, upward-mobile Negro women living in integrated neighborhoods were more inclined to change their child-rearing practices. (Blau, 1965)

In a study of migrant families, recent migrants to a large California city, each with a history of frequent moves on short notice, had no difficulty in moving into new communities quickly and without effort. The 100 families showed a very high degree of independence, self-reliance, and the ability to adapt to tension- and stress-producing situations. Apparently one learns by moving. (Landis, 1966)

Intellectually superior male high school students declared an overwhelming preference for their fathers. The brighter the student, the closer the child was to his parents and his father's ideologies. (Copper, 1962)

One hundred and fourteen mathematically gifted high school seniors were compared with a similar, but nonmathematically gifted, group of high school seniors. The mathematically gifted group showed very strong autocratic feelings, somewhat negative attitudes toward things in general, and indicated that their family relationships involved high-achievement demands from parents and strong fixed routines. (Kennedy, 1963)

The effect of the parents' concept of the family as a unit on child adjustment is a unique one. One factor usually found is the degree of agreement between the father and the mother and its direct bearing on the child's personal adjustment. (Ferber, 1967) In almost all cases, the higher the degree of parental agreement as to how the family should operate, the better the social, emotional and academic functioning of the child. (Higgins, 1967) (Hurley, 1967) (Preston, 1966) The evidence seems to be that when the mother and father agree as to how they should enact their roles and how the family should operate as a unit, there is a beneficial effect upon the children. (van der Veen, 1965) (Frye, 1965) (Rebhun, 1967) (Stacey, 1967)

Are mothers good therapists for their own children? It was found that the mother's social behavior did function as a powerful force upon the child's behavior returning to "normalcy." The study consisted of only 3 children and their 3 mothers. (Wahler, 1965)

What are the long-time effects of incest upon the child's later behavior? Two cases reported from Turkey state that "the children were not seriously or permanently impaired psychologically." (Yorukoglu, 1966) There are a few longitudinal studies from this country on the long-term effects of incest.[1]

How do families interact when they make decisions? One study considered the family triads (father-mother-child) and what happened when they made decisions. The study involved 125 families. Fifty families were considered normal in their living pattern and 75 were considered abnormal or neurotic. Two results seem to stand out: (1) the normal families were more spontaneous in their likes and dislikes prior to making the decisions and were more efficient in coming to a decision; (2) the schizophrenic families were unable to agree on likes and dislikes or how to proceed in making a decision. (Ferreira, 1965)

A unique study was reported in which parents attempted to control their children by calling upon God to punish them if they misbehaved. These "coalitions with God" did control the child's behavior. There was an effect on the child's behavior and on his personality. However, parents who called upon God as a punishing agent were ineffectual and powerless kinds of people both within their family and the world at large. (Nunn, 1964)

Duvall suggests six areas that are unavoidable in the influence parents have in molding the behavior of their children.

1. Parents must make some decisions as to what control and what freedom their teen-age children are to have.
2. Parents must decide how much responsibility is to be vested in the teen-agers and how much responsibility should remain with the parents. This connotes who is to be blamed when things go wrong.
3. Decisions must be made between the parents and children on school social activities and the degree of emphasis on academic achievement.
4. Parents must make the decision as to how mobile the child is to be. Shall he come and go with no or little accountability?
5. An ever-present problem is to keep open the lines of communication between the parent and the child. This is based on the respect each has for the other.
6. Values that the parents and teen-ager hold are considered to have two factors: those used for momentary decisions (day-to-day living) and those that go beyond and into causes bigger than the family or the self.

(Duvall, 1965)

[1] Representative studies may be found in R. E. L. Masters. *Patterns of Incest*. New York: Julian Press, 1963, and S. K. Weinberg. *Incest Behavior*. New York: Citadel Press, 1966.

The father's occupation does influence the offspring in many subtle ways. The not-so-subtle ways are obvious: the higher the father's income the greater the child's chances for attending college, traveling, eating, and living on a higher scale. The more subtle influences indicate that sons are more than likely to choose an occupation quite similar to the father's (76,000 students). (Werts, 1967) Paternal occupations also influence the child's attitudes, role expectations, work habits, and type of family structure. (Barth, 1967) (Paine, 1967) (Podell, 1967) (De Shazo, 1966)

IS BEING A GRANDPARENT PLEASANT OR A PROBLEM?

Grandparenthood is the supreme second chance. Being once removed from the direct responsibility, blame, and day-to-day wear and tear of bringing up a child can create wonders in changing attitudes toward child-rearing. Many grandparents whose own children were raised in strict conformity to rules and regulations suddenly become relaxed and lenient about their grandchildren's misbehaviors and pranks. This change in attitudes is not uncommon.

Traditionally, grandma and grandpa are considered to be benign, gray-haired angels with enormous compassion and capacity for use and abuse. There seems to be evidence that this picture, if not fictional, is certainly growing out of focus. Some evidence seems to indicate that grandparents no longer cherish or even willingly submit to unannounced babysitting chores and the like. Some writers feel that the modern-day grandma and grandpa much prefer short visits and to be left alone to pursue their own interests.

The intergenerational conflicts still persist. There may be evidence, however, that as the foreign-born grandparent is gradually passing from the scene, the rigidity reflected in their own upbringing and projected toward their own grandchildren is slowly abating. Replacing this are the more modern grandparents, whose home is well kept, who travel widely, and who have friends of their own and are not so dependent on their children for social contact.

There are cases in which the grandparents are more apt to buy the affection of both their children and their grandchildren rather than to actively engage in the day-to-day upbringing of the little children.

In 1900 fewer children knew their grandparents because longevity was so much shorter. In 1950, on the other hand, many more children not only knew, but had 5 to 10 years of grandparents. At least 50 percent of the grandparents, when they lived near enough, took over babysitting and child-care responsibilities. The conclusion was that the parental roles of grandparents have increased and been strengthened

since 1900. However, there exists the long and strong cultural gap between the children and their grandparents. The permissiveness that
may exist in 1960 is far different than the maxim, "Children should
be seen and not heard," of the 1900s. In 1900, grandparents had more
authority and a stronger hold on the inherited wealth of the family
structure. In towns and cities the vertical joint-family relationship was
replacing the horizontal joint-family of the smaller towns and villages
and farm. Because grandparents live longer, and there are more three-
and four-generational families these days, there is less dependence
upon cousins and relatives of the same age bracket for social contact
than there was in the past. There is less and less of the so-called family
reunion than there has been in the past. Supplanting this is the gathering of a single family unit, usually during vacation time and under the
auspices of the grandparents who wish to bring all the children together
for one short, hectic, frenetic, and reacquaintance time. Neutral
grounds provide less disruption of the pattern of any single family
involved. Not too infrequently the grandparents may pay a large portion of the vacation resort bill. (Friedman, 1963)

In a 1964 report by Neugarten, each member of 70 pairs of middle-
class grandparents was interviewed at some length regarding how he
felt about his grandchildren. The primary considerations were the
degree of comfort he felt in his grandparent role, how significant he
felt the grandparent role to be, and the style in which he felt most
comfortable in enacting his senior role. The most frequent pattern was
that of the grandparent-grandchild relationship as fun seekers. The
pattern of fun seeker and of distant figure (so characterized by the
grandchildren) was much more frequent in grandparents who were
under the age of 65 than in those who were over the age of 65.
Neugarten wisely points out that one of the areas requiring study as a
phenomenon of middle age is that of the grandparenthood role.
(Neugarten, 1964b)

Hader feels that grandparents have a modulating effect on the
lives of their children and grandchildren. Their presence may act as
sort of a judicial board of review. No matter what the age of the adult,
if his parents are alive there is always someone older with more experience to tell him when he is doing foolish things, whether he
appreciates the advice or not. (Hader, 1965)

Whether being a grandparent is a pleasant situation or a problem
situation would, of course, depend upon many things. Primary to this
would be whether the spouse is alive or dead. Being an "only" as a
grandparent may make significant differences in the enjoyment or rejection of the role. (Kalish, 1967) A further consideration could be how
much money the grandparents have. They may indulge in buying
things for the comfort of their grandchildren and their children, or

they may retreat through travel from the harassment of their children and their children's children. Whatever the effect of grandparenthood is, it seems to be changing.

IS THE IN-LAW SITUATION ALL BAD?

Someone should change the old slogan to read, "Nothing is certain in life except death, taxes, and in-laws." For adults, one of the most prevalent facts in life is the in-law situation. Marriage begets in-laws. It becomes a case of "instant relatives." Just add marriage vows with or without a ring. After 20-to-25 years of married life, those in-laws who are still surviving have now been sorted out as to the good, the bad, the supportive, the carping, the covetous, and all the gradations in between. In the author's own counseling experience, nothing is more traumatic and vicious than to have two sisters-in-law each compare the progress and lack of progress of her own children to the other's children. This cousin comparison too often leads to strife and false achievement if not downright lying to each other.

The structure of most families changes in middle life. Having adjusted to one's past in-laws, the adult parents now must adjust to the new in-laws accrued through the marriages of sons and daughters. There appears to be some evidence that adjustments to the in-law problem brought into the family by the first marriage will be different than the adjustments required for the in-law gained through the last marriage of a child. In most cases there seems to be a honeymoon, not only for the newly married child, but for the new in-law. Strife and stress with in-laws may be postponed indefinitely or until financial stress strikes the young married couple.

It has been suggested that the mother-in-law has a harder time than the father-in-law in learning her new role, regardless of whether it is a son-in-law or daughter-in-law that she now has. The father-in-law appears to have an easier time with his new role. With a daughter-in-law he may feel slightly romantic as he overindulges his new and probably pretty daughter by marriage. With a son-in-law he may overdo the role of "buddy" in seeking to establish some comfortable relationship with the man who has married the "apple of his eye." (Wallin, 1963)

The acceptance of a new in-law may depend upon four factors: similarity in ethnic group, similarity in religious background or belief, similiarity in class level, and similarity in educational level. (Wallin, 1963)

It may be easier for a wealthy girl to marry a poor boy than for a poor girl to marry into the family of a wealthy boy. Occupational success may be the key to satisfaction in the in-law relationship. It is possible for the poor boy to gain upward mobility with the help of a wealthy father-in-law. Because of a poor girl's restricted background, she may have a more difficult time with her wealthy husband's mother-in-law and particularly sisters-in-law. A woman sets the tone of the home (selects the furniture, rearranges the furniture, does the shopping, dresses the children, and so on). Having always shopped with a careful eye to value in the discount stores, her purchases may not carry the prestige value that her female in-laws feel is proper.

Most writers agree that a courtship of at least 1 year helps to ease the in-law acceptance. Elopement predicts an unhappy in-law relationship, which seems obvious. In the author's counseling experience, a unique phenomenon seems to occur, however, whether the courtship has been long or short or whether elopement created the marriage, with the arrival of the first child. Parents frequently play a wait-and-see role *until the first grandchild is born*. There seems to be something that happens upon the introduction of a tiny child. Even if they still have a very jaundiced view of the marriage, they rarely seem to "take it out" on the child. The tiny, defenseless grandchild seems to be living proof that the marriage, although disapproved of in the beginning, may eventually be a successful union.

The question of compatibility with in-laws may be in direct relationship to the geographical distance from the parental home. The further the distance, the greater the reliance on faith and sentimentality. There is some evidence that the young husband is in more jealous conflict with his father-in-law than his mother-in-law. Conversely, the young bride is inclined to say, "Your dad is a dear, but your mother is too nosey. She asks about everything, even the curtains."

Many marriages can expect some degree of rivalry between the two sets of parents. Rivalry manifests itself in competing with each other for the newlyweds' benefit (giving furniture, money, donating a car, or selling it for a ridiculously low price instead of trading it in). Decisions are forced as to whose parents are going to be visited during the Christmas and Easter holidays, especially if children are involved. In-laws may be influential in selecting a place and a type of residence. Considerations must be made in the type of work the husband does. In the latter case, each father feels his own occupation is a better one than the opposing father-in-law.

Parents feel better and closer to their married children when giving financial aid. The cliché is, "The kids may as well use the money when they need it and not have to wait for us to die off, hey, Mother?" It takes a wise and sometimes suffering father-in-law/son-in-law combination to agree on how such a money gift is spent when values differ widely. Some counselors suggest that parents are more inclined to help daughters financially than they are sons. Financial help is influenced by the birth of the first child and the addition of more children. Young couples having refused financial aid now accept it "for the children's sake." (Wallin, 1963)

One psychiatrist believes that the in-law problem is a question of "timing." The timing factor is in relation to the visits by the parents to the young married people. The visits should not be too long or too short and certainly should be timed so that they are convenient to the young married couple and not to the older parents who happen to have a free Sunday afternoon. (Mulvey, 1963)

Probably one of the most outstanding characteristics of older married adults is being surrounded by in-laws. Frequently the older married adult has the brothers- and sisters-in-law gained with his own marriage, the parents in-law of his spouse, and a son- or daughter-in-law. Being surrounded by in-laws may be more stressful for women than for men.

The adjustment of in-laws living in the home in a three-generation home appears to depend upon early experiences with the parent. If the parents have been harsh and demanding, the resentment is stronger toward them in later life. Adjustments are also easier when both the mother- and father-in-law have approved of the marriage. Probably most outstanding in adjusting to older in-laws living with the family is the degree of success with which one has learned to play the in-law role early in the marriage. (Wallin, 1963) (Koller, 1954)

The in-law situation has changed in the past 100 years. When this nation was more rural than urban, it was customary for the oldest son, when married, to remain with the parents and work the farm. This followed the custom of primogeniture. "Today, however, if an old parent lives with his or her relatives the chances are 55 to 45 it will be with a daughter rather than a son." Particularly if the older parent is dependent financially upon others, ". . . it is safer to be dependent on a daughter than on a son . . . since the woman usually sets the tone of the home." In comparing 1900 to 1950, living arrangements for older in-laws may be in reverse. In 1900, with farm homes, rooms were added to the parents' home for the children to reside in. However, in 1950 just the opposite seems to be in vogue: rooms are added to the children's homes for the parents to reside in. (Friedman, 1963)

What are the insights of the middle-aged child concerning the parents in a home for old people? Subjects who were interviewed felt that putting their parents in a home was an honest thing to do. The placement was accepted intellectually, but not emotionally by a majority of the aged parents. Most of the children felt that they should be doing more for their parents. The adult children felt frustrated in knowing just what to do and in feeling caught between their responsibilities to their parents and their primary responsibilities to their children and spouse. (Noll, 1965)

In a survey of approximately 500 Pennsylvania families, interviews were conducted in 1949 and 1950 in regard to family plans for later years. The conclusions were that about 75 percent of the respondents had had some experience in living with relatives; however, most had made no specific plans for retirement. The data indicated that couples maintained a closer relationship with the parents of the wife than with the parents of the husband. All of the respondents, both aged and children, felt that the government should take a greater step in aiding the aging. (Smith, 1954)

The picture is certainly not all bad. Many adults relate with pride that they are more effective and have greater understanding with their son-in-law or daughter-in-law than they do with their own child! At times, the parents express gratitude to the son-in-law or daughter-in-law for having achieved changes in behavior of their child, which the mother or father were never able to bring about. Conversely at times, the children in the relationship of being an in-law have felt more affectionate and closer to their new-found in-law than to their own blood parent. This may not be unusual. Both individuals are adults, both are putting forth more than average effort to get along with each other, and all the painful problems of growing up, which the real parent has had to cope with, are now things of the past. Therefore the new father and the new son seek each other out, meet each other, and operate toward each other with maximum adult effect.

All in-law situations begin with the son's or daughter's dating. All the questions of who, when, where, how, and why are the beginnings of the in-law situation. The first reactions of the middle-aged mother and the middle-aged father are usually quite different. Father frequently asks, "What does his/her father do?" This is how father measures his fellow man and how he in turn is measured by his fellow man. Given a man's occupation, his clubs, his church, father feels he can get a fairly accurate measure of what the potential son-in-law is worth in background. The middle-aged mother, particularly if she is a middle-class mother, usually phrases her questions around two areas: economic and educational. She wants to know what the young man or woman's level of and plans for education are, specifically if it is her daughter who is involved with a fiancé. In the same light and from her own experience she very much wants to know what the economic security would be for the future of her daughter. Mother's questions regarding her sons' fiancée are not as pointed. The middle-aged mother would rather see the prospective daughter-in-law in action. To do this, she must invite the young lady to the home for a meal or a week end for suitable scrutinizing. It is at this time the mother can observe whether the girl helps with the dishes, is neither overdressed nor underdressed, and, whether she realizes it or not, reflects something of the mother's image at that age.

It should be pointed out that compatibility or criticism is no indicator of future relationships. The wedding ceremony in and of itself does nothing toward changing the personalities of the bride and the groom. It may be, however, that once the marriage is consummated, the wedding ceremony will have an effect on the in-laws' relationships to the newly wedded couple after the honeymoon. Now the situation is *fait accompli*. It is no use hoping and wishing. The deed has been done. All of the critical remarks that were once made are now wiped clean. The best possible start is intended.

Do ideal-mate images influence the selection of one's mate? In a study of 90 engaged couples, the conclusions were that ideal-mate images are probably of little importance in mate selection. What one considered as an ideal mate and what one actually selected as a mate did not seem to agree. (Udry, 1965)

College women were questioned as to their attitudes toward mate selection. Of 200 women students, approximately 60 percent said they would obey their parents if the parents objected to their choice, while 15 percent thought they would disobey their parents. (Mahajan, 1965)

The in-law situation for adults is certainly interesting and very pervasive. Apparently it runs all the gradations from love to loathing. There are no specific answers to the in-law situation for adults. Either one enjoys in-laws, tolerates them, or avoids them.

ARE CHILDLESS MARRIAGES ESPECIALLY DIFFICULT?

There are no carefully conducted studies concerning childless couples who are in later adult years. What does exist are a number of clinical impressions. Whether it is fair or not, society seems to assign a subsidiary role to those married people who do not have children.

In the case of the woman, other women seem to be the primary arbiters for the status of the childless wife. Many times she is given a classification of second-class citizen. The impression is that a childless woman, particularly in her middle years, has really "nothing to do." It is the childless woman who is considered to be eligible for committee work because she has so much free time on her hands according to, at least, those who have children. Having children seems to connote that one suffers more and is burdened more and has a harder time in life. Whether this is true or not has nothing to do with the reputation given gratis for the adult woman without children. Hers must be an easy and a casual, free life, with long hours of eating bonbons. Many overburdened mothers with children of their own will further hope to strengthen and compensate for their own plight by assuming, and it is a rank assumption, that the childless woman is automatically envious of anyone who has children. There is no research to support the above hypothesis.

In the case of the husband in middle age without children of his own, not quite the same dynamics seem to apply. To his fellow males he is judged more by his success in an occupation than by his success as a father. Also, he is assumed to have more money, since he does not have to pay for the care and education of children. His reputation with middle-aged mothers, on the other hand, appears to be quite unstructured. They take him for what he is and how he behaves, particularly toward his wife, rather than judging him as a fatherless middle-aged man. Again, whether it is fair or not is beside the point. Society seems to prefer to blame childlessness more upon the woman than the man. The woman is the receiver and the giver of an embryo while the man is simply the instigator of a new life.

Purely from the author's clinical experience, many childless women relate as a mother to their husbands. Since this is the only other human in the home environment, they may lavish their unexpressed feelings for maternal care upon the man they live with. He becomes the woman's child. She may fuss, she may fret, and she may plan for his comfort and welfare.

It is not uncommon for a childless middle-aged couple to introduce into their home favorite nieces and nephews. This may be done during trips or vacation periods by the lavish giving of presents or frequent visits.

It is also not unknown for the childless middle-aged couple to use animals as substitute love objects for children of their own. This is a case where a dog or a cat is pampered and petted beyond the understanding of others, who may feel that the situation is ridiculous, despite the fact that it may be of no harm to them and in a narrow sense none of their business.

Some psychologists dealing with human behavior frequently consider the childless middle-aged couple to have a very close, affectionate, compatible marriage, with many reinforcements for the two people involved. Not having children to rear, or think about, obviously leaves more time for each other. These childless middle-aged couples have and usually do take extensive trips together. They are strongly supportive of each other's efforts. They reinforce the affection and the ambitions of each other. This is not surprising, because they have learned to value and adjust to the strengths and weaknesses of each other. Although it is conjecture, it is quite possible that middle-aged childless couples know each other far better than those who have children and are unable to devote as much exclusive time to each other.

The general conclusion, we feel, is that although society assigns a subsidiary role to the childless middle-aged couple, quite the opposite may be true in the couple's regard for each other. Society may not know it and may not want to recognize it, but childless middle-aged couples can be very happy with their station in life and not feel they are suffering every single day because there are no children in the home.

Probably the real tragedy of childless couples comes after the death of one of the partners, when there is no one else in the home to absorb the remaining partner's interests, although, and as is frequently the case, there are always relatives with whom a life may be shared. Unfortunately the attractiveness of widowed individuals is based upon the amount of money they have and their willingness to spend it on relatives.

ARE THERE MEASURABLE DIFFERENCES BETWEEN FATHERS AND MOTHERS?

Obviously there are some differences between being a mother or a father. Primary among these is that each is of an opposite sex.

The question of which parent holds the dominant role is a highly individualistic issue. Naturally it depends upon who is married to whom and how they have managed to adjust to each other for at least 20 to 25 years of married life.

There has been comment in psychological literature, particularly in regard to our Western industrial society, as to whether we have a matriarchal or patriarchal culture. There are theories but very few studies that help to clarify the situation. Some writers assume that our society is a matriarchal-centered one. This is usually construed as being bad for everyone. There is no clear research to prove this is true or untrue. Wylie's *Generation of Vipers* may be of interest and in its day certainly caused sharp comments and rebuttals. It does not prove, however, that women have softened up society to the detriment of everyone.

One gains the impression that the middle-aged father is more affected by economic conditions and historical influences than is the mother. The mother's role is possibly more stable and not so prone to be affected by conditions outside of the home. She still feeds, clothes, and ministers to her husband and children, whether there is prosperity or recession.

One writer, Nash, after reviewing all the relevant literature came to the tentative conclusion that our modern Western industrial society may be "decidedly matricentric" and that most of the studies done concerned the mother's role more than the father's role. Nash feels that there has been a relevant neglect of studying the father's position in society as such. (Nash, 1965)

Stineman did an interesting study in trying to analyze the evaluation made by city and farm boys of their fathers. Three hundred boys in elementary Catholic rural schools in the Midwest were matched with the same number of boys of Catholic schools in two large metropolitan areas. All the subjects were living at home with both natural parents. Stineman's conclusions indicate the primary differences were not between rural and urban groups, but between age groups. However, there were indications that more young city boys thought of their fathers in a desirable light than did the young rural boys. Of the total group of farm boys, less love was expressed as being present in their fathers when compared in general to what was thought about their fathers by the city boys. Still, the final conclusion was that rural and nonrural differences, at least according to this study, seemed to be fast disappearing. (Stineman, 1961)

A short, but pertinent study done on what was called the ponderal index of fathers and the sex ratio of their children was reported in 1965. Ponderal index appears to mean the degree of stockiness of the men. Two thousand men had been measured in physical characteristics at Harvard between 1880 and 1912. During a twenty-fifth class reunion, these weight-height figures were correlated with the sex of 3350 children. The researchers wisely conclude that their present findings may be premature and certainly have not been confirmed by others, but they did find indications that stockier men tended to have more sons. (Damon, 1965)

Another study attempted to find the effect of the intermittent absence of fathers on their children's perceptions of them. The children involved were second-grade public school students. The specific question raised was whether the intermittent prolonged father absence in any way affected the child's perception of him as a love object and a figure of authority. The results seemed somewhat at variance with other reported studies. In fact, the differences between children whose fathers were always present and children whose fathers were frequently absent were very small and generally nonsignificant. (Crain, 1965)

One final note may be added concerning the health of fathers during the wife's pregnancy. In a study of 327 husbands during the wife's pregnancy, approximately 10 percent of the "expectant" fathers had physical symptoms, functional disturbances of the alimentary tract, and some ambivalence about their father role. This is not a new phenomenon, since there have been primitive races where it was the custom after the birth of a child for a father to take to his bed as if he had actually given birth to the child. Freud also found this behavior in some of his patients. This male-pregnancy syndrome is known as "couvade." (Trethowan, 1965)

There can be no doubt that menopause has some effect on the mother's ability to play her role satisfactorily during the middle years. Mother's job, even in the middle years, continues to be that of nurturant. Historical influence and societal pressures seem to touch her less.

Turning to research studies, we find very few that apply directly to the adult mother. A short study using 18 pairs of identical female twins, both married and never married, attempted to investigate their parent identification and which parent they thought was the most dominant. The investigators hypothesized that the married twin would have more mother identification and feel both parents were equally dominant and that the never-married twin would have father identification and feel that the mother dominated the family. The results of this investigation did not support the hypothesis. On the other hand, there was a tendency the investigators noted for the never-married twin daughters to have a closer identification with their mothers. For both the married and the nonmarried twin daughters, both parents were conceived as being equally dominating. (Brooks, 1965)

Hetherington investigated the effects of the sex of the dominant parent on the sex-role preferences for boys and girls, that is, the relationship of the similarity between a parent and a child and the child's imitation of the parent. She used three age groups. Some of her findings indicated that boys and girls do imitate the dominant parent. In the case where the mother appeared to be the most dominant of the two partners, there was some disruption in the ability of the boy to fulfill an adequate sex role. This is in keeping with other studies. There appeared to be a greatly increased similarity between a father and a daughter when the father was the dominant figure in the family. (Hetherington, 1965)

In a study designed to answer the question why college-trained mothers work, the investigations came to the tentative conclusions that full-time employed mothers as compared to nonemployed mothers appeared to be brighter, at least as measured on an aptitude test, and that the full-time employed mothers were less satisfied with their marriages and with life in general. When compared to the nonemployed mothers, the full-time employed mothers were more likely to have a higher level of education than their husbands. The subjects in this study were 240 women who had been students at the University of Minnesota. (Rossman, 1965)

Finally, a study using subjects from India felt that "the phenome-

non of sex role identification is a crucial one in personality theorizing." "Identification with the same sex parent results in normal adult
sex role behavior, while identification with the opposite sex parent
leads to inverted sex role behavior." This follows in the line of thinking of the psychoanalysts. The thesis has some support from studies in
Western culture. (Dixit, 1964)

In the final analysis, the older father's life may be reaching its
peak as far as earning power and status on the job are concerned. On
the other hand, the older mother is having to convert sooner into
"retirement," as her children leave the family, her husband does not
seem to need her as much as his job, and she herself is going through
whatever trials and tribulations there are for her in menopause.

VILL THE OLDEST CHILD BE DIFFERENT THAN THE YOUNGEST CHILD IN THE FAMILY?

Periodically psychologists get interested in an Alfred Adler idea that
a person's personality may be influenced by their order of birth in the
family. This is sometimes called ordinal psychology. Currently there is
a renewed interest in this aspect of human behavior and we shall only
touch upon a few representative studies in this field. (Chopra, 1966)

One study, which attempted to explore the effect of age changes
and ordinal positions of sex-role identification, utilized 250 college
students as subjects. All the college students came from two-child
families. The conclusions were roughly that ordinal position is important at age 6, but the sex of the sibling is more important at ages 10
and 20. (Sutton-Smith, 1965)

Another study found that the oldest child was probably more
vulnerable to mental illness, particularly when there were three or
more brothers and sisters. It was felt that this might be because of the
oldest child's dependency and efforts to maintain some kind of family
tradition rather than to act more in an individual capacity or to change
the family's value systems. (Sharadamba, 1965)

What are the importance of the parents as models, the ordinal
position of the children, and the sex of the child? Some of the findings
indicated that identification with a more masculine father for the boys
or with a more masculine mother for the girls were associated with
good adolescent adjustment. In regard to ordinal position, it was
tentatively found that only children (boys) and first-child boys who
had sisters seemed to be more highly identified with their mothers.
(Heilbrun, 1965b)

Most of the evidence of these studies on ordinal positions indicate
some kind of difference between at least the oldest and the youngest,
but the investigators do not attribute any causes for this difference. The

studies will continue and the results are often confusing in that each investigator may be asking different questions and obviously getting different answers than the other investigators. Consequently, much of the research data appear to be contradictory at this point. The range of research interests is international. The relationships explored between birth order and other factors are enormously wide and prolific. As an illustration, the following items will give some indication of the breadth of interest: Australia (Wilson, 1966), Canada (de Lint, 1967), Taiwan, China (Tsuang, 1966), Great Britain (Berg, 1967a) (Granville-Grossman, 1966b), India (Sinha, 1967) (Sundararaj, 1966); and in subject interests, such as *motivation and achievement* (Bartlett, 1966) (Farley, 1967) (Moran, 1967) (Oberlander, 1967) (Rosenfeld, 1966) (Singer, 1967), *children's behavior* (Stewart, 1967) (Tuckman, 1967) (Vernon, 1967), *anxiety and psychopathological behavior* (Allen, 1967) (Eisenman, 1966a, b) (Eisenman, 1967a, b) (Solomon, 1967), *personality dynamics* (Dohrenwend, 1967b) (Hamilton, 1967) (Sampson, 1967), *suicide* (Lester, 1966), *aesthetic judgments* (Eisenman, 1967c), *honesty* (Wuebben, 1967), *scientific attainment* (Datta, 1967), *college attendance* (Bayer, 1966), *choice of college major* (Altus, 1967), *unwed mothers* (Wohlford, 1967), and finally, *lesbians and nonlesbians* (Gundlach, 1967). It may be of interest to note that the above listing is only for 2 years: 1966 and 1967.

ARE CHILDREN DIFFERENT NOW
THAN THEY WERE 25 YEARS AGO?

There is probably not a single home in the United States of America where the parents have not said at least once, "Well, it certainly was different when I was a kid."

One of the difficulties in studying the contrast has been to find a common base of measurement for a cross-sectional study or to locate enough subjects who were studied years ago and who are still available for restudy at a later date.

One author contends that a child of 9 today is probably equivalent physically to those of 10 years of age 30 years ago. The same author hazards a guess that we might find higher average intelligence quotients in the contemporary 10-year-old as compared to a 10-year-old 30 years ago. (Birren, 1964b)

Mussen reported a study conducted on boys who were rated on the degree of masculinity. When these same boys were in their 30s, they were restudied. The findings indicated that those who had been low in masculinity as adolescents were found to be still low. The more masculine boys became the more masculine adults. (Birren, 1964b)

In 1942 a questionnaire was given to 337 boys and 363 girls in grades 6, 9, and 12. In 1963 the same questionnaire was administered to approximately 1000 boys and 1000 girls in grades 6 through 12 of the same school. A reliably greater proportion of adolescents in 1963 made choices concerning the other sex than did those in 1942. If nothing else has changed, at least girls and boys seem more interested in each other than they used to be, according to this study. (Kuhlen, 1965)

Certainly the child of today lives in a different time than the child of 40 or 50 or 60 years ago. How much difference this makes no one knows precisely. The question still goes unanswered.

Research Suggestions

1. What would longitudinal data reveal about the continuity of change in behavioral patterns of parents to their children? of children to their parents?
2. Do discrete personality differences exist between fathers whose children call them Father and fathers whose children call them Dad or Pa, and so on? What about mothers?
3. What measurable changes occur when a man becomes a father (or a woman a mother), especially for the first time?
4. As people get older, do they get to be more and more like they remember their parents to be?
5. Are parents more likely to help sons or to help daughters financially?
6. What is the effect of social class on in-law relations?
7. Is the childless woman envious of those who have children?
8. What is the effect of childlessness on happiness in a marriage?
9. How do parents differ in their treatment of the first and second child? the last?

CHAPTER 6

Vocations
and
Avocations

PART A

Vocations

IS WORKING A WAY OF LIFE?

In 1917 Dr. William Lowe Bryan, then the president of Indiana University, gave the commencement address. His wisdom is reflected in the text of his address.

> It is your good fortune to have a wide choice of occupations among which to choose. It is no light matter to make the choice. It is to elect your physical and social environment. It is to choose where you will work—in a scholars' cloister, on a farm, or in the cliffs of a city street. It is to choose what you will attend to, what you will try for, whom you

will follow. In a word, it is to elect for life, for better or worse, some one part of the whole social heritage. These influences will not touch you lightly. They will compass you with subtle compulsions. They will fashion your clothes, and your looks, and your carriage, the cunning of your hands, the texture of your speech, and the temper of your will. And if you are wholly willing and wholly fit, they can work you this miracle: They can carry you swiftly in the course of your single life to levels of wisdom and skill in one sort, which it has cost the whole history of your guild to win. [Rees, 1920]

Many adult workers know that Dr. Bryan's commencement comments are true. (Hollender, 1967) By now the adult individual realizes, "These influences will not touch you lightly. They will surround you with subtle compulsions." Most middle-aged male workers have been employed probably for 20 years in one occupation. They realize the clothes they wear, the way they walk, the cunning of their hands, the kind of speech patterns they use, and many of their friends are the direct result of the occupation they are in. In other words, it is more than a salary that a man is now making, it has become his way of life. All too frequently the high salary that the male has worked so hard to attain is used in many ways to escape from the boredom, the frustrations, the conflicts, and the high degree of competition he finds in his everyday job. He spends all of his high salary in escape mechanisms. He goes fishing, hunting, retreats to a summer home, travels, drinks heavily, in summer moves his family miles away from his place of work so that he can get as far as possible from the frustrations of his present employment during short week ends.

Oscar Wilde is reputed to have said: "It is an occupation that illustrates the two tragedies of life: not getting what you want and getting it." (Ogilvie, 1962)

Birren adroitly states in his excellent book *The Psychology of Aging,* "Young men tend to change jobs for the better, older men for the worse." (Birren, 1964a)

McFarland, a Harvard professor, once commented at a meeting in 1955, "Earlier this morning it was suggested that we ought to fit men for jobs—perhaps the jobs ought to be fitted for men." (Anderson, 1956)

Birren makes two other very pertinent remarks in regard to occupations. He feels that in some ways the modern worker in our society is more of a controller of production than an actual producer. Birren goes on to point out, "It has been said that a good set of ideas used to last a man a lifetime; now they last merely a generation or perhaps only a decade." (Birren, 1964a)

To the present writer, the adult years in regard to men and their vocations appear to be "a time of truth." Dreams and aspirations may

have carried the man well through his 20s, 30s, and into his 40s. H
was going to be the president of the firm, he would make a millio
before he was 40, the entire Western United States would be his a
General Sales Manager, and so on. When a man gets to be 50 or so h
settles his brains, if he is wise, to the realities of life. *He must learn t*
cooperate with the inevitable. Whatever it was he had in his younge
days that gave him the confidence to plan or to dream may not hav
been adequate for the advancement he sought in his occupation. Man
men when faced with this time of truth may seek solace in at least on
of two ways: compensation or rationalization. Men compensate fo
their lack of status in an occupation by participating in a devote
manner in clubs and organizations, which eventually give them roles o
leadership. Barring this, they may turn to recreation and play t
alleviate the disappointments they may have found in their jobs. Me
will also find reasons, genuine or artificial, to rationalize away the
failure to achieve the occupational success they once assumed wa
theirs in early working years. No one has, to date, made an adequat
survey as to the prevalence of how men adjust to their feelings o
failure in middle age about their jobs. From the writer's own coun
seling experiences and obviously from a very limited sampling, h
would hazard the guess that at least 50 percent of middle-aged men ar
disappointed by not having reached the goals they once set for them
selves in the world of work. They feel "locked in" their jobs, with n
way to go except toward retirement.

Hurlock suggests five factors that influence the adjustment o
adults toward their jobs, particularly middle-aged workers.

1. *Increasing life span*—We live longer. At least this is a Unite
States phenomenon. In 1900 the life expectancy was approximately 4
years of age and only 10 percent of the male population exceeded wha
we now call middle age. A man worked for a living until he collapse
or deteriorated and died. In contrast, approximately 80 percent of th
male population today live to be around 60 years old. Instead o
hanging on to the job, hard and menial as it may have been, the prob
lems are now quite unique. Now the problems are to hold on to th
job, to keep younger men from taking it away, and to hold out only s
long until one can retire with a big fat pension.

2. *Social attitudes toward middle-aged workers*—Society consider
the middle-aged worker, particularly one above the age of 50, to hav
a slower pace, to be much less adaptable to changing business custom
and industrial techniques, to have lost initiative to try new things o
to accept them, to be in such physical shape as to be absent more ofte
because of sickness, and to be somewhat fearful lest his job cease an
he become unable to be rehired because the business world is ver
chary of hiring new employees beyond the age of 45 years.

There are at least six factors that would mandate against society's critical attitudes toward the middle-aged worker:

   a. Statistics indicate that 95 percent of middle-aged workers are not disabled.
   b. Middle-aged workers are frequently superior, particularly when the experience they have gained is considered.
   c. Middle-aged workers have a much better attendance record than younger workers and are rarely late to work.
   d. The middle-aged worker is a conscientious worker. He has pride in what he does, having learned it in the days before craftsmanship (which meant "pride in what you do") was replaced by "quality control," or how much sloppy work can you get away with before the other fellow catches you.
   e. The middle-aged worker is less impatient. He has been around for quite awhile now. He sees that it takes time to make changes, to progress, to fulfill plans.
   f. Hurlock also maintains that the middle-aged worker's attitude is much more stable. He has lived through the gossip and the changes in personnel procedures and he feels less threatened by rumors because he has lived through at least 10 to 20 years of all of these things. He may at times frustrate his younger worker by not seeming to care.

3. *Hiring policy*—Hurlock readily admits that management takes a dim view, if not a totally negative view, toward hiring middle-aged workers. The reasons for this are not only the cost of retirement pensions soon to be furnished, but in the social attitudes discussed in point 2 above. Hurlock, however, feels that in unions particularly the policy of seniority helps the middle-aged worker. However, management still considers that hiring a middle-aged worker gives them 10 to 20 years less of usefulness toward the company. Management persists in thinking that the middle-aged worker is less adjustable and more "set in his ways." And it may be true, certainly for men, probably not for women, that the middle-aged worker has advanced his salary to a level that makes it much more economical to hire a younger worker.

4. *Changes in work conditions*—Another factor for older adult workers is a new emphasis on team work rather than on individual work. The production line is an example of this. Most research, as we shall see in Chapter 8, does indicate that sensory and motor skills do decrease. There may be resistance in learning new techniques, especially when advanced by other men and not properly explained, which seem to the middle-aged worker to be no better than the tried and true way he knows will work. Many industries must, to stay alive, stress changing quickly to new models, new procedures and new manufac-

turing techniques. In the rush to have planned obsolescence and to se
more products always exceeding the previous year's quota, it is easy t
believe that the stress would be on speed instead of quality. And finally
Hurlock believes that as work conditions change, the middle-age
worker grows intolerant toward his younger workers, who seem bras
and not properly respectful of their elders.

5. *Compulsory retirement*—This, too, creates an enormous adjus
ment for a middle-aged worker as he progresses to his late 50s an
early 60s. (Hurlock, 1959)

As stated in the beginning of Chapter 4, probably two of th
greatest risks that one may take in the course of living are marriag
and the character of the primary job held through most of the adu
years. Working for a living is more than a paycheck. Work is a powerfu
force in shaping many of the facets of the individual's personality an
behavior.

WHAT ARE THE PROBLEMS OF AN
ADULT IN THE WORLD OF WORK?

Probably the most vital problem of the older adult in the world of wor
is to keep on working. In England over 50 percent of the unemploye
were over the age of 40. (Benaim, 1967) Loss of a job at age 50 mean
trying to live without an income, loss of status and pride, and the in
evitable problem of trying to get another job. All of these factors ca
be a devastating experience to a middle-aged man. Much has bee
written about the reluctance of employers to hire the "older workers.
To this end, the federal government has now enacted the Age Discrim
ination in Employment Act of 1967, which went into effect on June 1.
1968. The legislation hopes to correct the inequalities of the situatior
The basic provisions of the bill are as follows: Help-wanted ads are no
permitted to state age specifications; employment agencies may no
classify applicants on the basis of age or refrain from referring worker
to prospective employers because of age; labor unions may not exclud
from membership workers in the 40-to-65 age bracket; employer
involved in interstate commerce may not refuse to hire qualifie
workers aged 40 to 65; and most important, employers may not fir
workers aged 40 to 65 solely on the basis of age and are prohibited fro
discriminating against "older" workers in salary, seniority, or prom
tions. (Porter, 1968) The effects of this bill on alleviating discriminator
practices against older workers are yet to be determined.

Other evidence indicates that young adults may "resent the powe
that old people have" in business. (Bromley, 1966)

Welford, an English researcher, distinguishes two methods c
measuring the adult's ability to perform on the job and elsewhere. On

method is to measure the *optimum* pace (work that is congenial and efficient) and the other is to measure the *maximum* (or stress) pace, which is the very upper limit of performance one is capable of prior to collapsing at the task. Impairment in aging-adult performance is best measured by the maximum pace. "As age advances, the difference between optimum and maximum levels of performance decreases." Welford considers biological/psychological changes in adults' capacities to have five factors: (1) the adult may fail completely; (2) efficiency will be drastically reduced but failure may not follow; (3) by being more efficient, good adjustment may take place despite a reduction in capacity; (4) performance may not suffer, because the job is still within the older adult's optimum capacities; and (5) by overcompensating the aging adult, he may actually improve performance. (Bromley, 1966) (Welford, 1958, 1964, 1965)

Finally even the term *older worker* is in some dispute. The United States Department of Labor refers to *all* workers aged 45 to 64 as "older workers," whereas some writers strongly urge that "middle-aged worker" be introduced for those adults aged 45 to 64. (Sprague, 1968)

MENTAL ABILITY   Although the rise and fall of mental ability will be dealt with more fully in Chapter 8, there are some facts pertinent to occupations that should be dealt with here. The entire field of mental measurement continues to be a puzzling one, despite the valiant efforts of psychologists and others to measure this aspect of man's personality. If it is difficult to adequately measure children's basic brain power, it is even more difficult to measure intelligence in adults. One author, after reviewing hundreds of studies, decided: "We have taken intelligence-test studies of a cross-sectional nature as far as we can and have been left asking why people do less well on them with age." (Farnsworth, 1965)

What happens when adults, particularly older adults, take an intelligence test? A number of problems immediately emerge. For one thing, most intelligence tests were designed originally for children and adapted later for adults. The types of activities seem silly and of no utility to the adult. Remembering digit symbols, putting blocks and cartoons together, and similar items strike the adult as childish. He feels it has so very little to do with the way he has to use his brain to solve most of his adult problems: raising children, holding and advancing in a job, getting along with a spouse, trying to pay off a mortgage, and so on.

McFarland asks:

When in the aging processes is physiological and psychological deterioration no longer compensated for by past experience? Chronological age alone is rarely a reliable index of an individual's physical or mental development. In industry, it would be more appropriate to say that worker is as old as his vision, his motor skill or his mental adaptabilit as they relate to the performance of his duties. [Anderson, 1956]

One study, indicative of many, performed by a British psychol ogist used a test that would allow the assessment of differential change in auditory and visual short-term retention to three groups: young middle-aged, and elderly adult. The results indicated that *all* subject found it more difficult to handle visual information as opposed t orally presented information. However, the decline in visual retentio was found to increase with age, being most noticeable after the age o 60 years. (Lawson, 1965)

The initial level of ability was found to be extremely crucial i learning. Bright people continued to stay bright throughout the spa of life. Those with the high IQs were retested and "showed progressiv gains in comprehension, vocabulary, and arithmetic." Phrasing it a other way, a bright 70-year-old man was still better than the averag 20-year-old. (Levine, 1963)

Some of the studies become involved in determining the differenc between measured intelligence according to the traditional type o mental ability test and wisdom. In addition to measured menta ability, such factors as knowledge (information), experience (wisdon or knowing what to do with knowledge), solutions (problem-solving o everyday events), and having power (the authority to do right an wrong acts in regard to self and others) may come into importance fo the adult. Thus verbal, practical, affective, cognitive, and social skill may better describe the adult's mental ability than converted score on an IQ test. (Bromley, 1966)

Latimer cited various refutations by psychologists that aging an mental decline are synonymous. Some decline is highly related to en vironmental factors. Working at a dull repetitive job may reduce mind of formerly fairly high mental ability to a dull repetitive mind Many psychologists consider intelligence tests to be more of a school learning test than a test of ability to solve problems in life. Latime felt there was great confusion among psychologists and lay people i confounding measured intelligence with the ability to learn. Whe certain phases of learning are in constant use, they increase with age Many criticisms were lodged against both the procedures and th samples employed in measuring intelligence. (Latimer, 1963)

Adult subjects who had been given a Binet Test of intelligence i childhood were tested with a Wechsler Adult Intelligence Scale 25 year later. The scores of the two tests correlated at .85. The average intelli gence-quotient increase from adolescent to adulthood was eleve points. There was some indication that the intelligence quotient fo men gained more than those for women. This may indicate that men in their occupations may have more practice than do women with the kinds of items that occur on intelligence tests. The least amount of intelligence-quotient increase was among women who originally had very high intelligence quotients. The items on the test that seemed to increase the most for all subjects were related to abstract reasoning and vocabulary. The items that seemed to decrease the most pertained to rote memory and practical reasoning as measured by the test. Conclusions were that patterns of individual differences showed some stability: high IQs stayed high and low IQs stayed low. (Bradway, 1962) Two other studies indicated similar results. The maintenance of intellectual ability had a small decline for high IQs, more decline for middle IQs, and a very rapid decline for low IQs. (Tibbitts, 1962) Birren found that the Digit Span section in the Wechsler Test, an item designed to measure the ability to remember numbers forward and backward, "does not show appreciable change with age." Birren felt, "In language functions older adults perform better, whereas measures involving psychomotor speed and perceptions frequently favor young adults." (Williams, 1963a) A study reported in 1964, concerning the stability of average intelligence, used 25 subjects whose measured IQs were 100 at the age of 6. The subjects were retested at the average age of 33. The spread of IQs of the 25 subjects retested approximately 25 years later was from 90 to 132, with the average IQ being 107. Keeping in mind that all of the subjects had an IQ of 100 at the age of 6, the diversity of scores suggests caution in planning the futures of average children. (Charles, 1964) Reitan found that impairment on nonbrain-damaged adults appeared after the age of 45. Although Reitan found that aging does affect test performance, there was as much dispersion in scores for 60-year-olds as there was for 30-year-olds. This is in keeping with other studies. (Tibbitts, 1962)

What happens when a longitudinal study is done on the intellectual changes in aging twins? A study reported in 1962, done over a 10-year-period (1947–1957), tested 268 senescent twins. All the twins, over age 60 at the time of the first testing, were literate, white, English-speaking, and appeared to be in satisfactory health. Due to difficulties, only 48 of the twins completed all the tests. The reported results of the experiment were that "The performance of the twins (age 60–90) equalled or exceeded the norms established for the general population at a younger age (50–54 and 55–59), despite similar educational histories." They were retested again after a one-year interval. There was a general increase in scores, which marked a stability of the functions tested as well as some influence in being test-wise. "It seems that there is a positive relationship between test score and survival." This is not to say that bright people always live longer, but possibly the opposite, that very dull people have shorter lives. (Jarvik, 1962)

Hirt reporting in 1964 used the United States Government's widely given test, the GATB, which is administered through the Department of Labor in State Employment Offices. The General Aptitude Test Battery was given to 400 subjects divided into four age groups. Those parts of the test that had to do with general mental ability, verbal ability, numerical ability, and spatial ability were affected by age. In this study, the higher the age, the lower the score. (Hirt, 1964) Two earlier studies were conducted, using the same government test (GATB). One in New York State sampled the performance of approximately 700 males and 700 females in the period 1954–1957. A second study (1955–1960), consisting of approximately 1000 males and 1000 females from California, Iowa, Michigan, and Pennsylvania, indicated that there was no difference between the New York subjects' scores and those from the other four states. All the aptitudes measured, except verbal aptitudes, showed a decline in the average score with age. There was a large variation for the aptitudes measured with regard to the age of onset of the decline of that particular aptitude. For example, intelligence and numerical aptitude showed no decline until about the age of 42. As is usual, individual variations were quite wide. The authors concluded that predictions about the nature of change in aptitude scores with age for a particular individual would be ridiculous. Many older individuals scored higher than many younger ones. It would be most inappropriate to make a generalization. About all one can do is study a single individual. The average, or the norm, may give a totally false picture. (Droege, 1963, 1967)

Turning our attention now to a third aspect, having covered intelligence and aptitude, we may now take a look at the ability to learn. Lorge states, "The psychology of adult learning too often is based on the way young adults in college behave at the request of professors." Lorge continues with a very interesting comment. "I am on a committee on aging, studying methods for teaching older adults in industry: I have canvassed many industries in the New York area to discover that there is no interest in this problem. Why? Because they don't have a problem in teaching older people." (Anderson, 1956) An investigation using 14½-to-15-year-old school dropouts and comparing their performance to 40-to-50-year-old trainees for the general Post Office letter sorters' jobs indicated that the older group were significantly poor in all types of rote learning. (Moore, 1965b)

> Changes with age in primary ability to learn are small under most circumstances . . . at the present time there is little evidence to suggest that there is an intrinsic age difference in learning capacity over the employed years; i.e. up to the age 60 . . . years of schooling is a more

important variable than is age in relation to learning over the work life. [Birren, 1964a]

The difference in learning to perform successfully on the job as contrasted to the ability to take a test indicates these two fatcors may have very little bearing on each other.

RETRAINING   Some studies seem to contradict each other. (Jamieson, 1966) One study reports on retraining done with a petroleum company. "The older instrument workers were, if anything, somewhat better than the young (under 40) in the training courses." On the other hand, women being retrained from long-distance phone operators to new IBM techniques did not do as well as younger women. (Birren, 1964a) Foremen's ratings of retrainees stated the older men were much slower and lower in their ability to learn new jobs. (Elliot, 1966) Belbin and Entwhistle found that older men can be successfully retrained, although no direct comparisons were made with younger men. (Farnsworth, 1965)

PRODUCTION   Although related to mental ability and retraining, production has a quality of immediacy not found in other categories. A man at work must produce or he is no longer a man at work. Productivity and the energy required to produce have undergone tremendous changes as the world and its workers have gotten older. In 1850 human beings supplied about 13 percent, animals about 52 percent, and inanimate sources about 35 percent of the energy used toward producing in the world. In 1950 humans and animals supplied less than 1 percent of the energy needed for production. Thus 99 percent of the energy used to produce goods in the world was derived from inanimate sources. Studies of production in other parts of the world indicate similar results. (Buhler, 1961)

Surveys indicate productivity remains rather stable up through the age of 55, with some falling off after that. The amount of productivity varies widely with the type of job being done. For example, women office workers show very little change as they grow older in productivity. "Much of the evidence from industrial studies indicates that little change in worker performance is found up to age 60 or 65." Such studies are not conclusive because older workers have a survivor bias. It is assumed here that the good may not die young, but those who are good mentally and physically probably last longer in life. Therefore, people who are in good health and have good brains do not suffer in their production level. (Birren, 1964a)

Thirty elderly men and 30 younger men were asked to pace their own work. Both groups had been equated as far as possible in intellectual capacities. Older subjects did best when they could pace themselves and indicated significantly faster learning than when the younger subjects were asked to pace themselves. (Canestrari, 1963) One of the "cleanest" studies reported on productivity used 123 industrial workers from four Chicago factories. All the subjects were white with a minimum of 1-year incentive production prior to the test. The workers were arranged in matched pairs, with one coming from the age group of 40–45 and the other from the age group 60–65. Matching took into consideration place of work, kind of work, sex, occupation, marital status, education. Conclusions were from all four plants: (1) No significant differences were found in the average productivity scores between the two age groups. (2) There were no significant differences between how widely spread each group was in ability to produce. (3) There were no significant differences in the variance of monthly scores of production of the matched individuals. In short, there were no differences in productivity between men aged 40–45 and men aged 60–65. (Breen, 1960) A productivity study, in relation to age and sales effectiveness asked three questions: Is there any relationship between sales effectiveness and chronological age? Is there any particular age period related to peak effectiveness in saleswork? At what age should most salesmen expect to reach their peak? The major conclusions were that sales effectiveness on the average is related to age, with a peak occurring around the age of 40. Salesmen over the age of 45 may be less effective as a group in saleswork than their younger co-workers. However, an individual salesman over 45 may be far better than any individual under that age. (Kirchner, 1960)

We return now to the question: Can the older worker keep on producing the way he did in his early 30s? He may or he may not. As usual, it depends on a number of variables. Who is the individual worker? What kind of work does he do? How is productivity measured?

SELF-APPRAISAL   The higher the occupational and/or educational level the more the employee is inclined to perceive his productivity as high just prior to retirement. There appears to be no significant difference between male and female adult workers in self-perception. The older the employee the more he perceives himself as productive, particularly starting with the age of 60 and older. (Saleh, 1966) Older workers in one plant seemed to be more satisfied not only with their jobs but with life in general than did a comparable group of younger workers. (Meltzer, 1965a) A group of 140 workers in an industrial setting were asked to rank-order the best years of life for themselves and how they thought others would rank the best years. The years most preferred were in the span 20–35 for self and up to 20 for others. Most respondents felt the unfavorable years began at 45. From this study we may assume that factory workers have a youth-oriented society. (Meltzer, 1962) Paper-company employees (age range 19–77) were asked questions about job satisfaction. The older worker was credited with having increased feelings of having a good share of happiness, more significant work to do and less spare time, more concern in steady work, and a lessened interest in advancement. (Meltzer, 1963) Terman's long-range investigation of the gifted at middle age indicated that approximately half of the men expressed deep satisfaction and interest in their work while only a small minority (6 percent) reported themselves as being seriously discontented with their work. Gifted women were even more content in their vocational choices than men—over 55 percent found deep satisfaction in their vocations. Three percent reported serious discontent. There was also some evidence in Terman's study that the lower the salary the workers had the less satisfied they were with their jobs. (Terman, 1959)

The older adult employee may or may not have an honest opinion of his work but it seems to be as honest as his younger co-worker. There still appears to be a youth-oriented concept that as you get older you get worse. The older worker may feel quite to the contrary. He knows what he can do and he may even enjoy doing it. (Bell, 1967)

SALARY INCREMENT   The peak income comes between the ages of 40 and 50 for most people. The productivity peak is reached about the age of 30. It takes approximately 10 years for the salary and other remunerations to catch up with productivity. Total family income (children's and a working mother's salary) is at the peak in the parents mid-50s. (Birren, 1964a) Some sources indicate that the peak income comes shortly before retirement, as many occupations continue to increase their employees' salaries primarily because of longevity on the job. (Wallin, 1963)

For 1956 the estimated lifetime income for different levels of education were as follows:

Education	Total Lifetime Income
None	$ 58,000
1–4 years	72,000
5–7 years	93,000
8 years	116,000
High school—1–3 years	135,000
High school— 4 years	165,000
College —1–3 years	190,000
College — 4 years	268,000

The above figures are truly estimations. They in no sense reflect what a single human is going to make. Since the table was constructed in 1956, salary ranges, basic wage rates, and all the multitude of things that influence an expanding economy date the above figures. They are submitted as an example of the relationship between education and total lifetime income. Probably one of the most misunderstood clichés is, "Get a good education and you will make a lot of money." This is not necessarily so. Education and mental ability go together. Putting it another way, if you are not very bright you cannot go very far in school. Therefore, it is not the education as such that gives a higher salary, but the fact that you have to have brains to go up the educational ladder. Thus brainy people have a better chance of making a higher salary than not-so-brainy people.

The frightening thing about the previous table to the older adult worker is, "Where in the name of all the saints above did that money go?"

ACCIDENTS   Ross McFarland concludes:

> For example, the fact that the older person is a safer worker was brought out earlier. I have about 15 charts here all based on independent studies which show clearly that the accident rate is lower among older industrial workers than among younger ones. Even when time of exposure and other factors are equated. Moving picture studies of men working in industry show not only that the older worker's tempo is different, but that he is safer. For instance, the older person will never let his hands get out of sight while operating complicated machinery. [Anderson, 1956]

For those who do sustain injuries, some attempts are made to retrain and place the injured worker in less strenuous jobs. (Luchterhand, 1966)

ABSENTEEISM   Two occupational psychologists analyzed the personnel records of over 300 men for a period of 10 years in regard to their absence history. The aim was to check age differences that might contribute to absenteeism. There was an aging effect found for "certified sickness." The emphasis is upon certified sickness, not on willful absenteeism or malingering. The data indicated that, "High absence frequency, however, was not age-related." (Mare, 1961) Kleemeier felt that "middle-aged men are more likely to work full-time the year around than either young or older men." He found middle-aged workers were less likely to experience unemployment than the younger or older workers. The data come from a study of the United States labor force from 1890 through 1955. (Buhler, 1961)

At this point a pertinent question is how to define absenteeism. If it involves only absence from work for certifiable physical reasons, it may be true that the older worker is absent more frequently. (Cooper,

1965) However, if absenteeism includes purposeful absence from work for no certifiable or logical reasons, the older worker's record is an enviable one. Playing "hookey" from school and from work appears to be a younger man's syndrome.

MENTAL HEALTH

> The industrial elderly worker is jealous of his dignity. When a man works for years making objects that disappear as soon as made, he has nothing tangible left to indicate his expenditure of energy. His only remaining gauge of success or failure is the attitude shown toward him by his superiors and his fellow workmen. The symbols about him do not add up into something personally important. Though he would deny this vehemently, his job and his home have become worn and threadbare. [Wolff, 1959] [1]

STATUS   One author contends that middle-aged and middle-class men may feel the stress of success in business more strongly than other social classes. Part of the stress may be based on a fear of being replaced on the job. Further stressors may be that middle-class people need more reinforcement for their ego strength. There is also the threat of younger men coming up in a rapid manner. Lower-class workers with minimal salaries may develop a "so what" feeling. If you have little in life, you can lose little. Wealthy upper-class middle-aged men feel no threat for a number of reasons. It is assumed that in the course of their last 20–30 years of work, they have risen to a position where they are able to use the talents of others and to control the working lives of many other people. "By his forties the white-collar worker may even measure his progress in his career by how many men are under his control." (Benaim, 1967) The primary protection comes, of course, from enough accumulated wealth, which gives them some assurance of being able to tide over everything but a very prolonged setback. (Hurlock, 1959) "Failure to reach early goals would be a psychological problem for the aspiring middle-class man about to retire, but not for the lower-class man who would probably blame his employers or others for what he might consider a 'bad deal.' " (Birren, 1964a) Many social psychologists and sociologists consider the middle-class individual to have achieved that status by having come up from a lower-class level. No contention is made that all middle-class people have been at one time in a lower social class. Most of the studies of vertical social-class mobility will frequently show contradictory results. The primary problem is one of defining terms. One set of investigators may use the term

---

[1] K. Wolff. *The Biological, Sociological, and Psychological Aspects of Aging,* 1959, Charles C Thomas, Publisher, Springfield, Ill.

middle-class far differently than a second set of investigators. It is our own tentative conclusion that most middle-aged men, in what may be loosely defined as middle class, are going to stay there. Whether they have come from a lower class to middle or from an upper class down to middle, the reinforcements of a middle-class type of existence seem to give some stability.

CREATIVITY   One general conclusion is pertinent. For almost all of the professional fields, running the gamut from art and music to the physical sciences of physics and chemistry, the greatest period of productivity and creativity, usually measured by publications and discoveries, lies between the years of 25 to 40. (Birren, 1964a) (Lehman, 1953, 1965) Oberg, studying the performances of engineers in the oil industry, suggested that there was a high creativity period prior to age 40 and that then the major emphasis was upon production and management to the age of 60. (Farnsworth, 1965)

It is interesting to make conjectures about why famous people do not seem to produce much after the beginning of the middle years. Perhaps this may be relative to something that happens in the field of psychology. Many outstanding psychologists who have made extremely worthwhile contributions to the field in their earlier days very often wind up being administrators of other psychologists. Thus a man is removed from the thing he does best to supervising other young men who need his guidance and administrative skills. The same thing happens to good teachers. They become deans in colleges and universities, principals of buildings, or superintendents of schools. This removes them from that which they do best: teach. It is our own prejudicial set that being good at one type of work within an organization does not of itself indicate skill in an administrative position within that organization.

Actually there is no age limit for man's creativity. The human being is creative almost all of his life. Depending on the definition used for creative behavior, many authorities believe that childhood is the most creative period in life and that the formalized educational systems suppress this creativity in children never to have it emerge again. Perhaps we should say that *recognized* creativity reaches its peak at approximately 35 years of age or that acknowledged contributions to society are highest in early adulthood. Quantity and quality are also intermixed. Certainly some kinds of productivity, whether creative contributions or achievements, do continue until the very end of a long life, as the following list emphasizes.

1. Michelangelo completed the dome of St. Peter's at age 70.
2. Sophocles wrote *Oedipus Tyrannus* at age 80.
3. Goethe, past 80, completed *Faust*.

4. Gladstone became prime minister at age 84 for the fourth time.
5. Handel, Haydn, and Verdi created immortal melodies after the age of 70.
6. Hobbes wrote productively until age 91.
7. Franklin served as an influential member of the Constitutional Congress at age 81.
8. Jefferson was inventive and active until death at age 83.
9. Tennyson continued to write poetry until after age 80.
10. Churchill became prime minister at age 77.

Creative powers and artistic greatness are not bound to any age. It seems to be mainly an affair of sheer will power, working strength, endurance and not least of all, enthusiasm. (Wolff, 1959) (Stewart, 1966) (Bromley, 1966)

EARLY RETIREMENT   The issue of retirement as a reality is covered in Chapter 9: the adult is retired. The treatment in this chapter emphasizes preretirement. "The whole idea of planning for retirement may well be a middle-class concept." (Kleemeier, 1961) Many older workers may want to retire early. They may talk about it, savor the deliciousness of not having to work anymore, and even go so far as to make tentative plans. There is one enormous obstacle: "The employee who retires more than a year or two before the normal retirement receives a substantially reduced pension." If one retires at age 60, he reduces his pension to 63 percent of what he might have gotten at age 65. If he retires at age 55, he further reduces his pension to 43 percent of what he might have gotten at age 65. (Kleemeier, 1961) There is an interesting side note to early retirement. "It is worth noting that most federal civil servants do not wait until the compulsory retirement age." No reason is given for this statement. (Birren, 1964a)

This author, as well as many others, frequently has heard the statement the only thing that holds a man together is his job. The assumption is that the moment he retires, he will disintegrate and die. In regard to this phenomenon one author states, "Health as it has been shown is not so much a result as a cause of retirement. There is also some evidence of a tendency for health not to deteriorate but actually there may be some tendency for health to improve upon retirement." (Reichard, 1962) As a participant in an American Psychological Association Symposium of 1955, Dr. Birren had some very worthwhile things to say about the myth that if you retire early you will die.

We thought that longitudinally this could be checked. As a matter of fact, that is how the Cornell study of retirement began. They indicate that the myth is really a myth and that the relationship of the variable is just the reverse if anything. It is poor health that leads to (early) retirement which in turn is followed by what seems to be a premature death. [Anderson, 1956]

At the same conference, McFarland pointed out that in World War II many older people were brought back into work. They did succeed in great numbers and were very successful and certainly useful to the total war effort. (Anderson, 1956) In England the preparation for retirement is a widely recognized necessity. (Bromley, 1966) The same is true in the United States. (Heron, 1962a)

RETIREMENT—FIXED VERSUS FLEXIBLE   There are two schools of thought on retirement. (Kreps, 1968) The most prevalent one is to establish a fixed age, usually 65, and force all employees to retire at this time. The second one is to offer a flexible retirement age in which the worker himself decides whether to retire before or after age 65, with the employer furnishing his pension or the federal government supplanting it with Social Security. Most flexible-age retirements are based on one of two reasons. In some cases, there is a free choice because the pension is large enough, the work seems obnoxious enough, and security, at least at that time, seems to be established for the future. In other cases, flexible-age retirements may be mandated because of the individual's inability to work, primarily due to physical rather than mental reasons.

Compulsory retirement can and does deflate the adult's self-image, particularly when it comes at a time of a "well established social role and self-image." (Brehm, 1968) (Cavan, 1962)

It is the present writer's feeling a fixed-age retirement is, when all things are considered, preferable to a flexible-age retirement. Self-choice or flexible retirement age has merit while the worker still has sense and health enough to do something else. This is laudable, but only when the individual is actually changing jobs rather than retiring from work entirely. It is not uncommon on the other hand for a worker to retire on the "downbeat." He retires as something of a failure. The world is too much with him, and he wishes to withdraw only to sit and rock. It strikes us that self-choice in retirement is actually no choice at all. It is almost impossible to say, "I'm through now." This is something like asking a fisherman to set his own limit for the good of others when the fish are still biting strong. The "just one more" syndrome is too powerful to deny. In some cases, the older you get the less capable or wise you are to make a decision of such a vital nature.

Other considerations perhaps not as powerful to the individual for his own needs are still worth considering:

1. Fixed retirement at age 65 can be planned on by management and others and does keep the labor force moving. Younger men want

to know if there is room at the top. They have to have hopes or they may leave the organization and go to one where they know what the future will be.

2. When a man knows his fixed age for retirement, planning for it becomes mandatory. He must then ask himself the question "*What am I going to do?*" rather than "*When am I going to do whatever it is I'm going to do?*" In this case, the "what" a person is going to do in retirement seems more important than the "when" of retirement.

3. Retirement at age 65 may force the worker into planning economic security as best as is possible. Flexible-choice retirement leaves the worker with a feeling that there is not enough. It is a behavioral truism that there never is enough at any time of life as the self estimates the quantity of enough. For example, no matter what salary one makes, nobody ever refuses a raise. What we are saying is that it is not possible for the individual to say I will retire when I have enough money. There never is enough money. There can only be reasonable estimates as to guessing what the future will be.

4. Actually, fixing ages to control human behavior is not a new idea. We start school at the age of 6; we drive cars at the age of 16 or so, depending on state laws; we all vote at 21; individuals become eligible for public office at certain prescribed ages, and the most definite of fixed-age considerations comes from insurance companies. Your insurance rates are fixed, and very stringently, upon age principles.

5. In the writer's own counseling experience, many people quit just a shade this side of exhaustion. The all-too-familiar story of planning the trip, the ideal retirement home, and so on, and then the individual, who had crawled along until he thought he had enough money for all of this, stops living 6 months after retirement.

6. Fixed retirement is probably democratic and fair. If the president of General Electric and the man on the assembly line get equal treatment as far as age of retirement is concerned, we have an honest approach to the problem. On the other hand, it would be ridiculous to ignore the fact that the president of General Electric retires at a higher salary than the production-line worker. The rebuttal is that General Electric Company thought the president was worth more to them than the production-line worker.

7. Perhaps the most pertinent question of all is how much above subsistence level, rather than when, is the individual going to have to retire. Fixed or flexible retirement age means absolutely nothing if the worker is forced to retire at a less than subsistence level.

In the final analysis, retirement may be a middle-class phenomenon. The rich could have enough money not to worry about it. The poor have so little to retire on that the question may be an academic one.

DOES THE FATHER'S JOB AFFECT HIS
CHILDREN'S OCCUPATIONAL THINKING?

The influence of the father's occupation upon his children's behavior is also discussed in Chapter 5: "What Influence Do Parents Have on Their Children?"

Ninth-grade girls from a rural midwestern school were asked what kind of work their parents did, what kind of work they wanted to do after graduation from school, and what were the demands the parents placed upon them. The girls wanted higher vocations than their fathers or their mothers. Both the parents wanted the daughter to advance beyond the father's occupational level. The girl's level of aspiration agreed quite well with her parents' wishes for her. (Hanson, 1965) Boys are much more likely to attempt college if their fathers were foremen rather than laborers. If the mother was employed as a white-collar worker and married downward, (husband's occupation lower than hers), the father was very dissatisfied with his job. In these situations the parents applied pressure in early life for the son to attend college. Fathers are much more likely to consider the son's future vocation in a very pragmatic sense. Mothers were much more inclined to consider the son's future status, which would include more than the vocation. (Cohen, 1965)

WHAT IS THE EFFECT, VALUE, AND
FUTURE OF WORKING ADULT WOMEN?

Sylvia Porter, a widely read and influential financial/economics newspaper columnist, presents a striking example of the position—past, present, and future—of the value and place of women in today's world of work. Porter considers the problem of the "empty nest" as an emerging issue for American women to face in the near future. (Porter, 1967)

Kleemeier, in discussing recreation and leisure and aging, first finds some interesting statistics about women in the labor force.

> The life cycle in labor force participation in women has undergone a striking change since 1890. Whereas, formerly the proportion of women in the labor force reached a peak in the age group of from 20 to 24 and then dropped off, a second peak has appeared in recent decades as more and more middle-aged women have moved into the labor force. If recent trends continue, this second peak at ages 45–54 is before long likely to be substantially higher than the earlier peak from age 24. However, the bi-peaked cycle applies only to married women who tend to have substantially lower labor force participation rates than women without a spouse. [Buhler, 1961]

The same author goes on to say:

> The additional jobs in prospect for 1965 and beyond will largely be filled by persons 45 years of age and older—if we maintain high levels of economic activity in the coming years. Moreover, it is clear that a large part of the increase will be due to the increase in number of women over 45 who remain in the labor force. Almost one out of two women in the age group of 45–54 is now in the labor force, and one in three of those 55–64 age is employed. The very highest labor force participation among women is among the better educated. [Buhler, 1961]

Birren confirms the above by noting that employment for women drops radically after the middle 20s and then rises dramatically to a second peak after the age of 45, wherein the women are more stable, more mature workers, and without the drive to achieve higher jobs. They seem to make comfortable, conscientious, and highly dependable workers. There also seems to be some evidence the women who are age 45 and older are in a much better position than men in that age bracket as far as getting a new job. (Birren, 1964a)

Another interesting bit of evidence seems to indicate that women retire much more easily than men. (Bromley, 1966) Reasons for this might be that a woman is probably more used to the dual role of housekeeper and worker. When she retires, she knows what to do about the garbage, shopping, bed-making and all the details that go toward maintaining a home. Further evidence seems to indicate that single women upon retirement have, because of lack of families, gathered about them a comfortable coterie of friends throughout their working years. Many of these friends, of course, retire at or about the same time, so that the single woman is now protected from loneliness to a much better degree than possibly some other retirees. A third reason for women seeming to retire much more easily than men is that most of them have had less than executive positions. The transition from giving orders, managing other humans, and descending from high-status positions is not their wont. (Birren, 1964a)

In one of the studies designed to investigate the vocational pattern of middle-aged women, the study utilized questionnaire data submitted by 475 middle-aged women. These women seemed to have followed specific career patterns for at least 20 to 27 years after high school. Of the 475 women, about 12 definite career patterns emerged. The career patterns seemed to revolve around four factors: marriage and work, acceptance of work as a primary or secondary method of seeking identity of self, work as a method or level of adjustment for personal problems, and work as a pure and out-and-out career choice. (English, 1963)

Neugarten, in commenting about the above study, reported in

1961, found that intelligence was of the least importance in influencing the choice of career lines. (Birren, 1964b)

One statement concerning women schoolteachers may be of interest at this point. "In contrast with men teachers—married women teachers began to be anxious to retire nearly ten years earlier than men —and the desire is stronger." The same desire for earlier retirement also seems to apply to unmarried women teachers. From this one report we gather that men teachers seem to be most anxious to retire at 55, but following 55 retirement did not seem as favorable as it did at 55. On the other hand, the woman's strong desire to retire did not decrease. She still wanted to leave the teaching field and apparently did not change her mind as she got older after the age of 55. (Hurlock, 1959)

Despite the levity in the question, "How does one get promoted from motherhood?" it appears that the older woman may find a job and even gain more status than she ever had as a mother. (Dainton, 1967) Whatever successes and whatever triumphs she has are her own and not to be shared with youth workers, teachers, and society in general when her children happen to do something laudatory. It seems apparent at this point in time that the story of the working middle-aged woman is far from over. Most statistics indicate that women, despite federal legislation to the contrary, are not paid as much as men for comparable work. If and when this ever changes, the statistics may be even more difficult to find. As to why women work—only the individual woman could give an answer to that. (Harmon, 1967) (Pallone, 1967) Most older women would be adamant in saying, "I have always worked" (cooking, cleaning, raising children, and so on). What is being discussed now is working outside the home. Surveys of psychological literature on working women indicate the following reasons for working. The list concerns primarily married women.

1. Housekeeping may not be any easier today than it was 50 years ago. The pressures of running a home may be even more harrowing than in the past. What does seem to be present is that the work, though not easier, can be done more quickly. Prepared foods, appliances that wash, drain, drip, dry, shred, and do everything but make the garment, newer types of pressed fabrics, and on and on and on, all seem to have cut down the time of housework but, as we have stated, have not necessarily made it any more fun or easier to do.

2. There is some evidence that earlier marriages, with consequently earlier child-bearing, cause the children to be in school while the mother is still relatively young. Thus mother finds more free time on her hands earlier in life, when she may be healthier and have more vigor.

3. At least currently no one can argue the high cost of living. Some women work simply to pay bills.

4. It is in the nature of man to want to embellish what he is doing. When he first begins to walk he wants to skip, once he skips he wants to dance. Man is not satisfied with simple clothing. He wants to adorn himself. Man wants more than hair on his head, he wants it pomaded, permanented, and prettied up. The same dynamics may occur for the individual who wants a higher standard of living. One trip leads to two trips leads to three trips leads to Europe. An appliance seems obsolete when a new appliance comes out. The family goes from one car to two cars. Is there something genetic in the desire for wall-to-wall carpeting, moving furniture, and wanting to buy newer, fresher furniture and materials for the home? Entertainment is a factor in our wanting, if not a higher standard of living, a more expensive standard of living. This applies to color television, subscriptions to the opera, theater, lecture and entertainment series, memberships, and country clubs. And the ultimate for the middle-classed, middle-aged: a swimming pool of your very own in your very own backyard. All this despite the fact that in many cases the neighborhood children make greater use of the pool and neither the husband nor wife particularly like to get wet, especially after the wife's visit to the hairdresser's. So, older married women may work to embellish the lives of their families and themselves.

5. Many middle-aged women, at least in the experience of this professor who questions students in college, are working simply to pay their children's way through college.

6. Ego and status reasons may move a middle-aged woman to a job and keep her there quite happily.

7. In the writer's own counseling practice, which is restricted to clients who are middle-aged, the number of cases of middle-aged women who work purely to escape boredom has been very impressive.

8. In some suburban circles, it appears to be the fashionable thing to do to talk about one's job, even though it is a part-time job in a large shopping center selling clothing. Such interests as discounts and inside information into new styles have for some suburban groups taken the place of energy formerly directed into PTA, bridge, and golfing at the country club.

9. Some of the best evidence seems to indicate that as more and more girls go through college and get higher educations, particularly in the field of schoolteaching, they become dissatisfied with their housework and wish to continue in an occupation for which they had a great deal of enthusiasm in college. To many women it seems like a waste to have attended 4 years of college and have earned a degree and not to use it at all.

10. The entire question of older women entering the job market comes up at all because currently there are more jobs. Since World

War II, this country has been on a phenomenal economic rise. The want-ad section of any metropolitan newspaper will attest to the fact that employers are, and in some cases desperately, seeking workers. The entire consideration and conception of women working, especially middle-aged women, may fast disappear if the country sustains any kind of long economic depression. It should be well within the memory of the middle-aged individual to remember the Depression years of the early 1930s, when women schoolteachers, for example, were not permitted to work if they were married. The slogan seemed to be, "One job, one family." Thus, whatever position women take in society today as wage earners may change drastically if we all go through another dismal depression.

The effect upon the children of working mothers appears to indicate that the children are not unduly harmed. The children develop no differently than do those of nonworking mothers. Essential to the problem is the understanding by the children of *why* their mother is working and for what goals. The single factor of outside employment by the mother is insufficient to explain maladaptive behavior in the children. "When children of working mothers do have difficulties, these are likely to arise from factors which also have an adverse effect on the children of home-bound mothers (factors such as poverty, marital discord, a broken home)." (Jersild, 1968) Similar conditions were found in England, where "no firm evidence has been produced to support the accusations against the working mother." (Benaim, 1967)

For those who are interested in a statistical treatment of women's position in the world of work, their attention is directed to *American Women: Report of the President's Commission on the Status of Women, 1963*. This is available through the Superintendent of Documents, Washington, D.C., 20402. The price is $1.25 per copy.

WHAT ARE WORKERS LIKE
OUTSIDE OF THE UNITED STATES?

More and more studies of workers and their conditions are being conducted outside of the continental United States. The results indicate both similarities to and differences from the American worker. The similarities, however, appear to be more prevalent. Perhaps work is work the world over.

ENGLAND   Stacey, reporting in a British psychology journal, studied the psychological aspects of intergenerational and occupational mobility. The evidence was examined under five headings: (1) the influence of the family, (2) the role of intelligence, (3) the motivation to achieve, (4) the deferral of personal gratification, and (5) other factors. The author found in his study that the family plays a very important role in the mobility process of either going up or down in an occupation. One of the primary factors indicated that personality plays a large part in determining whether a man stays on the same level of job or goes up or down the occupational ladder. Three factors were highly related to upward mobility in an occupation: a high degree of intelligence, a strong desire to achieve, and a willingness and ability with the family's help to defer gratifications until a later date. Other factors of a much less significant nature were the social skills the individual had, his physical characteristics, his physical attractiveness, and the disabilities he may have had of a physical, mental, or social nature. (Stacey, 1965) A second study done in England, reported in 1961 by Heron and Chown, interviewed foremen as to their opinion of the efficiency of middle-aged workers. The foremen in general responded that there was some slowing down but this was more than offset by a greater conscientiousness to the job. (Farnsworth, 1965) Managers and foremen in England and Wales were asked when they thought the aging process would interfere with production. The foremen estimated from age 46 to 55. Managers gave a higher age level: 51–65. Both foremen and managers expected their workers to be much slower on the job after age 50 and that compensations would have to be made. Both groups agreed that the decrement in productivity was extremely small. The foremen and managers felt the problem of slowing up could be accompanied by and handled with tolerance from them. They also felt supervising the older worker was much easier because the worker was more reliable, much more reasonable to talk to, highly conscientious about his work, and appeared to be much more interested in his work than workers who were under the age of 40. The authors point out, however, what we might expect: older supervisors are more kind to older workers and younger supervisors are more kind to younger workers. Throughout the study the data indicated enormous individual differences for middle-aged workers in England. The general recommendation was to not transfer an older worker but to modify his present job in as informal a way as possible. (Williams, 1963a) Another study done in England had some unusual conclusions, "Industry in general simply does not acknowledge a problem of aging—the effects of aging are very gradual." Whether industry recognized or acknowledged the problem of aging, it did exist when the workers were asked about the abilities of older workers. "The power of ancient cliches is tremendous: 'old dogs can't learn new tricks, too old at 40, older people are set in their ways, training is for the young, light work for the elderly!' " The final conclusion from this study of aging workers was that tl ey were discriminated against when recruitment, promotion, and training were being considered. (Tibbitts, 1962)

SWEDEN   A short study done in Sweden concerning occupational mobility indicated that conditions there may be no different than they are in this country. It was found that it was easier to transfer down in a job and much more difficult to transfer up. (Tibbitts, 1962) Swedish workers also appear to have problems similar to American workers. (Seeman, 1967)

FRANCE   Turning now to France, a study concluded, "In industrially developed countries the work rates by age produce a declining curve beginning at about 50–55 years." (Tibbitts, 1962)

WEST GERMANY   Three studies now follow, which were conducted in West Germany since World War II. Thomae reports on a study done with 150 white-collar workers whose ages ranged from 35 to 55. Conclusions were that there were vast, significant differences on the attitudes toward jobs of those over 50 and those under 40. The main difference seemed to be that workers under the age of 40 were looking for a chance for some positive change, were more interested in an active kind of job, and much preferred jobs that had contact with people. German white-collar workers in this study who were over age 50 indicated attitudes that stressed security and independence from supervision on the job. A study reported in 1961 stated that approximately 50 percent of the workers were satisfied with their jobs until about the age of 30. However, after age 45, the highest level of job satisfaction came between ages 50 to 60. (Tibbitts, 1962) A final report on a West German study proposes a very interesting idea for further research concerning the efficiency of middle-aged workers when compared to younger workers. "Many tests of work capacity measure maximum rather than 'occupational' or permissable daily occupational work. The ratio between maximum and occupational work capacity varies with age. A more appropriate test is described." The authors then go on to explain that a younger worker may be much faster but he does not necessarily *get as much work done in the total span of a week.* When the younger worker works he does so at an accelerated rate, but he does not keep it up. The thesis is that an older worker paces himself and in the end will have produced more work even though he works more slowly. (Muller, 1962)

ISRAEL   One study published in 1965 measures the personalities and the work functionings of Israeli males during middle age. The subjects consisted of 62 Israeli men whose ages ranged from 39 through 61 years. All the workers were relatively similar in background and had similar occupational status. The results showed a reduced motivation for achievement, a relative withdrawal from social interaction, an increased discouragement with most of life's goals. "These findings are similar to those reported by American workers." (Shanan, 1965) The reader at this point may want to go back and reread the British studies mentioned above.

INDIA   Ramamurti reports that in tasks for the worker that required considerable physical movement, speed, and accuracy, the older worker's performance was poor. Where speed is not stressed there is no significant difference between the old and the young. In situations that were new and needed visual or verbal material to organize, the older people took much more time to relate the new data to the relevant material. "However, their deficiency in learning new material is counterbalanced by superior quality and accuracy in performance once the material is learned." This study of Indian workers also found that mental functions such as reasoning and judgment and comprehension did not show appreciable changes until very old age. Further, the author felt that the facts themselves do not support the view that older men are more accident prone than youngsters. He concludes, "A number of studies have shown that absenteeism decreases with age, and the causes of absence are very much different for the older than for the younger workers." (Ramamurti, 1965)

Our general conclusions are that workers work around the world. (Daniel, 1967) We must admit that in some countries what could be considered an old worker might be, for example, age 45; whereas to call a 45-year-old man an "old" worker in this country is to heap an insult upon his head.

PART B

Avocations

IS THERE A DIFFERENCE IN OUR MODERN SOCIETY BETWEEN WORK AND PLAY?

At first glance the above question seems rather odd. Of course there is a difference between work and play. Any individual knows when his 2-week vacation comes. The other 50 weeks of the year he works. But perhaps the work/nonwork issue is not as simple as that. (Angrist, 1967) Most modern middle-agers grew up at a time when work and play were distinct entities: Dad worked most of the year and the other time was spent at the summer cottage (for the lucky few), traveling to visit relatives, or there was time for lawn and lemonade. Current thinking seems to have changed our approach to work and play. "It is true as David Reisman notes (1950) that work and non-work are less distinguishable than in the past." Max Kaplan, author of the above statement, says this might not hold so true for the wage earner or lower-class employee as it does for the professional person who has "more difficulty in making such distinctions." (Buhler, 1961)

Continuing this theme just a step further, we rely heavily on the work of Kleemeier and his excellent presentation in *Aging and Leisure,* a 1961-published book. "What we are saying is this: there was a lot of non-working time in the past just as there is in the present. It is not the total amount of free time, but the way it is distributed that is of greatest significance to us here." (Buhler, 1961) What the author is talking about is the number of irregular jobs in the past. In the old days a thresher might work 16 hours a day, but threshing only took 3 or 4 weeks a year. The point is that in the old days the irregularity and variety in kinds of jobs would have given free time in between. Now the working man has to leave early, stay all day, and come home late at night so that he has less free time. (Nothing is said about coffee breaks.) The journey back and forth to work is a necessary part of the constraint of free time.

> It is generally assumed that contemporary Americans have much more free time than was the case for their forbears or the people of other cultures. Of outstanding importance is the fact that in many low energy societies the concepts of work time and free time hardly exist. A man does what is expected of him which we Westerners may refer to as the performance of ritual or ceremony. What is expected may also include the occupation time in conversation, sleep, recreational activity, singing, dancing or what not. A man in such a culture (low energy) may feel as constrained by the necessity to do one or the other. It is only when we classify this time into categories meaningful to us that work becomes defined. But, if we say that he is working only when he is gaining sustenance, then many primitive men had far more work-free time than we have. [Buhler, 1961a]

The work/nonwork issue may not seem as simple to delineate as it seemed on first thought. (Nealy, 1967) The issue has immediate pertinency because we are all told that modern man has more "free" time than he ever had before. This becomes even more relevant because the longer one works, the longer the vacation time he is granted by his employer. Middle-agers have worked longer than young adults. Yet, in an oblique way we find that existence—in work and play—is more than physical endeavor, more than exercise. "For in our day, as of old, the race is still to the swift and the battle to the strong: but the

battle of life is now waged with the *brain* for weapon; it is health
rather than strength that is required." (Italics added) (Ogilvie, 1962)

Returning to Kleemeier's theme, "In summary, traditionally and
in large measure today as well, there is no problem of spending leisure
time for the middle-aged and the elderly Eskimos of St. Lawrence
Island. They simply continue doing what as adults they always have
done (sew, mend, hunt food) then one day they die." (Buhler, 1961)

Is leisure an older-adult problem more so than for younger adults?
What do middle-agers do with their spare time? "Donahue urges research on the ability of adults to learn some of the things needed for
the enjoyment of leisure." (Anderson, 1956)

Returning to our original question, as yet we do not know if there
is much difference in our modern society between work and nonwork.
(Anonymous, 1967) (Dumazedier, 1967)

DO ADULTS PLAY LIKE OTHER PEOPLE
OR IS THEIR PLAY DIFFERENT?

For some years now psychologists have had various theories about
why people play. (Suits, 1967) Most of these theories concern themselves with play as a technique of therapy for disturbed children. The
following six theories of play are by no means exhaustive but do
illustrate the approaches psychologists make in considering play as a
human behavioral dynamic.

1. *Surplus energy*—This theory holds that many individuals have
so much energy and if work and other activities do not use up this
energy, they must simply expend it, and play is the best avenue to
get rid of surplus energy.

2. *Instinct/Practice*—This theoretical position holds that play,
and in this case particularly children's play, is one of the best ways to
prepare for adult life. By playing and observing rules and having to
learn how to adjust to the personalities of other players, the child is
led in the best possible way to get ready for the exigencies and the trials
and tribulations of being an adult.

3. *Need for relaxation*—Some theorists feel that man has to have
a change of pace. He cannot continue the same activity for too long a
period. Thus play may be even more physically vigorous than what the
individual does for a living, but it consists of doing something different. Also pertinent is the fact that in play the individual has a choice
and does not have to do it for a living.

4. *Phylogenetic*—In some ways this might be the most important
of the theories about play. It states that children, as they go through
stages of play from infancy to childhood to adolescence, recapitulate
the evolution of the race. They go from solitary, rough, barbaric kinds

of ego-centered play and gradually evolve through rules and systems and referees into a type of play that supposedly emulates present society.

5. *Catharsis*—This theory, held by some therapists, is that man must use play as an outlet for his emotional tensions built up by whatever situation he has in life. Thus, if the individual is thwarted and frustrated by others he may, through the displaced-aggression approach, engage in very vigorous kinds of play, which then makes up for the things he cannot do in his normal life.

6. *Self-expression*—This theory suggests that through forms of play the individual can really find and identify his own true self and personality. Because other forms of behavior are so highly structured, this may not be entirely possible except as he learns to do it in his early childhood and adolescent years.

Using these theories now to attempt some explanation of the value of play for middle-aged adults, we may use the first, third, fifth, and sixth theories. Perhaps the adult plays because he has energy that is not utilized in his occupation or, for the housewife, in conducting the affairs of the home. It may be sensible to consider play and recreation as a definite need for relaxation or a change of pace from the ordinary routine of life. Most therapists would probably believe that play is a catharsis from the frustrations and anxiety of everyday life. We may assume play and recreation help adults to identify and create further personality patterns for themselves by self-expression.

Another approach may be hypothesized although no research exists to prove or disprove the contribution. Games may be divided into two categories: parallel and reciprocal. Bowling, golf, fishing, and hunting may be considered typical parallel games. In these sports certain characteristics are evident: (1) the individual may participate by himself, (2) keeping score or a record of performance is a personal choice, (3) no human opponent is necessary to participate in the activity, (4) rules may often be ignored or adjusted to the individual's desire. Football, boxing, baseball, bridge, tennis, handball, and any contest where a winner is declared may be considered as reciprocal activities. Characteristics of these activities usually require (1) an opponent who must reciprocate any action you take *and* whose actions mandate some kind of reciprocal response from you, (tennis, boxing, bridge, football, and so on), (2) a score or record of performance must be kept in order to establish a winner and a loser, (3) rules must be established and maintained so that the contest is orderly and fair to both opponents. Obviously many parallel games become reciprocal in nature because the participants wish to make a contest of the activity. But, to participate in a parallel game, one may ignore all of the reciprocal-game requirements if he wishes to do so and still enjoy the activity. The opposite is not true for reciprocal games: football requires an opposing force, as does tennis, baseball, bridge, and so on. Not having an opponent merely means practice for the real event to come. The point of this long explanation of two possible types of recreation is to present an hypothesis in question form. Is it possible that the older humans become the more they eliminate reciprocal games from recreational repertoires? Is reciprocity in recreation an adolescent and young-adult syndrome? Do certain types of personalities insist on making *all* parallel games into reciprocity situations, namely, "Let's have a little money riding on the golf game." Or do certain types of personalities absolutely shun reciprocal games from childhood on and persist in keeping parallel games nonopponent oriented well into adulthood? No one knows. It is possible that most researchers could not care less. Yet, if Wilma Donahue, cited previously, is correct in stating that we need research on adults' leisure patterns the above hypothetical questions stand ready to be answered.

Still another system may present insight into adult play and the contrasts with other age groups. Perhaps it is possible to classify leisure under two rubrics: work/leisure and leisure/leisure. (Kleemeier, 1961) In the former we mean the activity is considered to be productive. Gardening, forms of creative hobbies (knitting, sewing clothes, carpentry, do-it-yourself projects), and all forms of activities done while not on the job and not necessary to sustenance of life could be considered work/leisure. In short, work/leisure consists of those activities we often see others doing, which make us wonder why they "work" so hard at having fun. The participant feels that moving tons of flagstone in making a patio is not work in the usual sense but healthy and well worth doing. In the latter (leisure/leisure) no real productive end is intended. In fact, the opposite is true. If the leisure-time activity begins to become "hard work," it is dropped immediately. Tom Sawyer and the delightful incidents of the whitewashed fence is an example of work/leisure. Loafing on the sun-kissed sands of a beach is an example of leisure/leisure, especially when a companion suggests a rigorous swim to the raft. "It's too much like work," makes it definitely a leisure/leisure association. Again a theory of adult play emerges. Do children indulge in leisure/leisure recreation more than adults? Is a growing propensity to indulge in more and more work/leisure a true dynamic and a unique one for adults? The hypothesis is in want of acceptance or rejection.

Buhler, an astute student of human behavior, makes a contribution along the above theme:

> Leisure occupation is not necessarily play. People use leisure time
> for educational purposes or self-expressive accomplishments in art or

even activities that might be called work, such as charity work, baby sitting, research work, and others. The main point about leisure occupations is that they are freely chosen and serve no necessity. But, to be meaningful, leisure occupations must fit into a person's life. It seems that people who pursue their fulfillment successfully know how to choose their leisure occupations and find the right rhythm between work and leisure. [Buhler, 1961]

Is this a method of measuring success in aging?

Barber makes some provocative statements in a chapter from Ogilvie's 1962 book, *Fifty: An Approach to the Problems of Middle Age.*

The essence of a hobby is that is should occupy the mind. Sir Thomas Browne in the 17th Century wrote, "He who must needs have company must needs have sometimes bad company. Be able to be alone." A pastime, which is merely recreation, has not the dignity or importance of a hobby. A hobby influences a man's character. Samuel Johnson remarked, "No man is a hypocrite in his pleasures." There are middle-aged men who claim they have never had time for anything but their work. It is the fault of their character. Regard old age as one of the bad habits which a busy man has no time to form. [Ogilvie, 1962]

We conclude Barber's contribution with his directive of what a hobby should have. "Hobbies," he states, "must have self-discipline and regularity. The dilettante who tinkers with this and that should not boast that he has a hobby." (Ogilvie, 1962)

One source takes a deeper analytical look at avocations.

For some people, jobs and hobbies serve as neurotic compensations for emotional difficulties. Where a person escapes his poor marriage or a marital sexual problem by staying on the job, his retirement may bring the difficulty closer to home, and the deceptive neurotic mechanism may ultimately decompensate following which the true state of affairs will be exposed. [English, 1963]

Following this, the authors discuss a John and Mary case in which the husband vigorously pursued hobbies in order to avoid intimate and prolonged contact with his wife. "He persevered in putting her off. Insiduously, quarrels broke out between them, and after a few years, they were rarely on speaking terms with each other." (English, 1963)

Birren makes some interesting observations in his *Psychology of Aging* regarding the possible male avocational interests. Males tend to become more feminine in their off-the-job interests over the life span. As aging increases many of them become more interested in raising flowers, yard work, museum visiting, collecting things, and avocations with far less excitement and vigor than in their young manhood periods. It should be pointed out that less strenuous activities are considered to be partially synonymous with femininity and do not connote an effeminate "sissy" accusation. (Birren, 1964a)

On the other hand, White in his work *The Study of Lives* states, the "major conclusion . . . is that aging has a rather insignificant influence upon people's recreational patterns and preferences." (White, 1963)

Kleemeier suggests that most adults mark off small units of time and then are faced with the necessity of filling them up. Adults have a leisure pattern that is unique to the "tyranny of the clock" but that may not apply to children, adolescents, or possibly very old adults. The middle-aged adult says, "Well, we have a few extra hours to kill, what shall we do?" The child naturally flows from one play activity to another as his skill, interests, and companions dictate. He plays unstructured when not influenced by adults or educators' school schedules. The very old adult sits, ruminates, lets come what may and couldn't care less if he does not accomplish so many things in so much given time. What adults do with leisure and particularly the values they place on leisure may be controlled by the "tyranny of the clock."

With the exception of Kleemeier, probably no one contributes more to the considerations of leisure in middle age than Havighurst, Neugarten, and the Chicago group on adult studies. The group confined their studies to adults aged 40 to 70. In seeking to define the values and qualities of leisure activities for these people, they devised twelve specific scales based in most cases on polar dimensions and two general scales also based on polar dimensions.

A condensed version of the scales appears below, followed by a very brief description of the findings:

1. *Autonomous versus other directed*—Means choosing activities with a purpose, acting on own initiative, while other-directed means being pushed toward activities by circumstance or position in society.

2. *Creativity (new solution or novel behavior)*—Means behavior not completely stereotyped, need for an element of novelty, interested in producing different but interesting results, rearranges activities for sheer novelty.

3. *Enjoyment versus time killer*—Means it is fun to do or because there is nothing else to do.

4. *Development of talent*—Means going from very simple noncomplex activities to learning totally new and difficult activities.

5. *Instrumental versus expressive*—Means manipulation of an object to meet self-needs to expressing an emotion as an end in itself (learning to sew versus acting in amateur theater).

6. *Physical energy input*—Means running the range from passive spectator (TV watching) to maximum physical activity (water skiing).

7. *Relation of leisure to work*—Means recreation that grows out of

one's job and which may make the individual more successful (reading for a scholar, golfing for business contacts, coaches attending events they coach, but also relief from work worries by contrast—salesman avoids people by fishing alone).

8. *Gregarious versus solitary*—Means the gamut from family re-unions to hiking alone in the mountains.

9. *Service versus pleasure*—Means from PTA to pinochle.

10. *Status or prestige*—Means the value others place on the activity.

11. *Relaxation from anxiety-producing tensions*—Means what it says.

12. *Ego Integration versus role fusion*—Means the person is better for having participated or does not fit the person's life style.

The two general scales for leisure style were:

   a. *Vitality versus apathy* (from true enjoyment to just filling in time).

   b. *Expansion versus constriction* (from very broad enjoyment to being an expert in a very narrow precise field).

Some of the results (in the same order as the scales were presented) are briefly summarized in the following section:

(Autonomous versus other-directed)   Upper-lower-class people were less autonomous than the middle-class subjects. The middle-class subjects chose recreations that had some bearing on their personal life. The lower classes chose recreation because of propinquity—it was near to the house. There were no age or sex differences.

(Creativity)   There was an enormous difference between the middle classes (middle-middle and upper-middle) and lower classes. The former were very creative, did and tried new things. The latter made a habit of recreation without fully realizing why. Again no age or sex differences.

(Enjoyment versus time killer)   Same result as above was found.

(Development of talent)   The middle-class subjects almost felt a compulsion to achieve a talent while the lower class were not interested. Though there was no age trend, there was a marked difference between men and women. Men wanted to "improve" their scores, made objects, and hoped to increase their skills. "Women are rated more frequently at points indicating less talent or less desire to develop talent but keep the talent they have as a status quo."

(Physical energy input)   There were no class differences here, but men were much more active in seeking recreation.

(Relation of leisure to work)   Again there were no age difference
or social-class differences. Women were more prone to fit recreation
into their housework while men wanted recreations that were a relief
or contrasted drastically from their jobs.

(Service versus pleasure)   There were no class differences or age
differences. Women were rated much higher in service recreations than
men.

(Vitality versus apathy)   The higher social classes were much
more vigorous and active pleasure seekers. (Perhaps they do not have to
work as hard.) Lower-status people were much more apathetic toward
rigorous recreation.

Who are the successful users of leisure? "They were generally
middle-class people." And finally, Havighurst gives a partial answer to
the original question of pages ago ". . . use of time, whether meaningful
or meaningless, remains on a plateau with respect to age from 40 to
65 or 75. It is part of one's personality." (Tibbitts, 1962) (Buhler, 1961)

By way of summarizing the Havighurst and co-workers' studies on
leisure patterns for adults, we turn to another source.

> [We] . . . need a new view of the life cycle. Not to divide life hori-
> zontally into discrete stages: childhood (play), adolescence (study), adult-
> hood (work), and old age (retirement) each with its special concern.
> Rather we need a view of the life cycle as a three dimensional combina-
> tion of play, study and work in appropriate portions at each age.
> [Tibbitts, 1962]

Some of the avocations indulged in by most adults are represented
in the following list: (1) club and organization memberships, (2) camping, (3) traveling—domestic and foreign, (4) fishing, (5) bowling, (6)
conversation, (7) visiting friends and relatives, (8) shopping (see later
comment), (9) hobbies—collecting and creating things, (10) do-it-
yourself home-improvement projects, (11) reading (see later comment),
(12) writing (see later comment), (13) gardening and horticulture, (14)
sports—participant and spectator (see later comment), (15) bridge and
allied table games (see later comment), (16) movies, and (17) television
(to be covered in a later section). There are very few studies concerning
games that adults play most. Writing in this field concerns itself with
a nonresearch approach: rules of games, how to play the game, and so
on. Very few psychologists investigate why adults play games or what
games they prefer. Most of the research concerns children, who are
easier to manipulate for research purposes.

In a survey of 6848 adults it was demonstrated that in intracultural
and cross-cultural samples men play more games of physical skill and
women more games of strategy and chance. (Sutton-Smith, 1963) A

primary factor concerning free time or time for leisure indicates our values on avocations have changed. Instead of sitting and resting we may get into things that call for participation such as golf, do-it-yourself household jobs, and so on. (Buhler, 1961) Birren points up some historical differences concerning recreation. He estimates that the number of free hours for adults in 1960 has probably doubled since 1900. This causes adults some uncertainty as to how to spend the expanding free time: the shorter the work week the longer one must think about what to do with the free time. The reduction in physical activity and organic demands on the body may create leisure for athletic hobbies. Because the average life span is increasing, the amount of time outside the job has increased to a point where more clock hours are spent on nonjob activities than job activities. (Birren, 1964a)

The peak of memberships in organizations is between the ages of 30–44. After the forty-fifth year there is a slight decline until age 60. At this time the individual withdraws from many organizations of a recreational nature. Attendance at meetings follows a very similar path. (Tibbitts, 1962) With the advent of large supershopping areas it may take more "consumed time" to buy the groceries than in the days of telephoning the grocery store to have the delivery boy do the traveling for you. Whereas current travel time to the supermarket is constraining free time, it may also be maintained that many individuals "love to shop for bargains." What is a chore to one may be a lark to another. (Buhler, 1961) "Of all skills, that of writing offers the highest reward in savoring and slowly re-educating the brain as an infinitely variable yet always individual instrument of precision." (Ogilvie, 1962) There appears to be a trend as the adult ages to increased interest in "cultural" reading and a decreased interest in being amused by literature. (Birren, 1964a) As the adult gets older he does more reading but limits himself to a few favorite topics. The adult in his reading development becomes more and more discriminating about what he will spend reading time on, with some indication that nonfictional books are preferred, especially over romantic fiction. History and accounts of events in one's own life span are slight favorites in preference. Much of these data come from middle- and upper-class subjects. Television seems to supplant reading for the lower socioeconomic brackets. (Vincent, 1961) One article presents an intriguing title, "On Play and the Psychopathology of Golf." Golf has a "wide range of intrapsychic meanings," and though other games may have certain common symbolic meanings, "golf has no simple meaning even for the same individual." (Adatto, 1964) Bridge, for some women, may be a "social ritual," which along with "do-gooder clubs" staves off a feeling of uselessness if the individual happens to have no marketable social talents or skills. Usually the enterprise is not very satisfactory because the benefit to others may be only marginal at best. As a consequence some women may try very hard to find a social utility for their avocational interests, whether it exists or not. Thus they may have further failures and become a "caricature" and "play at being Girl Scouts again with service points instead of merit badges." (Levine, 1963) In Terman's group of highly intelligent men and women, studied in their late 30s and early 40s, hobbies and other avocations increased considerably as the individual grew older. The three leading hobbies for men were sports, music, and gardening. For women they were music, gardening, and what Terman called "domestic arts and handwork." Reading was listed by two-thirds of the group as the most-liked avocation. Detective fiction ranked very high in regard to type of reading done most. (Terman, 1959)

WHAT DOES TELEVISION DO FOR THE ADULT?

Older adults rarely figure as the central figures in most television programming. TV appears to be a youth-oriented device. (Anast, 1966) (Stephenson, 1967) The primary emphasis is on the problems of romantic love concerning young handsome subjects in fictional situations. A second recurring theme is related to violence, also youth oriented. The problems of an aging adult are rarely portrayed to the television audience in fictional form. Occasionally documentary films illustrate the problems of the very old and their infirmities. (Anderson, 1962) Rarely are they given a positive treatment. Television "without creating anything new provides a compelling way to spend time." There appears to be a direct relationship between age and the number of hours of viewing television for men. Men aged 19 to 30 watched an average time of 2.35 hours. Men over age 60 watched an average of 3.75 hours. Adults over 50 spent more time during the week viewing television than those under age 50. Ten factors seem to predispose the aging adult toward increased addiction to watching television: (1) sedentary life, (2) more free time, (3) less contact with the world, (4) helps to kill boredom, (5) omnipresent nature throughout the nation, (6) 24-hour programming, (7) rigid time schedules help to impose some structure to a structureless life ("It's time for the ten o'clock news, mother, and then let's get some sleep."), (8) the only physical energy needed is eyelid control, (9) once the set is purchased all further entertainment is free, (10) TV entertains, stimulates and distracts from life's problems. (Buhler, 1961)

The time spent in television viewing remains approximately the same "throughout the life span." Older viewers like nonfictional programs (quiz shows, variety and talent shows) better than romantic or fantasy programs. (Birren, 1964a)

A West German study reported in 1964 questionnaired parents of 942 children. The children's ages ranged from 6 to 16. Thirty-eight percent had no TV set. The average estimated weekly viewing time was 7 hours for West Germany, 11 hours for England, and 22 hours for the United States. (Kurth, 1964) Other studies comparing United States children with other lands do exist. Himmelweit's study is outstanding. However, in this field of research last year's results have little meaning for foreign studies. The number of sets increases so rapidly that to make viewer-survey judgments is to have them change again and again.

Research Suggestions

1. How do men adjust to their feelings of vocational failure?
2. Can an IQ test be designed specifically for middle-aged people? For elderly people?
3. Do dull people die sooner than bright people? If so, why?
4. How can researchers on middle-age aptitude, intelligence, personality, and so on, get a more representative sample?
5. Can good psychological data be obtained on the training of older workers?
6. What aspects of jobs affect a worker's mental health most?
7. On what is creativity based? How does this change with age?
8. What are the differential effects between a fixed and a flexible age for retirement?
9. What are the leisure patterns of the middle-aged? of the elderly? What are the differences between social classes?
10. Can objective studies prove any of the theories on why people play?
11. Do people who utilize reciprocal play differ from those who use parallel play? In what ways?
12. What do personal differences between work/leisure and leisure/leisure indicate?
13. Is it a measure of maturity to be able to find the "right rhythm" between work and leisure?
14. Are hobbies and recreational activities more an indication of one's personality than many so-called personality tests?
15. What precisely is the effect of age on one's recreational patterns?

55	1911	1934	32	Grandchildren are too "wild" and need discipline.	No money, low pay—springs eternal, De-pression, NRA, orange-crate furni-ture, short honeymoon if at all.	"How old can you get?" "World is going to Hell in a wheelbarrow," don't struggle at work, relax, protect your seniority.	Best wife a man could have had con-sidering, of course, all things.
60	1906	1929	37	Might now be a great-grandfather, relaxed and more tolerant of kids, enjoys their occa-sional triumphs.	Dated in the Roaring Twenties, Stutz Bear-cat and raccoon coats, make it big in the stock market, peace forever.	"They should lower medicare age," dis-plays watch for 40 years plus of service to employer, "Who's retiring where and how do others like it?"	Now we are free and the kids can do what they want.

CHAPTER 7

Friends
and
Fellow
Citizens

WHO ARE THE ADULTS' FRIENDS?

Methods and characteristics

Although there are concentrated efforts to study the friendship patterns of children and adolescents, not much research exists to tell us with whom, for how long, and when adults form friendships. (Berg, 1967b) The age levels with the most flexible and shortest friendship alliances are studied the most: elementary and secondary school students. These individuals make and break friendships faster than their parents can account for.

"Why don't you ask Mary over?" suggests the parent.

"Oh, Mother, not her."

"Why not? She was your best friend last week, wasn't she?"

"You don't understand, Mother. Mary and Sally have lockers next to each other. They are together all the time. Haven't you noticed?"

"Oh," says Mother, wondering who is next to be the best friend.

Most of the techniques used to measure the friends of children and adolescents are called sociometric devices. The usual pattern is to ask the individual a semidisguised question such as, "Who would you like to have sit next to you on the school bus?" There are no specific techniques to measure the friendship patterns of adults. If definitive research is to be done on adult friendships, there needs to be more specific or unique devices for doing the data gathering. The major references about an adult's friends seem to come from cartoons: cartoons that usually depict some scene as a husband inviting an old army buddy into his home for an evening meal without prior permission from his wife. And yet—making and keeping friends is a large part of the social life of the adult. Who are his friends? How many are there? How long do friendships last in the middle years of life? Is friendship different for middle-aged people than for other age periods? What fosters making friends in adulthood? There are few answers to the above questions that come from psychological research. All we can do is observe the human scene and make certain assumptions about the process of friendship for young, middle-aged, and older adults. Much of what follows comes within these restrictions.

Friendships for adults may serve the following purposes: intimacy, admiration and ego-building, identification, dependency needs, decision-making, encouragement, solace in time of sorrow, sounding board, and warding off loneliness even if one is not uncommonly fond of the "friend." (Benaim, 1967)

Williams and others use the term *life space* to indicate "the number of people with whom the respondent interacts in a week." (Williams, 1963a) This term helps to determine how active one might be in social intercourse, or how inactive one is by the extent to which he withdraws from human contact, but it tells us little about the nature and depth of these contacts. Life-space dimensions give a quantitative measure, but leave the qualitative dimensions of friendship untouched.

The following considerations suggest many forces that operate in friendships, but proves none of them. Possibly the value of the list is in the direction it may give to research efforts rather than in its factual accuracy.

1. Probably the best single source of measuring longevity of friendships is in the list of Christmas cards sent and received; providing, of course, that one indulges in this annual end-of-the-year tribal custom.

Some enterprising young social psychologist wanting to corral a research niche for himself should study a representative sample of adult people and note the insertion and deletion of names in their Christmas lists, upon what basis these decisions were made, and then tell all of us what he found out. It might be a fruitful avenue for studying the flow of friendships for people from young to old adulthood.

2. It is the present writer's contention that many male adult workers frequently have very personal and reciprocal friendship contacts with their fellow workers but that these friends with whom they share confidences and intimate thoughts are only names to their wives. Certainly it is possible that an adult worker can and frequently does spend more waking hours from Monday to Friday with fellow workers than he does with his own spouse. This is particularly true of the commuting worker who leaves on the 7:55 A.M. train and arrives home after returning on the 5:15 P.M. train, which permits him to walk in the front door at 6:20 P.M. Is it possible that many middle-aged males now in their twentieth to twenty-fifth year of employment have spent more hours with and have conversed to a greater degree with their fellow working friends than they have with members of their own families? Some psychologist should research this area and tell us. It may be a factor in middle-age adjustment heretofore unacknowledged. Is it possible that a man's fellow working friend knows him better than his family does? Is it possible a "fellow at work" is more influential in decision-making processes than a man's own wife? (Who helps the husband to decide when and what kind of a new automobile to buy?) Can a man you have worked with for many years be more influential in having you see a medical doctor than your wife has been able to be despite her hours of coaxing? How does an adult male get his information and form his opinions on political campaigns and issues: from his wife or from his co-workers? Who do adults tell their troubles to—wife or fellow worker?

3. How important is nearness to the "holding power" of friendships? Is propinquity a powerful factor or are some friends "just as good as ever" minutes after seeing them again despite months and even years of separation? What factors make the difference between acquaintances and friends? Do adults have more acquaintances than friends as they grow older and older or is it the other way around? We do not know. We need some social psychologist to give us the answers.

4. There may be evidence married couples have "his" friends and "her" friends and "our" friends. It is not a question of compatibility but a factor of differing life space for each spouse. What we do not know is which friendship group is the most influential: in directing the lives of each spouse, in the manner in which they enact their parental roles, in the degree to which they keep up contacts and hold

on to their friends. After 25 years of marriage are "his" former frien
or "her" former friends more inclined to be still invited to the hom
Or do middle-aged couples create a new circle of "our" friends, wit
very few of the old "his/her" friends involved?

Relatives

The cliché that a man chooses his friends but inherits or marries h
relatives has some pertinency in a study of primary friends and ki
(For a full delineation of the differences between primary friend
secondary friends, and acquaintances, the reader may want to stuc
further the literature of social psychology. The differences are tc
complex to be spelled out here.) As is usual the subjects came from th
middle-class stratum. Husbands rather than wives were more likely t
initiate primary friendships for the couple at all stages of the fami
cycle. Couples in their 40s and 50s had the same number of primar
friends as did recently married couples. Most couples studied had tw
very close and deep friends who lived locally. The majority of th
husbands and wives claimed they did not have a single primary frien
who was not also a friend of their spouse. Children in the famil
neither enhanced nor constrained their parents' ability to entertain c
be with the couple's closest friends. The relationship between frienc
and relatives was not the same. The number of times one visited c
was visited by relatives had no relationship to how frequently th
couple visited and entertained close friends. (Babchuck, 1965)

Developmental levels

It is assumed that acquaintanceship with and knowledge of relative
remains constant throughout the three levels of adulthood: youn;
middle, and older. What seems clearer, however, is that nonrelatio
friendships do change in intensity as the couple grows older.

YOUNG ADULTS   Other than the aforementioned relatives—wh
come in all ages, variety of interests, and degrees of compatibility—th
young married couple have friends very close to their own ages. Thi
may result from a number of factors. College-educated couples ar
bound to have carryovers from friendships formed at that time. Th
contacts of serving in various capacities for each others' wedding cere
monies may help to enhance and prolong the friendships. These tie
may weaken very rapidly, however. The young groom's employer ma
mandate frequent and long-distance moves from the original hom
territory as the groom attempts to climb the occupational ladder o
success. (Beshers, 1967) Noncollege-educated couples may pursue di

fering friendship contacts, which revolve around the church, the husband's job, and certainly neighborhood friends of long standing from high school.

With the advent of children, friendship patterns may change radically. Now the couple will be involved almost weekly in church education, Brownies and/or Cub Scouts, baseball, camping, and PTA groups. Thus direct contact with other parents evolves into friendship patterns: They all have an absorbing, concerned confrontation with the same problems, revolving around the question, "What's the best thing for our kids?" Young married couples' lives revolve around the welfare of their children at least for the middle class. "The home-centered style" of entertainment was not by choice but necessary because of having young children. (Buhler, 1961) The cost and trouble of baby sitters' fees may drastically curtail the social life of a formerly hyperactive couple. Children are more than blessings. They are burdens to country club socials, bowling leagues, extended vacations, expensive visits to the theater, and dining out.

The unmarried young adult probably finds friendship through two pervasive contacts: fellow employees and dating. In the former pattern there is most likely to be like-sexed activities—joint vacations, attending theater, movies, sports contests, and the like. In the latter there are the usual attempts to seek out a marriage prospect, which become particularly poignant as the individual approaches and passes the mid-30s.

Both married and unmarried young adults use this period of life to learn how to give parties with their own facilities, both materially (setting the table, preparing the menu, and so on) and personally (organizing games, providing entertainment, and so on). This age represents education for host and hostess. Social contacts mandated by occupational reasons become more of a "contract" than a contact. (Hurlock, 1959)

MIDDLE-AGED ADULTS   By the time middle age is upon the married couple, they have established and maintained a form of entertainment compatible with their skills, facilities, and income. They maintain these factors with small deviation for the next 20 years or until approaching retirement curtails the amount of money they wish to spend on entertainment. Socializing with relatives may alter a little. The middle years appear to be a "plateau period for social competence." (Havighurst, 1957) And, ". . . at least until the mid-sixties, average persons maintain social competence in the face of considerable biological change," and, "in the face of considerable personality change." (Williams, 1963a) The gradual decline in social involvement of all types as couples progress through the 40s and 50s is attributed to a "reduction in drive level" or reduction in "ego energy." The couple may realize suddenly that they are spending more and more Saturday evenings alone at home (their children are living away from home or otherwise socially engaged), which fact may disturb them somewhat. They should expect to entertain and be entertained less as they near the mid-60s. It is not a question of loss of friends or decreasing popularity; it is the phenomenon of aging best expressetd by many middle agers' motto, "Do we have to go out again tonight?" (Birren, 1964a) Thus we find, "Membership in formal clubs and groups reaches its peak at the end of the middle adult years." (Pikunas, 1961) (Havighurst, 1953b) However, we find also, "The 204 men and women who were interviewed with regard to their experiences and attitudes in the area of social participation did not suggest many changes as they grew older." (Zborowski, 1962) It is of note that this study done in New England does not support the Kansas City studies which found a "disengagement" factor as aging progressed. (See Chapter 3, "Is Disengagement a Special Kind of Self-image?") The contradictions lead to some pertinent questions. Are the midwestern people of Kansas City different than New Englanders? Does the disengagement theory depend upon the initial level of engagement? Is Kuhlen's question applicable: How can you disengage from something not fully engaged in originally? (Cumming, 1960) (Phillips, 1967)

"Married women showed a peak in civic and organizational activities at about age 50." (Anderson, 1956) As previously stated, there is a sense of expanding social activities and occupational activities after the children leave home and the mother is left more to her own devices. (Anderson, 1956) Involved also is the decrease in neighbor involvement and child-involved friends after the children leave home for college or marriage. (Buhler, 1961)

Eventually all parents, if they live long enough, graduate from their roles as participants in parent/teacher groups and similar organizations wherein they became involved, made new friends, all because of children now past the eligible age. Nevertheless, though the middle-aged parents may now be PTA alumni, their teen-aged children continue to demand and need social involvement from their parents. Chaperoning "Y" dances, driving to Friday night basketball games, advising fraternity or sorority organizations, eliminate the past overnight hikes and camping, Sunday school teaching, Little League summers, and kindred children's activities. As the parent grows older in the middle years, the child's demands upon time and very active involvement are supplanted by greater and greater demands on the family financial resources. The checkbook takes the place of the buddy system. Dad's Day for fall football may be the closest link to the past camaraderie of camping. Finally, the child's marriage climaxes the effect the child had upon the parents' friendship circle. Traditionally, and without question, psychological research to the contrary, the preparation of the guest list for the wedding is the grandest effort ever made to decide one's hierarchy of friends. At no other time is friendship so devastatingly adjudicated. All decisions about wedding guests lists become dichotomized: invite or not invite. Friends and acquaintances become labeled and separated in actual fact: the former attend the wedding and the reception, the latter attend only the reception. This is a true example of an operational definition.

The social position of unmarried middle-aged persons is inextricably involved with their marital status. Thus much depends upon having been divorced, widowed, or never married. The friendship patterns of each group are highly tinctured by their present marital status. Much has been said concerning this in Chapter 4. Summarizing this material, we find that the divorced individual, where children are involved, is extremely curtailed in finding free time for friendships and socializing. Unless baby sitters are involved, older children can be parent surrogates or are sufficiently old enough to remain alone; otherwise the divorced woman has little free time. It appears the divorced middle-aged man assiduously seeks out younger female friends and little or no contacts with like-aged male friends. His friendships revolve around seeking a woman for a wife, which quest, if successful, brings him into many new acquaintances (not always friends) almost all of whom are younger than he is in years. In spirit he attempts to create a younger image for himself than that of his former marriage. When neither divorced man nor woman remarry, the circle of friends diminishes radically. Relatives frequently become closer friends than ever before. This is true mostly of the more sympathetic in-laws. Children become the avenue toward closer contact with one's own or the ex-spouse's parents.

Middle-aged widowed adults have an equally difficult time maintaining friendship contacts. Again the problem of free time from children must be solved. For widows, the children become the entree into new friendship circles. Her married friends do not abandon her; in point of fact, shortly after bereavement she may be overindulged with invitations, but in time invitations proffered her are built around the concept of the "extra." She is chosen to fill out the natural twosomeness of most couple-oriented social occasions at her age in life. The invitation to the widow comes because a fill in is needed for the temporary absence of a sick or traveling husband or wife among the guests. For some, two single women are invited to comprise a couple. If the entertainment is bridge, one of the ladies is allotted the role of a male partner. Thus society absorbs its friends who are widows. The widow, as time passes, entertains less and less in her own home. Many widows finally contrive a small social group of unattached like-aged women, also widowed or divorced or never married, around whom they build friendships whether the group is particularly compatible or not. The qualifications are being unattached rather than comparability of interests and affections. The middle-aged widower with children to raise seems to plunge into keeping his activities centered exclusively around his children whether they want it or not, particularly when the children are well toward postadolescence or early adulthood. The widowed male rarely seeks the friendship of similar-situated males. His friends are numbered largely among his co-workers and a diminishing number of couples uniquely close from prebereavement days. His best friend's wife frequently substitutes as a mother to his children most often during holidays such as Christmas, birthdays, and so on. If he remarries, and he frequently does as we have seen in Chapter 4, it is most often to a long-known friend who knows and appreciates his problems.

The never-married middle-aged adults, both male and female, have been working on friendships since early adulthood. Their friends come from both married and unmarried, with the greatest emphasis on the latter. Being middle-aged varies their friendship patterns very little if at all. Never-married middle-aged women have long had an intimate coterie of female friends with whom they have traveled, socialized, and turned to in time of sickness and trouble. No clear pattern of social behavior and friendships emerges for the male counterpart. He is a bachelor and probably more marketable on the social scene. His friendships may be considered far fewer and not of long standing. The never-married middle-aged male may have more acquaintances and less friends than the female counterpart at this age level.

Does the entertainment at adult parties change for all adults as they get older? Yes. They "often refuse to play a game in which they are not at home" or familiar with. They no longer like to "put on stunts" at a party or social gathering. (Hurlock, 1959) From the high social interest of the late teens and early 20s, there seems to be less interest in extensive social interaction with large number of people and a "shift to a greater liking for closer relationships with fewer people." In middle age there is a strong tendency to engage in solitary pursuits rather than getting involved in large groups. However, as Havighurst indicates, the values of leisure and solitary pursuits are more related to social class and to personal degrees of adjustment than to aging or sex. (Birren, 1964a) "The peak of activity takes place in the 50's and early 60's followed by a slow withdrawal." (Havighurst, 1953b)

OLDER ADULTS   The friendships and social participation of adults over 65 will be more fully discussed in Chapter 9. At this point it should be recognized that much of the picture changes with advancing old age: Because of retirement there is less income for socializing, the inevitable death of a spouse restructures friendship patterns as we have previously described, the health and vigor for social activities continues to diminish, changing the residence to a warmer climate has a strong effect on departing from old friends to successfully or not successfully making new friends, and the possible personality changes that come with extreme old age are also involved. "In general, the older you get the more mellow you become toward the underprivileged and ostracized racial groups." Aging begets sympathy and empathy rather than centripetal concern for self. (Birren, 1964a)

Although voting behavior is certainly an aspect of adult life it is not dealt with herein because it more rightly belongs in the field of sociological and political behavior than in that of psychological behavior. For an elaboration of voting behavior of older adults see Rose and Peterson, *Older People and Their Social World,* and Schmidhauser, "The political influence of the aged" as starters. (Rose, 1965) (Schmidhauser, 1968)

WHAT EFFECT DOES SOCIAL CLASS HAVE ON SOCIAL PARTICIPATION AND MOBILITY?

Apparently economic status has significance in the friendship patterns that adults form. (Dohrenwend, 1967a) Mobility and freedom in forming friendships appear to be easier for middle-class adults. The very wealthy and the extremely poor adults are less inclined to change their patterns of friends. The wealthy form a pattern of exclusion on their own terms, whereas the poverty-stricken adult is excluded but not on his terms. By and large, it is the middle-class adults who seem to have greater freedom and equality in moving up and down the social ladder for friendships.

Mobility on the social scale (perhaps a nicer name for "keeping up with the Joneses") appears to be more of a young-adult- than an older-adult-type of behavior. One can surmise that it is at its highest during the middle-adult years. Normally when social mobility is being studied by social psychologists, the emphasis is placed on the degree to which mobility occurs upward or downward but not on *why* people want to change the status quo. Also missing is the severity of the competition to possess something other people have. In short, although students of social behavior have conducted studies on social mobility and with better than average skill, we still know little concerning the inner dynamics of why people covet their "neighbor's house, his field, or his manservant, or his maidservant, his ox, his ass, or any thing that is thy neighbors." (Deuteronomy 6:21). Apparently the behavior is as old as

Moses and the Ten Commandments. Assuming covetousness and keeping up are somewhat synonymous, we know even less about these actions for middle-aged adults. Some of the more traditional studies (Prairie City, Elmstown, and so on) suffer from antiquity. Life and times in the United States have changed from the Depression of the thirties and the World War II frenzy of the forties. "Sex differences in mobility are not reliable, though there is a tendency in women to show more downward mobility than men before age fifty and more upward mobility than men after age fifty." (Havighurst, 1953b) But mobility and social striving are not closely synonymous, so we do not know much more.

It is this author's pet hunch, not even in the hypothesis stage, that competition that leads to covetousness and "keeping up" must eventually include the relationship between married sisters, neither of whom wishes to have a lesser life than the other. One wonders what pressures are perpetrated on children to keep up with their similar-aged and similar-sexed cousins. Also, is it possible for the mother of two middle-aged married daughters to be impartial toward the condition of their homes, especially when one home is clean while the other daughter's home is chaotic? Is it possible to become *nouveau riche* and not want what the established rich have had all along? *If* middle age is that period in life when all the hard work of previous years comes to full fruition, could it be, therefore, the highest stage of "keeping up with the Joneses"? Is middle age the time to "trade up to a bigger car," to wall-to-wall carpet the entire living room and dining room, to take the first trip abroad, to wear the first mink stole, to proudly possess the first set of matched irons? If it is, then middle age may be the peak years of "keeping up with the Joneses." Who are the Joneses? They may be the middle-aged middle-class couples of America. (Mayer, 1967a)

Probably the most pronounced phenomenon of parent/child involvement in youth-serving organizations is that of social class. It appears to be almost exclusively a middle class activity. What little evidence exists indicates that very poor people rarely, if ever, serve in any capacity for their children's organization. What little that is done by way of supervising poor children is often the work of social workers and paid community house recreational personnel. The extremely wealthy, on the other hand, also have their children guided and directed by paid professional specialists. However, in the former case a governmental agency pays the expenses while in the latter case the family pays for the tennis lessons, summer camping, golf lessons, ballet lessons, and music lessons. The evidence seems to be that the rich and the poor have their children serviced by professionals (only the mode of financing differs) while the middle class "do it themselves."

WHO DO THE SERVICE CLUBS SERVE?

First of all, the constituency of service clubs is, as Kuhlen's 1950 study suggests, comprised of middle-aged people. "Middle-age is the time for service." (Hurlock, 1959) Prior to middle age the male or female are probably much too busy to become overly involved in service club projects; she with her children and emerging home patterns and he with an ambitious effort to succeed in business. Civic work increases in the early 40s and then declines after a period of about 10 years. The general trend is to go from social participation in large groups to involvement in smaller organizations. In the early 40s there is more time, money, and skill for service club work. Aside from the Junior Chamber of Commerce-type organizations (upper age limit of 35) and veterans groups, most of the evidence seems to indicate that service clubs are most popular for the early stages of middle age. This is particularly true when the service club demands full attendance at all of its meetings and also engages in projects that require some vigor.

"It is evident that association (in clubs) decreases with decreasing social status and with increasing age." Havighurst finds that most urban areas offer less associational life for men than women. Churches, as we shall see, offer no more than a possible monthly men's brotherhood meeting. Service clubs, by placing heavy emphasis on regular attendance and active committee work, may lose all but the most active men. Consequently, older fraternal orders have lost much of their aggressive program vigor. To exist, male service clubs need new, younger, vigorous membership. (Havighurst, 1953b)

There is almost no reputable research being done on the dynamics of service clubs. Although most service clubs are meant for males there are those designed for women also, even though they do not receive the publicity given such groups as the Lions, Kiwanis, or Rotary. (Rarely does one see an announcement for a women's service club advertised on the billboard along the highway while driving into a city.) What little that has been written about service clubs from a psychological frame of reference can easily be divided into two divergent viewpoints: very negative or extremely laudatory. The emphasis depends upon, apparently, the viewpoint of the writer. The writing is usually journalistic in style and not based on reputable research as far as we can ascertain.

The positive statements generally emphasize the great benefits others receive from the service club's selfless efforts. Hospitals for crippled children, creation of new playgrounds, loans and scholarships for indigent students, free medical and dental services for destitute families, especially for children, free swimming lessons, are but a few

of the laudatory activities performed by service clubs for the welfare o
others.

The negative comments range from the mildly critical to the
deeply sarcastic criticisms: "playing boy scout again," "nothing but a
luncheon club looking for an excuse to exist," "arrested adolescence,"
"horseplay by fat, balding men under the disguise of helping others,"
"pretending phony philanthropy paid for by nonmembers."

None of the above positive or negative statements seems to com
from a dispassionate investigative source. Apparently, it depends upon
whether one is a member or nonmember when appraising the role o
service clubs for adult men and women.

WHAT IS THE RELIGIOUS BEHAVIOR OF ADULTS?

Whereas active involvement in service clubs seems to decrease along
about the middle part of middle age, some sources feel ". . . the area
of civic and church activity would seem to be ones in which an increase
of activity might occur." (Havighurst, 1953b) Another source states
". . . church membership and church attendance rise sharply in the
40's and 50's . . ." but both attendance and membership decline after
60. (Vincent, 1961)

". . . the average older person is a regular attendant of church
services, but takes no leadership or responsibility." (Havighurst, 1953b)
However, it seems to make a difference as to whether the adult is male
or female.

> Older women often find themselves in demand for service at church
> dinners as well as for sewing, quilting, and other church projects. Older
> women are generally of more use in a church than older men, and for
> this reason: they get more out of church life. . . . Older men drop out o
> church activity more rapidly than women do. Probably because their
> activities are more involved with administrative and teaching positions
> in which there is considerable turnover with new officers being elected
> annually. Women, on the other hand, have the women's organizations to
> keep them occupied and even though they may drop out of leadership
> roles, they have many meetings to attend during the week. [Havighurst
> 1953b] [1]

Lehman felt that churches and organized religion might properly be
named "Gerontocracies." In short, the older people get, the more
regularly they attend church services and become involved in the mean
ing of religion for themselves and others, except at the very late period
of life when there is a general decline in church going and participa

---

[1] Used by permission of David McKay Company, Inc.

tion. That is, attendance holds up, but active participation in church programs drops off. (Birren, 1964b)

Second, we find that ". . . interest in religion and all that it involves seems to increase as the individual goes from early adulthood to middle adulthood if they are poor or of average income while there is no pattern of increase for the very wealthy." (Hurlock, 1959) There is evidence from other fields that worship patterns do change according to social class structure. (Goode, 1966)

Religious behavior as it relates to personality factors in 500 psychiatric patients indicated that patients who expressed a great amount of dependence on God were not poor prognostic risks. Paranoid patients rejected the image of a Heavenly Father. Psychotics were not aware that they had "excessive religious experiences" counter to the generally held view that they do. (Lowe, 1966)

Social factors and religious-behavior studies disclose a number of elements that operate in modern society. Religious beliefs, size of community, and social issues were studied. The community size correlated negatively to acceptance of certain current social issues. (Photiadis, 1967) Studies begun in 1955 comparing children and their parents' attitudes on accepting desegregation in schools indicated favorable attitudes toward desegregation were associated with high economic status and increased activity in church affairs. (Sartain, 1966) However, another study indicated that "on the average churchgoers are more prejudiced than non-churchgoers." Parishioners with extrinsic religious orientation were more prejudiced than those with intrinsic religious orientation. These findings confirmed previous studies. (Allport, 1967) Still another study failed to find signfiicant differences in religious activity and social influences. (Barocas, 1967)

Comparisons between Catholic, Protestant, Jewish, and other religions have been undertaken with these results: Protestants appear to be less passive and more "present oriented" while Catholic subjects appeared to be more sensitive and given to habit formations. (Bronson, 1966) The differences and unity between Jews, Catholics, Protestants, Bahais, and nonbelievers revealed multiple factors, which indicated that studies of religious beliefs failed to distinguish deeper variables than ordinarily considered in research designs. (Keene, 1967) Jewish couples seemed to be more realistic in the joint feeling the husband and wife had in regard to family size. Catholic couples were more acceptant of undesired pregnancies. (Stimson, 1966) What factors may be present when couples of different faiths marry? Babchuck found that in highly stable marriages there is a stabilizing effect if the couples have a common religious affiliation. In couples where one of the partners changed church membership the change was usually to the spouse with the highest educational level. (Babchuck, 1967) More interfaith

marriages in contrast to intrafaith marriages were conducted in a civil
ceremony. Interfaith marriages were also found to have a dispropor
tionately higher rate than intrafaith in premarital pregnancies. The
data come from a statewide survey of marriages in Indiana, one of the
two states that requires a statement of religious affiliation on marriage
registration forms. (Christensen, 1967)

For readers who wish to explore in much greater detail some of
the former studies in religious experience and behavior, Clark's book,
The Psychology of Religion is still a standard work. (Clark, 1958) For
those concerned with a newer approach to ethics, Fletcher's *Situation
Ethics,* may be of interest. (Fletcher, 1966).

Growth and development must occur from the agnosticism and
atheistic feelings of adolescents to the deep-seated and complex beliefs
that so frequently occur in adults whose adolescent years so typically
followed the feelings of disbelief. It appears that "God is dead" strikes
closer to the adolescent heart than the adult mind. Is it possible
middle-aged adults do not feel "God is dead" when they have just
found Him after 50 years of trial and tribulation on this earth? The
concept of God is never pictured as a pimply faced teen-ager. It is not
so much, "Of course, she is black" but "Of course, all gods are thought
of as old and wise and experienced and settled." Just like an older
adult!

Research
Suggestions

1. Can a device or technique be developed to adequately measure the friendship patterns of adults?
2. Is there a correlation between the quantity or quality of a man's personal
   friendships and his feeling toward people in general?
3. What are the factors that influence adult friendship formations the most?
4. Can friendship be measured?
5. How long do friendships last? What causes friendships to be broken?
6. What is the influence of age differences on friendship? of social class?
   of economic status?
7. As adults get older, do they tend to have more friends than acquaintances
   or vice versa?
8. Do the requisites for friendship vary for different age groups?
9. Can a valid study be made of the dynamics of service club membership?
   Are there underlying aspects of personality that sway people toward
   joining service clubs?
10. How important is nearness to the "holding power" of friendship?

CHAPTER 8

The Body – the Brain – and Behavior

THE BODY

Shall we bless this house and all within?

In sickness and in health

Health at fifty is an amalgam of three elements: the physical condition of the body determined chiefly by the habitual way of life; activity of the mind best preserved by interesting and absorbing work and stimulated hobbies and holidays; spiritual insight and inspiration to be sought either in religious faith or in sympathy with others. [Ogilvie, 1962]

An interesting statement is made in Robert Burton's book, *The Anatomy of Melancholy*, "He who lives medically lives miserably." This we assume to be the hypochondriac's hurdle. The same author feels, "At fifty personal habits and way of life are much more important than medicine in the preservation of health." He feels that health, like happiness, is a by-product of activity and not of the drugstore. An interesting comment in regard to cigarette smoking and the incidence of cancer is also made. Although the evidence certainly seems to be overwhelming that smoking induces lung cancer in some manner, "If a man of 50 has smoked cigarettes for 30 years, little can be done to lessen the risk because damage likely to ensue has almost certainly been done." Pathologists with newer research and data would certainly want to contradict this statement. (Ogilvie, 1962)

Most writers agree that a concise definition of health is rather difficult. Generally it is assumed that soundness of body is indicative of good health. "But was Nelson at Trafalgar (blind in one eye and only one arm) an unhealthy man?" Arthur Thomson feels:

> There are in truth three aspects of human health: the physical, displayed by due discharge of bodily function, by rapid adaptation to environmental change, and also by capacity to work at an activity appropriate to the age, race, and development of the individual; the mental or intellectual aspect with qualities of curiosity, patient inquiry, and judgment; and finally the spiritual which comprises sensitivity to beauty, loyalty to truth, courage in adversity, consciousness of fellowship with mankind and faith in the purpose of life. [Williams, 1963a]

It seems obvious that the matrimonial phrase, "in sickness and in health" is not an easy phrase to understand. Just exactly what is sickness, and conversely, just exactly what is health? We find the state-of-health determination to be a very complex question to try to answer and one that brings out no definite answer. In trying to determine a state of health, at least eight factors must be considered.

1. Days in bed.
2. The number and amount of doctor and medical bills.
3. Incapacitation for all work or certain types of work (The experience of World War II, which accepted workers for certain kinds of employment but would not have accepted the same workers according to prewar or postwar standards).
4. Insurability.
5. Objective (physician) versus subjective (self) evaluations.
6. Comparative factors, such as comparing one's feeling of health with that of one's own age group versus comparing one's feeling of health with that of young adults or adolescents. Thus

we have chronological changes as a factor in trying to define health.

7. Whether the ailment is mild or severe.
8. An injury that may heal with proper care versus the impairment of an organ or limb.

(Williams, 1963b)

Kurt Wolff, a medical doctor, helps to give us some idea in approaching a definition of health by suggesting that aging, particularly in the middle years, produces a decrease in at least eight organic functions or areas: in the elastic properties of connective tissues, in the cellular elements in the nervous system, in the number of normally functioning cells, in oxygen utilization, in the amount of blood pumped by the heart under resting conditions, in the amount of air expired by the lungs, in muscular strength, and in the excretion of hormones, especially the sex glands and the adrenal gland. Does anything increase? Yes, says Wolff, the amount of fat on our bodies. (Wolff, 1959)

Since Gompertz' mathematical theory on aging in 1825 there have been many theories proposed on why human tissue ages. (Curtis, 1966) The theories are far too numerous to be adequately discussed here. Theories on biological aging range from homeostatic ("homeostasis is less efficient in older people"), to "wear and tear" and accident and stress theories. One of the most recent ones to gain considerable interest was proposed by a nuclear physicist, Szilard, in 1959. Szilard suggested that as the adult tissue grew older an accumulation of "genetic faults" occurred. He felt these "somatic mutations" accumulated at about the same rate that Gompertz had earlier suggested in 1825. Curtis and others evidence that the more frequently genetic mutations occur, the shorter the life expectancy of the species. (Blumenthal, 1968) The entire concept in all theories of aging "is under re-examination." (Birren, 1968a) The complex cellular structure of man may penalize his possibilities for longevity. "Cold blooded animals age more slowly at reduced body temperatures than at more elevated ones." Single cells may "possess a longer life-span" than the organism in which they live. (Strehler, 1962) The premise is that the single cell in a sense never dies but splits into two cells and thus retains a vestige of life. When the housing organism (the human body) ceases to exist the complexity of the system causes all of its organic components (the cells) also to end existence as viable organisms. In addition to biological aging there are the aspects of psychological and sociological aging to be considered. The theories on aging are extremely complex. New ones are still being proposed. The interested reader is advised to read other literature for a more complete treatment on theories of aging. Space limitations prohibit it here.

Older retired individuals seemed to be much more realistic about their health than younger nonretired individuals. "Younger respondents were more likely to employ active measures to maintain or improve their health such as diet, exercise, medication and so on." Efforts to preserve health may represent a somewhat realistic effort to preserve youth; however, when the fact of aging came to be accepted, preoccupation with very subtle physical and psychological changes diminished. (Reichard, 1962) Two age groups (40–59 years and 60–82 years) indicated no relationship between age and health status and age and socioeconomic status. On a subjective health-rating scale the sick saw themselves as more healthy than the well. A small percentage in both groups considered their health as being less than excellent or good. (Mason, 1966) Very few adults, if any, reach the 40s and certainly the 50s without some physical problems to contend with. (Hurlock, 1959) (Espenschade, 1966) (Malhotra, 1966)

At this point the middle-aged reader already knows that his health and physical vigor, his speed in motor skills, has certainly diminished, but then he must ask himself, "So what's new?" The important question seems to be what you do with what you have in the way of a body. Health difficulties may be less important than adjusting to decreased physical capacity and particularly to the change in appearance. The middle-ager may be fat and flaccid, but is it all that important? It would appear to be important only to those middle-aged individuals who have become brainwashed by the youth-oriented society. In some ways to look younger than one is, is a false approach to honest living. The factor of appearance also seems to have strong connotations of economic class. The data seem to indicate that the lower classes and some of the middle classes care less about appearance than the upper classes. (Hurlock, 1959)

Sensitivity to pain appeared to be constant for each individual up to and around the age of 50. There was a decline in pain sensitivity, but the decline differed for parts of the body. (Farnsworth, 1965)

Orthopedically disabled patients whose ages ranged from 15 to 79 underwent physical rehabilitation training at two centers. There was "little evidence of age alone as a factor of therapeutic performance." What seemed to be most important were the disabled patients' concepts of themselves, the kinds of social activities they had previously engaged in, and particularly the family solidarity, which could help or hinder their rehabilitation training. (Litman, 1964)

A German journal reports on observations in Europe and Africa that lead to the conclusion that recovery from illness depends on the magnitude and number of deficiencies—physiological, psychological, and social. Older people with specific illnesses in one organic area recovered much faster if deficiencies in the other areas were eliminated. (Le Compte, 1965) "It is estimated that for each five years of life, one can add a day to the period of recuperation from illness or disability." (Levine, 1963) Low-income males have a higher number of hospital days per illness than low-income females. High-income females spend more hospital days per illness than comparable males. One reason for this is that occupational hazards for low-income males are much higher. In short, they have more accidents. (Birren, 1964a) Most sources seem to agree that the middle-aged man or woman is rather safe from accidents, except for home accidents. Injuries do not appear to increase with aging. (Pikunas, 1961)

The head

As adults grow older there is a decrease in the size of the brain, especially after the age of 30. It was "pointed out that while the ventricles of the brain enlarge in old age, and the total volume of cerebrospinal fluid increases, the brain tissue itself contracts." There is an accumulation of moisture in the gray matter of the cerebral cortex at the expense of solid elements: more water and less weight. (Wolff, 1959)

A study reported in 1964, which attempted to relate decision time and brain waves, found that decision time was related to age. However, when the EEG frequency was held constant the relationship vanished. Fifty-four subjects whose ages ranged from 34 to 92 years of age were used in the study. In a further study the subjects were asked to decide between two choices and there was "evidence to support the hypothesis that subjects with slow brain waves required longer to make decisions than do subjects with faster brain waves." (Surwillo, 1964b)

Dr. Walter Alvarez, long famous for his work at the Mayo Clinic, wrote an article on the many causes of migraine in middle-aged and elderly women. There were many causes, ranging all the way from overconsumption of soft drinks to tight girdles. He felt there may be evidence that migraines are inherited. He further advanced the hypothesis that 95 percent of the time migraines will occur in women who are socially attractive, of about average intelligence, quick in bodily movements, and have small, trim, feminine bodies with well-formed breasts. "Knowing these attributes, a physician should suspect migraine the minute an alert and attractive woman walks into his office." (Vedder, 1965)

A questionnaire was submitted to Scottish subjects, in which the respondents indicated that there was a vast difference, as far as they were concerned, in the amount of sleep they needed as age progressed. Generally there was less need for sleep as the individual got older. The answers given to the questionnaire indicated that sedatives were more frequent for women than for men. There was evidence that, "Advancing age sleep patterns change without too much difficulty. But probably ages 60–70 require less sleep than earlier ages." (McGhie, 1962)

The psychological literature on the kinds of sleep, sleep deprivation, need for sleep, and learning during sleep is rather large, but does not directly deal with the effects of age on sleep behavior. For the reader interested in sleep behavior, the outstanding work of N. Kleitman and his former student W. C. Dement as well as the work of H. W. Magoun are recommended. Especially recommended for its consolidation of data is Kleitman's article in the November, 1960, issue of *Scientific American*.

The heart

Although there are always wide individual differences in the characteristics of any kind of human behavior, the evidence seems to be overwhelming that men, especially in the middle ages, are more prone to heart attacks than women. Many contributory causes are given for coronary heart disease. The etiological picture may be complex. (Russek, 1967) "Four out of five heart cases in middle-age are men." (Vincent, 1961) Much of the literature about heart disease is written by men, for men, and about men. For example, we find:

> From the literature one gathers that the high mortality from cardiovascular disease results from a confluence of many factors, diet, urbanization, occupational strain, body type, heredity, and still others. Some of these imply origins in early life, tubescence or earlier and suggest that we should continually broaden the search for factors and conditions throughout the life span. Masculinity, high activity or drive, productivity, and responsibility appear positively related to the development of cardiac disease. Apparently constitutional factors, that is, body build, temperament, and psychological activity suggest a precursor factor which might be distinguishable in use. [Birren, 1964b]

Again, another study concerns itself with men. The author Brozek was especially interested in the development of hypertension in comparing younger with older men. He studied 119 college students whose average age was 22 years and then studied 200 business and professional men whose average age was 50 years. All the subjects had normal blood pressure and were considered to be in a good state of health. The men involved came from a midwestern metropolitan community. The results indicate two items of interest. There appeared to be some success in predicting hypertension among the college-age men as they were compared to their opposites of middle-aged men. The factors most useful in tracing these age changes and personality were: health, recreation forms, the types of home and family they had, the degree of self-confidence they had, their emotional adjustment or lack of adjustment, and their standards of conduct in regard to other people. (Brozek, 1952) A 1965 reported study using a sample of over 100 pilots showed that age differences and the ability to make quick decisions and receive and retain information are less impressive than might be expected. The study attempted to show age differences in sequential decisions and cardiovascular status among these 100 pilots. The pilots whose ages were over 40 were relatively more susceptible than the younger pilots to information overload, especially in trying to remember short term recall. The cardiovascular status among these perfectly healthy men was a high factor in their efficiency. (Szafran, 1965b) In a study done in England, the hypothesis was advanced that men in physically active jobs would have a lower incidence of coronary disease in middle age than men who were physically inactive in their jobs. Three studies were conducted that advanced the acceptance of the above hypothesis. At 45–64 years of age, heavy workers had half the mortality rate from coronary disease than light workers. Heavy workers died less often than light workers in the first clinical attack of a coronary heart disease. Bus conductors on double-decked vehicles had less coronary disease than the single-deck bus conductor and also than the less active bus drivers. Other findings indicated that postmen have less heart disease than telephone operators or civil service officers or desk-bound clerks. Some of this data also supported a study done in Sweden, which indicated the same kind of relationship between the intensity of physical activity and work and the incidence of symptoms of coronary diseases. (Stringer, 1961)

Two representative recent studies are indicative of many many studies on the effects of exercise on heart rate. Almost all of the studies show that the older the adult the longer it takes for the heart to recover after strenuous exercise. (Montoye, 1968) (Daly, 1968)

The sexes—female

During the middle years of life, one undeniable aspect of female existence is the "change of life" called the menopause. Probably no other adult period of life has more written about it than menopause. The words, spoken and written, range all the way from old wives' tales to highly sophisticated scientific studies. Unfortunately, much of what has been said or written is more fiction than fact. Even the term *change of life* connotes a dramatic cleavage from one stage to another stage. This is not necessarily true. In twenty percent of the women the "process is smooth and uneventful." (Bromley, 1966) Menopause is a transition from the ability of women to bear children to the inability to ovulate in regular monthly periods and gradually to cease to ovulate entirely. Menopause is not a sudden departure from child-bearing one day to nonchild-bearing the next day. In a similar vein, at one time adolescence was considered to be universally a time of *Sturm und Drang*—storm and stress. Recent evidence refutes this concept that all adolescents are automatically going to go through a period of misery and misunderstanding. Too many people do too many things in too many different ways, making universal laws of behavior most difficult. In much the same fashion, menopause has as many variations on a theme as does adolescence. (Cristenson, 1965)

Menopause usually begins some time in the early 40s. "Irregularities in ovulation usually occur for 1½ to 2 years." It usually ceases anywhere from 45 to 60. In one study (Kinsey, 1953) the age range was from 40 to 60. Data from a study in 1952 found no relationship between a delayed first menstruation (menarche) and early menopause. (Vincent, 1961)

It is unfortunate, but some writers freely ascribe the term *menopause* to any kind of disability or stress that a woman may have between the ages of 45 to 55. Consequently the term *menopause* is frequently used to describe any kind of behavioral difficulty in women as they enter into the middle years. Along the same lines a hysterectomy (removal of the womb), although difficult and painful as is any major surgery, does not remove the ability to enjoy sexual intercourse. Frigidity following a hysterectomy is psychological in origin. (Bromley, 1966) (Masters, 1966)

Using data primarily gathered in Norway and other European countries, the age of menarche (the first time a girl ovulates) has been decreasing. The average age for menarche, or first menstruation, was 17 years of age in 1844. In 1950 it was 13½ years of age. This study supported data from Germany, Finland, Sweden, Great Britain, and the United States. "There is little evidence at present that the trend has stopped." We also find some limited evidence that girls with precocious sexual development who start to menstruate quite early in life need not necessarily have an earlier menopause. A unique example was given of a woman who began to menstruate at the age of 2, had a stillbirth at age 9, menopause at 52, and died at the age of 75. A case was found where menstruation began at age 2 and continued until age 53, with eight pregnancies during that period. In another case, menstruation began at the age of 30 months and continued until age 53, with nine pregnancies. Admittedly, these are unusual cases. However, "Such startling exceptional cases suggest that the early onset of reproductive life in the female has little relation to total life span and certainly need not be accompanied by earlier menopause." (Birren, 1964b) Early menstruation also seems to have very little to do with a girl being sexually precocious or overly interested in boys. This is particularly true in all of the 50 examples studied, in which only 1 girl who had gone through early menstruation showed any real interest in the opposite sex. In a study reported in 1950, there was evidence that the reproductive period, which begins with the menarche and is climaxed by the menopause, need be no different than any other kind of physiological process. (Benedek, 1950)

There may be a direct relationship between the manner or ease in which a woman accepts her menstrual cycles and her acceptance or rejection of the pain of child-bearing. Those women who moan and groan about how difficult it is to give birth to a child, how unfair it is for women to have to bear this great burden in life, and what a sad state of affairs it is that men do not have to bear the pain of ugly "periods" as do women, appear to be better than average candidates for involutional melancholia. Involutional melancholia, better called involutional psychotic reaction, is a mental disorder developed and related to the climacteric found in women who are going through menopause. The outstanding characteristics of involutional melancholia are frequent symptoms of insomnia, worry, strong guilt feelings, much anxiety and agitation with some delusional ideas and frequently accompanied by hypochondriacal behavior. Apparently the ease with which a woman manages to go through the period of menopause depends primarily upon her state of mental health. If in the past the woman has collapsed emotionally every time an incident of stress or anxiety occurred, the indications are that she will have a difficult time in menopause. If, on the other hand, there is enough ego strength so that the woman has been able to master most of the traumatic incidents in her past life and appears to have made a sensible solution to most of life's problems, she may pass through the physical parts of menopause and accept it as not much different than other problems of life. It is not the intent herein to minimize menopause. Despite a good quality of ego strength, it can be a period of adjustment for many middle-aged women. As she enters her 40s, a number of activities may take place that make the adjustment even more difficult. Let us assume that she is now approximately 45 years of age. She has three children with whom she has spent considerable time in bringing them through all the crises of sickness, disappointments, tribulations, and so on. She has spent many, many nights sitting up with them through sickness and scrimped and saved for their welfare. She has given unstintingly of her time and talents to these three children. Now she is 45 and is beginning to feel older and unwanted, with a body and a skin texture that are not what they were when she was 20. She begins to look around for reinforcement and love. The obvious objects are her children, for whom she has done so much. What are they doing? If they are somewhat normal, they are absorbed in college or work, falling in love with other human beings, and rather disinterested in how "ma" feels. Failing to gain reassurance and the quota of affection she feels should be given her by her ungrateful children, she may now turn to her husband, who is also having some difficulties in getting through the 40s or 50s. This man whom she has married, slept with, worked alongside of, shared successes and failures through life with, may also seem indifferent to her demands for extra affection. Because she feels denied by her children and her husband, the human beings who mean the most to her, the middle-aged woman going through menopause may seek other avenues to make herself feel more wanted and to enhance her feeling of fading beauty and value. To accomplish this end she may plunge herself into civic and philanthropic activities, get a job outside of the home, where at least her employers and customers may appreciate her, redecorate the house with wall-to-wall carpeting and new furniture, restructure her personality, dye her hair a different color, or simply wait it out as many women do until the whole menopausic period is over. Or, as is the case so many times, she may eventually become a grandmother. Now she has a new little human that can love her and want her and give her a sense really of being important once again.

The sexes—male

In the same way that women go through menopause, men also go through a period wherein their endocrine systems are readjusting in the span of life. This factor for men is usually called the climacterium. However, the term *climacterium* is used for women as well as men. The dynamics of the male climacterium are not the same as they are for women. The best evidence seems to be that there is less physiological involvement. The changes are less abrupt. The period probably lasts longer than it does for women. The end of fertility for males frequently is long drawn out.

One study reported in 1955 asked the question, "Is there a male climacteric?" The authors felt that the concept of a male climacteric was quite misleading and could be dangerous if it fostered an indiscriminate administration of androgens to men over the age of 50. They felt that androgen therapy was "contra-indicated" in most males over the age of 50 except in the very few cases of true testicle insufficiency. It was felt there was more than a calculated risk for stimulating prostatic carcinoma. (Hess, 1955) The controversy appears to be quite strong as to whether middle-aged men should take testosterone. One group of medical experts advocate a free use of testosterone but caution care. "It is almost impossible to over-treat an individual as long as recommended dosage schedules are followed and a basic 20–1 ratio maintained." However, others feel:

> There has been a recent enthusiasm for balanced androgen/estrogen therapy as it is called. And this, too, has been proposed for the male climacteric, even as it has been proposed for a multitude of vague complaints. The average urologist is poorly qualified to evaluate the complex hormonal interrelationships that are thrust at him by endocrinologists and the drug company detail men. If estrogens are good for prostatic carcinoma and androgens are bad for it, what happens when the two are given together?
>
> •   •   •
>
> We believe androgens alone or in combination with estrogens are contraindicated for use in the male over 50—recognition of the risk regarding cancer of the prostate. [Vedder, 1965]

Still others feel that the "problem of male impotence, when it occurs, is so complex that not much in the way of scientific findings is available." (Vincent, 1961)

In a 1966 study, 22 couples who had requested sterilization for the male (vasectomy) were interviewed and tested with psychological tests, both prior to the operation and two years later. This group of 22 couples were closely matched with 22 couples who had elected ovulation suppression for contraceptive purposes. The results indicated roughly that the couples for whom the male had an operation reported poor psychological functioning and much less marital satisfaction. In point of fact, the husbands frequently began to avoid any nonmasculine behavior. (Ziegler, 1966)

The senses—taste

Just as does all machinery as it gets older and older, the taste buds of the aging individual lose some of their efficiency. (Bromley, 1966) (Glanville, 1964, 1965) One study, for example, indicates, "There may be no basic differences in the four basic tastes (sweet, sour, salt, and bitter) but there definitely appears to be a loss in the nuances and the threshold of being able to delineate these tastes." (Farnsworth, 1965) "Generally, not much change was seen in taste thresholds up to the age of 50. After the late 50's, however, a decline in sensitivity was noted for all taste qualities." (Cooper, 1959)

Not necessarily related to taste but in a study regarding appetite and digestion, 20 percent to 30 percent of the men over age 30 were found to be obese. Obesity was defined as more than 15 percent excess over derived body weight for the age. Diabetes also seemed to reach a peak between the ages of 50 and 60. Conclusions were that men are far more susceptible to digestive diseases than are women. (Vincent, 1961)

The senses—touch

Two studies seem pertinent here: the first is a dissertation completed in 1964 in which 75 adult men and women whose ages ranged from 31 to 80 years were given a special test that required tactual and visual functioning. The test was originally designed to diagnose cortical brain damage. The subjects did show a systematic loss of efficiency on this test as a direct function of age. Both speed of response and quality of response were affected as age advanced. However, intelligence was found to correlate positively with the quality of performance in these 75 adult men and women. Further, it was found that subjects with better than an eighth-grade education performed much more efficiently at any age than those with less than 8 years of education. (Berg, 1964) In the second study, 786 normal, healthy, white subjects were studied in regard to age and sex differences in the palmar sweat print. "Females were found to have greater palmar sweat than males." The general hypothesis that the sweat glands decrease with age was corroborated. The applicability of this study to adults is not direct because the oldest subjects were 8 years of age. However, the investigator did find that palmar sweat increased rapidly from birth to about the age of 7 and decreased slowly from then on. (Ferreira, 1965)

The senses—smell

Although it is generally considered that smell and taste are uniquely correlated, they are treated here differently only because the research evidence seems to indicate a clearer understanding if this is done. One study is pertinent here. Four groups, 13 men in each group with the age ranges being 43–49, 50–59, 60–69, and 70–82, were measured for the absolute olfactory thresholds. The evidence seemed to indicate that there was a reliable threshold increase, that is to say, as age advanced the subjects were able to smell with less efficiency. However, the investigators state that it depends on what you smell as well as how old you are. (Kimbrell, 1963)

The senses—sight

The human being is rare who has lived past the age of 40 without realizing that visual acuity decreases with age. Bifocals and trifocals are the order of the day. Most middle-aged readers of this book probably join the author in having a stiff neck while trying to read a large metropolitan newspaper. The characteristic bending back of the head while trying to get a clearer view of the paper through the lower part of the bifocals is indeed a measure of middle age. However, even though this is known, there are a number of psychological research studies that may be of profit. Almost all studies show that visual efficiency declines rapidly after the age of 40. (Pikunas, 1961) (Agrawal, 1966) (Burg, 1967) (Leibowitz, 1967a and b) (Melton, 1966) (Meneghini, 1967)

The decrease in vision after the age of 40 or at least beginning at the age of 40 appears to reflect at least four different factors as reflected in 4 research projects. English studies indicate there is a change in the pupil diameter, in a strong yellowing of the lens, in an increase in sensitivity to glare, and in an ability of people past age 40 to adapt to the dark. All of this appears to have some significance for wearing colored glasses or having tinted windshields and for the middle-ager's reluctance to drive at night. (Farnsworth, 1965)

Presbyopia or farsightedness is referred to as "old sight." Thus the need for reading glasses should be very universal in middle-aged people. The degenerative and functional changes in vision are due to four factors: (1) decrease in pupil size, (2) loss of visual acuity, (3) strong resistance to glare and bright lights, and (4) a strong tendency toward glaucoma. The loss of elasticity of the lens structure is a strong factor in visual problems of the middle-aged. On the other hand, color vision seems to hold up fairly well through the ages. (Hurlock, 1959)

Vision was studied in 215 individuals whose ages ranged from 1 month through 81 years of age. There appeared to be a rapid increase in which brightness sensitivity (amplitude) reached a maximum at about the age of 6. This was considered to be about twice as large in visual efficiency as for older age groups. "With children seven years of age and older there was a rapid decline in amplitude until ages 13–14 when an abrupt increase in amplitude appeared." The ability to see well then appeared to stabilize around the age of 16. In older subjects (average age of 60 and beyond) there were great significant changes in lack of efficiency for vision. (Dustman, 1966) Adults and children made judgments in regard to the brightness of a target. The adults showed greater consistency than the children in their ability to perceive when the targets were presented one at a time, but the differences between the adults and the children were not significant. The results indicated the importance of cues in a perceptual situation wherein adults may be better at comparing perceptual differences, but children did remember differences from one single stimulus to a second single stimulus. (Beck, 1966) Men, ages 20–69, were asked to pick a specific numeral from "irregularly varied digit patterns changed at 3 average rates. Performance at the medium and slow rates did not change systematically with age; at the fast rate omission errors increased progressively with each decade." The decrease in efficiency with age as speed increased was not due to visual acuity properties but rather to "changes in the decision processes" within the brain. (Talland, 1966a) Visual acuity falls off with age, but too little attention has been paid to its implications in regard to the amount of light required for older subjects. Even where contrast is good, people of ages 60 and over require an illumination factor of several thousand lux if they are to have normal visual acuity. There should be a certain margin of safety between what can be seen and what must be seen, particularly if the individual's job consists of performing a continuous visual task. If the margin is not wide enough, the deficiency will have to be made up by extra mental effort on the part of the older individual. We may find a reason here for older subjects being very reluctant to drive at night while in the past it did not bother them at all. It looks like they have to have more light to see better. (Fortuin, 1963)

A West German study attempted to study the influence of age on the performance of visual differential sensitivity. The subjects were 48 individuals divided into four age groups (15–16, 30–35, 55–60, and over age 70). The age group that seemed to perform best on all of the six tests used was between ages 30 and 35. There was a pronounced difference between the sexes, with women appearing to have a little better vision at all ages than men. As we may assume, subjects over the age of 70 were the lowest in performance level. (Kovác, 1965)

Although not specifically concerned with the efficiency of vision, an interesting study of "normal" males and females hypothesized that males spend relatively more time viewing female pictures while females do the opposite. The results failed to support the hypothesis. (Leckart, 1966) The work of Hess may be interpreted differently.

The senses—sound

Along with taste, touch, smell, sight, and a few other things, including sex, the individual also loses some of his capacity to hear the world around him. Most authorities agree that the ability to hear high-pitched sounds is lost first and usually after the age of 40. The majority of the adults, however, rarely lose the full ability to hear low-pitched tones. (Pikunas, 1961) (Hurlock, 1959) Hearing loss was far greater for men than for women in the adults years. This might have been caused by the fact that men have more exposure to noise because of their occupations. (Farnsworth, 1965)

The ability to listen is sometimes called auding. As we may expect, adults' ability declined in efficiency with age. (Craik, 1965)

There seems to be no doubt that adults gradually lose their ability to hear. (Inglis, 1967) (Sataloff, 1966) The crucial question seems to be what they do about it. Most evidence indicates that unless the hearing-aid device can be cleverly disguised the majority of middle-aged and older-aged adults are very reluctant to be identified as having lost their hearing ability. The higher the degree of vanity the less the willingness to accept the device that will help in making up the loss of hearing. This does not seem to be true for eyeglasses. Currently, manufacturers are becoming more clever in disguising the device, either in the bows of eyeglasses or in very small transistorized hearing aids of minute proportions.

The appearance

Probably one of the factors the aging individual becomes most acutely sensitive to is the face or appearance. Face and figure and skin texture are most apparent in the aging process. What the individual does about it seems to have a unique relationship to his social class: lower, middle, or upper. In that order there is a growing emphasis upon face and figure.

"Until we are 35 or 40, our faces are those God gave us; after that they are the faces which we make for ourselves." (Vincent, 1961) This is remindful of Abe Lincoln's oft-quoted, "After 40 a man is responsible for his own face." It would seem apparent, then, that a dissolute past will be written upon the faces of those who indulge themselves in wasteful pursuits.

Middle-aged men and women are said to "stop growing at both ends and to grow in the middle." This seems to be a fairly common factor of the middle years as far as appearance is concerned. It should always be brought to mind that physiological aging and appearance have the same individual differences as are found in children. The average adolescent has approximately 10 percent of his total weight in body fat. The average middle-aged adult, man or woman, has approximately 20 percent of the total weight in body fat. (Hurlock, 1959)

The consensus is that men in our culture show signs of aging sooner than women. Among the reasons for this seem to be that women pay more attention to their appearance and have more devices, such as beauty shops, to help them. Another reason advanced by some is that men work harder in occupations, which influences their appearance. This would certainly be true of laboring and farm-employed individuals. Again, we find socioeconomic differences in the appearance of aging men and women. Higher occupational levels prefer to appear younger than their age. Lower occupational levels almost always look older than their age. Such generalizations must be carefully interpreted because of individual differences.

The muscles

The muscular portions of the body consist of voluntary or striped muscles and involuntary or smooth muscles. Striped muscles are found in the legs, arms, and other parts of the body. Smooth muscles are found in the intestines, stomach walls, and most of the internal organs and blood vessels. Aging effects are not as crucial to the functioning of smooth muscles as they are to striped muscles. Although lack of bladder sphincteral control is involved at late senescence adult individuals do suffer from bowel and bladder incontinence. However, the peak period of striped muscle strength is usually reached between the ages of 25 to 30 for most persons. After that, loss of elasticity depends largely upon sustained physical activity. The striped muscles may increase "in bulk and intensity up to about the age of 50." Later there is an increase in atrophying of these muscles. Posture changes and coordination with age are the results of daily habits and neural efficiency. (Bromley, 1966)

The bones

One of the most fruitful and dedicated organizations in studying longitudinal affects on human behavior is the Fels Institute in Ohio. In one of their projects, 462 white subjects were examined for change in bone structure. ". . . the decrease (in bone structure) from 40 to 45 is small, while the decrease from 45 to 60 is relatively large, . . . older women have smaller bones with greatly decreased structural strength." Bone loss in strength and size was by no means peculiar to the post-menopausal female. Bone loss took place in both sexes, but to a greater and faster pace in the aging female. There was some evidence that brittle bones are inherited. (Birren, 1964b) The peak of bone density occurs around the age of 35 years. Arthritis begins shortly after the age of 40, with some evidence of emotional factors being involved in developing arthritis. Muscle strength, as a general rule, is at its maximum between the ages of 25 and 30, with about a 10 percent loss between the ages of 30 to 60; however, wide individual differences exist. Most writers conclude that the decline in muscle strength is most to be found in the back muscles and the leg muscles and less in the arm muscles. (Vincent, 1961)

The breath

Without considering the medical entities such as emphysema and other abnormalities and the effects of smoking, it stands to reason that the aging adult breathes harder and with less satisfaction than in earlier years. After the age of 40, basal metabolic rate (oxygen consumption for the entire body) gradually declines. There is a very rapid rate decrease after the age of 80. (Wolff, 1959) One short study, conducted with 6 men and their adaptation to high altitudes, was done in California. Adaptation was compared to their responses to high altitudes 27 years before. In general it appeared that overall adaptation (headache, breathing, loss of sleep) was slower than when they were 27 years younger "but that this was not due to the respiratory system." (Birren, 1964b)

The voice

Professional singers and speakers are aware of the fact that the voice no longer has the timbre and quality that it once had. This is certainly in keeping with the loss in efficiency of all parts of a piece of apparatus such as the human body. "The voice becomes more highly pitched as the person progresses from middle to old age." (Bromley, 1966) However, one short study found that there was "no evidence of so-called senile voice among the subjects." "Speaking pitch level of women probably varies little throughout older life." (McGlone, 1963) On the contrary, another study found that there was a "difference in voice quality with age." The ability of 10 listeners was tested to differentiate the voices of younger adults (under age 35) from older subjects (over age 65) on the basis of a prolonged vowel, a reading example played backward, and a reading example played forward. Listeners were able to differentiate the voices of younger adults from aged speakers "with impressive accuracy under each of the three successive listening conditions of decreasing difficulty." (Ptacek, 1966)

THE BRAIN

Can an old dog learn new tricks?

Although we have handled similar data in regard to being able to teach an old dog new tricks in Chapter 6, Part A, "Vocations," there are certain aspects of adult mental behavior that do not belong properly within the rubric of vocational pursuits. The area of measuring adult mental ability is one that has had much emphasis by developmental psychologists and others. Almost all the results indicate that adults are gradually getting to be less and less bright. Some writers feel that mental ability becomes more differentiated as the adult ages but that in old age the "process of intellectual differentiations reverses" and specialized abilities decrease, although the hypothesis is only in the formative stage. (Bromley, 1966) Other studies give evidence that sensory and muscular processes do decline with age but that there are very few changes in the central nervous system with advancing age until late into senility. (Welford, 1958, 1964, 1965)

Problems in measurement

The problems of measuring mental ability, or as it is frequently called, intelligence, are enormous. The problem is a complex one and needs to be very thoroughly studied before understandable and acceptable answers can be obtained. (Botwinick, 1968b) The usual criticisms of measuring the adult's mental ability are that most intelligence tests are made for, standardized on, and in general given to children and thus are not appropriate for adults. "The content of adult intelligence tests has been rightfully criticized as an unthoughtful borrowing from children's tests." (Birren, 1964a) Bromley concludes that there "is as yet no adequate theory of intelligence." (Bromley, 1966)

Cattell has introduced the concepts of "fluid" and "crystallized" intelligence. Fluid general intelligence is primarily innate and adaptive toward all types of problem-solving. Crystallized general intelligence represents somewhat the exercise of fluid intelligence in past applications, such as school subjects. "It appears in such tests as vocabulary and numerical ability measures." Fluid intelligence reaches maturity for humans between the ages of 14 and 16. As the adult ages, then, we may assume a gap is developing between fluid and crystallized intelligences. (Cattell, 1965) Horn's work corroborated some of these findings. Subjects whose ages ranged from 14 to 16 years indicated that fluid intelligence was consistently higher for young adults while crystallized intelligence was consistently higher for older adults. Perhaps Cattell's contribution may prove to be a stepping stone to better understanding of adult mental ability. (Horn, 1967)

Again Botwinick makes a valuable contribution to delineating and understanding many of these problems in his useful book, *Cognitive Processes in Maturity and Old Age*. (Botwinick, 1968a)

Adult performance on intelligence tests calls for certain attributes such as being interested, persisting in the task, cooperating with the psychometrist, and certainly having some comfortable familiarity with the test items.

One author advances seven problems when using intelligence tests on adult populations.

1. By the time any human is an adult, whatever individual differences they had may have become even stronger so that one finds a considerable difference in the behaviors in testing adult populations.
2. "Aging occurs along a single dimension, measured best by blood pressure, lens accommodation, and sound threshold and less well by ability and speed tests." It is this factor of speed on a test that seems to have an enormous effect on the supposedly low ability of adults to take intelligence tests.

3. Aging adults want a higher chance for "success before they will approve a high risk, high reward course of action."

4. Sometimes in subjects up to age 65 their "years of education show a greater relationship to mental abilities than does chronological age." We will find, as we go through this chapter, that initial intelligence and particularly high level of education make a vast difference in performance on intelligence tests. The brighter you are, the brighter you remain.

5. There are no simple answers "to the question of whether problem solving and intellectual capacity rises or falls over the adult years."

6. Intelligence is difficult to define for children and more so for adults.

7. Good problem-solving, which is required of any mental-ability test, may be related to (a) the health of the individual, (b) high initial ability, (c) good education and, (d) supporting environment through the adult years: in short, to an enriching life rather to than a dull pedestrian-type existence.

(Birren, 1964a)

A West German psychologist finds that intelligence in adults and older persons is closely related to changes in ego strength during the lifetime. The usual intelligence tests are very inadequate for middle- and older-aged individuals. Intelligence as it applies to adults requires adaptive behavior to specific situations in everyday living rather than responses on a paper-and-pencil test. (Skawran, 1965) Wesman's presidential address to Division 5 of the American Psychological Association's 1967 meeting stressed some of the same issues. "Most individuals have not failed to learn more with added years." He felt that "older people do less well on tests designed for younger adults." He refuses to accept without reservations the "gloomy dictum" that after age 18 or 35 mental ability is all downhill. The relevancy of tests for adults is in question. (Wesman, 1968) The present author would support this thesis. In some ways it does not seem that much intelligence is used by the intelligence testers in testing intelligence for adults! To put it another way, it is just as fair to give an adult a child-oriented intelligence test as it would be fair to give a child an adult-oriented intelligence test that concerned itself with income-tax filing, behavior on a highly complex job, driving an automobile, and all of the things that an adult must do in using his mental ability to exist in this world. Obviously it is ridiculous to assume that a child could drive an automobile or fill out an income-tax form. However, many do not regard giving an adult a child's test as being equally difficult. Despite the fact that most intelligence tests do not adequately measure adult intelligence, there appears to be a decline in the performance of most adults in mental measurement endeavors.

Constancy of intelligence

We turn to the excellent Fels Institute for statements in regard to changes in intelligence quotients.

> A variety of studies have explored and attempted to explain the basis for IQ changes. Howell (this was reported in 1955) compared the performance of 50 men and 50 women on six subtests of the Wechsler-Bellevue Intelligence Test. His groups were equated for age over a range of 60 to 89 years, and there was no significant sex difference in the decline which he found. In addition, the decline was independent of education achievement and level of intelligence. Doppelt and Wallace reported in 1955 on research with a rather homogeneous sample of men and women from Kansas City aged 60 to 75 and found no significant differences in decline between sexes or for controlled speed versus non-speed tests. They did, however, find a slightly greater and earlier decline on performance subtests than on verbal tests. Eisdorfer also discovered a greater performance decline on 130 subjects over 60 years old. He divided his group by sex, race, socio-economic level, intellectual level, and health but found that none of these variables could explain the differential decline. Ghiselli, unlike the investigators already mentioned, noted no downward trend in a group of 1,400 subjects aged 20 to 65. His testing conditions put no premium on speed and he used well educated subjects—both crucial factors with I.Q. change according to his hypothesis. Over 1,000 rural New England villagers, aged 10 to 60, were studied by Jones and Conrad using the Army Alpha Test. Their overall finding was that peak performance occurs between 18 and 21 years with a gradual decline to 50 years of age. These investigators were unable to explain their findings on the basis of lack of motivation, lack of testing practice, remoteness from school, speed control, or failing perceptual abilities. They did not point out, as other investigators have, that the decline varied among subtests and that there were greater individual differences within adult age groups than between the ages. [Birren, 1964b]

Test results for older individuals were more homogeneous than for younger individuals. This is a contrary finding to the one cited above, wherein individual differences seemed to be wider as the individuals grew older. (Merz, 1965) Subjects randomly selected to represent inhabitants of the Netherlands (ages 12–77) found that the subject's best performance on a Netherlands Intelligence Test was reached at about the age of 20 and then remained fairly level until about the thirty-second year, after which there was a gradual decline in ability to perform on this test. As we might expect, test items that represented some school experience were performed less and less better as age progressed. The performance curve of superior persons maintained a very high level much longer than that of the nonsuperior individuals. A strong plea was made to define what is meant by intelligence in light of the fact that the age differential and the impact of age role is so uniquely tied up with what may be considered "functioning" intelligence and "academically orientated" intelligence. (Verhage, 1965)

Two groups of elderly males, approximately ages 65 to 70, drawn from a Veterans Administration Hospital were tested. One group was given the Wechsler-Bellevue Test. This group was retested at about an average interval of 8½ years. The group showed a *decline,* which was significant at all levels of intelligence. The largest decline occurred at the higher IQ levels. A second group drawn from the same hospital with approximately the same ages was given the Wechsler Adult Intelligence Scale. This group was retested about 105 days later. This second group showed a significant *increase* in their IQ scores. This increase is such as might be found when testing and retesting younger people. (Berkowitz, 1965b) Fels Institute tested 72 women and 59 men with the Otis Mental Ability Test. Contrary to the study cited above, there was no significant change in the average level of IQ over a period of approximately 17 years. Even though the group average did not change, there were many individual changes in IQ scores both upward and downward. Further analysis indicated that women, when considering their personality types, changed in IQs very similar to children's IQ changes as to personality types. Women who were highly social and quite dependent were more likely to have a declining IQ (Birren, 1964b)

What happens when an intelligence test is given to the same people 25 years apart? The Stanford-Binet test was administered for the first time either in preschool periods or at the adolescent level. Twenty-five years later, both the original test and the Wechsler Adult Intelligence Scale were given. The males showed significantly more IQ gain from adolescence to adulthood than did the females. Both males and females increased in abstract reasoning and vocabulary and decreased in rote memory and practical reasoning. The correlations between preschool IQs and adult IQs were .59 for women and .64 for men. The correlations for adolescent IQs with adult IQs were considerably higher, being .85 for women and .80 for men. On the average, there was an increase of about eleven IQ points from adolescence to adulthood. Predicting adult scores showed some stability in comparing the differences between verbal and nonverbal items on the test. (Bradway, 1962) One study was done with 96 men who had taken a very early form of intelligence test, called the Army Alpha, in 1919. They took this test again when they were 50 years old, in 1950, and again in 1961 at age 61.

The results indicate, among many things, that most of the scores on the eight subtests did decline between the first and second time of testing but not significantly. Analysis of the data suggested that most of the subjects were near their peak of test-performance curve at the age of 50. "The period from ages 50 to 60 did not adversely affect the maintenance of mental abilities." A direct comparison between the 1919 and 1961 scores performance showed an increase on the verbal items, a constant on the reasoning items, and a significant decline on the numerical items on the test. (Kelley, 1965) (Owens, 1966)

Undoubtedly the mental ability psychometric device that has been used the most consistently to measure decline in intelligence is the 1955 Wechsler Adult Intelligence Scale (WAIS). The test author has proposed a "Hold"-"Don't Hold" value for some of the ten subtests. Adults appear to "Hold" up their ability on three tests: Vocabulary, Information, and Comprehension. They "Don't Hold" up in performance level on the Object Assembly, Digit Symbol, and Block Design subsections of the WAIS. Although all test scores on the WAIS decline with age, the Performance Section shows greater loss than the Verbal Section. (Wechsler, 1958) The WAIS has become a favorite instrument to measure adult loss of mental ability. The psychological literature during the late fifties and early sixties became crowded with such studies. Now we find some of the earlier work being challenged, which is healthy and in the tradition of psychological-research efforts. Bromley suggests a more meaningful classification would be "more resistant" and "less resistant" to change, primarily because "Vocabulary," "Information," and "Comprehension" reflect intellectual *attainment*, whereas "Object Assembly," "Digit Symbol," and "Block Design" represent intellectual *ability*. An additional function of speed is also required in the latter but not in the former. (Bromley, 1966)

Two other English psychologists, Savage and Britton, using as a basis Cattell's "fluid" and "crystalline" proposal, found a factorial structure on the WAIS of a general factor, a Verbal-Performance factor and a Picture-Completion specific. They also produced a "verbal" bias and a "performance" bias in factor-analyzing the data for 86 subjects of both sexes, all over the age of 80. The latter finding is not surprising, since the WAIS itself is structured on Verbal and Performance tests. It would be more startling not to get that bias. (Savage, 1968)

Finally, Birren a valuable contributor to the field, reviews the current status of the aspects of aging and intellectual functioning and finds that "at the present time, we know little about the distribution of deficit states in the population." (Birren, 1968b) The statement is a judicious one because it comes from a research specialist on aging and maturity whose work is well worth reading.

Two studies wrestled with the problem of the difference in loss of mental ability between very bright individuals and not-so-bright individuals. The results of these two studies seemed to be in conflict. One study, reported in 1959, compared test scores of shifts in IQ as measured in 1919 and again in 1950.

> Thus far, it has been a rather generally accepted view that age is kinder to those gifted few. The present results, on the other hand, suggest that this not the case, and that increments and decrements in test scores from age 20 to age 50 are roughly comparable at all levels of initial ability. [Owens, 1959]

The study was unable to give much evidence as to what relationship exists, however, after the age of 50. (Owens, 1959) The Terman study of the gifted in midlife finds contrary results to the study cited above. The Terman study seemed to indicate that mental ability or intelligence continues to increase at least through the age of 50. The data concerned 1103 adults, which included the original 768 children selected by Terman in 1927 as well as 335 of their spouses. After $3\frac{1}{2}$ decades, or 35 years, the author states, ". . . the records show that the gifted subjects in overwhelming numbers have fulfilled the promise of their youth in their later life achievements." There were some sex differences, but the results were not conclusive. (Terman, 1959) (Bayley, 1955)

The outstanding longitudinal study on mental growth is the work of Nancy Bayley and her co-workers. Beginning in 1933 she has studied the same subjects for a span of 36 years. Originally there were 74 subjects tested as babies. The latest report indicates 54 subjects were tested. Bayley makes no conclusions on her data. What follows is a very brief report of some of her findings.

1. ". . . females mental abilities stabilize at an earlier age, while the males exhibit greater stability later."
2. Early emotional experiences do make a difference in performance if the experiences occur at critical periods: Girls appear to be more resilient, while boys are more affected by early experiences.
3. Verbal scores are more stable than performance scores for both sexes.
4. Verbal scores were more efficient in prediction of personality variables and in mental ability.
5. The data after 36 years were very little different than after 18 years.   (Bayley, 1968)

Reaction time

Reaction times were measured for 480 women whose ages ranged from 6 to 84. Reaction times improved from childhood up to about the age of 19. Reaction times remained constant until the age of 26 and showed a slow decline after the age of 26 on through the age of 84. (Hodgkins, 1962) Another interesting study along the same lines as the one cited above had the subjects measured for "vigilance," which meant they spent 60 minutes watching a clock and being tested during that interval as to how quickly they could respond to starting and stopping times by the clock. Two groups of subjects were used. One group consisted of 53 individuals whose average age was about 43 and a second group of 53 individuals whose average age was about 71. The results indicated that the older subjects were just as vigilant as the younger subjects in the initial stages of "watch-keeping" but that after 45 minutes their ability or vigilance declined to a significantly lower level. It appears then that for at least three-fourths of the time the 71-year-olds were doing as well as the 43-year-olds, after which they seem to tire or lose interest in the task. (Surwillo, 1964a) Powell and Ferraro studied women school-teachers and their ability to respond to certain types of words. The criterion used was the reaction time in responding to certain words. The teachers' ages ranged from 20 to 59. Older-women schoolteachers took longer to respond to emotionally charged words such as *worry, afraid, unhappy, restless, anxious.* Reaction time had some relationship to personality variables. (Birren, 1964b) Four-second- and ten-second-paced verbal-learning tasks under experimental stress situations also revealed personality concommitants. (Troyer, 1967)

Finally, an unusual kind of test for measuring the effects of aging on motor tasks and motor speed was reported in 1966. Two tasks were involved: One employed the ability of subjects to stand erect and hold perfectly still (the amount of body sway was measured by a stabilo-meter); the second involved rapidly climbing a free-standing ladder. The 192 male and female subjects' ages ranged from 26 to 50 years. The evidence indicated no sex differences in the "rate" of learning "and that it may also be independent of age." (Bachman, 1966) Also, the "amount" of learning was not related to age.

The problem of reaction time in response to stimuli seems to be not in the "velocity of the peripheral nerve fibers" but that the "synapse may increase" in conduction time between the nerve fibers. (Bromley, 1966) Botwinick adds a very valuable note to the numerous studies on reaction time and the effects of aging. In studying the responses of athletes and nonathletes he finds the obvious result that older subjects were considerably slower than younger subjects; however, when comparing the older subjects' reaction time to younger subjects who were "non-athletes" "they *were not significantly slower.*" The contribution is a valuable one. Obviously, cross-sectional studies on reaction time should carefully examine the backgrounds of the subjects in the study. In this one study older people reacted as well as younger people when the younger subjects were identified as nonathletes. Thus, Botwinick wisely suggests that we must "evaluate individual differences" as well as "habits of exercise" in conducting research on the effects of reaction time and aging. (Botwinick, 1968b)

Memory

Subjects were used whose ages ranged from 25 to 75 years old. They were shown word lists on a screen at 4-second intervals. Involved in the study was the ability to "recognize" words first seen and then later seen and also the ability to "recall" words first seen and then seen a second time. The results suggested that the aged showed special defects in remembering recently acquired material. This was felt to be due to loss of ability to retrieve memories rather than an actual deficiency in the neural or storage system itself. (Schonfield, 1965, 1966b) On the other hand, two Canadian psychologists feel it is not the loss in the retrieval system but "that of a defect in the storage system itself." Thus one group of investigators feel the system (neural synapses, and so on) is at fault, while another group of investigators feel that the storage area (cerebral cortex, and so on) hinders the aging adult's ability to remember recent events. (McNulty, 1966) (Schonfield, 1966a)

Two British psychologists used 120 normal subjects with ages ranging from 11 through 70 years. This study consisted of reproducing digits. As we might expect, the ability to reproduce these digits in different circumstances was reduced as age continued. (Inglis, 1965b) What effect does age have in dialing performance on a telephone set? Thirty-six men whose ages ranged from 45 through 60 were used as subjects. The subjects heard the numbers they were to dial or they saw the numbers they were to dial. The results do not seem to indicate any difference in age brackets. The auditory method seemed to be better than the visual method. (Heron, 1962b) Subjects were asked to recall a list of words and then repeat them later on. This study indicated that subvocal rehearsal (saying words to oneself) and vocal enumeration (saying the words out loud) both "shrank" with age. (Talland, 1965) One study concerned itself with a repetitive task that was associated with sound. The interesting finding in this study was not so much the fact that younger subjects could do better than older subjects but that younger subjects were more inclined to take a gambler's chance on their responses, whereas older subjects were less concerned with immediate feedback and considered the response of the whole pattern. (Rabbitt, 1965b)

The psychological literature on both short-term and long-term memory is voluminous. Much of it concerns techniques on subjects of school age. The bulk of the studies seems to report that the older the adult becomes the poorer becomes the short-term memory. However, much of what has been done depends on what has been asked, by whom, and for what purpose. If it is true that short-term memory decreases with age, then in writing for older people sentences should be short, simple, and presented in ways easy to understand. This does not appear to be the case. Conversely, longer, complex, and obtruse sentences should be easier for young people to understand. Most high school teachers would maintain that this does not appear to be the case either. Once again individual differences may have to be considered in short-term laboratory research. (Isotti, 1966) They are not too frequent. Perhaps older subjects in laboratory experiment situations do poorly because they are more cautious. So, a recent study indicates, "short-term memory of trigrams was not a function of age." (Kriauciunas, 1968) The older the adult gets the poorer becomes his memory. (Costa, 1967) (Enesco, 1967) (Davis, 1966) (Friedman, 1966) (Hulicka, 1966) (Warburton, 1967) The same thing may be said, of course, of any old machine: the older the mechanism the greater the loss of efficiency.

One final note may be added on memory and forgetting as they affect the aging individual. We refer to two generalizations that are somewhat outmoded. The first is called Jackson's Law. It states the principle that when mental functions are impaired or lost through disease, the first to disappear are those that were the last to appear in the individual's development. In other words, the order of degeneration is the reverse of the order of ontogenesis. This tells us we may expect as the individual gets older, and specifically if disease is involved, that forgetting will take place first on current events, while the individual is still able to remember events that occurred as many as 30, 40, and 50 years ago. A second generalization, somewhat along the same lines, is called Jost's Law. This presents the generalization that whenever there are two associations or two memory stems that appear to have the same strength but are of unequal age (one was learned much before the other), we may expect two phenomena: that repetition will increase the strength of the older more than the younger memory stem and that the older of the two learned things will fall off less rapidly or be forgotten less rapidly in a given length of time.

Both Jackson's and Jost's generalizations fit somewhat in the pattern of Linden, who felt that late adulthood was not a second childhood but "childhood in reverse."

Problem-solving

One study reported in 1964 used 3 male groups whose ages were 20, 40, and 60. The problem was to work on a switchboard panel. "The results indicated nonsignificant age differences in level of performance." (Wetherick, 1964) While in a large study reported in 1963, 211 subjects whose ages ranged from 18 to 85 worked on a questionnaire and a complexity test. "The results do not support the hypothesis of a decrease in optimal level of complexity with advancing age." (Collins, 1964) An Australian psychologist studied children's and adults' ability to learn under two different training procedures. One method asked the subjects to anticipate events to be learned according to a fixed sequence of presentation of words. The second method measured the subjects' ability to learn dependent upon their previous responses to words. "Adults performed better under the former condition (words presented in fixed sequence), but children performed equally well under both." (Winefield, 1966) The ability of 30 young subjects and 23 old subjects to associate syllables was reported in 1966. Older subjects were less capable on this test, both in the ability to respond quickly as the test became more complex and in the variety of their responses. (Riegel, 1966) Still another study used 18 elderly and 18 young subjects whose job it was to generalize in a spatial-relation problem. The results are not entirely clear-cut, but there was evidence that "The data revealed that the elderly subjects make the necessary discrimination and exhibit more stimulus generalization than do younger subjects." (Canestrari, 1965) One study hoped to compare the abilities of young, middle-aged and old subjects on learning letter combinations by means of flash cards. There were 11 men in each of the samples, aged 20, 40, and over 60. The study seems to indicate that the older subjects had difficulty in flexibility in learning. They took less advantage of information that was of a negative nature and seemed to prefer information or reinforcement that told them they were doing the right things. They were much less willing to change their concepts that were adequate for them in the past. (Wetherick, 1965) In a report of 1963, utilizing teaching machines, it was found that linear-type teaching machines were much less effective for people 50 years and older, whereas 20-year-old subjects were able to utilize all types of teaching machines much better. (Farnsworth, 1965)

In many ways it is a moot point whether young adults solve problems better or worse than old adults. As contrived in a laboratory situation, old adults are not as efficient as young adults. Whether this applies to pragmatic everyday life situations, no one knows as yet. The evidence seems to indicate that young adults do not appear to solve the problems of everyday living any more efficiently than do much older adults. Equally pertinent may be the quality of mental ability. Age to the contrary, bright people appear to solve problems better than dull people. Data do not exist to tell us how well single individuals solve problems throughout their entire life span. Most studies are cross-sectional in nature (Appleton, 1967) (Riegel, 1967a), use infrahumans (Doty, 1966), or are oriented toward a specific technique. (Laurance,

1966) (Schwartz, 1967) (Zaretsky, 1968) The previous studies are a representative sample. Some of the effect of age on problem-solving is
"caused by motivation and attitude." (Bromley, 1966)

And so we come to the general conclusion the old dog can learn
new tricks but the answer is not a direct and simple one. It appears that
the old dog is reluctant to learn new tricks. He is less likely to gamble
on the results, particularly when he is not convinced that the new trick
is any better than the old tricks, which served him so well in the past.
He may not learn the new trick as rapidly as he did in the past, but
learn it he does. Further, the best evidence seems to indicate that if he
starts out as a clever young pup, he is very likely to end up as a wise
old hound.

AND BEHAVIOR

Will you come quietly?

Many authors feel that the physical changes that come in adult aging
will be much easier to adapt to than the psychological changes.
Contrary to this viewpoint, other authors feel that adulthood is no
different concerning emotional disturbances than any other age period.
One author believes that the neuroses do reach "a sharp peak around
35 years of age" while the deeper emotional difficulties such as psychoses increase steadily to the remaining years of life. It may be true
that if any individual lives long enough, he will eventually succumb
to senile psychosis.

Mental health

In general, most writers concerned with mental health feel that there is
not too much evidence that middle age, per se, shows an increase in
mental illness. (Kraines, 1966) Usually they feel when the breakdown
does come there is a "history of unresolved problems." (Hare, 1966)

In the writer's own experiences with clients, women whose attitudes are negative concerning childbirth and who bemoan their painful fate as child-bearing individuals very frequently appear to have
incipient involutional melancholic manifestations. As stated before in
the present book, we appear to build on the strengths of the past or
fall on their weaknesses. This is much in the general framework of
what Alfred Adler called "the life style." (Hurlock, 1959) (Spitzer,
1966) (Williams, 1966) On the other hand, prediction of emotional
disorders in adults has met with very little success. (Kane, 1967)
(Lowe, 1967)

If parents are addicted to grinding their teeth at night or talking
in their sleep, will this affect their children? One short study feels that

there is a better than even chance that the children will be similarly afflicted. It was suggested that this type of behavior may even be "influenced by genetic factors." Approximately 33 percent of the adults who were childhood teeth-grinders persisted in this in adult life. One out of every 4 sleep talkers retained the habit into adult life. (Abe, 1966)

One problem that is ubiquitous in all considerations of mental difficulties concerns itself with "the obscure agreement on definitions or terms" between psychiatrists themselves. The psychologist Wilma Donahue feels that there is no dichotomy in the psychopathologies between youth and old age. Other writers suggest at least four implications of diagnostic difficulties. The labels that are often used for psychotics come under four headings: (1) descriptive implications— "Give a short picture," (b) prognostic implications—"The likely course or outcome of the disease," (c) etiological implications—"The cause or precipitants," (d) therapeutic implications—"What may be done about the disorder." It depends, therefore, upon which of the above implications or labels one is using and how they may effect the differences between mental disease in youth and old age. (Williams, 1963a)

There appears to be evidence from hospitals in England and Sweden that adult schizophrenia (called at times "paraphrenia") is the result of social isolation rather than the reverse, that schizophrenia causes isolation. In short, the isolation comes before the mental disease. (Williams, 1963a) If this be true, then we may find older people being more isolated and thus more prone to the mental disorder of schizophrenia than are younger people who are more actively engaged in society, the point being that older individuals should not isolate themselves because this may increase their probabilities for mental difficulties.

Most therapists feel that relatively little work has been done by the psychoanalysts with middle-aged or older adults. Freud in one of his earlier papers, "On Psychotherapy" (1904), discussed the application of analytic techniques as a therapeutic measure. "Near and above the 50's, the elasticity of the mental processes on which the treatment depends is, as a rule, lacking. Old people are no longer educable, and on the other hand, the mass of material to be dealt with would prolong the duration of the treatment indefinitely." (Freud, 1959) On the other hand, Dr. Charlotte Buhler states, "It seems to me, personally, that neuroses in our time has often less to do with sex, inferiority or conscience problems which psychoanalysis has taught us to understand, than with problems of a lack of direction, lack of self-understanding, and lack of purpose for the own inner self." (Buhler, 1961) This is very much in keeping with the theories of Karen Horney, who also felt that the pansexualism of the psychoanalytic position was very much overdone. Horney emphasized the pressures of an industrialized society and the individual's inability to get along with his fellow man as primary causal factors in an emotional breakdown. (Bischof, 1964)

In interviews with 118 people the differences between age groups were in attitudes toward issues relatively outside of the personality. The few sex differences that did emerge between the men and women had to do primarily with specific role perceptions and with structuring of interpersonal relations. The aging process did not appear to affect mental health either favorably or unfavorably in the years between 40 and 65. (Peck, 1959) Middle-aged conflicts for lower- and middle-class men were based primarily upon family, relations with younger business associates, and attempts to prove sexual abilities by extramarital affairs. (Billig, 1957) A research project using 240 men whose ages ranged from 20 to 79 and 240 women of the same age range indicated that males were very similar in their emotional adjustment in the younger groups. As men grow older there is more dissimilarity in their ability to adjust emotionally. Women appeared to be similar to each other in emotional adjustment, both in the younger group and in the older group. (Wallin, 1963) One small study reported in 1965 used 40 neurotic female patients whose ages ranged from 16 to 65. In a second experiment using somewhat the same techniques, but using 30 neurotic and 30 nonneurotic normal females of the same age range, the results indicated that in both groups (normals and nonnormals) there was a distinct difference in the ability to respond as age increased. The older subjects were less able to perform the experiment, whether they were neurotic or not. (Davidson, 1965) Does being a former adult mental patient affect your ability to bear children? No, states one research report that studied the fertility of 164 female patients after they had been discharged from the hospital. Forty-two of the former patients were unmarried. The incidence of promiscuity was "negligible" in the latter group. (Bean, 1966)

Anger certainly runs the gamut for all types of humans. Two groups of researchers were curious about the incidence of anger as an individual grows older. One group felt that "temper outbursts were remindful of early years of childhood" and seemed to give some indications that a "low boiling point" was more of a "life style" than related to age changes. (Pikunas, 1961) A second group of researchers, using subjects aged 46 through 65 and subjects aged 66 through 86, asked, "Is it ever right to be angry?" The younger subjects frequently said yes, that it was all right to be angry, whereas the older subjects did not. Further analysis of the data found that the older subjects thought of themselves as being "furious" but not necessarily justified in being so. The younger subjects more often considered themselves as "rebellious" about their anger and that it was justified. (Friedman, 1963)

Daydreaming

When James Thurber created the wishful-thinking character of Walter Mitty and his "tapockatapockata" existence, the theme struck a highly responsive note for many adults. Others have felt, "The ability to fantasize is the ability to survive." Or, "Man must dream or die." Most theoretical positions considering the value of daydreaming are based on one or all of the following: compensation, entertainment during periods of boredom, reduction of anxiety, mood change, problem-resolving, or social withdrawal. As can be expected, introverts are better at fantasizing than extroverts. Other evidence indicates "only" children and nonachievers are more adept at creating images for daydreaming. The facility and ease of fantasizing apparently is the result of practice and begins with parent models via such things as story-telling and make-believe bedtime stories.

The phenomenon of daydreaming appears to be more associated with younger people than older people. There appears to be some evidence that as we grow older we daydream less and less. "The peak of daydreaming seems to be in mid-adolescence, and then it falls off gradually, although fantasy persists well into old age. In later years daydreaming takes on a retrospective quality for future possibilities are not only limited but rather frightening to the aged." If there appears not to be much future, daydreaming may be supplanted by sentimentality toward the past. It is true, of course, that sentimentality toward past events may, through the years, be coated over with more and more wishful thinking so that old memories become more distorted and more palatable. (Zybon, 1966)

Some authors feel that daydreaming is neither trivial nor pathological. It becomes a very important part of human ability and, in fact, needs to be practiced at length in order to be developed. One author feels that daydreaming is not to be confused with mind-wandering, which may be more appropriate to older people. The author feels that one should develop skill in daydreaming because it enhances and enriches life.

> The position that I have taken is that daydreaming is a neutral skill available for the active enrichment of the life of otherwise ordinary persons as well as being a manifestation in many persons of escape, evasion of responsibility, or self-dissatisfaction. Self-examination and skill in daydreaming are important assets for most humans, but they cannot compensate for restricted and drab life experiences. Nor can they take the place of extensive reading or commitment to some cause which involves meaningful experiences. [Singer, 1966]

There may be evidence that daydreaming for women is considered beneficial whereas men consider it to be a sign of weakness and "giving up." (May, 1968) (Singer, 1963)

Suicide

The psychological literature is beginning to emphasize the phenomenon of suicide. Many writers find it very difficult to define suicide from a medical viewpoint. Psychiatrists themselves disagree as to the description, the causes, and of what they like to call "deliberate accidents." Many times the statistics do not adequately represent true data. Primarily most suicides must fit a police classification system plus the fact that many families hide the circumstances of what actually was a true suicide. Thus we find suicide rates differing according to countries, sections, socioeconomic levels, and so forth. Some data from the World Health Organization indicate that there may be a higher incidence of suicide in women who are middle-aged and that this rate decreases as women grow into later years. One report indicates a high increase in suicidal rates as they were reported from 1861 to 1948 in England and Wales. In these two areas there was a great increase in suicide in women after the age of 55. Other data indicate that high economic levels appear to have a low percentage of suicidal rates, whereas the very poor individuals have a much higher percentage of suicide. Most statistics indicate that in times of stress, such as England's difficulties during World War II, there was a very large decrease in the incidence of suicide. It was also indicated that physical illness may not be as important a factor in suicide rates as social isolation as individuals grow older. (Williams, 1963b)

Almost all studies indicate that there is always a lower incidence of suicide by married people, especially when children are involved, whereas the highest incidence is in divorced adults, followed by single adults, and then widowed adults. "Suicide, at all ages, however, is found more frequently among men." (Bromley, 1966) Finally we find that the older people get the more they succeed in their attempts to commit suicide. Old people rarely publicize their attempts and their suicidal behavior. It appears that they go quietly about the business of taking their own life without too much publicity. Again we should like to emphasize, however, that the statistics on suicidal rates are very confusing and it is dangerous to make generalizations. (Williams, 1963b) (Shneidman, 1963, 1957)

Driving

As our world gets older and older, the percentage of people driving automobiles becomes higher and higher. (McFarland, 1964) We should like to examine this as much as the data permit from the viewpoint of aging. Driving an automobile is an essential fact of adult life often consuming many hours of time. Not many studies concern themselves with the effect of aging on driving efficiency and accident prevention. (Greenshields, 1967) In trying to uncover statistics and dynamics about this behavior, the writer finds that many times a single incident becomes enumerated so often that it soon becomes a generalization. The stereotype is that adult drivers are stodgy and "accident producing." They may not have an accident themselves but will create accident situations for others. Many states require citizens who wish to renew their driver's licence after the age of 65 to take a periodic examination.

Going back to a study done in 1938, in which the millions of miles driven per fatality was used as a criterion, the investigators found that ". . . safety of driving increases up to about the age of 50." This was true even though the physiological components of driving fitness (glare, vision, eye-hand coordination, and brake-reaction time) did show a decrease along with other sensory motor capacities. In spite of this, the authors felt that safe driving increased to the age of 50 and then appeared to decrease "very slowly." (Anderson, 1956) A study reported in 1960 found that drivers below the age of 24 years and over the age of 60 years had the worst accident records. Middle-aged adults were the safest drivers of all. The type of accidents for older drivers was much different than for younger drivers. Younger drivers were involved more in single accidents at high speeds than older drivers. The number of drivers over the age of 60 in 1960 had increased 100 percent in the last 20 years. (McFarland, 1964) In 1960 the safest drivers were between the ages of 40 and 60, regardless of whether they were men or women. Even though an individual had had a high accident rate prior to the age of 40, the rate declined dramatically for ages 40 to 60. (Birren, 1964a) Lauer, in a very large study reported in 1959, gave data that we should like to report rather thoroughly. This study was undertaken to answer two fundamental questions: Are reported accidents equally distributed among the population in regard to age, and are accidents distributed equally among licensed drivers when mileage was held constant? Lauer also considered what percentage of drivers was to be found in each age group. The study included approximately 15,000 drivers who lived in Iowa. The statistics were gained from the driver license files in that state. The files contained information on all accidents, violations, and revocations made since the driver license law became effective in Iowa in 1933. The investigators sent a post card to each person, requesting further information regarding the mileage they drove annually by day and by night. Other questions were asked about the way the person learned to drive, mileage on the car, age of car, model, ownership of car, and other related data. The data were analyzed for age groups, sex groups, and location within the state. The conclusions were that there was a preponderance of evidence that male drivers age 30 and under contributed most heavily to the accident total. Male drivers spent about 6 years from the time they first began to drive before there was any improvement noticeable in their reported accident records. Women, on the other hand, improved their record from the very beginning of their driving period, at least for the first 17 to 20 years. The women did differ from the men at various age levels with respect to the kind of accidents they had, which pertained to questions of judgment rather than of speed. One factor that did not relate to age at all appeared to be that the more densely populated areas had a higher incidence of accidents. The final conclusion is not a startling one. "One of the most serious problems is that of youthful male drivers." (Lauer, 1959) Most studies indicate that factors other than age are primarily responsible for auto accidents and poor driving records. (Nash, 1966) (Waller, 1966)

Crime

The Federal Bureau of Investigation study published in 1963 indicates sex crimes appear to be a young man's crime. In the types of stealing for men over the age of 40, the following criminal activities in ascending order were: burglary 1 percent, auto theft 3 percent, robbery 6 percent, larceny 11 percent, stolen property 14 percent, forgery and counterfeiting 19 percent, embezzlement and fraud 27 percent. The FBI statistics for individuals, all men over the age of 40, also indicate the following: narcotic arrests 10 percent, liquor law violations 21 percent, disorderly conduct 29 percent, vagrancy—driving while intoxicated—gambling 44 percent, and the highest incidence of arrests for males over age 40 was for drunkenness, which was at 66 percent. Most writers conclude that middle-aged individuals are by and large extremely law-abiding when compared to other or younger age groups. However, when they do break laws, the penalties are not as harsh as they are for younger individuals. Perhaps juries, being made up primarily of young to middle-aged adults, are more sympathetic to one of their kind than they would be toward a younger offender. Other traces of evidence seem to indicate that criminal activities for the middle-aged individual are subtle and less violent than criminal activities for individuals in their teens or in the bracket of 20 to 30.

Keller and Vedder bring the study of crime and its relationship to aging in much sharper focus by their excellent analysis of the 1964 *Uniform Crime Reports* (data from the Federal Bureau of Investigation and the United States Department of Justice). First it should be noted that there is a difference between being arrested and being committed to a penal institution. Thus some statistics reflect no difference in age levels, particularly "where alcohol is involved" in the number of arrests, while other statistics do indicate age differences when considering penal populations and types of major crimes. In generalizing it may be said that older people commit the quieter crimes (drunkenness and disorderly conduct not included) while young adults commit the more violent crimes, although unanimity of opinion on this by criminologists does not exist. The subject of age and crime is a complex one. At least two factors help to complicate interpreting the data: uniformity in reporting data does not always exist, and as history progresses different crimes are committed (horse thefts versus car thefts and depression-type crimes versus prosperity-type crimes). For students greatly interested in this area, the source cited is excellent and scholarly. (Keller, 1968)

Research
Suggestions

1. How do concepts of health differ with age? Do men see "health" differently than women?
2. How accurately do people judge their own health?
3. Do concepts of physical beauty change with age? How? Do men view physical beauty differently than women?
4. What is the relative importance of factors such as diet, occupational strain, socioeconomic status, recreational patterns on the development of heart disease?
5. To what extent are emotional factors involved in arthritis?
6. What is the relationship between problems in pregnancy and susceptibility to involutional melancholia?
7. Is there a reliable correlation between metabolic rate and aging?
8. If it is true that intelligence decreases with age, what causes this decrease?
9. What is the locus of recent memory loss with age?
10. Would longitudinal studies on average people confirm the intelligence decrement with age as obtained from cross-sectional studies?
11. To what extent can psychological studies of suicide be refined?
12. What is the importance of daydreaming in our lives? Is there a relationship between daydreaming and creativity? daydreaming and happiness? daydreaming and age?
13. Do we really need less sleep as we get older? What is the importance of sleep in our lives?

CHAPTER 9

The Next Steps

WHAT ARE OLDER PEOPLE LIKE?

In a sense all of Chapter 9 attempts to answer the question of what older people are like. As we shall see, perception may have a strong influence in answering the question. Much depends on whether you are young and studying adults older than 65 or whether you are past 65 and looking at people your own age. In the former case the age level often looks bleak. In the latter case life still appears to be fruitful but also frustrating—just like it has always been. The younger adult may ask, "Who would want to live to be 98 years old?" The older adult has one answer, "The person who is 97."

Walt Whitman poetically stated:

> Youth, large, lusty, loving—youth
> Full of grace, force, fascination.
> Do you know that old age may come
> After you with equal grace, force, fascination?
> *Youth, Day, Old Age, and Night* (1881)

Probably the only nonage-biased examination of aged populations comes from census data. (Davidson, 1967) But it must also be understood that the dynamics of aging are not found in a statistic.

Theories

As has been mentioned, a theoretical position on the processes of old age may depend on the theorist's age. "Ideally the investigation of the aging process should begin with the beginning of life." (Birren, 1964b) This tells us that old age is theoretically no different than any other stage of life. Human beings are continuously getting older and forever do so until death stops the process. (Platt, 1968) Thus, "an individual lives his life in a forward direction from its beginning." (Birren, 1964a)

Some investigators theorize old age comes at a time when the old adult is least fitted to meet new demands, be flexible and adaptive to situations never faced before in life. (Jones, 1961) Others consider the theory that old age consists of two factors: adaptation, which has neutral value (keeping alive), and adjustment, which has positive value (enjoying life in the same measure as earlier). (Anderson, 1956) Similar in nature is the postulation that theories of aging conflict. One theory assumes the aging individual is as goal-directed as he has always been while the other theory centers around the concept of "disengagement," which assumes the individual and society mutually seek to decrease the interaction between them. It must be recognized, however, that wanting to disengage may itself be a goal. (Birren, 1964b) (Neugarten, 1965b, a)

Peck and Buhler, utilizing Erikson's neo-Freudian psychoanalytic approach, consider it a valuable theory to a true understanding of aging. "Erikson's conception of the life cycle is a truly developmental one and he has been the first of the psychoanalytic theorists to carry us beyond the age of genital maturity." (Birren, 1964b) "Erikson's description of the healthy resolution of the last great developmental crisis (integrity vs. despair)—the fruit of the seven stages—is a magnificent concept. 'I know of no better word for it than integrity.' " Erikson is stating in the last of the seven life stages that the individual now must accept himself or despair. If he accepts himself in the last stages of his life for what he is, then he can truly (integrity) see his position in the entire cosmos: his life as one segment of history and his ability to put all the pieces together at the end of life. If he does not accept himself as he is, life then ends on a note of despair.

Peck suggests that the final stage of 40 years is too long, covering "More time than is covered by all his preceding six stages." He presents three dichotomized factors that may delineate the 40-year span into more meaningful dimensions of time. The first is Ego Differentiation Versus Work Role Preoccupation: Am I valuable as a human or valuable only because I can work? The second is Body Transcendence Versus Body Preoccupation: Can I accept my aging body for what it is and enjoy it, or will I become overly preoccupied with my state of health and sicknesses real or imagined? The third dichotomized factor is Ego Transcendence Versus Ego Preoccupation: "The task here is that of positive adaptation to the certain prospects of personal debt—'the night of the ego'—success may be measured 'both in terms of the individual's inner state of contentment or stress and his constructive or stress inducing impact on those around him.' " (Birren, 1964b)

The Developmental Tasks (Havighurst, et al.) add another theoretical dimension to the concept of aging in the final years of life. The last stage he calls "Later Maturity." The tasks are as follows: (1) adjust to decreasing physical strength and health, (2) adjust to retirement and reduced income, (3) adjust to death of spouse, (4) establish affiliation with one's age group, (5) meet social and civic obligations, (6) establish satisfactory living arrangements. (Havighurst, 1953a)

Developmental psychologists continue to pursue a theoretical basis to explain the process of aging in the human and other species. The theories range from biological (that of gene mutations is currently in vogue) to sociological to psychological to combination theories. All appear to be worth pursuing at this stage of research on aging. No one theory has overwhelmed the others. However, practically all theories about aging invariably focus on the aged person and not on aging as a lifetime process. (Busse, 1967) (Pincus, 1967) (Verwoerdt, 1967) At this point the most eclectic and complete work on theories of aging is the work of Kastenbaum, a very valuable contribution to the field. (Kastenbaum, 1965b)

Research methods and bias

Professionally the study of old age is divided into two categories: geriatrics, the science and art of medically treating the old, and gerontology, the psychological and sociological study of old age processes and problems. Instrumentation for geriatric studies is essentially all that of the biologist, physiologist, and medical practitioner. Tools and techniques employed in researching old age by the gerontologist may include some of the former but primarily the major devices are the interview, questionnaires, surveys, and all the armamentarium of the researcher. (Gergen, 1966) (Havighurst, 1966b) (Kutner, 1956) (Postema, 1967) (Hamlin, 1966)

The crucial factor in studying old age is not what is used but by whom and with what biases. "One difficulty in providing information, if not answers to our questions, is that, 'Actually, results obtained under laboratory situations . . . cannot be translated directly into terms related to daily behavior.' " (Birren, 1964a) Havighurst notes there are at least three propositions that should guide research on human gerontology: The social environment must be considered as a determinant in the aging of the individual; the biological and psychological functioning are essential to understanding old age; and also important to consider is how the older adult feels about society as much as what society demands of him. (Havighurst, 1965a) One author, Blenkner, feels that the psychoanalysts have made it difficult to create theories and test them. Two factors emerge: the neo-Freudian emphasis on early-life influences with little interest or data concerning the eventual adult behavior of the child, and the strong viewpoint that life is something to be defended against rather than something to be mastered. Ego-defense mechanisms supplant ego mastery. ". . . the overwhelming emphasis on defense may have a good deal to do with the fact that most social workers shun work with the aging." Too much work on the aged is on psychopathology. Very few old people are studied as normal relatively healthy people. (Birren, 1964b) On the other hand, "It should be noted that current studies all point toward the health, not the pathology of the aged. None uphold the prevailing stereotype." The prevailing stereotype is usually that of the old being very infirm and weak. Attitudes of social workers, physicians, and nurses emphasize difficulties in the aged. (Munch-Petersen, 1966) Attitudes of research-oriented social scientists may conflict with the stereotype.

> In thinking of the aged, it is perhaps too easy to slip into thinking of them as all being in extreme condition. Actually, only two per cent of the group 65 and over are bed-ridden. Less than 10 per cent are in institutions. Relatively few ever become senile. Many older people reach the end of life without ever having been physically or mentally infirm. [Reichard, 1962]

It is refreshing to note that there is a growing emphasis on the training of personnel specifically in the field of social gerontology. (Kushner, 1967)

And, finally, two delightful retirees, Alice and Sidney Pressey, former Ohio State University professors, 79 and 77 years of age in 1967, illustrate that the most qualified experts on old age may be, indeed, old people themselves! As we have seen, data coming from "oldsters" can be interpreted by "youngsters" in a negative sense.

> . . . both teaching and research dealing with aging should occasionally be an "inside job." Medicare and other services for the old should give able elderly people certain opportunities for usefulness for which their own age should give special understanding . . . *almost all the huge literature on that subject* (old age and its problems) *is by people who have never been there.* [Italics added] [Pressey, 1966b]

Physical attributes

It would be meaningless to dispute the fact that in old age the body and its tissues have lost much of their functional efficiency. (Henley, 1967) (Nodine, 1967) (No one claims a 50-year-old automobile operates as powerfully as a new automobile, even though the ancient car may have much charm, usefulness, and comfortable familiar habits.) Old machinery does not operate as well as new machinery. Great expensive research efforts are not needed to reveal this fact. What is needed are the knowledge and patience to keep the old machine in good repair for maximum usefulness. This is the province of both the geriatrician for physical know-how and the gerontologist for psychological acceptance of a fact. It may help if the oldster knows what to expect and thus prepare intelligently for decreasing physical efficiency.

The vast literature on physical conditions in the aged is the province of geriatrics, and the reader is directed to those sources for information. (See Preface.) The emphasis here is on the psychology of old age. "Sensory changes begin to be particularly striking after the age of 70." (Birren, 1964a) It would seem that 70 is a kind of watershed for sensory processes: hearing, tasting, feeling, smelling, and seeing. Always there is the individual's unique adaptation level. ("Grandpa never wore glasses and had all his teeth when he died at 98 years of age.") But some behaviors may persist through time. "The impromptu speaking and oral reading rate were found to be rather high, about 137 words per minute, in subjects over the age of 65." (Mysak, 1958) And "after many years the speed of writing may become relatively fixed for an individual in that he will rarely write much faster or slower than his characteristic speed." (Botwinick, 1959b) In a sense, getting old physically does not seem to threaten the old adult. It is the probability and the possibility of extended illness that are the greatest single threat to their peace of mind. "Most people in the older age group have worked out some way of life, and even those with very small incomes make the best of their negligible resources: but the threat of illness remains." (Birren, 1964b) A synonym for medicare may be peace of mind rather than physical treatment for the aged. (Srour, 1966)

Two physicians make the unique suggestion of a possible "third sex." "The fundamental concept upon which our entire investigative effort has been based is the conviction that there is a third sex existent in our society today. This so-called 'neutral gender' may be considered to encompass roughly all persons who have reached an average age of 60." (Vedder, 1965) (Masters, 1955)

Selye feels that in old age (beyond 70) there is a deficit in the "adaptation energy." Death does not come because the body organs wear out but because these organs have lost their ability to adapt to stress. This seems to be the price human beings pay for the evolution from a single cell into a highly complex interrelated cellular organism. "Unicellular animals never die because they divide and their parts live on." (Wolff, 1959)

Attitudes and adjustments

In the beginning of the chapter the premise was made that research conclusions on old age may depend very much on the age of the researcher. This is specifically involved in measuring attitudes of the aged and in determining their ability to adjust to the problems of that age level. Beyond ability we also find advice on "how to" grow old gracefully, which advice varies from the grandiloquent to the dismal advice —it can't be done. (Bromley, 1966)

> Thus, basic personalities significantly determine the individual's style of adjustment to aging. Those who grow old gracefully do so in different ways. Some find happiness in remaining active, others like to take it easy. There is no single formula for successful aging; each individual must find the formula that best fits his needs. [Tibbitts, 1962]

Most of the advice on how to adjust to old age and grow old gracefully follows the general precepts of mental hygiene for all age levels. The following list highlights most of the pertinent advice for old-age adjustment.

1.

> Your retirement will be most satisfying . . . if you will stop fretting about having a lot of friends after age 65. So, maybe you retired people who are depressed and rattling around because you don't have many friends and who are embarrassed because you think you aren't popular any more, should get the monkey off your back. Most retired people, particularly the most sophisticated ones, have given up on "friends." [Collins, 1965]

2. "The older person adapts to his slowness of response by avoiding situations with unusual time pressures." (Birren, 1964a)
3. "It is not so much the person's way of adapting to his life

situation which is important, but rather his retaining the offensive in his approach to life, so as to maintain activity and expansion." (Singer, 1966)

4. "The way a man grows old depends to a degree on his personality—on what his psychological drives are and his ability to satisfy them in old age." (Reichard, 1962)

5. "Old age is a possibility and a probability, the need remains to use what there is with a sense of mastery." (Birren, 1964b)

6. From Germany, the advice is to restore the capacity to work and to keep on working so that one may enjoy life to its very end. (Scheidler, 1965)

7. From England, the advice on the way to retire gracefully and be happy in it is to keep on working at some other job, providing the salary is not too small. (Welford, 1966)

8. Assess your life's goals and if you have not completed them, work to catch up with the things you did not do in your younger age. (Birren, 1964b)

9. However, contemplation and religious meditation are also of high value in old age even though "the aged and retired rarely wish to lead a life of contemplation." Action ranks too highly in our culture system, whereas passivity is not appreciated. Our action-packed "let's do something" society forces old people to continue in the mold. Retirement should be a time for thinking and contemplating about the verities of life. (Buhler, 1961)

10. Old age and inevitable death may be easier to accept if the individual strives to leave behind a lasting memorial and remembrance of his time on this earth: a trust fund, cemetery monument, endowment for college scholarships, memorial fund, and so on.

11. The way to grow old gracefully is to be the "successful isolate." (Birren, 1964a)

12. "The secret of retaining youth and happiness after middle life is to occupy the mind." (Ogilvie, 1962)

13. Daydreaming and fantasy are suggested for living through the last years, although research does indicate "greater poverty of imagination and the projective story telling of this group." "The aged person who never developed a taste for inner living may now, with help, be more ready for this experience," and thus achieve tranquility, more "than he might have in his middle years." (Birren, 1964b)

14. Prevent unhappiness in old age before it begins. (James, 1967)

15. Alter the social organization so the aged can become useful to society. (Butler, 1967a)

16. "Congregate living" in tax-built apartments in conjunction

with a highly selected population was successful in Sa
Antonio. (Carp, 1966)

17. Do not "infantalize" the aged but help them to become com
munity oriented and to strengthen their self-respect. (Forma
1967)

18. Anxiety was reduced in a VA Hospital with as little as on
activity hour per week. (Kaiman, 1966)

19. One hundred middle-class men and women aged 60 to 6
indicated in a longitudinal study that men were "more posi
tively oriented" toward the future but women were no
Health, socioeconomic status, physical activity, and intelli
gence seemed to be some of the ingredients for thinkin
positively. (Lehr, 1967)

20. "The older person must learn how recreation can becom
re-creation" by developing new capacities for creativeness
(Fromm, 1966)

Finally, reference is made to two studies involving the use of re
port wine given to elderly patients in a geriatric hospital: "Wine an
fellowship in aging: an exploratory program." It was felt that th
"intaking" of wine induced a sufficiently pleasurable reaction amon
the patients and toward the staff that further research in this type o
liquid therapy might deserve more study. (Kastenbaum, 1965b)

Old age with or without advice on how to be happy is considere
to have some assets. Again it may depend crucially upon the age of th
eye of the beholder. (Hickey, 1968) Old age may be a time when th
person does not get excited and hyperemotional at times of catastro
phies or extreme stress. He may have lived through many similar crise
and emerged unharmed. Old people may be tranquil and lack th
hyperemotionality of the young. The old have just so much emotiona
energy to invest and do not waste it on nonessentials. (Farnsworth
1965) "Results showed that some of the older men appeared to be mor
satisfied with their earlier lives than were the younger men." The
were more "benign in their view of early family life than were th
younger men." (Birren, 1964a) (Reichard, 1962) (Tibbitts, 1962) Fo
those who have worked extremely hard and now are very wealthy, ol
age may have many benefits; the fruits of labor, the time to travel an
indulge oneself, the final payoff for a life of sacrifice and labor.

Most authorities, however, judge old age to be an unhappy period
But not all. Thirty-six men, all considered to be social science expert
on the aging process beyond age 70, were interviewed in regard to thei
fields of expertise. Their opinions differed widely concerning what th
aging process was like. They had strong stereotyped opinions on th
state of being aged; old age was an emotionally charged period of lif
and not a particularly happy state of existence. (Arnhoff, 1960) Middle

aged adults' attitudes toward growing old were studied in a large metropolitan area (625 men and women in the age range 40–70). Evidence indicated that fear of aging was consistent for all respondents. Major worry was based on becoming dependent upon others either through loss of income, loss of health, or both. (Neugarten, 1959)

A group of 92 subjects (ages 70–84) ranked age periods in regard to their estimation of time passing quickly or slowly. Fifty percent selected age 60 and over as a period when time passed most quickly. Forty percent felt time passed most slowly in the after-60 period. Ten percent selected an earlier period. The essential finding was associated with their feelings of being active or inactive as a judgment of time passage. (Tuckman, 1965a) Other studies on time estimation show that children and very old subjects "did poorly in estimating time in 16 minute and one minute intervals." (LeBlanc, 1966) Time in a non-laboratory sense but within the context of time in the future calls for the ability to use "partners" along with integrating life in the future. Adults who can integrate past and future appear to be better adjusted. (Kastenbaum, 1966b) The perception of "filled" and "vacant" time as a function of age shows that being occupied reduces the estimate of time lapsed, but older subjects (average age 78) perceived time not much differently than younger subjects (average age 22). (McNanamy, 1968)

In a review of many studies about aging published in 1965 the reviewer found "a change in the definition of loneliness was noted. For older people it was absence of activity rather than absence of people." (Farnsworth, 1965) One investigator found that when people become old and are institutionalized, men tend to perceive this as physical isolation, women as social isolation. (Williams, 1963a) Another summary of studies states, "Evidence presented thus far indicates rather clearly that, as people get older, they are less happy, have more negative concepts, and have experienced a loss of self confidence." (Birren, 1964b) "A good deal is left unexplained in the processes affecting the adjustment of the aged." However, the older the individual felt and the more negatively he reacted toward old age, the more these feelings affected his adjustment to situations. If you feel old you will be unhappy. If you feel young you will adjust much better to old age. (Phillips, 1961) Twenty-three old men were compared with a matched group of 23 old women on dimensions of superego strength. There appeared to be "increased homosexuality in old men" but not in old women after being observed for one year. (Hader, 1966) And finally, on the negative side of old age:

> The sadness of old age, real old age, is that all our life is behind us, really behind. Skills have gone. Interests have gone. Friends have gone. We are no longer important. We cannot lead again or command. We can get

respect if we deserve it, and love if we have earned it, but not admira tion. We are alone except for those equally old, and they, like us, ar more interested in themselves than us. Happiness and serenity are al that we need, and they are obtainable if we live for others. *The only ur forgivable vice of old age is to be a bore.* [Italics added] [Ogilvie, 1962

The types of adjustment to old age have received some emphasis The Kansas City study of adult life identified four personality types o adjustment: integrated, armored or defendant, passive-dependent, an unintegrated. (Birren, 1964b) (Neugarten, 1965b, a) Buhler identifie four types of adjustment patterns to old age as follows: those who ar content to rest and relax after completing life's work, those who striv to the very end of life because "life's work is never done," those wh are resigned unhappily to old age but wished they had the strength t keep going, and "those who led thoughtless and meaningless lives anc who are now not only frustrated, but bothered by guilt and regret." (Birren, 1964b)

What may we expect from marriages, usually remarriages, in late years of life? "Remarriages in later maturity are often stable and har monious. The decrease in the psychological component of aggressior that is concomitant with aging, very frequently makes sex life after 65 both ardent and concordant." Marriages and remarriages after the age of 65 very frequently are happy unions. (English, 1963)

One of the earlier talented researchers, Cavan, found there were unique adjustment problems for older women in our current society more so than in the past. Women today are released much earlier from mothering care, which produces child-free homes for a much longer period. The woman in today's society must make adjustments to chil dren's maturity, to widowhood, to possible employment problems, and, because she lives longer, a certain amount of physical disability not heretofore known. Thus the longer the woman lives the more adjust ments she must make. (Cavan, 1952)

One author maintains that after age 65 people become a quasi- minority group, which creates adjustment problems. Involved are stereotypes created by those younger and discrimination in positions and power in society. Just like all minority groups the over-65 individ uals will create their own defensive reactions toward society. Also similar to other minority groups, aged people create their own stereo types about themselves. (Tibbitts, 1962)

Longevity

Very, very old people give as many answers as to why they lived to 98 as there are people asked. The answers run the gamut from humorous to hearty. Everything from heavy indulgence in liquor, labor, or love to the avoidance of these factors is given as reasons for having obtained longevity in life. Actually scientists do not know precisely why some live to be very old whereas others perish much younger barring, of course, accidents and traumatic events. (Karp, 1967) One position is, "Early social class and his social mobility influence not only his behavior as he grows older, but also his length of life." (Birren, 1964a) Some people live longer than others because they live safer lives. Most researchers feel that longevity is directly attributed to heredity: having ancestors who have continuously managed to live a long time enhances one's own chances for longevity. (Selye, 1956) Such data come from studies of longevity tables of family geneologies. An experiment of inbreeding stocks of long-lived mice produced unusually long-lived and vigorous offspring. These were called "super-mice." (Birren, 1964b) Bromley feels there is small chance of longevity increasing much but the real effects should be expended in making old age more enjoyable rather than longer. (Bromley, 1966) Probably there is another pertinent answer to the child's question, "Grandpa, how did you get to be so old?" The answer is, "I didn't die."

IS OLD AGE AN AMERICAN PROBLEM?

One forthright answer is that old age may always be a problem. Equally pertinent is, whose problem is it: the aged's, their children's, society's and so forth? The basic premise of the question, however, revolves around the concept that citizens of this country live longer than do citizens of other countries. It is true that tables of longevity indicate Americans are longer lived than natives of many other countries. As one might expect not all nations keep accurate statistics on longevity. Comparisons made on average age at death do not reveal the problems of aging any more than the average age of an automobile at a trade-in reveals the problems the motorist may have had with his car. The initial interest in the question arises from the premise that in backward undeveloped nations an individual may be "old" at age 40 and lucky to be alive after age 50. The vicissitudes of life under conditions of poverty reduce the chances of long life. The assumption is that Americans increase their chances for living longer because of better medical care and may be financially more capable of supporting life after retirement from an occupation. As an average this is true but fails to reveal other important dynamics: there are underprivileged adults also in the United States; a "used up" body whether through hard living or through old age is still a problem to contend with, and not all the aged people in the world live in this country. The chances of living to a ripe old age are better in this nation than most other

nations but the problems of old age may be no more unique f
American adults than any other nation's adults.

There seems to be evidence that the aged in the world in whatev
nation they reside must still cope with at least five adjustment area
death of spouse, loss or reduction of employment income, physical i
firmities, affiliation with older people, and maintenance of some stan
ard of food intake and satisfactory living arrangements. Beyond the
basic needs are two methods of approaching patterns of behavior in o
age. Most American aged adults tend toward the "stay young/kee
active" mode while Europeans and Asians may tend toward the "roc
ing chair" approach to aging. These are generalizations based on th
American youth-oriented charisma and the over-all economic status
this country. Exceptions always exist in generalizations. (Havighurs
1949)

In Germany the loss of status has been deeply felt by older peop
since the cataclysms of World War II. The prior authoritarian patr
archal type of family has diminished. Losing the war, housing shor
ages, and the general tenor of the times have re-created the "father
all" image. The general impression of gerontological problems wit
the aged in Switzerland is usually approached with the negative thoug
of what to do with old people before they die. Studies there indica
that as people become older they move from extroversion to intr
version. Again from Switzerland, "The more diversified the previo
interests the more nearly intact the personality remains." French med
cal men feel, "one grows old as one has lived." Studies of aged Chine
adults in Hong Kong indicate there is a rapid change in the concep
of reverence for older people. Asiatics, too, appear to be becoming
youth-oriented culture. Old oriental women have a much more dif
cult time than do old oriental men. (Tibbitts, 1962) (William
1963a, b)

Returning to the question, "Is old age an American problem?
there is no direct answer. Although the United States may have pr
portionately more octogenarians and nonagenarians than other n
tions, old age is what the aged make of it throughout the world.

WHAT RIGHTS AND PRIVILEGES
DO OLD PEOPLE HAVE?

As a group the aged may have no greater rights and privileges than an
other age group. The deciding factor may well hinge on the age of th
individual answering the question. If the adolescent boasts that he doe
not trust anyone over the age of 20 or 21 or 22, depending upon h
nearness to that divisive age, the 80-year-old may respond in kind, "
don't trust anyone who hasn't lived long enough to know what life

like." To the adolescent the world's troubles are due to adult misman-
agement. To the old people the world's troubles are due to the inability of the young to learn from their wisdom and experience. This may
be a right and privilege that old people have.

The articulate Presseys forcefully express the viewpoint that gerontology should concern itself also with the assets of the "oldsters." Old
people have a modicum of social intelligence that they have had to
learn through the years. Old people may have that precious commodity
called character. Many people in their world are benefitting from the
inventions, discoveries, paved streets, school construction, parks, homes,
and so on, that old people leave as a legacy to the world at large. It may
not be possible to count all the individuals who are "riding on the
backs" of their predecessors still alive but too old to participate. Old
people once clothed, fed, sheltered, supported, suffered, for those
younger than they. Sidney and Alice Pressey suggest that achievement
should earn a few accolades. This may be a right and privilege of old
people. But, gratitude is not a forte of the young. (Pressey, 1966a, b,
1967)

It may be that old people may not be given any rights and privileges for being old but they may through sheer numbers demand these
as their due. A 20-year-old man in 1900 could anticipate on the average 2.0 years of retirement before he died. A 20-year-old man in 1955
could anticipate at least 6 years of retirement. In 1900 less than 2 of
every 5 men would reach the age of 65. Currently 3 out of 5 reach age
65. The prospect is, through preventive medical care, that at least 4
out of 5 can be expected to reach age 65. The number of old people is
increasing. Perhaps their power is increasing proportionately. Social
Security, Medicare, income tax reductions after age 65, construction of
decent retirement homes, all of these and more attest to the emerging
power for rights and privileges for the aged. (Buhler, 1961)

Perhaps it is a right for the not-so-old to expect a better old age
than was previously possible. One very intensive study conducted by
22 scientists upon 47 men (ages 65–92) found the men to differ very
little medically from a group of men average age of 21. The older men
were found to be mentally flexible, alert, vigorous, interesting, and
"deeply involved in everyday living." These older men were found to
be significantly superior to the younger men in verbal intelligence. The
one factor that seemed outstanding from this study indicated that the
elderly are remarkably young if they retain their health with advancing
age. "It is predicted that with the promise of control of diseases of old
age, more individuals will be old in years, but functionally young by
present standards." (Birren, 1963)

The old have more free time, may even carry out new careers not
possible before, play the role of sage, give advice welcome or not, and

especially gain some degree of freedom from the mores of society tha
so highly mandate behavior, dress, speech, and all of the enforced code
of structured living. "Leave him alone. He's old enough to do what h
wants. He has earned the right to act foolish." And, finally, life's goal
and life's problems may seem more meaningful at the end of life. Thu
hindsight is a right and privilege. (Williams, 1963b)

Perhaps the list may increase as society continues to have an ir
crease in the number of senior citizens.

1. "Our honorary appointment as advisor-in-chief of lifemanship.
   (Ogilvie, 1962)
2. "It must be recognized that persons who survive into old ag
   may be psychologically stronger than those who do not.
   (Birren, 1964b)
3. The older individual has rights and privileges as a trustee, no
   over social values particularly, but specifically over cultura
   values. Old people give a true sense of tradition to society.
4. At the back end of life it is an obligation to forgive and forge
   earlier errors. Mellowness may be rendered unto old memories
5. "To teach the rest of us how to die and thereby give us a
   philosophy by which to live." This is a true right and privilege
   (Birren, 1964b)

WHAT ARE THE PLEASURES
AND PROBLEMS OF RETIREMENT?

Much has been written about retirement but very little of the materia
comes from retired people themselves. Again we have someone telling
how they think it is rather than the involved individual telling what
retirement actually is like.

Unpublished research data of this writer going back through the
mid-1940s indicate certain occupations retire much easier than others.
Ease in retirement was ascertained through interviews and modified
TAT procedures.[1] Criteria were based on satisfaction with past occupation, satisfaction with present status, and outlook for the future.
Teachers (elementary, high school, and college) and ministers seemed
to be the best adjusted and happiest about their retirement status.
Lawyers and medical doctors also appeared to accept retirement gracefully; however, as in the case of teachers and ministers, semiretirement
was often involved: the men continued to teach, preach, or practice
part time. The average age of the respondents was 72. The number of

[1] The subjects were asked to respond to photographs of retired persons shown in
advertisements. Stress level was measured in three ways: desire to travel, feelings of
financial security, depth of status feeling toward retirees, and the normal TAT
protocol evaluation—hero, thema, needs, press, prognosis.

subjects was 207 in all of the studies. Executives in industry, administrators of public or private enterprises, appeared to be less well adjusted
to retirement. The higher the level of authority and power to manipulate others the lower the factor of adjustment. High-salaried executives
gave evidence of being lost without their authority. At the opposite
end of the economic scale very low-salaried manual workers also had a
difficult time in retirement primarily for three reasons: very small
pensions; aching bodies, which had had to sustain hard labor for years;
and disinterest or inability to use mental pastimes (reading, nonphysi-
cal hobbies, and so on) to while away the hours. Televised afternoon
baseball games seemed to be a major activity.

For many men "retirement seems like the removal of the most
steadying thing of all, his destination." After retirement it is essential
that a retiree create a destination, a place to be occupied, an avenue to
use energy. (Wolff, 1959) Many studies indicate workers, particularly
low-skilled workers, are embittered and resentful of retirement. Nevertheless, "Once retirement has actually occurred there is a tendency for
anxiety to subside and for the individual to work out a mode of adjustment to his altered way of life." (Reichard, 1962) Reviews of many
studies on conditions in retirement indicate they group as follows: (1)
timing, (2) financial support, (3) discovering and adjusting to new roles
never played before, (4) maintaining old social contacts and making
new ones, (5) concern and maintenance of health, (6) living arrangements that do not demand extra effort to maintain and are within
reduced income, (7) nature of skills carried over from previous occupations to support future part-time employment, (8) family acceptance of
an inactive head, (9) marital-role adjustments, (10) reduction in standard of living, and (11) the concern and welfare orientation programs of
the former employer for their retired workers. (Tibbitts, 1954) (Kleemeier, 1961) (Kreps, 1968) (Vasey, 1968) (Ballweg, 1967)

Reichard and her co-workers suggest that retirees may be cate-
gorized into at least five types: the mature individual (constructive
approach in preretirement), the rocking-chair individual (passive attitude and leaned on others in the past), the armored individual (shelters
self or avoids any stress situation), the "angry men" (hostile, project
own weaknesses onto others, world's fault that they are aging) and, the
"self-haters" (have failed to achieve anything of true value now that
"life is over"). The first three types were considered to be successful in
retirement. The angry men and self-haters were not. (Reichard, 1962)

One study concluded that successful business and professional retired men had more satisfying hobbies than those with nonsuccessful
business careers. The explanation may be that successful workers have
more talent and ability and can carry this asset into the retired years.
(Vincent, 1961)

Factors in adjusting to retirement

Some employees would rather "die with their boots on" while others limp through the very last years of preretirement employment fervently wishing for the day when they may finally "put the boots away, punch the time clock for the last time, tell the boss to do it himself, and go fishing." Regardless of which end of the continuum the worker places himself, compulsory retirement for all but the self-employed is a fact. The question is what to do about it. Factors that indicate good adjustment or poor adjustment are summarized in the following list.

1. Adjustment to old age and retirement depends greatly on how one has adjusted to life in the past. If problem-solving has been overwhelming in childhood, adolescence, marriage, accepting decreasing physical vigor, retirement too will be difficult to solve. Those who have been able to meet most of life's problems with a degree of equanimity and courage will probably do the same after retirement. Thus we build on the strengths of the past or collapse on the weaknesses of the past. A familiar theme.

2. Those who were flexible to changes will no doubt retain their flexibility.

3. Historical data tell us very old age and retirement were not factors 100 years ago. Perhaps now the increase in number of retirees may help to create more agencies, more research, more techniques, more facilities to aid the adjustment of the retired. (Buhler, 1961)

4. In reference to the above, increased federal, state, and local aid may make retirement less dependent upon the accumulated wealth of the past or particularly upon the financial status of one's children.

5. Employers as a group are becoming increasingly involved and interested in the preparation for retirement and in the state of being retired for their employees present and past.

6. The pre-age 65 retired worker is becoming more and more acceptable in society.

7. Financial schemes such as deferred payment plans and variable annuity programs have helped greatly in alleviating the cost-of-living rises on fixed retirement incomes. In addition the gradual increases in Social Security benefits are factors in adjustment to retirement. Inflation is now a factor in the fiduciary systems for pension planning.

8. In contrast to the financial problems, most authorities feel that a "mental set" or "psychological preparedness" is equally or more important than financial security. Our society rarely

permits the aged to starve to death if society and its welfare agencies become aware of the problem. Perhaps there is an overemphasis on the amount of pension and not enough on the amount of psychological strength after retirement. Yet, most old people would prefer to be wealthy in retirement rather than destitute. Money may not buy happiness but it does alleviate suffering.

9. Most measured social attitudes toward the aging process beyond 65 are negative but there is some evidence to the contrary. Acceptance of mandatory preparation for retirement in middle age is growing. The prior conception to slow down or retire as an indication of loss of manliness has alleviated. Brains seem to have higher status than brawn as the world of work moves from the farm and factory toward clerks and computors. (Rose, 1966)

10. Longer vacations (4 months even for seniority in labor forces), higher mobility (Europe is no longer the exclusive province of the very wealthy), hobbies with greater finances and freedom to enjoy them (gardens, boating, power tools), and the ability to pay for better medical care are factors related to past retirement adjustments.

Thus the pleasures and problems of retirement in our emerging society may find the former increasing and the latter decreasing. At least we can hope.

WHAT DO OLDER ADULTS THINK ABOUT DEATH?

The subject of death is not a popular one but still a fact of human existence or, better stated, end of existence. Death can and does occur at any age level. For the individual who was fortunate enough to live a long time, death happens late in life. Without being maudlin, perhaps dying at an old age would be for the lucky ones. It is conceivable that those families who lose a teen-aged son or daughter might feel so. The relevant issue for the purposes of this chapter is how do aged adults think about approaching death, if they do, and when they do. Religious systems, philosophers, novelists, poets, playwrights, everyone at some time or other, grapples with a concept of death and what might happen afterward. For the child, the adolescent, the young and middle-aged adult it is not usually a vital thought. For the very old it is more a question of when or how far from now. Only recently, however, have social scientists begun to conduct surveys and research in this area. (Kastenbaum, 1966a)

Fromm, for example, feels that man is the only living thing that knows it is going to die. "Man is the only animal who finds his own existence a problem which he has to solve and from which he cannot escape. In the same sense man is the only animal who knows he must die." (*The Sane Society*, pp. 23–24) Man creates all kinds of theories and systems to explain why he must die, where he might go after he dies, and, while alive, what will things be like back on Earth because he lived.

How the human being approaches imminent death is, as we might assume, a very sensitive area for investigation. As late as 1963 the topic of death appeared in a book titled, *Taboo Topics.* (Farberow, 1963) How man feels about time has been researched but as time for staying alive runs out for the individual we know very little. (Kleemeier, 1961) Some feel that society has avoided and been quite ignorant of the basic orientations toward death. Dying, like all things concerning human behavior, is amenable to scientific research. Three recent books have now broken the barrier on death as a subject of research and subsequent reporting of the data. Verwoerdt's, *Communication with the Fatally Ill,* stresses the goals and guidelines to use in caring for the dying patient. (Verwoerdt, 1966) Hinton's book, *Dying,* surveys the concepts and available knowledge on the way people die, the hospital care of the dying, and the bereavement of the survivors. (Hinton, 1967) Anselm Strauss's, *Time for Dying,* a companion volume to *Awareness of Dying,* is a social psychological treatment of the subject by an astute observer of the human scene. (Strauss, 1968)

One study concerned itself with the concept of "will to live." Medical doctors rated 102 consecutive admissions to a geriatric hospital as to the doctors' estimate of life expectancy. These physicians were inclined to see their elderly patients as somewhat removed from actual death. In actuality death occurred substantially within the first month after admission into the hospital. (Kastenbaum, 1965c) Variations in the manner that hospital personnel handle terminal cases appear to be an important factor. The "social loss" factor makes a difference in how the patient is handled even though the difference may be subtle to all but the patient. "The morale of a dying patient needs to be maintained irrespective of, say, his age, social class, or personality." The bedside manner of hospital and medical workers toward a dying President, wealthy industrialist, famous figure will be in sharp contrast toward the indigent dying pauper headed for Potter's Field. Treatment of terminal cases depends on the "social loss" factor. In addition there is a "work loss" factor: the dead or dying patient represents a "medical failure" for the physicians and nurses. Medicare should concern itself to "offset the probable consequences for the aged of being a low social loss patient in a typical hospital." (Glaser, 1966) The medical professions might answer this charge with, "How many times can I suffer for people I never heard of before." Fiefel finds that even the most elementary questions about death are met with rigidity by hospitals and physicians. ". . . death is a dark symbol not to be stirred, even touched —an obscenity to be avoided. I remember how paradoxical it was that the problem (studying reactions and anticipations of death) was turning out to be not the patient, but the physician." The patient and the physician are on opposite sides of the fence in regard to their attitudes toward death. "A study I have just completed (1962) on the attitudes of forty physicians toward death indicates that, though physicians think *less* about death than two central control groups of patients . . . they are *more afraid* of death than any of the control groups." (Farberow, 1963)

Attempts to measure personality changes in dying patients have used figure drawings and some measures of mental ability. The evidence indicates that there is a severe inability to draw human figures as death comes nearer. The changes were irreversible. Mental ability also decreases dramatically as death approaches. (Birren, 1964b, 1968b) (Riegel, 1967c) Prediction of lifetime left, as evidenced by collapsing performance on a psychological test, has not been possible as yet. Other attempts to measure nearness to death have used the concepts of, beyond the obvious "biological death," "social death," and "psychological death." These precede the actuality of biologically dying. (Kalish, 1966)

A unique suggestion has been made in measuring aging and organizing psychological data about aging, which may be more meaningful than chronological age. "In viewing the dying process as extending over a long time, it is reasonable to say that psychological changes are specifically related to a *time line in terms of distance from death.*" (Italics added) It is not how long you have lived but how close you are to dying that may give meaning to a better understanding of aging and human responses. This subsumes, it seems, that the date of death is possible to know (Death Row and premeditated murders?). Or, research is reserved for ex post facto methods. (Lieberman, 1966)

As measured by social scientists, how do individuals themselves view and accept an ultimate death? Shneidman suggests five possible attitudes toward death. (1) Some may welcome death as an end to all their problems, pain, and unresolved anxiety. (2) Death is an eternal verity of existence. It is not welcomed, but what can you do about it? (3) Death is to be postponed, delayed, deferred at all costs humanly possible. Doctors, drugs, rare or exotic medical treatments, are frantically sought after. (4) Death is to be disdained. Never fear it. Meet death head on bravely and cavalierly. (5) The last attitude is one of quaking, trembling, quivering fear, even at the mere contemplation of death. (Shneidman, 1957)

"Retired respondents were more realistic and less anxious about death than nonretired respondents. The data suggest that after retirement, anxiety about death, like anxiety about aging in general, is reduced." (Ogilvie, 1962) "Lifelong adjustment patterns are predictive" of attitudes towards death. In facing death "the elderly person shows an accentuation of lifelong personality defenses." (Wolff, 1966) We die, apparently, as we have lived. (Eaton, 1964) To paraphrase T. S. Eliot, we may die with a whimper, not with a bang. Or, other literary works may exemplify our death attitudes: Mimi in the opera *La Bohème*, Silas in Frost's poem, "Death of the Hired Man," Gunga Din in Kipling's *Barrack Room Ballads*, and hundreds of war movies, tales of derring-do, and much of the folklore of every nation's heroes.

Does the dying patient want to be told the truth? Should cancer victims be informed of their condition? It is a highly personal question that requires a uniquely personal answer: it depends upon who you are. The dichotomy exists: the patient's privilege to know versus the physician's or family's reluctance to add shock to pain. However, some efforts have been made to help to answer the awesome question. "The great majority (82 percent) desire to be informed about their condition in order to: 'settle my affairs,' 'It's my life I have a right to know,' 'would have time to live with an idea and learn to die.' " "Most seriously ill and terminally ill patients prefer honest, plain talk from physicians and family about the seriousness of their illnesses." (Farberow, 1963) The question now becomes how can you know beforehand if the patient is capable of accepting the fatal news, or if he will collapse and only hasten the end in worse shape with knowledge than with ignorance and false hopes. This is a puzzle as yet unresolved. Kastenbaum concludes in his article "As the clock runs out" after his many interviews, observations, and experiences with very old institutionalized adults, that the meaning of impending death is directly related to the meaning of time left to live. The older the adult the less important and precious and fascinating time becomes. Death to the octogenarian is far less formidable than it is to young adults. (Kastenbaum, 1966c)

EPILOGUE

There are no conclusions or summaries to this book. It follows the adult as he proceeds through the long years of adulthood. Death concludes the story. There are no platitudes, no commandments, no exhortations: only the dynamics of living as an adult and dying as a decent human being.

There is no more appropriate ending than the quotation in London's Festival Hall.

> *And the end of our exploring will be to arrive*
> *to where we started and to know the place for*
> *the first time.*

Research
Suggestions

1. Can Selye's aging theory of "deficit in adaptation energy" be empirically tested?
2. To what extent does the age of a researcher on old age affect his conclusions?
3. What are the relationships between personality types and adjustments to aging?
4. Is there a way to test Birren's hypothesis that people who survive into old age are "psychologically stronger" than those who do not?
5. Is there a way to reliably measure psychological nearness to death?
6. Is there a way of determining beforehand how a patient will accept news of impending death?
7. Precisely what is the relationship between psychological factors and physical aging?
8. What psychological effect will increasing extent of body transplants have on older people?
9. Could preretirement counseling centers affect this country's attitude toward retirement?

Bibliography

Abe, K., and M. Shimakawa. "Genetic and developmental aspects of sleep-talking and teeth-grinding," *Acta Paedopsychiatrica*, 1966, *33*, 339–344.

Adams, B. N. "Occupational position, mobility, and the kin of orientation," *American Sociological Review*, 1967, *32*, 364–377.

Adams, E. B., and I. G. Sarason. "Relation between anxiety in children and their parents," *Child Development*, 1963, *34*, 237–246.

Adams, P. L., J. J. Schwab, and J. F. Aponte. "Authoritarian parents and disturbed children," *American Journal of Psychiatry*, 1965, *121*, 1162–1167.

Adatto, C. "On play and the psychopathology of golf," *Journal of the American Psychoanalytic Association*, 1964, *12*, 826–841.

Agrawal, K. G. "Age and color codability," *Manas*, 1966, *13*, 33–39.

Aisenberg, R. "What happens to old psychologists?" in Kastenbaum, R. (ed.). *New Thoughts on Old Age.* New York: Springer, 1964.

Aldous, J., and R. Hill. *International Bibliography of Research in Marriage and the Family, 1900–1964.* Minneapolis: The University of Minnesota Press, 1967.

Allen, C. E. "Birth order and reaction to threat: a comparison of self-evaluation and anxiety reduction motives," *Dissertation Abstracts,* 1967, *27,* 3510.

Allen, M. G. "Childhood experience and adult personality: a cross-cultural study using the concept of ego strength," *Journal of Social Psychology,* 1967, *71,* 53–68.

Allport, G. W., and J. M. Ross. "Personal religious orientation and prejudice," *Journal of Personality and Social Psychology,* 1967, *5,* 432–443.

Altus, W. D. "Birth order and choice of college major," *Proceedings of the 75th Annual Convention of the American Psychological Association,* 1967, *2,* 287–288.

Alvarez, W. E. "The duration of widowhood," *Geriatrics,* 1955, *10,* 297.

Ames, L. B. "Changes in Rorschach response throughout the life span," *Genetic Psychology Monographs,* 1966, *74,* 89–125.

Anast, P. "Personality determinants of mass media preferences," *Journalism Quarterly,* 1966, *43,* 729–732.

Anderson, A. W. "The relationship of age to adult Reading Scores," *Journal of Educational Psychology,* 1960, *55,* 334–336.

Anderson, J. E. (ed.). *Psychological Aspects of Aging.* Washington, D.C.: American Psychological Association, 1956.

Anderson, J. E. *A Survey of Children's Adjustment Over Time: A Report to the People of Nobles County, Minneapolis.* Institute of Child Welfare and Development, University of Minnesota, 1959. (Also in Iscoe, I., and H. W. Stevenson, eds. *Personality Development in Children.* Austin, Tex.: University of Texas Press, 1960.)

Anderson, J. E. "Aging and educational television: a preliminary survey," *Journal of Gerontology,* 1962, *17,* 447–449.

Angrist, S. S. "Role constellation as a variable in women's leisure activities," *Social Forces,* 1967, *45,* 423–431.

Anonymous. "Age and automobile accidents," *Geriatrics,* 1961, *16,* 271–277.

Anonymous. "The pleasure prinzip: a growing personnel problem and opportunity," *Personnel Journal,* 1967, *46,* 177–178.

Appleton, W. S. "Concentration: the phenomenon and its disruption," *Archives of General Psychiatry,* 1967, *16,* 373–381.

Arasteh, A. R. *Final Integration in the Adult Personality: A Measure for Health, Social Change, and Leadership.* Leiden, Netherlands: Brill, 1965.

Arenberg, D. "Anticipation interval and age differences in verbal learning," *Journal of Abnormal Psychology,* 1965, *70,* 419–425.

Arenberg, D. "Verbal learning and retention," *The Gerontologist,* 1967a, *7,* 10–13.

Arenberg, D. "Age differences in retroaction," *Journal of Gerontology,* 1967b, *22,* 88–91.

Arnhoff, F. N., and I. Lorge. "Stereotypes about aging and the aged," *School and Society*, 1960, *88*, 70–71.

Arpad, E. E. "Age changes in master chess performance," *Journal of Gerontology*, 1965, *20*, 289–299.

Astin, H. S. "Patterns of career choices over time," *Personnel and Guidance Journal*, 1967, *45*, 541–546.

Babchuk, N., and A. P. Bates. "The primary relations of middle-class couples: a study in male dominance," *American Sociological Review*, 1963, *28*, 377–384.

Babchuck, N. "Primary friends and kin: a study of the associations of middle-class couples," *Social Forces*, 1965, *43*, 483–493.

Babchuk, N., H. J. Crockett, Jr., and J. A. Ballweg. "Change in religious affiliation and family stability," *Social Forces*, 1967, *45*, 551–555.

Bach, L. Z. "Homeness: a centripetal counterforce to intrafamily mobility," *Dissertation Abstracts*, 1967, *27*, 3117–3118.

Bachman, J. C. "Influence of age and sex on the amount and rate of learning two motor tasks," *Research Quarterly*, 1966, *37*, 176–186.

Balinsky, B. "An analysis of the mental factors of various age groups from nine to sixty," *Genetic Psychology Monographs*, 1941, *23*, 191–234.

Ballweg, J. A. "Resolution of conjugal role adjustment after retirement," *Journal of Marriage and the Family*, 1967, *29*, 277–281.

Barclay, A. M., and R. N. Haber. "Personality patterns among religious personnel: a review," *Catholic Psychological Record*, 1965, *3*, 125–137.

Barger, B., and E. Hall. "The interrelationships of family size and socioeconomic status for parents of college students," *Journal of Marriage and the Family*, 1966, *28*, 186–187.

Barocas, R., and L. Gorlow. "Religious affiliation, religious activities, and conformity," *Psychological Reports*, 1967, *20*, 366.

Barth, E. A., and W. B. Watson. "Social stratification and the family in mass society," *Social Forces*, 1967, *45*, 392–402.

Bartlett, E. W., and C. P. Smith. "Childbearing practices, birth order, and the development of achievement-related motives," *Psychological Reports*, 1966, *19*, 1207–1216.

Battistella, R. M. "Social bases of medical care behavior among aged and middle aged persons: I–II," *Dissertation Abstracts*, 1966, *27*, 536–537.

Bayer, A. E. "Birth order and college attendance," *Journal of Marriage and the Family*, 1966, *28*, 480–484.

Bayley, N. "On the growth of intelligence," *American Psychologist*, 1955, *10*, 805–818.

Bayley, N., and M. H. Oden. "The maintenance of intellectual ability in gifted adults," *Journal of Gerontology*, 1955, *10*, 91–107.

Bayley, N. "The life span as a frame of reference in psychological research," *Vita Humana*, 1963, *6*, 125–139.

Bayley, N. "Learning in adulthood: the role of intelligence," in Klausmeier, H. J., and C. Harris (eds.). *Analyses of Concept Learning*. New York: Academic, 1966, pp. 117–138.

Bayley, N. "Behavioral correlates of mental growth: birth to thirty-six years," *American Psychologist,* 1968, *23,* 1–17.

Bean, L. L. "The fertility of former mental patients," *Eugenics Quarterly,* 1966, *13,* 34–39.

Beck, J. "Age differences in lightness perception," *Psychonomic Science,* 1966, *4,* 201–202.

Becker, D., and F. Margolin. "How surviving parents handled their young children's adaptation to the crisis of loss," *American Journal of Orthopsychiatry,* 1967, *37,* 753–757.

Belbin, E., S. M. Downs, and B. Moore. "Unlearning and its relationship to age," *Ergonomics,* 1964a, *7,* 419–427.

Belbin, E., and S. M. Downs. "Activity learning and the older worker," *Ergonomics,* 1964b, *7,* 429–437.

Belbin, E. "Retraining the middle-aged," *New Society,* 1964c, *3,* 6–8.

Belbin, E., and S. Shimmin. "Training the middle-aged for inspection work." *Occupational Psychology,* 1964d, *38,* 49–57.

Belbin, E., and S. M. Downs. "Interference effects from new learning: their relevance to the design of adult training programs," *Journal of Gerontology,* 1965, *20,* 154–159.

Belbin, E., and S. M. Downs. "Teaching paired associates: the problem of age," *Occupational Psychology,* 1966, *40,* 67–74.

Bell, G. D. "Self-confidence and persuasion in car buying," *Journal of Marketing Research,* 1967, *4,* 46–52.

Benaim, S., and I. Allen (eds.). *The Middle Years.* London, England: T. V. Publications Limited, 1967.

Benedek, T. "Climacterium: a developmental phase," *Psychoanalytic Quarterly,* 1950, *19,* 1–27.

Berg, I., *et al.* "Birth order and family size of approved school boys," *British Journal of Psychiatry,* 1967a, *113,* 793–800.

Berg, P. "Adult socialization and social work practice," *Social Work,* 1967b, *12,* 89–94.

Berg, W. "The effect of aging on tactual-motor and visual-motor performance," *Dissertation Abstracts,* 1964, *25,* 3105.

Berger, L., A. Berstein, E. Elein, J. Cohen, and G. Lucas. "Effects of aging and pathology on the factorial structure of intelligence," *Journal of Consulting Psychology,* 1964, *28,* 199–207.

Bergler, E. *The Revolt of the Middle-Aged Man.* New York: Grosset & Dunlap, 1954.

Berkowitz, B. "Changes in intellect with age: IV. Changes in achievement and survival in older people," *Journal of Genetic Psychology,* 1965a, *107,* 3–14.

Berkowitz, B., and R. E. Green. "Changes in intellect with age: V. Differential changes as functions of time interval and original score," *Journal of Genetic Psychology,* 1965b, *107,* 179–192.

Bernard, J. *Remarriage: A Study of Marriage.* New York: Holt, Rinehart and Winston, 1956.

Bernard, J. "Marital stability and patterns of status variables," *Journal of Marriage and the Family,* 1966, *28,* 421–439.

Beshers, J. M., and E. O. Laumann. "Social distance: a network approach," *American Sociological Review*, 1967, *32*, 225–236.

Beverfeld E., M. Nygard, and H. Nordvik. "Factor analysis of Wechsler Adult Intelligence Scale performance of elderly Norwegians," *Journal of Gerontology*, 1964, *19*, 49–53.

Bieliauskas, V. J. "Recent advances in psychology of masculinity and femininity," *Journal of Psychology*, 1965, *60*, 255–263.

Billig, O., and R. W. Adams. "Emotional conflicts of the middle-aged man," *Geriatrics*, 1957, *12*, 535–541.

Birren, J. E., and J. Botwinick. "Rate of addition as a function of difficulty and age," *Psychometrika*, 1951, *11*, 219–232.

Birren, J. E. *Handbook of Aging and the Individual*. Chicago: The University of Chicago Press, 1959.

Birren, J. E. "A brief history of the psychology of aging," *The Gerontologist*, 1961, *1*, 69–77, 127–134.

Birren, J. E., R. N. Butler, S. W. Greenhouse, L. Sokoloff, and M. R. Yarrow. *Human Aging: A Biological and Behavioral Study*, Public Health Service Publication, No. 986. Washington, D.C.: U.S. Department of Health, Education and Welfare, 1963.

Birren, J. E. *The Psychology of Aging*. Englewood Cliffs, N.J.: Prentice-Hall, 1964a.

Birren, J. E. (ed.). *Relations of Development and Aging*. Springfield, Ill.: Charles C Thomas, 1964b.

Birren, J. E., M. W. Bick, and C. Fox. "Age changes in the light threshold of the dark adapted eye," *Journal of Gerontology*, 1965, *3*, 267–271.

Birren, J. E. "Research on aging: a frontier of science and social gain," *The Gerontologist*, 1968a, *8*, Part I, 7–13.

Birren, J. E. "Psychological aspects of aging: intellectual functioning," *The Gerontologist*, 1968b, *8*, Part II, 16–19.

Bischof, L. J. *Interpreting Personality Theories*. New York: Harper & Row, 1964.

Blau, Z. "Class structure, mobility and change in childrearing," *Sociometry*, 1965, *28*, 210–219.

Blumenthal, H. T., and A. W. Berns. "Autoimmunity and aging," in Strehler, B. L. (ed.). *Advances in Gerontological Research*. New York: Academic, 1964.

Blumenthal, H. T. "Some biomedical aspects of aging," *The Gerontologist*, 1968, *8*, Part II, 3–6.

Blumenthal, M. D. "Mental health among the divorced: a field study of divorced and never divorced persons," *Archives of General Psychiatry*, 1967, *16*, 603–608.

Bolton, H., P. G. Britton, and R. D. Savage. "Some normative data on the WAIS and its indices in an aged population," *Journal of Clinical Psychology*, 1966, *22*, 184–188.

Borello, J. A. "Psychosocial factors related to reported marital adjustments and task-efficiency," *Dissertation Abstracts*, 1966, *27*, 1925.

Bortner, R. W. "The relationship between age and measures of id, ego, and superego functioning," *Journal of Gerontology*, 1963, *18*, 286–289.

Bortner, R. W. "Adult development or idiosyncratic change? A plea for the developmental approach," *The Gerontologist*, 1966, *6*, 159–164.

Bossard, J. H. S. "Marrying late in life," *Social Forces*, 1951, *29*, 405–408.

Bossard, J. H. S., and E. S. Boll. "Marital unhappiness in the life cycle," *Marriage and Family Living*, 1955, *17*, 10–14.

Botwinick, J., J. F. Brinley, and J. S. Robbin. "Maintaining set in relation to motivation and age," *American Journal of Psychology*, 1959a 72, 585–588.

Botwinick, J., J. F. Brinley, and J. S. Robbin. "Modulation of speed of response with age," *Journal of Genetic Psychology*, 1959b, *95*, 137–144.

Botwinick, J. "Research problems and concepts in the study of aging," *The Gerontologist*, 1964, *4*, 121–129.

Botwinick, J. "Theories of antecedent conditions of speed of response," in Welford, A. T., and J. E. Birren (eds.). *Behavior, Aging, and the Nervous System*. Springfield, Ill.: Charles C Thomas, 1965a, pp. 67–87.

Botwinick, J. "Perceptual organization in relation to age and sex," *Journal of Gerontology*, 1965b, *20*, 224–227.

Botwinick, J., and J. E. Birren. "A follow-up study of card-sorting performance in elderly men," *Journal of Gerontology*, 1965c, *20*, 208–210.

Botwinick, J.,. and L. W. Thompson. "Components of reaction time in relation to age and sex," *Journal of Genetic Psychology*, 1966, *108*, 175–183.

Botwinick J., and L. W. Thompson. "Practice of speeded response in relation to age, sex, and set," *Journal of Gerontology*, 1967, *22*, 72–76.

Botwinick, J. *Cognitive Processes in Maturity and Old Age*. New York: Springer, 1968a.

Botwinick, J., and L. W. Thompson. "Age difference in reaction time: an artifact?" *The Gerontologist*, 1968b, *8*, Part 1, 25–28.

Bradway, K. P., and C. W. Thompson. "Intelligence at adulthood: a twenty-five year followup," *Journal of Educational Psychology*, 1962, *53*, 1–14.

Braun, H. W., and R. Geiselhard. "Age differences in the acquisition and extinction of the conditioned eyelid response," *Journal of Experimental Psychology*, 1959, *57*, 386–388.

Braun, J. R., and J. M. Link. "Relation between self-acceptance, food and occupation aversions, and susceptibility to annoyance," *Journal of Clinical Psychology*, 1967, *23*, 24–26.

Breen, L. Z., and J. L. Spaeth. "Age and productivity among workers in four Chicago companies," *Journal of Gerontology* 1960, *15*, 68–70.

Bregman, E., E. Thorndike, and T. Tilton. *Adult Learning*. New York: Macmillan, 1932.

Brehm, H. P. "Sociology and aging: orientation and research," *The Gerontologist*, 1968, *8*, 24–31.

Brennan, J. F. "Self-understanding and social feeling," *Journal of Individual Psychology*, 1967, *23*, 53–57.

Brinley, J. F. "Cognitive sets, speed and accuracy of performance in the elderly," in Welford, A. T., and J. E. Birren (eds.). *Behavior, Aging, and the Nervous System*. Springfield, Ill.: Charles C Thomas, 1965, pp. 114–149.

Britton, P. G., and R. D. Savage. "A short form of the WAIS for use with the aged," *British Journal of Psychiatry*, 1966a, *112*, 417–418.

Britton, P. G., and R. D. Savage. "The MMPI and the aged: some normative data from a community sample," *British Journal of Psychiatry*, 1966b, *112*, 941–943.

Broadbent, D. E., and M. Gregory. "Some confirmatory results on age differences in memory for simultaneous stimulation," *British Journal of Psychology*, 1965, *56*, 77–80.

Bromley, D. B. "Some effects of age on short term learning and remembering," *Journal of Gerontology*, 1958, *13*, 398–406.

Bromley, D. B. *The Psychology of Human Aging*. Baltimore: Penguin, 1966.

Bromley, D. B. "Age and sex differences in the serial production of creative conceptual responses," *Journal of Gerontology*, 1967, *22*, 34–42.

Bronson, L. F. "Changes in personality needs and values following conversion to Protestantism in a traditionally Roman Catholic ethnic group," *Dissertation Abstracts*, 1966, *27*, 1615.

Brooks, M., and C. H. Hillman. "Parent-daughter relationship as a factor in nonmarriage studied in identical twins," *Journal of Marriage and the Family*, 1965, *27*, 383–385.

Brown, R. A. "Age and paced work," *Occupational Psychology*, 1957, *31*, 11–20.

Brozek, H. S. "Changes in sensory, motor, and intellective functions with age," *Geriatrics*, 1951, *6*, 221–226.

Brozek, J. "Personality of young and middle-aged normal men: an analysis of a psychosomatic inventory," *Journal of Gerontology*, 1952, *7*, 410–418.

Budoff, M., and R. B. Vacchiano. "Developmental study of ambiguity level in picture-story stimuli," *Journal of Projective Techniques and Personality Assessment*, 1965, *29*, 465–472.

Buhler, C. "Theoretical observations about life's basic tendencies," *American Journal of Psychotherapy*, 1959, *13*, 561–581.

Buhler, C. "Meaningful living in the mature years," in Kleemeier, R. W. (ed.). *Aging and Leisure*. New York: Oxford, 1961.

Burchinal, L. G., and J. E. Rossman. "Relations among maternal employment indices and developmental characteristics of children," *Marriage and Family Living*, 1961, *23*, 334–340.

Burchinal, L. G., and W. W. Bauder. "Decision-making and role patterns among Iowa farm and non-farm families." *Journal of Marriage and the Family*, 1965, *27*, 525–530.

Burg, A. "Light sensitivity as related to age and sex," *Perceptual and Motor Skills*, 1967, *24*, 1279–1288.

Burgess, E. W. (ed.). *Aging in Western Societies*. Chicago: The University of Chicago Press, 1960.

Busse, E. W. "Geriatrics today: an overview," *American Journal of Psychiatry*, 1967, *123*, 1226–1233.

Butler, R. N. "The facade of chronological age: an interpretative summary," *American Journal of Psychiatry*, 1963, *119*, 721–728.

Butler, R. N. "Crises and contributions in later life," *American Journal of Orthopsychiatry*, 1967a, *37*, 337–338.

Butler, R. N. "Aspects of survival and adaptation in human aging," *American Journal of Psychiatry*, 1967b, *123*, 1233–1243.

Byrd, E., and S. Gertman. "Taste sensitivity in aging persons," *Geriatrics*, 1959, *14*, 381–384.

Byrne, D., and B. Blaylock. "Similarity and assumed similarity of attitudes between husbands and wives," *Journal of Abnormal and Social Psychology*, 1963, *67*, 636–640.

Cahill, I. D. "Child-rearing practices in lower socioeconomic ethnic groups," *Dissertation Abstracts*, 1967, *27*, 3139.

Caird, W. K. "Aging and short-term memory," *Journal of Gerontology*, 1966, *21*, 295–299.

Caird, W. K. "Memory loss in the senile psychoses: organic or psychogenic," *Psychological Reports*, 1966, *18*, 788–790.

Cameron, P. "Masculinity-femininity in the aged," *Journal of Gerontology*, 1968, *23*, 63–65.

Campbell, D. P. "A cross-sectional and longitudinal study of scholastic abilities over twenty-five years," *Journal of Counseling Psychology*, 1965, *12*, 55–61.

Canestrari, R. E., Jr. "Paced and self-paced learning in young and elderly adults," *Journal of Gerontology*, 1963, *18*, 165–168.

Canestrari, R. E., Jr. "Age differences in paired associate learning as a function of response pretraining," *The Gerontologist*, 1964, *4*, 30.

Canestrari, R. E., Jr. "Age differences in spatial stimulus generalization," *Journal of Genetic Psychology*, 1965, *106*, 129–135.

Canestrari, R. E., Jr. "The effects of commonality on paired associate learning in two age groups," *Journal of Genetic Psychology*, 1966, *108*, 3–7.

Carlson, E. R. "Generality of order of concept attainment," *Psychological Reports*, 1962, *10*, 375–380.

Carney, R. E. "Sex chromatin, body masculinity, achievement motivation and smoking behavior," *Psychological Reports*, 1967, *20*, 859–866.

Carp, F. M. *A Future for the Aged: Victoria Plaza and Its Residents.* Austin, Tex.: University of Texas Press, 1966.

Cath, S. N. "Some dynamics of the middle and later years," in Porad, H. J. (ed.). *Crisis Intervention: Selected Readings.* New York: Family Service Association of America, 1965, pp. 174–190.

Cattell, R. B. *The Scientific Analysis of Personality.* Baltimore: Penguin, 1965.

Cavan, R. S. "Adjustment problems of the older woman," *Marriage and Family Living*, 1952, *14*, 16–18.

Cavan, R. S. "Self and role in adjustment during old age," in Rose, A. M. (ed.). *Human Behavior and Social Processes.* Boston: Houghton Mifflin, 1962.

Chapani, A. "Relationship between age, visual acuity and color vision," *Human Biology*, 1950, *22*, 1–33.

Chapman, H. P. "Factors associated with self-perceptions of age," *Dissertation Abstracts*, 1966, *27*, 1118.

Chapman, J. D. *The Feminine Mind and Body: The Psychosexual and Psychosomatic Reactions of Women.* New York: Philosophical Library, 1967.

Charles, D. C., and S. T. James. "Stability of average intelligence," *Journal of Genetic Psychology,* 1964, *105,* 105–111.

Chess, S., A. Thomas, and H. G. Birch. "Distortions in developmental reporting made by parents of behaviorally disturbed children," *Journal of the American Academy of Child Psychiatry,* 1966, *5,* 226–234.

Chopra, S. L. "Family size and sibling position as related to intelligence test scores and academic achievement," *Journal of Social Psychology,* 1966, *70,* 133–137.

Chown, S., and A. Heron. "Psychological aspects of aging in man," *Annual Review of Psychology,* 1965, *16,* 417–450.

Chown, S., E. Belbin, and S. M. Downs. "Programmed instruction as a method of teaching paired associates to older learners," *Journal of Gerontology,* 1967, *22,* 212–219.

Christensen, H. T., and K. E. Barber. "Interfaith versus intrafaith marriage in Indiana," *Journal of Marriage and the Family,* 1967, *29,* 461–469.

Christopher, S. A. "Perceived strength of interpersonal relationships and parental value orientation as factors related to academic achievement," *Dissertation Abstracts,* 1966, *27,* 666.

Chyatte, C. "Brain bloodshift theory: a preliminary test through correlations of age with alpha EEG and CRR," *Journal of Psychology,* 1965, *61,* 27–32.

Cijfer, E. "An experiment of some differences in logical thinking between Dutch medical people under and over the age of 35: a replication experiment," *Acta Psychologica,* 1966, *25,* 159–171.

Clark, A. L., and P. Wallin. "Women's sexual responsiveness and the duration and quality of their marriages," *American Journal of Sociology,* 1965, *71,* 187–196.

Clark, H. E. "The development of a needs and problems inventory for older women," *Dissertation Abstracts,* 1965, *26,* 1762–1763.

Clark, L. M. "Sex life in the middle-aged," *Marriage and Family Living,* 1949, *11,* 58–60.

Clark, M. "The anthropology of aging, a new era for studies of culture and personality," *The Gerontologist,* 1967, *7,* 55–64.

Clark, W. H. *The Psychology of Religion.* New York: Macmillan, 1958.

Clarke, A. D. B., and G. M. Cooper. "Age and perceptual motor transfer of training," *Perceptual and Motor Skills,* 1964, *19,* 849–850.

Clay, H. M. "The relationship between time, accuracy and age on similar tasks of varying complexity," *Gerontologia,* 1957, *1,* 41–49.

Clement, F. "Effect of physical activity on the maintenance of intellectual capacities," *The Gerontologist,* 1966, *6,* 91–92.

Cohen, E. G. "Parental factors in educational mobility," *Sociology of Education,* 1965, *38,* 407–425.

Cohen, W. J. "Improving the status of the aged," *Social Security Bulletin,* 1966, *29,* 3–8.

Collins, G. R. "Changes in optimal level of complexity as a function of age," *Dissertation Abstracts,* 1964, *24,* 5538.

Collins, T. *The Golden Years.* New York: John Day, 1956.

Collins, T. "The Golden years: but do you need a lot of friends?" *Chicago Daily News,* January 18, 1965.

Comalli, P. E., Jr., S. Wapner, and H. Werner. "Perception of verticality in middle and old age," *Journal of Psychology,* 1959, *47,* 259–266.

Comalli, P. E., Jr., D. M. Drus, and S. Wapner. "Cognitive functioning in two groups of aged, one institutionalized, the other living in the community," *Journal of Gerontology,* 1965a, *20,* 9–13.

Comalli, P. E., Jr., "Cognitive functioning in a group of 80–90 year old men," *Journal of Gerontology,* 1965b, *20,* 14–17.

Comfort, A. *Ageing: The Biology of Senescence,* London: Routledge, 1964.

Conway, J. A. "Protests, permissiveness, and the adolescent," *Child Study Bulletin,* 1966, *2,* 96–99.

Cooper, R. C., and R. L. Payne. "Age and absence: a longitudinal study in three firms," *Occupational Psychology,* 1965, *39,* 31–35.

Cooper, R. M., I. Bilash, and J. P. Zubek. "The effect of age on taste sensitivity," *Journal of Gerontology,* 1959, *14,* 56–58.

Coopersmith, S. *The Antecedents of Self-Esteem.* San Francisco: Freeman, 1967.

Copper, J. B., and J. H. Lewis. "Parent evaluation as related to social ideology and academic achievement," *Journal of Genetic Psychology,* 1962, *101,* 135–143.

Coppinger, N. W. "The relationship between critical flicker frequency and chronological age for varying levels of stimulus brightness," *Journal of Gerontology,* 1955, *10,* 48–52.

Correll, R. E., S. Rokosz, and B. M. Blanchard. "Some correlates of WAIS performance in the elderly," *Journal of Gerontology,* 1966, *21,* 544–549.

Corsini, R. J., and K. K. Fasett. "Intelligence and Aging," *Journal of Genetic Psychology,* 1953, *83,* 249–264.

Costa, P., and R. Kastenbaum. "Some aspects of memories and ambitions in centenarians," *Journal of Genetic Psychology,* 1967, *110,* 3–16.

Craik, F. I. M. "An observed age difference in responses to a personality inventory," *British Journal of Psychology,* 1964, *55,* 453–462.

Craik, F. I. M. "The nature of the age decrement in performance on dichotic listening tasks," *Quarterly Journal of Experimental Psychology,* 1965, *17,* 227–240.

Crain, A. J., and C. S. Stamm. "Intermittent absence of fathers and children's perceptions of parents," *Journal of Marriage and the Family,* 1965, *27,* 344–347.

Crawford, C. O. "Family attachment, family support for migration and migration plans of young people," *Rural Sociology,* 1966, *31,* 293–300.

Cristenson, C. V., and J. H. Gagnon. "Sexual behavior in a group of older women," *Journal of Gerontology,* 1965, *20,* 351–357.

Crovitz, E. K. "Visual discrimination learning in elderly subjects," *Dissertation Abstracts,* 1964, *24,* 3123–3124.

Crovitz, E. K. "Reversing a learning deficit in the aged," *Journal of Gerontology,* 1966, *21,* 236–238.

Cumming, E., L. R. Dean, D. S. Newell, and I. McCaffrey. "Disengagement— a tentative theory of aging," *Sociometry,* 1960, *23,* 23–35.

Cumming, E., and W. E. Henry. *Growing Old: The Process of Disengagement.* New York: Basic Books, 1961.

Curtis, H. J. "A composite theory of aging," *The Gerontologist*, 1966, *6*, 143–149.

Curtis, H. J. *Biological Mechanisms of Aging*. Springfield, Ill.: Charles C Thomas, 1967.

Dainton, P. M. "Women executives: is there room at the top?" *Personnel Management*, 1967, *49*, 15–19.

Daly, J. W., A. J. Barry, and N. C. Birkhead. "The physical working capacity of older individuals," *Journal of Gerontology*, 1968, *23*, 134–139.

Dame, N. G., G. Finck, B. A. Reiner, and B. Smith. "The effect on the marital relationship of the wife's search for identity," *Family Life Coordinator*, 1965, *14*, 133–136.

Damon, A. "Discrepancies between findings of longitudinal and cross-sectional studies in adult life: physique and physiology," *Human Development*, 1965, *8*, 16–22.

Damon, A., and R. L. Nuttall. "Ponderal index of fathers and sex ratio of children," *Human Biology*, 1965, *37*, 23–28.

Daniel, J., and M. Strizenec. "Experimental research into some aspects of the operator's activity: I," *Studia Psychologica*, 1967, *9*, 106–119.

Datta, L. E. "Birth order and early scientific attainment," *Perceptual and Motor Skills*, 1967, *24*, 157–158.

Davids, A., and P. K. Hainsworth. "Maternal attitudes about family life and child rearing as avowed by mothers and perceived by their underachieving and higher-achieving sons," *Journal of Consulting Psychology*, 1967, *31*, 29–37.

Davidson, M. "Social and economic characteristics of aged persons (65 years old and over) in the United States in 1960," *Eugenics Quarterly*, 1967, *14*, 27–44.

Davidson, P. O., R. W. Payne, and R. B. Sloane. "Conditionability and age in human adults," *Psychological Reports*, 1965, *17*, 351–354.

Davies, D. R. "A further note on the effect of aging on auditory vigilance performance: the effect of low signal frequency," *Journal of Gerontology*, 1963, *18*, 370–371.

Davies, D. R., and S. Griew. "Age and Vigilance," in Welford, A. T., and J. E. Birren (eds.). *Behavior, Aging, and the Nervous System*. Springfield, Ill.: Charles C Thomas, 1965. pp. 54–59.

Davis, C. *Room to Grow: A Study of Parent-Child Relationships*. Toronto, Canada: University of Toronto Press, 1966.

Davis, S. H., and W. D. Obrist. "Age differences in learning and retention of verbal material," *Cornell Journal of Social Relations*, 1966, *1*, 95–103.

Dean, D. G. "Emotional maturity and marital adjustment," *Journal of Marriage and the Family*, 1966, *28*, 454–457.

de Lint, J. "Note on birth order and intelligence test performance," *Journal of Psychology*, 1967, *66*, 15–17.

Denmark, F. L., and M. Guttentag. "The effect of college attendance on mature women: changes in self-concept and evaluation of student role," *Journal of Social Psychology*, 1966, *68*, 155–158.

Denmark, F. L., and M. Guttentag. "Dissonance in the self-concepts and educational concepts of college- and noncollege-oriented women," *Journal of Counseling Psychology*, 1967, *14*, 113–115.

Dennis, W. "Creative productivity between the ages of 20 and 80 years," *Journal of Gerontology*, 1966, *21*, 1–8.

de Saugy, D. "The alcoholic and his wife," *Hygiene Mentale*, 1962, *51*, 145–201.

De Shazo, D. "Vocational interest development as a function of parental attitudes," *Dissertation Abstracts*, 1966, *27*, 957–958.

Desmond, T. C. "America's unknown middle-agers," *The New York Times*, July 29, 1956.

Desroches, H. F., B. D. Kaiman, and H. T. Ballard. "Relationship between age and recall of meaningful material," *Psychological Reports*, 1966, *18*, 920–922.

Deutsch, M., I. Katz, and A. Jensen (eds.). *Social Class, Race, and Psychological Development*. New York: Holt, Rinehart and Winston, 1968.

De Wit, G. A. *Symbolism of Masculinity and Femininity*. New York: Springer, 1963.

Dicks, H. V. "Object relations theory and marital studies," *British Journal of Medical Psychology*, 1963, *36*, 125–129.

Dicks, H. V. *Marital Tensions: Clinical Studies Towards a Psychological Theory of Interaction*. New York: Basic Books, 1967.

Dixit, C. R. "The measurement of sex-role identification in children," *Psychological Studies*, 1964, *9*, 133–138.

Dohrenwend, B., and E. Chinshong. "Social status and attitudes toward psychological disorder: the problem of tolerance of deviance," *American Sociological Review*, 1967a, *32*, 417–433.

Dohrenwend, B., S. Feldstein, J. Plosky, and G. R. Schmeidler. "Factors interacting with birth order in self-selection among volunteer subjects," *Journal of Social Psychology*, 1967b, *72*, 125–128.

Donahue, W. "Relationship of age of perceivers to their social perceptions," *The Gerontologist*, 1965, *5*, 241–245.

Doty, B. A., and L. A. Doty. "Effect of age and chlorpromazine on memory consolidation," *Journal of Comparative and Physiological Psychology*, 1964, *57*, 331–334.

Doty, B. A. "Age differences in avoidance conditioning as a function of distribution of trials and task difficulty," *Journal of Genetic Psychology*, 1966, *109*, 249–254.

Doty, B. A. "Effects of handling on learning of young and aged rats," *Journal of Gerontology*, 1968, *23*, 142–144.

Downs, S. M., and B. Moore. "'Unlearning' and its relationship to age," *Ergonomics*, 1964, *7*, 419–427.

Downs, S. M. "Age in relation to part and whole learning," *Journal of Gerontology*, 1965, *20*, 479–482.

Dreikurs, R., and H. H. Mosak. "The tasks of life: II. The fourth life task," *Individual Psychologist*, 1967, *4*, 51–56.

Droege, R. C., A. C. Crambert, and J. B. Henkin. "Relationship between G.A.T.B. aptitude scores and age for adults," *Personnel and Guidance Journal*, 1963, *41*, 502–508.

Droege, R. C. "Effects of aptitude-score adjustments by age curves on prediction of job performance," *Journal of Applied Psychology*, 1967, *51*, 181–186.

Dumazedier, J. *Toward a Society of Leisure*. New York: Free Press, 1967.

Dunn, H. L. "Dynamic maturity for purposeful living," *Geriatrics*, 1966, *21*, 205–208.

Dustman, R. E., and E. C. Beck. "Visually evoked potentials: amplitude changes with age," *Science*, 1966, *151*, 1013–1014.

Duvall, E. M. "Family dilemmas with teenagers," *Family Life Coordinator*, 1965, *14*, 35–38.

Eaton, J. W. "The art of aging and dying," *Journal of Gerontology*, 1964, *4*, 94–112.

Edwards, J. A. "Maternal attitudes and social reinforcement as factors in mother-child interaction," *Dissertation Abstracts*, 1966, 27, 964.

Edwards, J. N. "The future of the family revisited," *Journal of Marriage and the Family*, 1967, 29, 505–511.

Egerman, L. E. "Attitudes of adult children toward parents and parent's problems," *Geriatrics*, 1966, *21*, 217–222.

Eisdorfer, C. "Verbal learning and response time in the aged," *Journal of Genetic Psychology*, 1965, *107*, 15–22.

Eisdorfer, C., and C. Service. "The effects of pace of verbal rote learning on intellectually superior adults," *The Gerontologist*, 1966, *6*, Part II, 27. (Abstract.)

Eisdorfer, C. "New dimensions and a tentative theory," *The Gerontologist*, 1967a, 7, 14–18.

Eisdorfer, C., and C. Service. "Verbal rote learning and superior intelligence in the aged," *Journal of Gerontology*, 1967b, 22, 158–161.

Eisenman, R., and R. E. Taylor. "Birth order and MMPI patterns," *Journal of Individual Psychology*, 1966a, 22, 208–211.

Eisenman, R. "Birth order, anxiety, and verbalizations in group psychotherapy," *Journal of Consulting Psychology*, 1966b, *30*, 521–526.

Eisenman, R. "Complexity-simplicity: II. Birth order and sex differences," *Psychonomic Science*, 1967a, *8*, 171–172.

Eisenman, R. "Birth order, anxiety, and verbal interaction in group psychotherapy," *Dissertation Abstracts*, 1967b, 27, 3670.

Eisenman, R. "Birth-order and sex differences in aesthetic preference for complexity-simplicity," *Journal of General Psychology*, 1967c, 77, 121–126.

Elder, G. H., Jr. "Role relations, sociocultural environments, and autocratic family ideology," *Sociometry*, 1965, *28*, 173–196.

Elliott, C. K. "Age and internal labour mobility of semiskilled workers," *Occupational Psychology*, 1966, *40*, 227–236.

Ellis, A., with J. Wolf and S. Moseley. *How to Prevent Your Child from Becoming a Neurotic Adult*. New York: Crown, 1966.

Enesco, H. E. "RNA and memory: a re-evaluation of present data," *Canadian Psychiatric Association Journal*, 1967, *12*, 29–34.

English, O.S., and G. H. J. Pearson. *Emotional Problems of Living*, 3d e New York: Norton, 1963.

Erfmann, I. "Age and manifestation of psychosomatic disorders," *Vi Humana, Basel,* 1962, *5,* 161–166.

Erikson, E. H. *Childhood and Society.* New York: Norton, 1950.

Erikson, E. H. "Identity and the life cycle: selected papers," *Psychologic Issues,* Monograph, No. 1, 1959.

Espenschade, A. S. "General activity measures of women 35–80 years of age *Perceptual and Motor Skills,* 1966, *23,* 718.

Farber, S. M., and R. H. Wilson (eds.). *The Challenge to Women.* New Yor Basic Books, 1966.

Farberow, N. L. (ed.). *Taboo Topics.* New York: Atherton Press, 1963.

Farina, A. J. "A study of the relationships between personality factors and pa terns of free-time behavior," *Dissertation Abstracts,* 1966, *26,* 4795–4796.

Farley, F. H. "Birth order, achievement-motivation and academic attainment. *British Journal of Educational Psychology,* 1967, *37,* 256.

Farnsworth, P. R., O. McNemar, and Q. McNemar (eds.). *Annual Review Psychology, Vol. 16.* Palo Alto, Calif.: Annual Reviews, 1965.

Faunce, W. A., and R. L. Fulton. "The sociology of death," *Social Force* 1958, *36,* 205–209.

Feifel, H. "Attitudes of mentally ill patients towards death," *Journal c Nervous and Mental Disease,* 1955, *122,* 375–380.

Feifel, H. (ed.). *The Meaning of Death.* New York: McGraw-Hill, 1959.

Feifel H. "Death—relevant variable in psychology," in May, R. (ed.). *Exister tial Psychology.* New York: Random House, 1961.

Feifel, H. "Attitudes toward death in older persons: a symposium," *Journa of Gerontology,* 1961, *16,* 44–66.

Ferber, A., D. Kliger, I. Zwerling, and M. Mendelsohn. "Current famil structure: psychiatric emergencies and patient fate," *Archives of Genera Psychiatry,* 1967, *16,* 659–667.

Ferguson, L. W. "Quantifying the family-life cycle," *Psychological Record* 1967, *17,* 219–227.

Ferreira, A. J., and W. D. Winter. "Family interaction and decision making," *Archives of General Psychology,* 1965, *13,* 214–223.

Ferreira, A. J., and W. D. Winter. "Age and sex differences in the palma sweat print," *Psychosomatic Medicine,* 1965, *27,* 207–211.

Fisher, J., and R. C. Pierce. "Dimensions of intellectual functioning of th aged," *Journal of Gerontology,* 1967a, *22,* 166–173.

Fisher, M. B., and J. E. Birren. "Age and strength," *Journal of Applied Psy chology,* 1947, *31,* 490–497.

Fisher, S., and H. Osofsky. "Sexual responsiveness in women: psychologica correlates," *Archives of General Psychiatry,* 1967b, *17,* 214–226.

Fitzgerald, M. P. "Sex differences in the perception of the parental role for middle and working class adolescents," *Journal of Clinical Psychology* 1966, *22,* 15–16.

Fitzhugh, K. B., and L. C. Fitzhugh. "Age difference on tasks of immediate problem solving and stored knowledge," *The Gerontologist,* 1964, *4* (3, Supple.), 38. (Abstract.)

Fletcher, J. *Situation Ethics: The New Morality.* Philadelphia: The Westminister Press, 1966.

Flint, A. A., Jr. "Crisis in marriage," *American Journal of Orthopsychiatry,* 1967, *37,* 335–336.

Forman, M. "Conflict, controversy, and confrontation in group work with older adults," *Social Work,* 1967, *12,* 80–85.

Fortuin, G. J. "Age and lighting needs," *Ergonomics,* 1963, *6,* 239–245.

Foulds, G. A., and J. C. Raven. "Normal changes in the mental abilities of adults as age advances," *Journal of Mental Science,* 1948, *94,* 133–142.

Frank, G. H., and S. Hiester. "Reliability of the ideal-self concept," *Journal of Counseling Psychology,* 1967, *14,* 356–357.

Frenkel, E. "Studies in biographical psychology," *Character and Personality,* 1936, *5,* 1–34.

Freud, S. *Collected Papers.* New York: Basic Books, 1959.

Friedman, A. S., and S. Granick. "A note on anger and aggression in old age," *Journal of Gerontology,* 1963, *18,* 283–285.

Friedman, H. "Memory organization in the aged," *Journal of Genetic Psychology,* 1966, *109,* 3–8.

Friedman, H. "Action patterns in the aged," *Journal of Genetic Psychology,* 1967, *110,* 153–157.

Friend, C. M., and J. P. Zubek. "The effects of age on critical thinking," *Journal of Gerontology,* 1958, *13,* 407–413.

Fromm, E. "Psychological problems of aging," *Journal of Rehabilitation,* 1966, *32,* 10–12.

Frye, R. L., D. R. South, and O. V. Vegas. "The effect of parental orientation on the development of the child's orientation," *Journal of Genetic Psychology,* 1965, *106,* 315–318.

Gagne, R. M. *Psychology and Human Performance.* New York: Holt, Rinehart and Winston, 1959.

Garfield District Staff of the Family Service Association (Cleveland, Ohio). "Infidelity in women as a manifestation of a character disorder," *Smith College Studies in Social Work,* 1962, *32,* 180–198.

Gavron, H. *The Captive Wife: Conflicts of Housebound Mothers.* New York: Humanities Press, 1966.

Gebhard, P. H. "Factors in marital orgasm," *Journal of Social Issues,* 1966, *22,* 88–95.

Gergen, K. J., and K. W. Back. "Communication in the interview and the disengaged respondent," *Public Opinion Quarterly,* 1966, *30,* 385–398.

Gergen, K. J., and S. J. Morse. "Self-consistency: measurement and validation," *Proceedings of the 75th Annual Convention of the American Psychological Association,* 1967, *2,* 207–208.

Gerontological Society, 19th Annual Scientific Meeting of the Gerontological Society, New York, November, 1966: Symposium on learning and memory, *The Gerontologist,* 1967, *7,* 3–30.

Giannitrapani, D., A. I. Sorkin, and J. Enenstein. "Laterality preference children and adults as related to interhemespheric EEG phase activity *Journal of Neurological Science,* 1966, *3,* 139–150.

Gibbs, C. B. "Probability learning in step-input tracking," *British Journal Psychology,* 1965, *56,* 233–242.

Gilbert, J. G. "Age changes in color matching," *Journal of Gerontology,* 195 *12,* 210–215.

Gilbert, J. G., and R. F. Levee. "A comparison of the personality structures a group of young, married and a group of middle-aged, married women *Perceptual and Motor Skills,* 1963, *16,* 773–777.

Gilmore, J. V. "Parental counseling and academic achievement," *Journal Education,* 1967, *149,* 46–69.

Gladis, M., and H. Braun. "Age differences in transfer and retroaction as function of intertask response similarity," *Journal of Experimental Ps chology,* 1958, *55,* 25–30.

Glanville, E., R. Fisher, and A. Kaplan. "Age, sex, and taste sensitivity, *Journal of Gerontology,* 1964, *19,* 474–479.

Glanville, E., R. Fisher, and A. Kaplan. "Cumulative effect of age and smol ing on taste sensitivity in males and females," *Journal of Gerontolog* 1965, *20,* 334–338.

Glaser, B. A. "The social loss of aged dying patients," *The Gerontologist,* 196(*6,* 77–80.

Glick, P. C., and E. Landau. "Age as a factor in marriage," *American Soci logical Review,* 1950, *15,* 517–529.

Glick, P. C. "The life cycle of the family," *Marriage and Family Living,* 195! *17,* 3–9.

Gogel, W. C., B. O. Hartman, and G. S. Harker. "The retinal size of a familia object as a determiner of apparent distance," *Psychological Monograph* 1957, No. 442.

Goldberg, P. A. "Ideology vs. primary group membership as determinants o political choice," *Psychological Reports,* 1967, *20,* 1058.

Golden, J. S., R. J. Silver, and N. Mandel. "The wives of 50 'normal' Amer can men," *Archives of General Psychiatry,* 1963, *9,* 614–618.

Goode, E. "Social class and church participation," *American Journal o Sociology,* 1966, *72,* 102–111.

Goodenough, F. L., and L. E. Tyler. *Developmental Psychology,* 3d ed. Nev York: Appleton-Century-Crofts, 1959.

Goodrick, C. L. "Operant level and light-contingent for process as a functio of age and deprivation," *Psychological Reports,* 1965, *17,* 283–288.

Gorer, G. *Death, Grief and Mourning.* Garden City, N.Y.: Anchor, 1967.

Granick, S., and A. S. Friedman. "Rate of decline in cognitive-perceptua functioning from middle to old age," *The Gerontologist,* 1966, *6,* Part II 27.

Granick, S., and A. S. Friedman. "The effect of education on the decline o psychometric test performance with age," *Journal of Gerontology,* 1967 *22,* 191–195.

Granville-Grossman, K. L. "Parental age and schizophrenia," *British Journa of Psychiatry,* 1966a, *112,* 899–905.

Granville-Grossman, K. L. "Birth order and schizophrenia," *British Journal of Psychiatry*, 1966b, *112*, 1119–1126.

Gravatt, A. E. "Family relations in middle and old age—a review," *Journal of Gerontology*, 1953, *8*, 197–201.

Green, R. F., and B. Berkowitz. "Changes in intellect with age: II. Factorial analysis of Wechsler-Bellevue scores," *Journal of Genetic Psychology*, 1964, *104*, 3–18.

Green, R. F., and B. Berkowitz. "Changes in intellect with age: III. The relation of heterogeneous brain damage to achievement in older people," *Journal of Genetic Psychology*, 1965, *106*, 349–359.

Greenshields, B. D., and F. N. Platt. "Development of a method of predicting high-accident and high-violation drivers," *Journal of Applied Psychology*, 1967, *51*, 205–210.

Greenwood, D. I., and C. Taylor. "Adaptive testing in an older population," *Journal of Psychology*, 1965, *60*, 193–198.

Griew, S., and D. R. Davis. "The effect of aging on auditory vigilance," *Journal of Gerontology*, 1961, *17*, 88–90.

Grinder, R. E., and V. C. Spector. "Sex differences in adolescence, perceptions of parental resource control," *Journal of Genetic Psychology*, 1965, *106*, 337–344.

Guilford, J. B. *The Nature of Human Intelligence.* New York: McGraw-Hill, 1967.

Gundlach, R. H., and B. F. Riess. "Birth order and sex of siblings in a sample of lesbians and nonlesbians," *Psychological Reports*, 1967, *20*, 61–62.

Gutman, G. M. "The effects of age and extraversion on pursuit rotor reminiscence," *Journal of Gerontology*, 1965, *20*, 346–350.

Haan, N. "Proposed model of ego functioning: coping and defense mechanisms in relation to I.Q. change," *Psychological Monographs*, 1963, *77*, 1–123.

Hader, M. "The importance of grandparents in family life," *Family Process*, 1965, *4*, 288–298.

Hader, M. "Homosexuality as part of our aging process," *Psychiatric Quarterly*, 1966, *40*, 515–524.

Hahn, M. E. "Forgotten people: the normal individual and, and in, professional psychology," *American Psychologist*, 1962, *17*, 700–705.

Hahn, M. E. *Psycho-Evaluation: Adaptation, Distribution, Adjustment.* New York: McGraw-Hill, 1963.

Hahn, M. E. *Planning Ahead After Forty: The Process of Psycho-evaluation with Self-Study Projects.* Beverly Hills, Calif.: Western Psychological Services, 1967.

Halloran, J. D. *Attitude Formation and Change.* Leicester, England: Leicester University Press, 1967.

Hamilton, M. L. "Affiliative behavior as a function of approach and avoidance affiliation motives, opinion evaluation, and birth order," *Journal of Social Psychology*, 1967, *72*, 61–70.

Hamlin, R. M. "Utility theory of old age," *Proceedings of the 74th Annual Convention of the American Psychological Association*, 1966, *1*, 213–214.

Hanson, J. T. "Ninth grade girls' vocational choices and their parents' occupational level," *Vocational Guidance Quarterly*, 1965, *13*, 261–264.

Harburg, E., N. F. McGinn, and J. B. Wigle. "Recalled treatment by parent among college males and blood pressure levels vs. variability," *Journal of Psychosomatic Research*, 1965, *9*, 173–183.

Hare, E. H. "Mental health in new towns: what next?" *Journal of Psychosomatic Research*, 1966, *10*, 53–58.

Harmon, L. W. "Women's working patterns related to their SVIB housewife and 'own' occupational scores," *Journal of Counseling Psychology*, 1967 *14*, 299–301.

Harris, S. J. *On the Contrary*. Boston: Houghton Mifflin, 1964.

Havighurst, R. J. "Old age—an American problem," *Journal of Gerontology* 1949, *4*, 298–304.

Havighurst, R. J. *Human Development and Education*. New York: McKay 1953a.

Havighurst, R. J., and R. Albrecht. *Older People*. New York: McKay, 1953b

Havighurst, R. J. "The social competence of middle-aged people," *Genetic Psychology Monographs*, 1957, *56*, 297–375.

Havighurst, R. J., and B. Neugarten. *Society and Education*. Boston: Allyn and Bacon, 1962.

Havighurst, R. J. "Factors which control the experience of aging," *Gawein*, 1965a, *13*, 242–248.

Havighurst, R. J. "Body, self and society," *Sociology and Social Research*, 1965b, *49*, 261–267.

Havighurst, R. J. "How does it feel to grow old?" *The Gerontologist*, 1966a, *6*, 130–131.

Havighurst, R. J., B. L. Neugarten, and V. L. Bengston. "A cross-sectional study of adjustment to retirement," *The Gerontologist*, 1966b, *6*, 137–138.

Havighurst, R. J. "Personality and patterns of aging," *The Gerontologist*, 1968, *8*, Part II, 20–23.

Heglin, H. J. "Problem solving set in different age groups," *Journal of Gerontology*, 1956, *11*, 310–317.

Heilbrun, A. B., Jr. "Sex differences in identification learning," *Journal of Genetic Psychology*, 1965a, *10*, 185–193.

Heilbrun, A. B., Jr., and D. K. Fromme. "Parental identification of late adolescence and level of adjustment," *Journal of Genetic Psychology*, 1965b, *107*, 49–59.

Heilbrun, A. B., Jr., and H. K. Orr. "Maternal childrearing control history and subsequent cognitive and personality functioning of the offspring," *Psychological Reports*, 1965c, *17*, 259–272.

Heilbrun, A. B., Jr., and H. K. Orr. "Perceived maternal childrearing history and subsequent motivational effects of failure," *Journal of Genetic Psychology*, 1966, *109*, 75–89.

Henley, B., and M. S. Davis. "Satisfaction and dissatisfaction: a study of the chronically-ill aged patient," *Journal of Health and Social Behavior*, 1967, *8*, 65–75.

Heron, A. "Preparation for retirement: a new phase in occupational development," *Occupational Psychology*, 1962a, *36*, 1–9.

Heron, A. "Immediate memory in dialling performance with and without simple rehearsal," *Quarterly Journal of Experimental Psychology*, 1962b, *14*, 95–103.

Heron, A., and S. Chown. *Age and Function*. Boston: Little, Brown, 1967.

Hess, E., R. B. Roth, and A. F. Kaminsky. "Is there a male climacteric?" *Geriatrics*, 1955, *10*, 170–173.

Hess, R. D., and J. V. Torney. *The Development of Political Attitudes in Children*. Chicago: Aldine, 1967.

Heston, J., and C. F. Connell. "A note on the relation between age and performance of adult subjects on four familiar psychometric tests," *Journal of Applied Psychology*, 1941, *25*, 415–419.

Heston, L. L., D. D. Denny, and I. B. Pauly. "The adult adjustment of persons institutionalized as children," *British Journal of Psychiatry*, 1966, *112*, 1103–1110.

Hetherington, E. M. "A development study of the effects of sex of the dominant parent on sex-role preference, identification, and imitation in children," *Journal of Personality and Social Psychology*, 1965, *2*, 188–194.

Hickey, T., and R. A. Kalish. "Young people's perceptions of adults," *Journal of Gerontology*, 1968, *23*, 215–219.

Hicks, R. A., W. Bramble, and S. Ulseth. "Socialization and time perception in aged subjects," *Perceptual and Motor Skills*, 1967, *24*, 1170.

Higgins, J. W. "Marital health and family planning," *Insight: Quarterly Review of Religion and Mental Health*, 1967, *5*, 12–14.

Hiltner, H. J. "Changing family tasks of adults," *Marriage and Family Living*, 1953, *15*, 110–113.

Hinchcliffe, R. "Aging and sensory thresholds," *Journal of Gerontology*, 1962, *17*, 45–50.

Hinton, J. *Dying*. Baltimore: Penguin, 1967.

Hirt, M. L. "Aptitude changes as a function of age," *Personality and Guidance Journal*, 1964, *43*, 174–176.

Hodgkins, J. "Influence of age on the speed of reaction and movement in females," *Journal of Gerontology*, 1962, *17*, 385–389.

Hoenig, J., and M. W. Hamilton. "Elderly psychiatric patients and the burden on the household," *Psychiatria et Neurologia*, 1966, *152*, 281–293.

Hoffman, M. L., and H. D. Saltzstein. "Parent discipline and the child's moral development," *Journal of Personality and Social Psychology*, 1967, *5*, 45–57.

Holland, J. L. *The Psychology of Vocational Choice*. Waltham, Mass.: Blaisdell, 1966.

Hollander, P. "Leisure as an American and Soviet value," *Social Problems*, 1966, *14*, 179–188.

Hollender, J. W. "Development of a realistic vocational choice," *Journal of Counseling Psychology*, 1967, *14*, 314–318.

Hollingshead, A. B., and F. C. Redlich. *Social Class and Mental Illness*. New York: Wiley, 1958.

Horn, J. L., and R. B. Cattell. "Age differences in primary mental ability factors," *Journal of Gerontology*, 1966, *21*, 210–220.

Horn, J. L., and R. B. Cattell. "Age differences in fluid and crystallized intelligence," *Acta Psychologica,* 1967, *26,* 107–129.
Howe, M. A. "The employment of older workers," *Personnel Practice Bulletin,*
1964, *20,* 33–39.
Hulicka, I. M., and L. D. Rust. "Age related retention deficit as a function of
learning," *Journal of American Geriatric Society,* 1964, *12,* 1061–1065.
Hulicka, I. M. "Age difference for intentional and incidental learning and recall scores," *Journal of American Geriatric Society,* 1965a, *13,* 639–649.
Hulicka, I. M., and R. L. Weiss. "Age differences in retention as a function of
learning," *Journal of Consulting Psychology,* 1965b, *29,* 125–129.
Hulicka, I. M. "Age differences in Wechsler Memory Scale scores," *Journal of
Genetic Psychology,* 1966, *109,* 135–145.
Hulicka, I. M., and J. L. Grossman. "Age-group comparisons for the use of
mediators in paired associate learning," *Journal of Gerontology,* 1967a,
22, 46–51.
Hulicka, I. M. "Age differences in retention as a function of interference,"
Journal of Gerontology, 1967b, *22,* 180–184.
Hulicka, I. M., H. Sterns, and J. Grossman. "Age group comparisons of paired-
associate learning as a function of paced and self-paced association and
response times," *Journal of Gerontology,* 1967c, *22,* 274–280.
Hunt, R. A. "Self and other semantic concepts in relation to choice of a voca-
tion," *Journal of Applied Psychology,* 1967, *51,* 242–246.
Hurley, J. R. "Parental malevolence and children's intelligence," *Journal of
Consulting Psychology,* 1967, *31,* 199–204.
Hurlock, E. *Developmental Psychology,* 2d ed. New York: McGraw-Hill, 1959.
Hurvitz, N. "Control roles, marital strain, role deviation, and marital adjust-
ment," *Journal of Marriage and the Family,* 1965, *27,* 29–31.

Illingworth, R. S., and C. M. Illingworth. *Lessons from Childhood: Some
Aspects of the Early Life of Unusual Men and Women.* Baltimore:
Williams & Wilkins, 1966.
Inglis, J. "Influency of motivation, perception and attention on age-related
changes in short-term memory," *Nature,* 1964, *204,* 103–104.
Inglis, J. "Immediate memory, age and brain function," in Welford, A. T.,
and J. E. Birren (eds.). *Behavior, Aging, and the Nervous System.* Spring-
field, Ill.: Charles C Thomas, 1965a, pp. 88–113.
Inglis, J., and M. N. Ankus. "Effects of age on short-term storage and serial
rote learning," *British Journal of Psychology,* 1965b, *56,* 183–195.
Inglis, J., and C. L. Tansey. "Age differences and scoring differences in dichotic listening performance," *Journal of Psychology,* 1967, *66,* 325–332.
Inselberg, R. M. "Sentence completion technique in the measurement of
marital satisfaction," *Journal of Marriage and the Family,* 1964, *26,* 339–
340.
Irving, S. G. "Parental empathy and adolescent adjustment," *Dissertation
Abstracts,* 1966, *27,* 967–968.
Isotti, E. G. "The relation of ego constriction and interest to recall in the
aged," *Dissertation Abstracts,* 1966, *27,* 1622–1623.

James, G. "Mental health services for older people," *Geriatrics,* 1967, *22,* 162–167.

Jamieson, G. H. "Age, speed and accuracy: a study in industrial retraining," *Occupational Psychology,* 1966, *40,* 237–242.

Jansen, E. F., Jr. "Employment participation behavioral relationships," *Dissertation Abstracts,* 1967, *27,* 2235–2236.

Jaques, E. "Death and the mid-life crisis," *International Journal of Psycho-Analysis,* 1965, *46,* 502–514.

Jarvik, L. F., F. J. Kallman, and A. Falek. "Intellectual changes in aging twins," *Journal of Gerontology,* 1962, *17,* 289–294.

Jeffers, F. C., C. Eisdorfer, and E. W. Busse. "Measurement of age identification: a methodological note," *Journal of Gerontology,* 1962, *17,* 437–439.

Jersild, A. T. *Child Psychology,* 6th ed. Englewood Cliffs, N.J.: Prentice-Hall, 1968.

Johnsen, K. P. "An analysis of factors contributing to within-class differences in maternal role change over two generations," *Dissertation Abstracts,* 1967, *27,* 2210–2211.

Jones, H. E., and H. S. Conrad. "The growth and decline of intelligence: a study of a homogeneous group between the ages ten and sixty," *Genetic Psychology Monographs,* 1933, *13,* 223–298.

Jones, H. E. "The age-relative study of personality," *Acta Psychologica,* 1961, *19,* 140–142.

Jones, M. C. "A report on three growth studies at the University of California," *The Gerontologist,* 1967, *7,* 49–54.

Josselyn, I. M. "Sources of sexual identity," *Child and Family,* 1967, *6,* 38–45.

Kahn, M. W. "Implications for a theory of adult personality from developments in psychoanalytic theory," *Comprehensive Psychology,* 1965, *6,* 85–93.

Kaiman, B. D., H. F. Desroches, and H. T. Ballard. "Therapeutic effectiveness of minimal activity in an aged population," *Psychological Reports,* 1966, *19,* 439–443.

Kalish, R. A. "A continuum of subjectively perceived death," *The Gerontologist,* 1966, *6,* 73–76.

Kalish, R. A. "Of children and grandfathers: a speculative essay on dependency," *The Gerontologist,* 1967, *7,* 65–69.

Kane, F. J., Jr., R. J. Daly, J. A. Ewing, and M. H. Keeler. "Mood and behavioural changes with progestational agents," *British Journal of Psychiatry,* 1967, *113,* 265–268.

Karp, S. A. "Field dependence and occupational activity in the aged," *Perceptual and Motor Skills,* 1967, *24,* 603–609.

Kastenbaum, R. *New Thoughts on Old Age.* New York: Springer, 1964.

Kastenbaum, R. (ed.). *Contributions to the Psycho-Biology of Aging.* New York: Springer, 1965a.

Kastenbaum, R. "Wine and fellowship in aging: an exploratory action program," *Journal of Human Relations,* 1965b, *13,* 266–276.

Kastenbaum, R. "The realm of death: an emerging area in psychological research," *Journal of Human Relations,* 1965c, *13,* 538–552.

Kastenbaum, R. "Death as a research problem in social gerontology: an over view," *The Gerontologist,* 1966a, *6,* 67–69.

Kastenbaum, R. "On the meaning of time in later life," *Journal of Geneti Psychology,* 1966b, *109,* 9–25.

Kastenbaum, R. "As the clock runs out," *Mental Hygiene,* 1966c, *50,* 332–336

Kastenbaum, R. "The impact of experience with the aged upon the time per spective of young adults," *Journal of Genetic Psychology,* 1967, *110,* 159–167.

Kaufmann, C. B. *Man Incorporate: The Individual and His Work in an Organized Society.* Garden City, N.Y.: Doubleday, 1967.

Keene, J. J. "Religious behavior and neuroticism, spontaneity, and world mindedness," *Sociometry,* 1967, *30,* 137–157.

Keller, O. J., and C. B. Vedder. "The crimes that old persons commit," *The Gerontologist,* 1968, *8,* Part I, 43–50.

Kelley, P. R. "Age changes in mental abilities and their life history anteced ents," *Dissertation Abstracts,* 1965, *26,* 1765.

Kennedy, W. A., and H. Willcutt. "Youth-parent relations of mathematically gifted adolescents," *Journal of Clinical Psychology,* 1963, *19,* 400–402

Kent, D. P. "Aging: fact and fancy," *The Gerontologist,* 1965a, *5,* 51–56.

Kent, R. "Children of mothers with authoritarian ideology," *Dissertation Abstracts,* 1965b, *26,* 2313.

Kephart, W. M. "Some correlates of romantic love," *Journal of Marriage and the Family,* 1967, *29,* 494–499.

Kidd, J. *How Adults Learn.* New York: Association Press, 1963.

Kimbrell, G. M., and E. Furchtgott. "The effect of aging on olfactory thresh old," *Journal of Gerontology,* 1963, *18,* 364–365.

Kinnane, J. E., and M. M. Bannon. "Perceived parental influence and work value orientation," *Personnel and Guidance Journal,* 1964, *43,* 273–279

Kinsey, A. C., W. B. Pomeroy, and C. E. Martin. *Sexual Behavior in the Human Male.* Philadelphia: Saunders, 1948.

Kinsey, A. C., W. B. Pomeroy, C. E. Martin, and P. H. Gebhard. *Sexual Be havior in the Human Female.* Philadelphia: Saunders, 1953.

Kirchner, W. K., C. S. McElwain, and M. D. Dunnette. "A note on the rela tionship between age and roles effectiveness," *Journal of Applied Psy chology,* 1960, *44,* 92–93.

Kiss, R. A. "Some effects of a skill learned in youth on relearning in later maturity and old age," *Dissertation Abstracts,* 1967, *27,* 2072.

Kleemeier, R. W. (ed.). *Aging and Leisure: A Research Perspective into the Meaningful Use of Time.* New York: Oxford, 1961.

Klonoff, H., and M. Kennedy. "Memory and perceptual functioning in octo genarians and nonagenarians in the community," *Journal of Geron tology,* 1965, *20,* 328–333.

Klonoff, H., and M. Kennedy. "A comparative study of cognitive functioning in old age," *Journal of Gerontology,* 1966, *21,* 239–243.

Knox, A. B., and D. D. Sjogren. "Achievement and withdrawal in university adult education classes," *Adult Education,* 1965a, *15,* 14–88.

Knox, A. B., and D. D. Sjogren. "Further evidence that young adults can learn as effectively as older adults," *High School Journal,* 1965b, *49,* 73–79.

Knupfer, G., W. Clark, and R. Room. "The mental health of the unmarried," *American Journal of Psychiatry*, 1966, *122*, 841–851.

Kobashigawa, A., K. Arakaki, and A. Awaguni. "Avoidance of feminine toys by kindergarten boys: the effects of adult presence or absence, and an adult's attitudes towards sex-typing," *Japanese Journal of Psychology*, 1966, *37*, 96–103.

Kogan, N., and M. A. Wallach. "Age changes in values and attitudes," *Journal of Gerontology*, 1961, *16*, 272–280.

Koller, M. R. "Studies of three-generation households," *Marriage and Family Living*, 1954, *16*, 205–206.

Komarovsky, M., with the collaboration of J. H. Philips. *Blue-Collar Marriage*. New York: Vintage Books, 1962.

Korman, A. K. "Ethical judgments, self-perceptions and vocational choice," *Proceedings of the 75th Annual Convention of the American Psychological Association*, 1967, *2*, 349–350.

Kotlar, S. L. "Middle-class marital role perceptions and marital adjustment," *Sociology and Social Research*, 1965, *49*, 281–294.

Kovác, D. "Einflus des Alters auf die Leistungen ver visuellen Untersheidungen" [Influence of age on the performance of visual differential sensitivity], *Studia Psychologica, 7*, 187–213.

Kraines, S. J., and E. S. Thetford. *Managing Your Mind*. Greenwich, Conn.: Fawcett, 1966.

Kral, V. A., C. Cahn, and H. Mueller. "Senescent memory impairment and its relation to the general health of the aging individual," *Journal of the American Geriatric Society*, 1964, *12*, 101–113.

Kreps, J. M. "Economic policy and the nation's aged," *The Gerontologist*, 1968, *8*, 37–43.

Kriauciunas, R. "The relationship of age and retention-interval activity in short-term memory," *Journal of Gerontology*, 1968, *23*, 169–173.

Kriesberg, L. "Rearing children for educational achievement in fatherless families," *Journal of Marriage and the Family*, 1967, *29*, 288–301.

Krugman, A. D. "A note on level of aspiration and aging," *Journal of Gerontology*, 1959, *14*, 222–225.

Kuhlen, R. G. "Age differences in personality during adult years," *Psychological Bulletin*, 1945, *42*, 333–358.

Kuhlen, R. G., and G. H. Johnson. "Changes in goals with adult increasing age," *Journal of Consulting Psychology*, 1952, *16*, 1–4.

Kuhlen, R. G., and N. B. Houlihan. "Adolescent heterosexual interest in 1942 and 1963," *Child Development*, 1965, *36*, 1049–1052.

Kuhlen, R. G., R. H. Monge, and E. F. Gardner. *Syracuse University Bibliography Learning and Cognitive Performance in Adults*. Syracuse, N.Y.; Adult Development Study, 1967.

Kumnick, L. W. "Aging and the latency and duration of pupil constriction in response to light and sound stimuli," *Journal of Gerontology*, 1956, *11*, 391–396.

Kurokawa, M. "Family solidarity, social change, and childhood accidents," *Journal of Marriage and the Family*, 1966, *28*, 498–506.

Kurth, E. "Fernsehen und Verholtensstörungen" [T.V. and behavior disturbances], *Zeitschrift für Psychologie*, 1946, *170*, 261–269.

Kushner, R. E., and M. E. Bunch. *Graduate Education in Aging*. Ann Arbor, Mich.: The University of Michigan Press, 1967.

Kutner, B., D. Fanshel, A. M. Togo, and T. S. Langner. *Five Hundred Over Sixty: A Community Survey of Aging*. New York: Russell Sage, 1956.

Ladd, C. E., and E. E. Levitt. "The EPPS heterosexual scale and marital status," *Journal of Clinical Psychology*, 1967, *23*, 192–194.

Landis, J. R., and L. Stoetzer. "An exploratory study of middle-class migrant families," *Journal of Marriage and the Family*, 1966, *28*, 51–53.

Landis, P. H. "Sequential marriage," *Journal of Home Economics*, 1950, *42*, 625–627.

Lane, G. "Adjustment to aging: some applications of learning theory," *The Gerontologist*, 1966, *6*, 88–89.

Lansky, L. "The family structure also affects the model: sex-role attitudes in parents of preschool children," *Merrill-Palmer Quarterly*, 1967, *13*, 139–150.

Latimer, J. "The status of intelligence in the aging," *Journal of Genetic Psychology*, 1963, *102*, 175–188.

Lauer, A. R. "Age and sex in relation to (road) accidents," *Traffic Safety*, 1959, *55*, 6.

Laurance, M. W. "Age differences in performance and subjective organization in the free-recall learning of pictorial material," *Canadian Journal of Psychology*, 1966, *20*, 388–399.

Lawson, J. S. "Changes in immediate memory with age," *British Journal of Psychology*, 1965, *56*, 69–75.

LeBlanc, A. F. "Orientation and estimation of time as a function of age," *Dissertation Abstracts*, 1966, *27*, 1624–1625.

Leckart, B. T., K. R. Keeling, and P. Bakan. "Sex differences in the duration of visual attention," *Perception and Psychophysics*, 1966, *1*, 374–376.

LeCompte, H. "Das Gesetz von LeCompte" [LeCompte's Law], *Zeitschrift für Alternsforschung*, 1965, *18*, 79–81.

Lehman, H. C. *Age and Achievement*. Princeton, N.J.: Princeton University Press, 1953.

Lehman, H. C. "The production of masterworks prior to age 30," *The Gerontologist*, 1965, *5*, 24–30.

Lehr, U. "Attitudes towards the future in old age," *Human Development*, 1967, *10*, 230–238.

Leibowitz, H. W., S. W. Pollard, and D. Dickson. "Monocular and binocular size-matching as a function of distance at various age levels," *American Journal of Psychology*, 1967a, *80*, 263–268.

Leibowitz, H. W., and J. M. Judisch. "Size-constancy in older persons: a function of distance," *American Journal of Psychology*, 1967b, *80*, 294–296.

Leonard, M. R. "Fathers and daughters: The significance of 'fathering' in the psychosexual development of the girl," *International Journal of Psycho-Analysis*, 1966, *47*, 325–334.

Lester, D. "Sibling position and suicidal behavior," *Journal of Individual Psychology*, 1966, *22*, 204–207.

Levine, A. J. "A sound approach to middle age," *Geriatrics*, 1957, *12*, 625–627.

Levine, J., C. Fishman, and J. Kagan. "Social class and sex as determinants of maternal behavior," *American Journal of Orthopsychiatry*, 1967, *37*, 397.

Levine, L. S. *Personal and Social Development*. New York: Holt, Rinehart and Winston, 1963.

Levinger, G. "Note on need complementarity in marriage," *Psychological Bulletin*, 1964, *61*, 153–157.

Levinger, G. "Altruism in marriage: a test of the Buerkle-Badgley battery," *Journal of Marriage and the Family*, 1965, *27*, 32–33.

Levinger, G. "Sources of marital dissatisfaction among applicants for divorce," *American Journal of Orthopsychiatry*, 1966, *36*, 803–807.

Levinger, G., and J. Breedlove. "Interpersonal attraction and agreement: a study of marriage partners," *Journal of Personality and Social Psychology*, 1966, *3*, 367–372.

Lewis, L. S. "Terms of address for parents and some clues about social relationships in the American family," *Family Life Coordinator*, 1965, *14*, 43–46.

Lichtenberg, P. "Reactions to success and failure during individual and cooperative effort," *Journal of Social Psychology*, 1957, *46*, 31–34.

Liebenberg, B. "Expectant fathers," *American Journal of Orthopsychiatry*, 1967, *37*, 358–359.

Lieberman, M. A. "Observations on death and dying," *The Gerontologist*, 1966, *6*, 70–72.

Litman, T. J. "Influence of age on physical rehabilitation," *Geriatrics*, 1964, *19*, 202–207.

Livson, N. "Parental behavior and children's involvement with their parents," *Journal of Genetic Psychology*, 1966, *109*, 173–194.

Lowe, C. M., and R. O. Braaten. "Differences in religious attitudes in mental illness," *Journal for the Scientific Study of Religion*, 1966, *5*, 435–445.

Lowe, C. M. "The relationship between marital and socioeconomic status and in-patient impairment," *Journal of Clinical Psychology*, 1967, *23*, 315–318.

Luchterhand, E., and D. Sydiaha. *Choice in Human Affairs: An Application to Aging-Accident-Illness Problems*. New Haven, Conn.: College and University Press Services, 1966.

Luckey, E. B. "Number of years married as related to personality perception and marital satisfaction," *Journal of Marriage and the Family*, 1966, *28*, 44–48.

Lynn, K., (ed.). *The Professions in America*. Boston: Beacon Press, 1967.

McCall, G. J., and J. L. Simmons. *Identities and Interactions: An Examination of Human Associations in Everyday Life*. New York: Free Press, 1966.

McClusky, H. Y. "Psychology and learning," *Review of Educational Research* 1965, *35*, 191–200.

McFarland, R. A., and M. B. Fisher. "Alterations in dark adaption as a fun tion of age," *Journal of Gerontology*, 1955, *10*, 424–428.

McFarland, R. A., G. S. Tune, and A. T. Welford. "On the driving of aut mobiles by older people," *Journal of Gerontology*, 1964, *19*, 190–197.

McGhie, A. J., and S. M. Russell. "The subjective assessment of norma sleep patterns," *Journal of Mental Science*, 1962, *108*, 642–654.

McGhie, A. J., J. Chapman, and J. S. Lawson. "Changes in immediat memory with age," *British Journal of Psychology*, 1965, *56*, 69–75.

McGinnis, R. *Your First Year of Marriage.* New York: Doubleday, 1967.

McGlone, R. E., and H. Hollien. "Vocal pitch characteristics of aged women, *Journal of Speech and Hearing Research*, 1963, *6*, 164–170.

Machotka, P., and A. S. Ferber. "Delineation of family roles," *America Journal of Orthopsychiatry*, 1967, *37*, 409–410.

Mackie, J. B., and E. C. Beck. "Relations among age, intelligence, and crit cal flicker fusion," *Perceptual and Motor Skills*, 1965, *21*, 875.

McKinney, J. C., and F. T. de Vyver (eds.). *Aging and Social Policy.* Ne York: Appleton-Century-Crofts, 1966.

McNanamy, E. W. "The effect of novelty on time judgment by young an aged persons," *Dissertation Abstracts*, 1966, *27*, 2167.

McNanamy, E. W. "Effect of novelty on time judgment by young and age persons," *Journal of Gerontology*, 1968, *23*, 41–44.

McNeil, J. S., and M. B. Giffen. "Military retirement: the retirement syn drome," *American Journal of Psychiatry*, 1967, *123*, 848–854.

McNulty, J. A., and W. K. Caird. "Memory loss with age: retrieval or stor age?" *Psychological Reports*, 1966, *19*, 229–230.

McNulty, J. A., and W. K. Caird. "Memory loss with age: an unsolved prob lem," *Psychological Reports*, 1967, *20*, 283–288.

Maddox, G. L. "Disengagement theory: a critical evaluation," *The Geron tologist*, 1964, *4*, 80–82, 103.

Maddox, G. L. "Fact and artifact: evidence bearing on disengagement theor from the Duke Geriatrics Project," *Human Development*, 1965, *8*, 117–130.

Mahajan, A. "A study of attitudes of women students toward mate selection, *Journal of Family Welfare*, 1965, *12*, 36–39.

Malhotra, M. S., S. S. Ramaswamy, G. L. Dua, and J. Sengupta. "Physica work capacity as influenced by age," *Ergonomics*, 1966, *9*, 305–316.

Malzberg, B. "Marital status and the incidence of mental disease," *Interna tional Journal of Social Psychiatry*, 1964, *10*, 19–26.

Mandell, A. J. "The value of variety in sexual behavior in the marital rela tionship," in Wahl, C. W. (ed.). *Sexual Problems: Diagnosis and Treat ment in Medical Practice.* New York: Free Press, 1967, pp. 62–70.

Mare, G. D., and R. Sergean. "Two methods of studying changes in absence with age," *Occupational Psychology*, 1961, *35*, 245–252.

Marmor, J. "The crisis of middle age," *American Journal of Orthopsychiatry* 1967, *37*, 336–337.

Martin, P. A., and H. W. Bird. "One type of the 'in-search-of-a-mother' marital pattern," *Psychiatric Quarterly*, 1962, *36*, 283–293.

Marzolf, S. S. "Parents behavior as reported by college students," *Journal of Clinical Psychology*, 1965, *21*, 360–366.

Mason, R. C. "Psychological aging as a function of chronological age and illness: retinal detachment," *Dissertation Abstracts*, 1966, *26*, 6852.

Masters, W. H., and J. W. Ballew. "The third sex," *Geriatrics*, 1955, *10*, 1–4.

Masters, W. H., and V. E. Johnson. *Human Sexual Response.* Boston: Little, Brown, 1966.

May, R. "Fantasy differences in men and women," *Psychology Today*, 1968, *1*, 42–45, 69.

Mayer, J. E. "People's imagery of other families," *Family Process*, 1967a, *6*, 27–36.

Mayer, J. E. "Disclosing marital problems," *Social Casework*, 1967b, *48*, 342–351.

Meer, B., and J. A. Baker. "Reliability of measurements of intellectual functioning of geriatric patients," *Journal of Gerontology*, 1965, *20*, 410–414.

Meier, E. G. "Adults who were foster children," *Children*, 1966, *13*, 16–22.

Meister, D. "A comparative study of figure-ground discrimination in preschool children and adults," *Journal of Genetic Psychology*, 1949, *74*, 311–323.

Melton, C. E., and M. Wicks. "Pilot vision considerations: the effect of age on binocular fusion time," *Office of Aviation Medicine Report*, 1966, No. 66-35.

Meltzer, H. "Age differences in status and happiness of workers," *Geriatrics*, 1962, *17*, 831–838.

Meltzer, H. "Age differences in happiness and life adjustment of workers," *Journal of Gerontology*, 1963, *18*, 66–70.

Meltzer, H. "Attitudes of workers before and after age 40," *Geriatrics*, 1965a, *20*, 425–432.

Meltzer, H. "Mental-health implications of aging in industry," *Journal of Genetic Psychology*, 1965b, *107*, 193–203.

Meltzer, H. "Memory optimism and pessimism of workers," *Perceptual and Motor Skills*, 1966, *23*, 997–998.

Meltzer, H., and D. Ludwig. "Age differences in memory optimism and pessimism in workers," *Journal of Genetic Psychology*, 1967, *110*, 17–30.

Meneghini, K. A., and H. W. Leibowitz. "Effect of stimulus distance and age on shape constancy," *Journal of Experimental Psychology*, 1967, *74*, 241–248.

Mensh, I. N. "Intellectual and other personality adjustments to aging," *The Gerontologist*, 1966, *6*, 104.

Mercer, C. V. "Interrelations among family stability, family composition, residence, and race," *Journal of Marriage and the Family*, 1967, *29*, 456–460.

Merz, F., and K. T. Kalveram. "Kritik der Differenzierungshypothese der Intelligenz" [An evaluation of the hypothesis of intelligence differentiation], *Archiv für die gesamte Psychologie*, 1965, *117*, 287–295.

Middleton, R., and S. Putney. "Student rebellion against parental political beliefs," *Social Forces*, 1963, *41*, 377–383.

Miles, W. R. "Measures of certain human abilities throughout the life span," *Procedures of the National Academy of Sciences*, 1931, *17*, 627–633.

Miller, R., and S. Wiesenfeld. "The treatment of 'moral' masochism in mothers who experienced the loss of a child," *Smith College Studies in Social Work*, 1966, *36*, 148–160.

Milt, H. *Middle Age, Threat or Promise?* New York: Public Affairs Pamphlets, 1960.

Mitchell, D., and W. Wilson. "Relationship of father absence to masculinity and popularity of delinquent boys," *Psychological Reports*, 1967, *20*, 1173–1174.

Montoye, H. J., P. W. Willis, and D. A. Cunningham. "Heart rate response to submaximal exercise: relation to age and sex," *Journal of Gerontology*, 1968, *23*, 127–133.

Moore, B. M., and W. Holtzman. *Tomorrow's Parents: A Study of Youth and Their Families*. Austin, Tex.: University of Texas Press, 1965a.

Moore, B. M. "Age and error in a rote learning task," *Ergonomics*, 1965b, *8*, 305–314.

Moran, G. "Ordinal position and approval motivation," *Journal of Consulting Psychology*, 1967, *31*, 319–320.

Morgan, D. D. "Perceptions of role conflicts and self concepts among career and non-career college educated women," *Dissertation Abstracts*, 1962, *23*, 1816–1817.

Morgenthau, H. J. "Death in the nuclear age," *Commentary*, 1961, *32*, 231–234.

Moriarty, D. M. (ed.). *The Loss of Loved Ones: The Effects of a Death in the Family on Personality Development*. Springfield, Ill.: Charles C Thomas, 1967.

Morrison, D. "Age and light deprivation in relation to reinforcing effects of light onset," *Journal of Comparative and Physiological Psychology*, 1965, *60*, 432–435.

Moulton, R. W., E. Burnstein, P. G. Liberty, and N. Altucher. "Patterning of parental affection and disciplinary dominance as a determinant of guilt and sex typing," *Journal of Personality and Social Psychology*, 1966, *4*, 356–363.

Muller, E. A. "Ocupational work capacity," *Ergonomics*, 1962, *5*, 445–452.

Mulvey, M. C. "Psychological and sociological factors in prediction of career patterns of women," *Genetic Psychology Monographs*, 1963, *68*, 309–386.

Munch-Petersen, S. "Problems relating to patients with senile dementia," *Acta Psychiatrica Scandinavica*, 1966, *42*, 99–103.

Mysak, E. D., and T. D. Hanley. "Aging process in speech: pitch and duration characteristics," *Journal of Gerontology*, 1958, *13*, 309–313.

Nash, H. "Psychological effects and alcohol-antagonizing properties of caffeine," *Quarterly Journal of Studies on Alcohol*, 1966, *27*, 727–734.

Nash, J. "The father in contemporary culture and current psychological literature," *Child Development,* 1965, *36,* 261–297.

Nealy, S. M., and J. G. Goodale. "Worker preferences among time-off benefits and pay," *Journal of Applied Psychology,* 1967, *51,* 357–361.

Nelson, T. *The Torture of Mothers.* Boston: Beacon Press, 1968.

Neubeck, G., and V. M. Schletzer. "A study of extra-marital relationships," *Marriage and Family Living,* 1962, *24,* 279–281.

Neugarten, B. L., and D. C. Garron. "Attitudes of middle-aged persons toward growing older," *Geriatrics,* 1959, *14,* 21–24.

Neugarten, B. L., R. J. Havighurst, and S. S. Tobin. "The measurement of life satisfaction," *Journal of Gerontology,* 1961, *16,* 134–143.

Neugarten, B. L., and Associates. *Personality in Middle and Late Life.* New York: Atherton Press, 1964a.

Neugarten, B. L., and K. K. Weinstein. "The changing American grandparent," *Journal of Marriage and the Family,* 1964b, *26,* 199–206.

Neugarten, B. L. "Personality changes in the aged," *Catholic Psychological Record,* 1965a, *3,* 9–17.

Neugarten, B. L. "Personality and patterns of aging," *Gawein,* 1965b, *13,* 249–256.

Neugarten, B. L., and R. J. Kraines. "Menopausal symptoms in women of various ages," *Psychosomatic Medicine,* 1965c, *27,* 266–273.

Nisbett, R. E., and A. Gordon. "Self-esteem and susceptibility to social influence," *Journal of Personality and Social Psychology,* 1967, *5,* 268–276.

Noble, C. E., B. L. Baker, and T. A. Jones. "Age and sex parameters in psychomotor learning," *Perceptual and Motor Skills,* 1964, *19,* 935–945.

Nodine, J. H., *et al.* "A double-blind study of the effect of ribonucleic acid in senile brain disease," *American Journal of Psychiatry,* 1967, *123,* 1257–1259.

Noll, R. P. "Insights of the middle-aged child concerning the parent in a home for old people," *Journal of Human Relations,* 1965, *13,* 62–79.

Norris, A. H., and N. W. Shock. "Aging and variability," *Annals of the New York Academy of Science,* 1966, *134,* 591–600.

Nunn, C. Z. "Child control through a 'coalition with God,'" *Child Development,* 1964, *35,* 417–432.

Nye, F. I. "Employment status of mothers and adjustment of adolescent children," *Marriage and Family Living,* 1959, *21,* 240–244.

Nye, F. I., and F. M. Berardo (eds.). *Emerging Conceptual Frameworks in Family Analysis.* New York: Macmillan, 1966.

Oakes, C. G. "Parental aspirations for children that are associated with emotional disturbance in young sons," *Dissertation Abstracts,* 1966, *27,* 835–836.

Oberg, W. "Personnel psychology," *Journal of Applied Research,* 1960, *13,* 245–259.

Oberlander, M., and N. Jenkin. "Birth order and academic achievement," *Journal of Individual Psychology,* 1967, *23,* 103–109.

Oberleder, M. "Effects of psycho-social factors on test results of the aging," *Psychological Reports,* 1964, *14,* 383–387.

Oberleder, M. "Psychotherapy with the aging: an art of the possible?" *Psychotherapy: Theory, Research and Practice,* 1966, *3,* 139–142.

Oberleder, M. "Adapting current psychological techniques for use in testing the aging," *The Gerontologist,* 1967, *7,* 188–191.

O'Connell, W. E. "Item analysis of the WHAT test," *Journal of Social Psychology,* 1962, *56,* 271–276.

Ogilvie, H. (ed.). *Fifty: An Approach to the Problems of Middle Age.* Springfield, Ill.: Charles C Thomas, 1962.

Olsen, I. A. "Discrimination of auditory information as related to aging," *Journal of Gerontology,* 1965, *20,* 394–397.

O'Neil, W. M. "The stability of the main pattern of abilities with changing age," *Australian Journal of Psychology,* 1962, *14,* 1–8.

Orshansky, M. "Counting the poor: another look at the poverty profile," *Social Security Bulletin,* 1965, *28,* 3–29.

Orshansky, M. "The poor in city and suburb, 1964," *Social Security Bulletin,* 1966, *29,* 22–37.

Osofsky, H. H., and S. Fisher. "Psychological correlates of the development of amenorrhea in a stress situation," *Psychosomatic Medicine,* 1967, *29,* 15–22.

Owens, W. A. "Age and mental abilities: a longitudinal study," *Genetic Psychology Monographs,* 1953, *48,* 3–54.

Owens, W. A. "Is age kinder to the initially more able?" *Journal of Gerontology,* 1959, *14,* 334–337.

Owens, W. A. "Age and mental abilities: a second adult follow-up," *Journal of Educational Psychology,* 1966, *57,* 311–325.

Paine, F. T., D. R. Deutsch, and R. A. Smith. "Relationship between family backgrounds and work values," *Journal of Applied Psychology,* 1967, *51,* 320–323.

Palermo, D. S., G. B. Flamer, and J. J. Jenkins. "Association value of responses in paired-associate learning of children and adults," *Journal of Verbal Learning and Verbal Behavior,* 1964, *3,* 171–175.

Pallone, N. J., and M. Hosinski. "Reality-testing a vocational choice: congruence between self, ideal, and occupational percepts among student nurses," *Personnel and Guidance Journal,* 1967, *45,* 666–670.

Paris, B. L., and E. B. Luckey. "A longitudinal study in marital satisfaction," *Sociology and Social Research,* 1966, *50,* 212–222.

Parke, R., Jr., and P. C. Glick. "Prospective changes in marriage and the family," *Journal of Marriage and the Family,* 1967, *29,* 249–256.

Pearl, R. "Variations and correlation in brain weight," *Biometrics,* 1905, *4,* 13–104.

Peck, R. F. "Measuring the mental health of normal adults," *Genetic Psychology Monographs,* 1959, *60,* 197–255.

Penrose, L. S. "The effects of change in maternal age distribution upon the incidence of mongolism," *Journal of Mental Deficiency Research,* 1967, *11,* 54–57.

Perdue, O. R., and C. D. Spielberger. "Anxiety and the perception of punishment," *Mental Hygiene,* 1966, *50,* 390–397.

Perry, J. B., Jr. "The mother substitutes of employed mothers: an exploratory inquiry," *Marriage and Family Living,* 1961, *23,* 362–367.

Peterson, D. R., *et al.* "Parental attitudes and child adjustment," in Endler, N. S., L. R. Boulter, and H. Osser (eds.). *Contemporary Issues in Developmental Psychology.* New York: Holt, Rinehart and Winston, 1968.

Peterson, E. T. "The impact of maternal employment on the mother-daughter relationship," *Marriage and Family Living,* 1961, *23,* 355–361.

Phillips, B. S. "Role change, subjective age, and adjustment: a correlational analysis," *Journal of Gerontology,* 1961, *16,* 347–352.

Phillips, D. L. "Social participation and happiness," *American Journal of Sociology,* 1967, *72,* 479–488.

Photiadis, J. D. "Community size and aspects of the authoritarian personality among businessmen," *Rural Sociology,* 1967, *32,* 70–77.

Pickford, J. H., E. I. Signori, and H. Rempel. "Similar or related personality traits as a factor in marital happiness," *Journal of Marriage and the Family,* 1966, *28,* 190–192.

Pickford, J. H., E. I. Signori, and H. Rempel. "Husband-wife differences in personality traits as a factor in marital happiness," *Psychological Reports,* 1967, *20,* 1087–1090.

Pikunas, P., and E. J. Albrecht. *Psychology of Human Development.* New York: McGraw-Hill, 1961.

Pinard, M. "Marriage and divorce decisions and the larger social system: a case study in social change," *Social Forces,* 1966, *44,* 341–355.

Pincus, A. "Toward a developmental view of aging for social work," *Social Work,* 1967, *12,* 33–41.

Pishkin, V., and J. T. Shurley. "Auditory dimensions and irrelevant information in concept identification of males and females," *Perceptual and Motor Skills,* 1965, *20,* 673–683.

Plag, J. A., and L. E. Hardacre. "Age, years of schooling, and intelligence as predictors of military effectiveness for naval enlistees," *USN Medical Neuropsychiatric Research Unit Report,* 1965, No. 65-19, 1–40.

Platt, J. J., and R. E. Taylor. "Homesickness, future time perspective, and the self concept," *Journal of Individual Psychology,* 1967, *23,* 94–97.

Platt, L. R., and A. S. Parkes (eds.). *Social and Genetic Influences on Life and Death.* New York: Plenum Press, 1968.

Plym, D. L. "Employee self-disclosure as related to illness-absenteeism, self-perceived wellness and job satisfaction," *Dissertation Abstracts,* 1967, *27,* 2617–2618.

Podell, L. "Occupational and familial role-expectations," *Journal of Marriage and the Family,* 1967, *29,* 492–493.

Porter, S. "Naming of women to high U.S. jobs linked to progress," *Chicago Daily News,* April 5, 1965.

Porter, S. "Stock up for empty nest," *Chicago Daily News,* October 4, 1967.

Porter S. "New law aids older worker," *Chicago Daily News,* May 16, 1968.

Porteus, S. D., and K. David. "Australian mental development and geriatric decline," *Perceptual and Motor Skills,* 1966, *23,* 75–87.

Posner, W. "Basic issues in case-work with older people," *Social Casework,* 1961, *42,* 235–240.

Postema, L. J., and R. E. Schnell. "Aging and psychopathology: some MMPI evidence for seemingly greater neurotic behavior among older people," *Journal of Clinical Psychology*, 1967, *23*, 140–143.

Poulton, E. C. "Letter differentiation and rate of comprehension in reading," *Journal of Applied Psychology*, 1965, *49*, 358–362.

Powell, M. H., C. Eisdorfer, and M. D. Bogdonoff. "Physiologic response patterns observed in a learning task," *Archives of General Psychiatry*, 1964, *10*, 192–195.

Pressey, S. L., and R. G. Kuhlen. *Psychological Development Through the Life Span*. New York: Harper & Row, 1957.

Pressey, S. L., and A. D. Pressey. "Two insiders' searchings for best life in old age," *The Gerontologist*, 1966a, *6*, 14–16.

Pressey, S. L. "Not all decline!" *The Gerontologist*, 1966b, *6*, 66.

Pressey, S. L., and A. D. Pressey. "Genius at 80; and other oldsters," *The Gerontologist*, 1967, *7*, 183–187.

Preston, C. E. "Self-reporting among retired and non-retired older subjects," *Journal of Gerontology*, 1967, *22*, 415–420.

Preston, C. E. "Subjectively perceived agedness and retirement," *Journal of Gerontology*, 1968, *23*, 201–204.

Preston, G. A. "Parental role perceptions and identification in adolescent girls," *Dissertation Abstracts*, 1966, *27*, 612–613.

Prothro, E. T. "Socialization and social class in transitional society," *Child Development*, 1966, *37*, 219–228.

Ptacek, P. H., and E. K. Sander. "Age recognition from voice," *Journal of Speech and Hearing Research*, 1966, *9*, 273–277.

Rabbie, J. "A cross-cultural comparison of parent-child relationship in the United States and West Germany," *British Journal of Social and Clinical Psychology*, 1965, *4*, 298–310.

Rabbitt, P. M. A. "Set and age in a choice-response task," *Journal of Gerontology*, 1964a, *19*, 301–306.

Rabbitt, P. M. A. "Age and time for choice between stimuli and between responses," *Journal of Gerontology*, 1964b, *19*, 307–312.

Rabbitt, P. M. A. "Grouping of stimuli in pattern recognition as a function of age," *Quarterly Journal of Experimental Psychology*, 1964c, *16*, 172–176.

Rabbitt, P. M. A. "Age and discrimination between complex stimuli," in Welford, A. T., and J. E. Birren (eds.). *Behavior, Aging and the Nervous System*. Springfield, Ill.: Charles C Thomas, 1965a, pp. 35–53.

Rabbitt, P. M. A., and M. Rogers. "Age and choice between responses in a self-paced repetitive task," *Ergonomics*, 1965b, *8*, 435–444.

Rabbitt, P. M. A. "An age decrement in the ability to ignore irrelevant information," *Journal of Gerontology*, 1965c, *20*, 233–238.

Rabkin, R. "Uncoordinated communication between marriage partners," *Family Process*, 1967, *6*, 10–15.

Radcliffe, J. A. "WAIS factorial structure and factor scores for ages 18 to 54," *Australian Journal of Psychology*, 1966, *18*, 228–238.

Raines, R. A. *The Secular Congregation*. New York: Harper & Row, 1968.

Rainwater, L. "Some aspects of lower class sexual behavior," *Journal of Social Issues*, 1966, *22*, 96–108.

Rajalakshmi, R., and M. A. Jeeves. "Changes in tachistoscopic form perception as a function of age and intellectual status," *Journal of Gerontology*, 1963, *18*, 275–278.

Rallings, E. M. "Family situations of married and never-married males," *Journal of Marriage and the Family*, 1966, *28*, 485–490.

Ramamurti, P. U. "Problems of aging in industry," *Journal of the Indian Academy of Applied Psychology*, 1965, *2*, 30–33.

Rebhun, M. T. "Parental attitudes and the closed belief-disbelief system," *Psychological Reports*, 1967, *20*, 260–262.

Reed, H. B. C., and R. M. Reitan. "The significance of age in the performance of a complex psychomotor task by brain-damaged and non-brain-damaged subjects," *Journal of Gerontology*, 1962, *17*, 193–196.

Rees, B. J. (ed.). *Modern American Prose Selections*. New York: Harcourt, Brace & World, 1920.

Reichard, S., F. Livson, and P. Peterson. *Aging and Personality*. New York: Wiley, 1962.

Reimanis, G. "Relationship of childhood experience memories to anomie later in life," *Journal of Genetic Psychology*, 1965, *106*, 245–252.

Reimanis, G. "Childhood experience memories: anomie in adults and college students," *Journal of Individual Psychology*, 1966, *22*, 56–64.

Reiss, P. J. "The trend in interfaith marriages," *Journal for the Scientific Study of Religion*, 1965, *5*, 64–67.

Rheingold, J. C. *The Mother, Anxiety and Death: The Catastrophic Death Complex*. Boston: Little, Brown, 1967.

Richardson, S. A., and A. F. Guttmacher (eds.). *Childbearing—Its Social and Psychological Aspects*. Baltimore: Williams & Wilkins, 1967.

Riegel, K. F., and R. M. Riegel. "Changes in associative behavior during later years of life: a cross-sectional analysis," *Vita Humana*, 1964, *7*, 1–32.

Riegel, K. F. "Age and cultural differences as determinants of word associations: suggestions for their analysis," *Psychological Reports*, 1965a, *16*, 75–78.

Riegel, K. F., and J. E. Birren. "Age differences in associative behavior," *Journal of Gerontology*, 1965b, *20*, 125–130.

Riegel, K. F., and J. E. Birren. "Age differences in verbal associations," *Journal of Genetic Psychology*, 1966, *108*, 153–170.

Riegel, K. F., and J. E. Birren. "Age differences in choice reaction times to verbal stimuli," *Gerontologia*, 1967a, *13*, 1–13.

Riegel, K. F., R. M. Riegel, and G. Meyer. "Socio-psychological factors of aging: a cohort-sequential analysis," *Human Development*, 1967b, *10*, 27–56.

Riegel, K. F., R. M. Riegel, and G. Meyer. "A study of the dropout rates in longitudinal research on aging and the prediction of death," *Journal of Personality and Social Psychology*, 1967c, *5*, 342–348.

Robbins, L. C. "The accuracy of parental recall of aspects of child development and of child rearing practices," *Journal of Abnormal and Social Psychology*, 1963, *66*, 261–270.

Rodman, H. "Marital power in France, Greece, Yugoslavia, and the United States: A cross-national discussion," *Journal of Marriage and the Family*, 1967, *29*, 320–324.

Roe, A. *Alcohol Science in Society*. New Haven, Conn.: Yale, 1945.

Rogers, R. *Coming into Existence: The Struggle to Become an Individual*. Cleveland: World Publishing, 1967.

Rokosz, S. F., and R. E. Correll. "Free association responses as a function of age and stimulus frequency," *Psychological Reports*, 1966, *18*, 195–199.

Rose, A. M. "Factors associated with the life satisfactions of middle-class, middle-aged persons," *Marriage and Family Living*, 1955, *17*, 15–19.

Rose, A. M., and W. A. Peterson (eds.). *Older People and Their Social World*. Philadelphia: Davis, 1965.

Rose, A. M. "Class differences among the elderly," *Sociology and Social Research*, 1966, *50*, 356–360.

Rosen, J. L., and B. L. Neugarten. "Ego functions in the middle and later years: a thematic apperception study of normal adults," *Journal of Gerontology*, 1960, *15*, 62–67.

Rosenbaum, S., and I. Alger. *The Marriage Relationship: Psychoanalytic Perspectives*. New York: Basic Books, 1968.

Rosenfeld, H. "Relationships of ordinal position to affiliation and achievement motives: direction and generality," *Journal of Personality*, 1966, *34*, 467–469.

Rosow, I. "Relationship of older persons to family and friends," *Welfare Review*, 1965, *3*, 7–15.

Rosow, I., and N. Breslow. "A Guttman scale for the aged," *Journal of Gerontology*, 1966, *21*, 556–559.

Rosow, I. *Social Integration of the Aged*. New York: Free Press, 1967.

Ross, H. A. "Protective services for the aged," *The Gerontologist*, 1968, *8*, Part II, 50–53.

Rossman, J. E., and P. P. Campbell. "Why college-trained mothers work," *Personnel and Guidance Journal*, 1965, *43*, 986–992.

Rothbart, M. K., and E. E. Maccoby. "Parents differential reactions to sons and daughters," *Journal of Personality and Social Psychology*, 1966, *4*, 237–243.

Ruch, F. L. "The differentiative effects of age upon human learning," *Journal of General Psychology*, 1934, *11*, 261–286.

Russek, H. I. "Emotional stress in the etiology of coronary heart disease," *Geriatrics*, 1967, *22*, 84–89.

Ryder, R. G. "Compatibility in marriage," *Psychological Reports*, 1967, *20*, 807–813.

Saleh, S. D., and T. G. Grygier. "Self-perception of productivity before retirement," *Personnel Administration*, 1966, *29*, 35–39.

Salzman, L. "Psychology of the female: a new look," *Archives of General Psychiatry*, 1967, *17*, 195–203.

Sampson, E. E., and F. T. Hancock. "An examination of the relationship between ordinal position, personality, and conformity," *Journal of Personality and Social Psychology*, 1967, *5*, 398–407.

Sanders, S., M. Laurendeau, and J. Bergeron. "Aging and the concept of space: the conservation of surface," *Journal of Gerontology*, 1965, *21*, 281.

Sanders, W. H. "A study of art attitudes and graphic expression among the retired: an experimental program in art education," *Dissertation Abstracts*, 1966, *27*, 371.

Sartain, J. A. "Attitudes of parents and children toward desegregation," *Dissertation Abstracts*, 1966, *27*, 1460–1461.

Sarvis, M. A., and S. Rauch. "Longitudinal study of a patient with premature ego development," *Journal of the American Academy of Child Psychiatry*, 1966, *5*, 46–65.

Sataloff, J., and L. Vassalo. "Hard-of-hearing senior citizens and the physician," *Geriatrics*, 1966, *21*, 182–185.

Savage, R. D., and P. G. Britton. "The factorial structure of the WAIS in an aged sample," *Journal of Gerontology*, 1968, *23*, 183–186.

Schaie, K. W., and C. R. Strother. "Models for the prediction of age changes in cognitive behavior," *The Gerontologist*, 1964, *4*, 14. (Abstract.)

Scheidler, K. "Die medizinischen und sozialen Probleme um den alten Menschen" [Medical and social problems about old people], *Zeitschift für Alternsforschung*, 1965, *18*, 82–94.

Schmidhauser, J. "The political influence of the aged," *The Gerontologist*, 1968, *8*, Part II, 44–49.

Schonfeld, W. A. "Body-image disturbances in adolescents: IV. Influence of family attitudes and psychopathology," *Archives of General Psychiatry*, 1966, *15*, 16–21.

Schonfeld, D. "Memory changes with age," *Nature*, 1965, *208*, 918.

Schonfeld, D., and W. Donaldson. "Immediate memory as a function of intraseries variation," *Canadian Journal of Psychology*, 1966a, *20*, 218–227.

Schonfeld, D., and B. A. Robertson. "Memory storage and aging," *Canadian Journal of Psychology*, 1966b, *20*, 228–236.

Schonfeld, D. "Memory loss with age: acquisition and retrieval," *Psychological Reports*, 1967, *20*, 223–226.

Schutz, W. C. *Joy: Expanding Human Awareness*. New York: Grove Press, 1967.

Schwartz, A. N. "The effects of illness and age upon some aspects of personality," *Dissertation Abstracts*, 1963, *24*, 386–387.

Schwartz, D. W., and S. A. Karp. "Field dependence in a geriatric population," *Perceptual and Motor Skills*, 1967, *24*, 495–504.

Sechrest, L., and J. Wallace, Jr. *Psychology and Human Problems*. Columbus, Ohio: Merrill, 1967.

Seeman, M. "On the personal consequences of alienation in work," *American Sociological Review*, 1967, *32*, 273–285.

Selye, H. *The Stress of Life*. New York: McGraw-Hill, 1956.

Shaffer, J. P. "Fisher's 'power orientation and concept of self height in men:' a comment," *Perceptual and Motor Skills*, 1965, *20*, 459–460.

Shagass, C., and M. Schwartz. "Age, personality, and somatosensory cerebral evoked responses," *Science*, 1965, *148*, Whole No. 3675, 1359–1361.

Shanan, J., and M. Sharon. "Personality and functioning of Israeli males during the middle years," *Human Development*, 1965, *8*, 2–15.

Sharadamba, R. "Sibling position and mental disorders," *Psychiatric Quarterly Supplement*, 1965, *39*, 27–47.

Shaw, M. C., and D. L. White. "The relationship between child-parent identification and academic underachievement," *Journal of Clinical Psychology*, 1965, *21*, 10–13.

Shepard, A. W., D. S. Abbey, and M. Humphries. "Age and sex in relation to perceptual-motor performance on several control-display relations on the TCC," *Perceptual and Motor Skills*, 1962, *14*, 103–118.

Sherwood, S. "Sociological aspects of learning and memory," *The Gerontologist*, 1967, *7*, 19–23.

Shipman, W. G. "Age of menarche and adult personality," *Archives of General Psychiatry*, 1964, *10*, 155–159.

Shneidman, E. S., and N. L. Farberow (eds.). *Clues to Suicide.* New York: McGraw-Hill, 1957.

Shneidman, E. S. "Suicide," in Farberow, N. L. (ed.). *Taboo Topics.* New York: Atherton Press, 1963.

Shock, N. W. "Gerontology (later maturity)," *Annual Review of Psychology*, 1961, *2*, 353–370.

Shostrom, E. L. *Man, the Manipulator: The Inner Journey from Manipulation to Actualization.* Nashville, Tenn.: Abingdon, 1967.

Silverman, I. "Age and tendency to withhold response," *Journal of Gerontology*, 1963, *18*, 372–375.

Simon, A. *The New Years: A New Middle Age.* New York: Knopf. 1968a.

Simon, A. "The geriatric mentally ill," *The Gerontologist*, 1968b, *8*, Part II, 7–15.

Singer, E. "Birth order, educational aspirations, and educational attainment," *Dissertation Abstracts*, 1967, *27*, 2638.

Singer, J. L. "A factor-analytic study of daydreaming and related cognitive and personality variables," *Perceptual and Motor Skills*, 1963, *3*, supplement.

Singer, J. L. *Daydreaming: An Introduction to the Experimental Study of Inner Experience.* New York: Random House, 1966.

Singer, J. L. "The importance of daydreaming," *Psychology Today*, 1968, *1*, 18–26.

Singleton, W. T. "The change of movement timing with age," *British Journal of Gerontology*, 1965, *20*, 483–488.

Sinha, J. B. "Birth order and sex differences in n-achievement and n-affiliation," *Journal of Psychological Researches*, 1967, *11*, 22–27.

Skawran, P. R. "Die Intelligenz als Werkzenzdes Ich" [Intelligence as a tool of the ego], *Psychologische Rundschau*, 1965, *4*, 263–281.

Skolnick, A. "Stability and interrelations of thematic test imagery over 20 years," *Child Development*, 1966, *37*, 389–396.

Slotkin, J. S. "Life course in middle age," *Social Forces*, 1954, *33*, 171–177.

Smith, P. M., Jr. "Personality rating of students whose fathers are professional or non-professional workers," *Journal of Educational Research,* 1966, *17,* 22–25.

Smith, W. C. *The Step-Child.* Chicago: The University of Chicago Press, 1953.

Smith, W. M. "Family plans for later years," *Marriage and Family Living,* 1954, *16,* 36–40.

Snider, A. J. "The ired wife in retired life—doctor describes forgotten women," *Chicago Daily News,* June 22, 1964.

Sobanska, J. "Problemy wzajemnych stuosunkau miedzy mlodzieza a rodzicami" [Relationships between adolescents and their parents], *Psychologia Wychowawcza,* 1965, *3,* 225–245.

Sobel, H. "When does human aging start?" *The Gerontologist,* 1966, *6,* 17–22.

Solomon, L., and R. Nuttall. "Sibling order, premorbid adjustment and remission in schizophrenia," *Journal of Nervous and Mental Disease,* 1967, *144,* 37–46.

Solyom, L., and H. C. Barik. "Conditioning in senescence and senility," *Journal of Gerontology,* 1965, *20,* 483–488.

Speakman, D. "The effect of age on the incidental relearning of stamp values," *Journal of Gerontology,* 1954, *9,* 162–167.

Spieth, W. "Cardiovascular health status, age, and psychological performance," *Journal of Gerontology,* 1964, *19,* 277–284.

Spitzer, E. P. "Counseling aging persons with self-bounded life styles," *Journal of Individual Psychology,* 1966, *22,* 104–111.

Sprague, H. D. "Perceptions of family life attitudes among male college students and their fathers," *Dissertation Abstracts,* 1966, *27,* 1273.

Sprague, N. "A note on terminology," *The Gerontologist,* 1968, *8,* Part I, 59.

Srour, G. M., R. J. Finnegan, and C. A. Delcioppo. "A new approach to recreational therapy with older chronically hospitalized patients," *Psychiatric Quarterly Supplement,* 1966, *40,* 10–16.

Stacey, B. G. "Some psychological aspects of inter-generation occupational mobility," *British Journal of Social and Clinical Psychology,* 1965, *4,* 275–286.

Stacey, B. G. "Some psychological consequences of inter-generation mobility," *Human Relations,* 1967, *20,* 3–12.

Stein, C. I. "The GATB. The effect of age on the intersample variation," *Personnel and Guidance Journal,* 1962, *40,* 779–783.

Steindl-Rast, D. F. "A deep bow," *Main Currents in Modern Thought,* 1967, *23,* 128–132.

Steiner, L. R. *Romantic Marriage: The Twentieth Century Illusion.* Philadelphia: Chilton, 1963.

Stephenson, W. *The Play Theory of Mass Communication.* Chicago: The University of Chicago Press, 1967.

Stewart, D. J., and S. Chown. "A comparison of the effects of a continuous and a linear programmed text on adult pupils," *Occupational Psychology,* 1965, *39,* 135–144.

Stewart, N., and W. J. Sparks. "Patent productivity of research chemists as related to age and experience," *Personnel and Guidance Journal,* 1966, *45,* 28–36.

Stewart, R. H. "Birth order and dependency," *Journal of Personality and Social Psychology,* 1967, *6,* 192–194.

Stimson, J. B. "Husband-wife similarity, agreement and fertility," *Dissertation Abstracts,* 1966, *27,* 834.

Stineman, W. F. "An analysis of urban and rural boys evaluation of their fathers," *Dissertation Abstracts,* 1961, *21,* 3184.

Stolz, L. M. *Influences on Parent Behavior.* Stanford, Calif.: Stanford University Press, 1967.

Stone, A., and L. Levine. "The dynamics of the marital relationship," *Mental Hygiene,* 1953, *37,* 606–614.

Strauss, A. L., and B. G. Glaser. *Time for Dying.* Chicago: Aldine, 1968.

Strehler, B. L. *Time, Cells, and Aging.* New York: Academic, 1962.

Strehler, B. L. (ed.). *Advances in Gerontological Research, Vol. 2.* New York: Academic, 1964.

Streib, G. F. "Intergenerational relationships: perspectives of the two generations on the older parent," *Journal of Marriage and the Family,* 1965, *27,* 469–476.

Stringer, L. A., and D. J. Pittman. "The unmeasured residual in current research on parental attitudes and child behavior," in Glidewell, J. C. (ed.). *Parental Attitudes and Child Behavior.* Springfield, Ill.: Charles C Thomas, 1961.

Strong, E. K., Jr. "Vocational interest of men and women," *Journal of Social Psychology,* 1936, *7,* 49–67.

Stump, W. L., J. E. Jordan, and E. W. Friesen. "Cross-cultural considerations in understanding vocational development," *Journal of Counseling Psychology,* 1967, *14,* 325–331.

Suits, B. "What is a game?" *Philosophy of Science,* 1967, *34,* 148–156.

Sundararaj, N., and R. R. Sridhara. "Order of birth and schizophrenia," *British Journal of Psychiatry,* 1966, *112,* 1127–1129.

Surwillo, W. W., and R. Quilter. "Vigilance, age, and response-time," *American Journal of Psychology,* 1964a, *77,* 614–620.

Surwillo, W. W. "The relation of decision time to brain wave frequency and to age," *Electroencephalography and Clinical Neurophysiology,* 1964b, *16,* 510–514.

Surwillo, W. W. "Age and the perception of short intervals of time," *Journal of Gerontology,* 1964c, *19,* 322–324.

Surwillo, W. W., and R. E. Quilter. "The relation of frequency of spontaneous skin potential responses to vigilance and to age," *Psychophysiology,* 1965, *1,* 272–276.

Surwillo, W. W. "The relation of autonomic activity to age differences in vigilance," *Journal of Gerontology,* 1966, *21,* 257–260.

Sussman, M. B. "The help pattern of the middle-class family," *American Sociological Review,* 1953, *18,* 22–28.

Sussman, M. B. "Intergenerational family relationships and social role changes in middle age," *Journal of Gerontology,* 1960, *15,* 71–75.

Sutton-Smith, B., J. M. Roberts, and R. M. Kozelka. "Game involvement in adults," *Journal of Social Psychology,* 1963, *60,* 15–30.

Sutton-Smith, B., and B. G. Rosenberg. "Age changes in the effects of ordinal position on sex role identification," *Journal of Genetic Psychology*, 1965, *107*, 61–73.

Swift, M. S. "Parent childbearing attitudes and psychological health of the parent," *Dissertation Abstracts*, 1966, *27*, 1274.

Swinehart, J. W. "Socio-economic level, status aspiration, and maternal role," *American Sociological Review*, 1963, *28*, 391–399.

Szafran, J. "Decision processes and aging," in Welford, A. T., and J. E. Birren (eds.). *Behavior, Aging, and the Nervous System*. Springfield, Ill.: Charles C Thomas, 1965a, pp. 21–34.

Szafran, J. "Age differences in sequential decisions and cardiovascular status among pilots," *Aerospace Medicine*, 1965b, *36*, 303–310.

Szafran, J. "Age differences in the rate of gain of information, signal detection strategy, and cardiovascular status among pilots," *Gerontologia*, 1966, *12*, 6–17.

Szilard, L. "On the nature of the aging process," *Procedures of the National Academy of Science*, 1959, *45*, 32–45.

Tabachnick, N. "Self-realization and social definition: two aspects of identity formation," *International Journal of Psycho-Analysis*, 1967, *48*, 68–75.

Talland, G. A. "The effect of age on speed of a simple manual skill," *Journal of Genetic Psychology*, 1962, *100*, 69–76.

Talland, G. A. "Three estimates of the word span and their stability over the adult years," *Quarterly Journal of Experimental Psychology*, 1965, *17*, 301–307.

Talland, G. A. "Visual signal detection as a function of age, input rate, and signal frequency," *Journal of Psychology*, 1966a, *63*, 105–115.

Talland, G. A. "Performance studies in human aging and their theoretical significance," *Psychiatric Digest*, 1966b, *27*, 37–53.

Talland, G. A. "Age and the immediate memory span," *The Gerontologist*, 1967, *7*, 4–9.

Talland, G. A. (ed.). *Human Behavior and Aging*. New York: Academic, 1968.

Taub, H. A. "Visual short-term memory as a function of age, rate of presentation, and schedule of presentation," *Journal of Gerontology*, 1966, *21*, 388–391.

Taub, H. A., and S. Grieff. "Effects of age on organization and recall of two sets of stimuli," *Psychonomic Science*, 1967, *7*, 53–54.

Teahan, J. E. "Parental attitudes and college success," *Journal of Educational Psychology*, 1963, *54*, 104–109.

Terman, L. M., and M. H. Oden. *The Gifted Group at Mid-Life*. Stanford, Calif.: Stanford University Press, 1959.

Tharp, R. G. "Psychological patterning in marriage," *Psychological Bulletin*, 1963, *60*, 97–117.

Tharp, R. G. "Reply to Levinger's note," *Psychological Bulletin*, 1964, *61*, 158–160.

Theobald, R. *Dialogue on Women*. Indianapolis: Bobbs-Merrill, 1967.

Thomas, J. M., and D. C. Charles. "Effects of age and stimulus size on perception," *Journal of Gerontology*, 1964, *19*, 447–450.

Thompson, J. L. "Stresses in middle life from the psychiatrist's viewpoint," *Geriatrics*, 1955, *10*, 162–164.

Thompson, L. W., S. Axelrod, and L. D. Cohen. "Senescence and visual identification of tactual-kinesthetic forms," *Journal of Gerontology*, 1965, *20*, 244–249.

Thompson, L. W., and S. W. Wilson. "Electrocortical reactivity and learning in the elderly," *Journal of Gerontology*, 1966, *21*, 45–51.

Thorndike, E. L., *et al. Adult Learning.* New York: Macmillan, 1928.

Thoroman, E. C. *The Vocational Counseling of Adults and Young Adults.* Boston: Houghton Mifflin, 1968.

Thumin, F. J., and C. Boeonke. "Ability scores as related to age among female job applicants," *Journal of Gerontology*, 1966, *21*, 369–371.

Thune, J. M. "Racial attitudes of older adults," *Journal of Genetic Psychology*, 1967, *7*, 179–182.

Tibbitts, C. "Retirement problems in American society," *American Journal of Sociology*, 1954, *59*, 301–308.

Tibbitts, C., and W. Donahue. *Aging in Today's Society.* Englewood Cliffs, N.J.: Prentice-Hall, 1960a.

Tibbitts, C. (ed.). *Handbook of Social Gerontology: Societal Aspects of Aging.* Chicago: The University of Chicago Press, 1960b.

Tibbitts, C., and W. Donahue (eds.). *Social and Psychological Aspects of Aging: Aging Around the World.* New York: Columbia University Press, 1962.

Tiktin, M. "Menstrual tensions and marital satisfaction," *Dissertation Abstracts*, 1967, *27*, 2520.

Time, July 1, 1966, p. 60.

Time, July 29, 1966, pp. 50–54 (1966b).

Trethowan, W. H., and M. F. Conlon. "The couvade syndrome," *British Journal of Psychiatry*, 1965, *111*, 57–66.

Troyer, W. G., Jr., C. Eisdorfer, M. D. Bogdonoff, and F. Wilkie. "Experimental stress and learning in the aged," *Journal of Abnormal Psychology*, 1967, *72*, 65–70.

Tsuang, M. T. "Birth order and maternal age of psychiatric in-patients," *British Journal of Psychiatry*, 1966, *112*, 1131–1141.

Tucker, C. W., Jr. "Occupational evaluation and self identification," *Dissertation Abstracts*, 1967, *27*, 3138.

Tuckman, J., and I. Lorge. "Attitudes toward old people," *Journal of Social Psychology*, 1953, *37*, 249–260.

Tuckman, J., and I. Lorge. "Classification of self as young, middle-aged, or old," *Geriatrics*, 1954, *9*, 534–536.

Tuckman, J., I. Lorge, and F. D. Zeman. "The self image in aging," *Journal of Genetic Psychology*, 1961, *99*, 317–321.

Tuckman, J. "Older persons' judgment of the passage of time over the life-span," *Geriatrics*, 1965a, *20*, 136–140.

Tuckman, J. "College students' judgment of the passage of time over the life span," *Journal of Genetic Psychology*, 1965b, *107*, 43–48.

Tuckman, J., and R. A. Regan. "Ordinal position and behavior problems in children," *Journal of Health and Social Behavior*, 1967, *8*, 32–39.

Tune, G. S. "Errors of commission as a function of age and temperament in a type of vigilance task," *Quarterly Journal of Experimental Psychology,* 1966, *18,* 358–361.

Tyler, B. B., F. B. Tyler, and J. E. Rafferty. "The development of behavior patterns in children," *Genetic Psychology Monographs,* 1966, *74,* 165–213.

Udry, V. R. "The influence of the ideal mate image on mate selection and mate perception," *Journal of Marriage and the Family,* 1965, *27,* 477–482.

Udry, V. R. "Marital instability by race and income based on 1960 census data," *American Journal of Sociology,* 1967, *72,* 673–674.

Uhlmann, F. W., and E. Saltz. "Retention of anxiety material as a function of cognitive differentiation," *Journal of Personality and Social Psychology,* 1965, *1,* 55–62.

U.S. Department of Labor. *American Women: Report of the President's Commission on the Status of Women, 1963.* Washington, D.C.: Superintendent of Documents.

U.S. Department of Labor. *Trends in Educational Attainment of Women.* Washington, D.C.: U.S. Department of Labor, 1967.

van der Veen, F., B. Huebner, B. Jorgens, and P. Nega. "Relationships between the parents' concept of the family and family adjustment," *American Journal of Orthopsychiatry,* 1964, *34,* 45–55.

van der Veen, F. "The parents' concept of the family unit and child adjustment," *Journal of Counseling Psychology,* 1965, *12,* 196–200.

Vasey, W. "Organization of community services for the aged," *The Gerontologist,* 1968, *8,* Part II, 54–56.

Vedder, C. B. *Problems of the Middle-Aged.* Springfield, Ill.: Charles C Thomas, 1965.

Verhage, F. "Intelligence and age in a Dutch sample," *Human Development,* 1965, *8,* 238–245.

Vernon, D. T., J. M. Foley, and J. L. Schulman. "Effect of mother-child separation and birth order on young children's responses to two potentially stressful experiences," *Journal of Personality and Social Psychology,* 1967, *5,* 162–174.

Veroff, J., J. W. Atkinson, S. C. Feld, and G. Gurin. "The use of thematic apperception to assess motivation in a nationwide interview study," *Psychological Monographs: General and Applied,* 1960, *74,* No. 12, Whole No. 499.

Verville, E., and N. Cameron. "Age and sex differences in the perception of incomplete pictures by adults," *Journal of Genetic Psychology,* 1946, *68,* 149–157.

Verwoerdt, A. *Communication with the Fatally Ill.* Springfield, Ill.: Charles C Thomas, 1966.

Verwoerdt, A., and C. Eisdorfer. "Geropsychiatry: the psychiatry of senescence," *Geriatrics,* 1967, *22,* 139–149.

Vince, M. A. "Corrective movements in a pursuit task," *Quarterly Journal of Experimental Psychology,* 1948, *1,* 85–103.

Vincent, E. L., and P. C. Martin. *Human Psychological Development.* New York: Ronald, 1961.

Vogel, B. S., and R. E. Schell. "Vocational interest patterns in late maturity and retirement," *Journal of Gerontology*, 1968, *23*, 66–70.

Vosen, L. M. "The relationship between self-disclosure and self-esteem," *Dissertation Abstracts*, 1967, *27*, 2882.

Wahl, C. W. (ed.). *Sexual Problems: Diagnosis and Treatment in Medical Practice*. New York: Free Press, 1967.

Wahler, R. G., G. H. Winkel, R. F. Peterson, and D. C. Morrison. "Mothers as behavior therapists for their own children," *Behaviour Research and Therapy*, 1965, *3*, 113–124.

Wainwright, W. H. "Fatherhood as a precipitant to mental illness," *American Journal of Psychiatry*, 1966, *123*, 40–44.

Wakefield, W. M. "Awareness, affection, and perceived similarity in the parent-child relationship," *Dissertation Abstracts*, 1966, *27*, 401–402.

Waller, J. A. "High 'accident' risk among middle-aged drivers and pedestrians," *Geriatrics*, 1966, *21*, 125–137.

Wallin, P., and A. L. Clark. "A study of orgasm as a condition of women's enjoyment of coitus in the middle years of marriage," *Human Biology*, 1963, *35*, 131–139.

Wallin, P., and A. L. Clark. "Religiosity, sexual gratification, and marital satisfaction in the middle years of marriage," *Social Forces*, 1964, *42*, 303–309.

Walton, W. G., Jr. "Visual problems of the institutional aged," *American Journal of Optometry and Archives of American Academy of Optometry*, 1967, *44*, 319–335.

Wapner, S., H. Werner, and P. E. Comalli. "Perception of part-whole relations in middle and old age," *Journal of Gerontology*, 1960, *15*, 412–416.

Warburton, J. W. "Memory disturbance and the Parkinson syndrome," *British Journal of Medical Psychology*, 1967, *40*, 169–171.

Warner, S. J. *Self-realization and Self-Defeat*. New York: Grove Press, 1966.

Warren, R. M., and R. P. Warren. "A comparison of speech perception in childhood, maturity, and old age by means of the verbal transformation effect," *Journal of Verbal Learning and Verbal Behavior*, 1966, *5*, 142–146.

Warriner, C. C., D. A. Foster, and D. K. Trites. "Failure to complete as a family characteristic: a college sample," *Journal of Educational Research*, 1966, *59*, 466–468.

Weale, R. A. *The Aging Eye*. London: H. K. Lewis, 1963.

Wechsler, D. *The Measurement and Appraisal of Adult Intelligence*, 4th ed. Baltimore: Williams & Wilkins, 1958.

Weiner, M. "Organization of mental abilities from ages 14 to 54," *Educational and Psychological Measurement*, 1964, *24*, 573–587.

Weinstein, S., E. A. Sersen, L. Fisher, and R. J. Vetter. "Preferences for bodily parts as a function of sex, age, and socio-economic status," *American Journal of Psychology*, 1964, *77*, 291–294.

Weinstock, A. R. "Family environment and the development of defense and coping mechanisms," *Journal of Personality and Social Psychology*, 1967, *5*, 67–75.

Weir, M. W. "Age and memory as factors in problem solving," *Journal of Experimental Psychology*, 1967, *73*, 78–84.

Welford, A. T. *Ageing and Human Skill.* London: Oxford, 1958.

Welford, A. T. "Experimental psychology in the study of ageing," *British Medical Bulletin,* 1964, *20,* 65–69.

Welford, A. T., and J. E. Birren (eds.). *Behavior, Aging, and the Nervous System.* Springfield, Ill.: Charles C Thomas, 1965.

Welford, A. T. "Industrial work suitable for older people: some British studies," *The Gerontologist,* 1966, *6,* 4–9.

Wertheimer, M. "Conception of chronological age as a function of chronological age," *Psychological Reports,* 1960, *7,* 450.

Werts, C. E. "Paternal influence on career choice," *National Merit Scholarship Corporation Research Reports,* 1967, *3,* 19.

Wesman, A. G. "Intelligent testing," *The American Psychologist,* 1968, *23,* 267–274.

Weston, H. C. "The effect of age and illumination upon visual performance with close sights," *British Journal of Ophthalmology,* 1948, *32,* 645–653.

Weston, H. C. "On age and illumination in relation to visual performance," *Transactions of the Illuminating Engineering Society,* 1949, *14,* 281–297.

Wetherick, N. E. "A comparison of the problem-solving ability of young, middle-aged and old subjects," *Gerontologia,* 1964, *9,* 164–178.

Wetherick, N. E. "Changing an established concept: a comparison of the ability of young, middle-aged, and old subjects," *Gerontologia,* 1965, *11,* 82–95.

Wetherick, N. E. "The responses of normal adult subjects to the matrices test," *British Journal of Psychology,* 1966, *57,* 297–300.

White, J. G., and S. J. Knox. "Some psychological correlates of age and dementia," *British Journal of Social and Clinical Psychology,* 1965, *4,* 259–265.

White, R. W. *Lives in Progress.* New York: Holt, Rinehart and Winston, 1952.

White, R. W. (ed.). *The Study of Lives.* New York: Atherton Press, 1963.

White, R. W. *Lives in Progress,* 2d ed. New York: Holt, Rinehart and Winston, 1966.

Whitman, H. *Your Middle Years.* Des Moines, Iowa: The Register and Tribune Syndicate, 1961.

Wiersma, W., and H. J. Klausmeier. "The effect of age upon speed of concept attainment," *Journal of Gerontology,* 1965, *20,* 398–400.

Williams, R. H., C. Tibbitts, and W. Donahue (eds.). *Processes of Aging: I.* New York: Atherton Press, 1963a.

Williams, R. H., C. Tibbitts, and W. Donahue (eds.). *Processes of Aging: II.* New York: Atherton Press, 1963b.

Williams, R. H., and C. G. Wirths. *Lives Through the Years: Styles of Life and Successful Aging.* New York: Atherton Press, 1965.

Williams, R. H. "A concept of style of life induced from a study of aging," *Journal of Individual Psychology,* 1966, *22,* 100–103.

Williamson, R. C. *Marriage and Family Relations.* New York: Wiley, 1966.

Wilson, P. R., J. R. Patterson, and A. M. Lysons. "Sex, birth order, and volunteer behavior," *Australian Journal of Psychology,* 1966, *18,* 158–159.

Wilson, W. R. "Correlates of avowed happiness," *Psychological Bulletin,* 1967, *67,* 294–306.

Winefield, A. H. "The learning of double alternation by children and adults under different training procedures," *Journal of Genetic Psychology,* 1966, *108,* 291–295.

Wittenberg, R. M. *The Troubled Generation: Toward Understanding and Helping the Young Adult.* New York: Association Press, 1967.

Wohlford, P., and M. R. Jones. "Ordinal position, age, anxiety, and defensiveness in unwed mothers," *Proceedings of the 75th Annual Convention of the American Psychological Association,* 1967, *2,* 177–178.

Wolfe, R. N., and J. A. Davis. "Intelligence and central life interests in two groups of older men," *Psychological Reports,* 1964, *14,* 847–852.

Wolff, K. *The Biological, Sociological, and Psychological Aspects of Aging.* Springfield, Ill.: Charles C Thomas, 1959.

Wolff, K. "Personality type and reaction toward aging and death: a clinical study," *Geriatrics,* 1966, *21,* 189–192.

Wolk, R. L., and S. L. Rustin. "Psychologic evaluation of a gerontologic population: comparison of results with the Raven Progressive Matrices (1947) versus the Wechsler Adult Intelligence Scale," *Journal of American Geriatric Society,* 1964, *12,* 807–809.

Wuebben, P. L. "Honesty of subjects and birth order," *Journal of Personality and Social Psychology,* 1967, *5,* 350–352.

Wyer, R. S. "Self-acceptance, discrepancy between parents' perceptions of their children, and goal-seeking effectiveness," *Journal of Personality and Social Psychology,* 1965, *2,* 311–316.

Yorukoglu, A., and J. P. Kemph. "Children not severely damaged by incest with a parent," *Journal of the American Academy of Child Psychiatry,* 1966, *5,* 111–124.

Young, M. L. "Problem solving performance in two age groups," *Journal of Gerontology,* 1966, *21,* 505–509.

Zaretsky, H. H., and J. L. Halberstam. "Age differences in paired-associate learning," *Journal of Gerontology,* 1968, *23,* 165–168.

Zborowski, M. "Aging and recreation," *Journal of Gerontology,* 1962a, *17,* 302–309.

Zborowski, M., and L. E. Eyde. "Aging and social participation," *Journal of Gerontology,* 1962b, *17,* 424–430.

Ziegler, G. J., D. A. Rodgers, and S. A. Kriegsman. "Effect of vasectomy on psychological functioning," *Psychosomatic Medicine,* 1966, *28,* 50–63.

Ziller, R. C., and S. A. Grossman. "A developmental study of the self-social constructs of normals and the neurotic personality," *Journal of Clinical Psychology,* 1967, *23,* 15–21.

Zinberg, N., and I. Kaufman (eds.). *Normal Psychology of the Aging Process.* New York: International Universities Press, 1963.

Zippin, D. "Sex differences and the sense of humor," *Psychoanalytic Review,* 1966, *53,* 45–55.

Zybon, G. "Role consensus, need complementarity, and continuance of marriage," *Dissertation Abstracts,* 1966, *27,* 826–827.

Index of
Names

Index of
Subjects